ARTHUR JAMES BALFOUR

PORTRAIT BY G. FIDDES WATT, R.S.A., PRESENTED TO ETON COLLEGE BY THE O.E. ASSOCIATION JUNE 4TH, 1920

34038

ARTHUR JAMES BALFOUR
First Earl of Balfour, K.G., O.M., F.R.S.

by
His Niece
BLANCHE E. C. DUGDALE

1906–1930

With 20 Illustrations

GREENWOOD PRESS, PUBLISHERS
WESTPORT, CONNECTICUT

Originally published in 1936
by Hutchinson & Co., London

First Greenwood Reprinting 1970

SBN 8371-2893-5 (SET)
SBN 8371-2892-7 (VOL. 2)

PRINTED IN UNITED STATES OF AMERICA

CONTENTS

CHAPTER I

A FAMILY PORTRAIT, 1906–1914 . . . . . . PAGE 13
The Gramophone. "Us Four." Whittingehame life. Balfour's conversation. Character.

CHAPTER II

OPPOSITION, 1906–1909 20
The new balance of Parties. Balfour and Chamberlain reach agreement. Balfour's views on the House of Lords at the opening of the Constitutional conflict. Action of House of Lords in Trades Disputes Bill. Death of Sir Henry Campbell-Bannerman. Mr. Asquith Prime Minister. Beginning of discontent with Balfour's leadership. Increases in Germany's Navy. Balfour urges naval increases.

CHAPTER III

DIE-HARDS 55
The Budget of 1909. Pros and cons of resistance by the House of Lords. Death of King Edward VII. The Constitutional Conference. Balfour's Memorandum on its break-down. General Election of December 1910. Balfour's views on the request of Ministers for a pledge from the King to create Peers. The Conservative Shadow Cabinet of July 21st, 1911. The "Die Hards" arise. Balfour's suppressed Memorandum on the Constitutional Crisis.

CHAPTER IV

MR. LLOYD GEORGE'S PROPOSAL, 1910 72
Mr. Lloyd George approaches Balfour, October 1910, with scheme for Coalition Government. Balfour's refusal. "I cannot be a second Sir Robert Peel." Balfour's commentary in after years. Balfour's views on conscription.

CHAPTER V

"B. M. G." BALFOUR MUST GO 81
Balfour advises the Peers to pass the Parliament Bill. Halsbury Club Dinner. Balfour departs for Bas Gastein. Determines to resign the leadership. Arguments and persuasions. Balfour tells his family. Announcement on November 8th, 1911.

CONTENTS

CHAPTER VI

	PAGE
OUT OF HARNESS, 1911–1914	93

Balfour and Bonar Law. " Nationality and Home Rule." The Unionists desire an election. Passions aroused by Home Rule Bill. Contrast with Unity in face of danger from Continental war. Balfour's memorandum on Anglo-French relations. New Year's Eve 1913–14. The Gifford Lectures.

CHAPTER VII

THE FIRST NINE MONTHS OF WAR, AUGUST 1914 TO MAY 1915 . 112

The first days of August. Balfour in London. Promise of Unionist support for the Government. Correspondence with Lord Haldane. Balfour's views of Sir Edward Grey and Lord Kitchener. The Passing of the Home Rule Bill. Balfour's visit to his nephew at Blackdown Camp. Dinner at the Automobile Club. Disquiet about war preparations. Balfour joins the " War Council." Visit to the Battle-cruisers. Letter from Lord Fisher. Balfour's views of war strategy. Balfour consults Mr. Bonar Law on his position in " War Council." Difficulties of the Unionists.

CHAPTER VIII

FIRST LORD OF THE ADMIRALTY, MAY 1915 TO DECEMBER 1916 . 137

Lord Fisher resigns. First Coalition Government formed. Mr. Asquith offers Balfour the Admiralty. Critics of Balfour's appointment. Admiralty problems. Appointment of Sir Henry Jackson as First Sea Lord. Departmental organisation. Sir John Jellicoe. Rise of the submarine menace. Balfour's view of Mr. Asquith and Lord Kitchener. Balfour's Memorandum on the Air Board. The Battle of Jutland. The Admiralty communique. Sir Edward Grey and Mr. Asquith insist on replacement of First Sea Lord. Sir John Jellicoe appointed.

CHAPTER IX

CRISIS AND RECONSTRUCTION. DECEMBER, 1916 166

Signs of break-up of the First Coalition. Lloyd George and Bonar Law present scheme of War Council Reform. Balfour falls ill. Balfour backs Lloyd George. His reasons. Correspondence with Asquith. Bonar Law and Lloyd George visit Balfour. They discuss alternatives. Balfour's account of Buckingham Palace Conference. Balfour accepts the Foreign Office. Balfour and Lloyd George.

CONTENTS

CHAPTER X

ENTER THE UNITED STATES, 1917 . . . . PAGE 186
Balfour's views on Peace Terms, December 1916. Balfour and Lord Robert Cecil. American misunderstanding of Allied aims. The Zimmermann Telegram. The U.S.A. enters the War. The "Balfour Mission" embarks for America. Balfour and President Wilson. The "Secret Treaties." Balfour addresses Congress. New York welcomes Balfour. Return of "Balfour Mission" to England. British need for money and ships. Balfour and the United States.

CHAPTER XI

CONTACT WITH JEWRY 213
Opposition of Jewish non-Zionists to Zionist idea. Sir Mark Sykes interprets Zionism to British Government. Balfour champions Zionist cause in Cabinet. Balfour's faith in Zionism. His attitude to Arab claims. His speeches to Zionist audiences. Zionists approach the British Government in 1914. Dr. Weizmann's conversations with Balfour. Zionist diplomacy in 1916. Balfour as Foreign Secretary discusses future with American Zionists. "Balfour Declaration" before the Cabinet. Weizmann and Trotsky. "Balfour Declaration" issued in November 1917.

CHAPTER XII

FOREIGN MINISTER IN WAR-TIME 236
Balfour's view of political bearing of military problems. Relations with Lloyd George. Sir Maurice Hankey. Balfour defends Lord Hardinge. Balfour's Memorandum on proposals of General Staff. Peace proposals of 1917. Balfour's view of them. The "Lansdowne Peace Letter." War Aims. Policy towards the Bolsheviks.

CHAPTER XIII

TREATY MAKING 263
Balfour's conception of responsibility. His attempt to deal separately with the Military Clauses. Departure of Signor Orlando. The "Council of Four." Work on the British Empire Delegation. Balfour's Memorandum on France and Germany. Balfour defends the Treaty of Versailles. Balfour becomes head of the British Delegation. The Treaty of Trianon. The "Anschluss." The Tyrol. Balfour's letter to Lord Curzon. Balfour leaves the Foreign Office. Lord Curzon and Mr. Lloyd George. Balfour at the Peace Conference.

7

CONTENTS

CHAPTER XIV

INTERLUDE, 1919 294

Balfour admitted to the Académie des Sciences Morales et Politiques. Letter on the death in action of a friend's son. Balfour's portrait unveiled at Eton. Chancellor of Cambridge University. Rockefeller gift to University Library.

CHAPTER XV

THE LEAGUE OF NATIONS 300

The Making of the Covenant. Balfour and Lord Robert Cecil. Balfour's anxiety at American defection. His view of the League's limitations. The First Assembly, 1920. Balfour's public speaking at Geneva. The British Empire votes as one. The Upper Silesian settlement. Balfour's use of League procedure. Balfour's defence of the League.

CHAPTER XVI

THE WASHINGTON CONFERENCE 315

Balfour heads the Delegation. The question of the Anglo-Japanese Alliance. The American proposal for Naval Disarmament. Balfour accepts it. The Japanese attitude. The French oppose limitation of submarines. The British case for it. The Four Power Treaty. Balfour's Speech on termination of the Anglo-Japanese Alliance. The Shantung Question. The Nine Power Treaty. Balfour returns home. The Garter and the Earldom.

CHAPTER XVII

LAST WORDS ON IRELAND 336

The treaty of 1922. Evolution of Balfour's opinions. Twenty years of "Resolute Government." Balfour's speech of 1911. "Nationality and Home Rule." Balfour refuses compromise.

CHAPTER XVIII

THE ELDER STATESMAN. PART I 344

Discontent of Conservatives with the Coalition in spring of 1922. Balfour supports Mr. Lloyd George. Reasons for Mr. Lloyd George's unpopularity. The "Balfour Note" on War Debts. Balfour and the League of Nations' Guaranteed Loan to Austria. The fall of the Coalition, October 1922.

CONTENTS

CHAPTER XIX

THE ELDER STATESMAN. PART II 358
Balfour and the House of Lords. Lord Curzon and the Premiership. Unionist defeat of 1923. Balfour visits Palestine. Lord President of the Council once more. Scientific research.

CHAPTER XX

IMPERIAL RELATIONS 374
The Imperial Conference of 1926. Its problems. Balfour's views of Imperial relations. The drafting of his Report. Effect upon the Dominions. Balfour in 1927. Essay on Francis Bacon. Balfour's views on Nationality.

CHAPTER XXI

THE LAST TWO YEARS, 1928–1930 389
First decline in health. Work on the Autobiography. Reminiscences. Attack of illness at Taplow Court. Recovery. The eightieth birthday. The last autumn at home. Move to Fishers Hill. Resignation of office. Visit to the King at Bognor. India Debate and letter to Mr. Baldwin. Conversations. The approaching end. Visit of Dr. Weizmann. Death, March 19th, 1930.

LIST OF ILLUSTRATIONS

PORTRAIT BY G. FIDDES WATT, R.S.A., PRESENTED TO ETON
COLLEGE BY THE O.E. ASSOCIATION, JUNE 4TH, 1920 *Frontispiece*

	FACING PAGE
WHITTINGEHAME HOUSE IN THE SNOW	14
A. J. BALFOUR, 1911	50
WHITTINGEHAME GARDEN AND TOWER	86
A. J. BALFOUR, 1917	104
A. J. BALFOUR AND D. LLOYD GEORGE VIEWING THE WRECK OF A ZEPPELIN, SEPTEMBER 1916	150
LORD ROBERT CECIL AND A. J. BALFOUR, 1914	188
THE "BALFOUR MISSION" ARRIVES, APRIL 20TH, 1917	198
A. J. BALFOUR AND JOSEPH CHOATE IN NEW YORK, MAY 22ND, 1917	208
A. J. BALFOUR AND LORD HAIG, 1918	238
BALFOUR'S SITTING-ROOM AT WHITTINGEHAME	254
THE FOREIGN SECRETARY IN PARIS, 1919	264
THE LORD PRESIDENT OF THE COUNCIL	288
THE TWO GERALDS	332
A. J. BALFOUR ON THE COURTS AT CANNES	360
KING GEORGE V AND LORD BALFOUR AT BOGNOR, MAY 11TH, 1929	400

Chapter 1

A FAMILY PORTRAIT
1906—1914

The Gramophone. "Us Four." Whittingehame life. Balfour's conversation. Character.

After the Election campaign of January 1906, Balfour went home to Whittingehame, to enjoy for a couple of weeks a freedom that he had not known for twenty years. Not one of the bevy of nieces who gathered at the door to greet his return had ever thought of him even momentarily as a private citizen. For the first time in their memory no Cabinet boxes, no cypher telegrams, could disturb the self-sufficing life at Whittingehame. The idea seemed a little comical and decidedly elating. The situation could not last—even the babies of the family knew that. But while it lasted the family was determined to make the most of it. He came home in the dark of a January evening, and as the head-lights of his car illumined the Approach, we rushed out of the house to greet him. I remember wondering ridiculously whether he would look different from what he had done as a Prime Minister. As the car drew up, children of all ages swarmed upon it like bees, and its door opened, to disclose a huge gramophone trumpet of shining brass. Behind this object (then something of a novelty) was the beaming face of A. J. B. He had bought the instrument in an interval

1906

1906 between Election speeches—whether in Manchester, or later in Nottingham or Glasgow, I cannot now say. It was in any case a result of the General Election, and the only one which at the moment seemed of the slightest importance to him or to his relations. Next day he accompanied a jubilant throng into Edinburgh, where we spent hours trying over records in Paterson's music shop in George Street. Laden with every sort of melody, from Beethoven and Handel, Annie Laurie, and the Choristers' Waltz, down to the lowest depths that could be reached in those pre-jazz days, we returned home, and the brazen trumpet blared by night and by day through the long corridors of Whittingehame House for the rest of the brief holiday.

The respite was short. Before the end of January Mr. Alban Gibbs, one of the two Members for the City of London, had offered to vacate his seat in Balfour's favour, and Balfour himself went to London, where pending his reappearance in the Opposition Leader's place, he plunged into the counsels of the Conservative Party.

Before following him there I would sketch him once more in his family circle. The years immediately preceding the Great War were years in which his enjoyment of his home was at its zenith. No touch of old age had as yet impaired his physical powers. At golf his game was as good as ever. His early zest for lawn-tennis had revived, as a new hard court in the grounds at Whittingehame bore witness. No separations, no anxieties, seemed impending on the horizon of private life. None of the economies which financial circumstances made necessary in later years interfered as yet with the improvements to the Whittingehame estate that were his constant joy, or with the full tide of life that surged through the big house itself. There was the continual

WHITTINGEHAME HOUSE IN SNOW

"US FOUR"

flow of high spirits in which he revelled—high spirits that took their tone from him, and in return fed the perpetual youthfulness of his own nature.

In this atmosphere, sparkling with conscious happiness, there was a rare companionship between generations. It has been explained earlier how the growing families of Balfour's two brothers made their home at Whittingehame for the half of every year. The children's wing of the house was still full when the elders of the tribe emerged into grown-up life. One group of nieces were so near of an age, and had from babyhood always so regarded themselves as an entity, that they were known to themselves and others by the name of " Us Four."[1]

Individually and collectively this quartette counted for more and more in Balfour's life as time went on. They were his partners and opponents at lawn-tennis and garden-golf, the initiators of the plans for every day of his holidays. He was the confidant, the enthusiastic commentator upon all their doings, which were as many and as varied as might be expected from four young women whose tastes were alike in nothing except the intensity with which they each pursued their chosen way. One of them had married, and another had begun a University career before the War, but two who were still at home were the first audience of Balfour's Gifford Lectures on " Theism and Humanism," which he read aloud to them before delivery in Glasgow in the winter of 1913–1914. Not because " Us Four " were in any sense metaphysicians, but because it was his theory that any intelligent person could understand anything,

[1] Ruth and Eleanor, daughters of Gerald Balfour. They married respectively Lieut.-Colonel E. W. S. Balfour, of Balbirnie, and the Hon. Galbraith Cole.
Joan and Alison, daughters of Eustace Balfour; afterwards the Hon. Mrs. Edward Lascelles, and Mrs. Arthur Milne.

provided it were sufficiently lucidly exposed. On this happy hypothesis the blame for a failure of comprehension lay with him and not with his listeners. But I never heard that the experiment brought any such failure to light!

A Whittingehame House hockey team, recruited from the family and the household, was an invention of " Us Four." The team went on one occasion to play the neighbouring house of Nunraw. Balfour accompanied it, and someone asked him whether he meant to take part in the game. " No, no," he said, " but if all goes well I am here to crown the hall-boy with laurel."

There was no detail about the Whittingehame estate that did not interest him, though he left its management more and more in other hands as the work of public office grew heavier, and home life and holidays became for him synonymous. His personal intercourse with the people mostly consisted of a pleasant word or two when they met. He seldom visited the cottages, except occasionally one where lived Mrs. Mercer, who had been nursery maid at Whittingehame House in Lady Blanche's day. But everyone about the place felt for him a proprietary affection and pride, and he was always in their midst at any gathering. He enjoyed curling, and his own pair of stones were always kept in the little wooden shed by the pond at Overfield farm. There was only one estate function that he attended without gusto, and upon pressure from Miss Balfour. This was the annual dance for the estate employees in the barn at the Home Farm, which used to plunge him for hours beforehand into a gloom so rare that it was known as the " Farm Ball mood." He was, however, a very competent performer in a foursome reel, having never forgotten the steps taught him in childhood by the old Edinburgh dancing master. Eightsome reels he despised as modern inventions.

There used to be lectures on improving subjects in the Parish Hall. One snowy night he and Gerald Balfour struggled forth on foot with their young relatives, to attend one of these gatherings. The brothers were at that time respectively Prime Minister and President of the Board of Trade. The family found itself composing the greater part of the listeners, and the chairman apologised profoundly to the lecturer for the "miserable quality" of the audience.

"No doubt our standards are high at Whittingehame," remarked Balfour rather plaintively afterwards, "but I personally should have directed my criticism to-night less upon quality than upon quantity."

It is a risky thing to try to revive scenes and memories whose very essence was the freedom from publicity which gives intensity to the home life of a public man. Yet that famous "charm," which was felt by nearly everyone who came in contact with Balfour, was so intensified for his family that it is only by describing him as he appeared at home that I, at any rate, can hope to convey any impression of it.

What was its secret? It did not lie solely in his conversation, brilliant as that always was. I have known other people—though not many—who could be as witty, as unexpected, as profound, as frivolous, as devastating, as gentle, as he could be in talk. I have never known anybody but him to whom all these moods were natural, nor anybody with as great a range of interests, or so adaptable to his company. But it was not from any of these qualities that the delight in his society was derived. It arose, primarily, I think, from the power he had of causing everybody else to be at their own best, in their own line, by his attentive, often eager, appreciation of their remarks. In conversation he was the most unselfish, un-self-conscious of artists. His social tastes were very catholic. He was not easily bored, though when that catastrophe occurred, he flew signals of distress terribly patent to all who knew him. But no one was ever more nimble to seize a life-line deftly flung from the other side of the table.

Personal gossip amused him, provided it was not purely malicious. But in this, above all other forms of talk, he thought it more blessed to receive than to give. He was the most discreet of men. He was the recipient of secrets innumerable, the active peacemaker or negotiator in many private troubles, of which few dreamed he was even aware. Often I have seen him expressing the appropriate astonishment, delight, or horror, at some piece of news affecting his friends, which one afterwards realised was no news at all to him.

He was less apparently careful about the secrets, or what were supposed to be the secrets, of political life, at any rate as regards his family. He was very apt, when in London, to bring colleagues home to luncheon, and to discuss business with them there. " Of course, this mustn't go further," he would remark casually, and once that word was said, it never did. We would as soon have cut out our tongues as forfeit that complete trust which was his greatest gift to those he loved. Once lost, nothing could have restored it. " I never forgive, but I always forget," he once said half in joke; but the remark was true. He seldom excited himself to genuine contempt or anger, but, once aroused, they remained, though their occasion might be forgotten beyond recall.

His sense of humour was like the rest of his mental equipment; its limits were hard to find. Only practical

SOLITARY AT HEART

joking lay completely beyond its scope. The best audience in the world for a good story, he was, partly for that very reason, a bad teller of stories, for he never could remember one. There was a collection, compiled by his nieces, known as the *Book of Bosh*, recording family incidents not always sufficiently respectful to their elders to be suitable for promiscuous reading aloud to any representative of that generation except Balfour himself. With due precautions, therefore, the volume used to be unlocked in his room every Christmas holidays. Old chestnuts and new delighted him equally.

Thus and thus could the pen run on, attempting to illustrate a personality that made all others by comparison seem limited and crude. And yet in the end the living portrait might not be recaptured. In this sketch of purely personal life I have dwelt upon the strength and warmth of his affections. Yet even here (and I include with his family the very small number of friends, men and women, who were admitted up to the very gates of his innermost citadel), even here there was an impenetrable place. Within was that refuge from inharmonious conditions, whether in public or personal life, that never failed him, and which may have been the secret of the unruffled grace and ease with which he walked through the world. His power of becoming aloof at will was perhaps the most important thing for an understanding of his character and the only way of explaining a paradox that lurked in the depths. He basked all his days in affection, and repaid it to the full. Yet no misfortune, no bereavement, could have broken him, for he was a solitary at heart.

Chapter II

OPPOSITION
1906—1909

The new balance of Parties. Balfour and Chamberlain reach agreement. Balfour's views on the House of Lords at the opening of the Constitutional conflict. Action of House of Lords in Trades Disputes Bill. Death of Sir Henry Campbell-Bannermann. Mr. Asquith Prime Minister. Beginning of discontent with Balfour's leadership. Increases in Germany's Navy. Balfour urges naval increases.

1906

The chapter of electoral defeat which concludes the first volume of this book leaves Balfour writing to Lady Salisbury of his vivified interest in the political scene. The mood reflects itself in various forms in answers to the condolences of friends, as in a letter to Lord Knollys of January 17th, 1906, conveying his thanks to the King for a message, and continuing:

> I have no reason to believe that there will be any special difficulty in getting me a fresh seat, though I am afraid hardly in time for the opening of Parliament,—which is a great pity. If you had asked me when we last met whether I should much mind permanently leaving politics, I should have answered in the negative. But I am so profoundly interested in what is *now* going on that I should return a very different answer to-day. We have here to do with something much more important than the swing of the pendulum or all the squabbles about Free Trade and Fiscal Reform. We are face to face (no doubt in a milder form) with the Socialist difficulties which loom so large on the Continent. Unless I am greatly mistaken, the Election of 1905 inaugurates a new era.

THE LABOUR PARTY

The first of Balfour's own correspondents to perceive the new portents was an observer from the other side of the Atlantic. Senator Lodge wrote from Washington on January 28th:

> With us such violent changes have usually been followed by equally violent and quick reactions; but the more significant feature of your Election seems to be, not the size of the Liberal majority—that will come and go—but the appearance of a large and compact body of Labour Members. I think it was certain to come, but I believe it portends a very radical alteration in your politics and the adjustment of parties.

Balfour dwelt on the same theme in a letter of January 24th to Lord Northcote, then Governor-General of Australia.

> The really interesting development is the organised Labour Party, a subject on which you in Australia will have a good deal to teach us. It is impossible as yet to say what perturbations this new planet, suddenly introduced into our political heavens, will cause in existing orbits, but certainly it is curious that while *you* are writing to me about your hopes of getting rid of the "third" Party system in Australia, *we* should suddenly find ourselves, for the first time, with a "fourth" Party system in Great Britain.[1]

Other letters of this period allude to the coming change in the balance of parties, all with the same absence of any note of lament. Balfour was soon called back from his political star-gazing by the immediate problems of organising the scattered fragments of the Unionists into an effective Opposition.

The first necessity was to find, in concert with Mr. Chamberlain, a common policy with regard to the fiscal question, and a formula capable of uniting the Party, to which they could both subscribe. They dined

[1] The Irish Nationalists were of course the "third" Party in English politics.

ARTHUR JAMES BALFOUR

1906 together on February 2nd, in Mr. Chamberlain's house in Princes Gardens, the only other persons present being Mrs. Chamberlain and Mr. Austen Chamberlain, and talked far into the night. Nothing was established that evening except the will to agree, which was to be the decisive factor in the discussions carried on by letter for the next twelve days.

For Balfour the main thing now was to strengthen the Party for approaching conflicts which would have nothing to do with Free Trade or Protection. Mr. Chamberlain's principal object might still be to achieve unity for a policy of tariffs, but the mutual determination to stand together was not affected by differences in its inspiration. Had there been any shadow of rivalry between them it would have appeared now, in the delicate situation created by Mr. Chamberlain's temporary leadership of the Opposition while Balfour was without a seat. At this moment efforts to exploit their differences were not lacking in sections of the press and the public. Rumours of disputed leadership were put about, ludicrous in the light of the correspondence that was passing in private. It was characteristic that while Mr. Chamberlain hastened to repudiate the idea that he should under any circumstances supplant Balfour, it was Balfour himself who pointed out to him that the course he was at first proposing to follow might result in making him leader against his own will.

Mr. Chamberlain was desirous of a Party meeting, and Balfour acquiesced. His first letter, dated February 6th, 1906, begins:

> This is not intended to reopen or continue our discussion of Friday night, as where conversation has *for the moment* proved a failure, correspondence is not likely to prove a success. I only wish to ask your opinion on subsidiary points.

BALFOUR AND CHAMBERLAIN

You know how strong my objection is in ordinary 1906 circumstances to a Party Meeting, and how reluctant I am to have all our differences dealt with in a manner which is certain to be published, and will probably be irritating. But, on carefully thinking over the whole situation, I have come round to your view that, *if you desire it*, a Party Meeting must be held. . . .

The most difficult of the questions we have to settle . . . relates to the procedure to be adopted when it does meet. There is no case in history, as far as I am aware, in which a Party Meeting has been summoned except to give emphasis and authority to a decision at which the Party have informally already arrived; still less is there an example to be found of a vote being taken at such a Meeting. How then are we to proceed on the present occasion? Are you and I to agree upon some question on which the Meeting can vote Aye or No? If so, what is this question to be, and how is it to be formulated? . . . These things puzzle me greatly, and I should be glad to have your opinion about them.

Mr. Chamberlain wanted a vote. He answered by return:

Of course there will be no question whatever as to Leadership, but . . . I think the Party as a whole should be asked to express freely their opinion as to the best policy for the future, and to vote as between the alternatives suggested.

I take it that, as matters stand, and assuming, *if I must assume*, that we can come no nearer, the choice lies between the " Half-sheet of Notepaper "[1] and the Glasgow Pro-

[1] The reference is to a speech by Balfour at Manchester on January 26th, 1905, in which he claimed that he could place his fiscal policy on a " half-sheet of notepaper." He proceeded to outline it as follows:
First, I desire such an alteration of our fiscal system as will give us a freedom of action impossible while we hold ourselves bound by the maxim that no taxation should be imposed except for revenue. I desire this freedom in the main for three reasons. It will strengthen our hands in any negotiations by which we may hope to lower foreign hostile tariffs. It may enable us to protect the fiscal independence of those Colonies which desire to give us preferential treatment. It may be useful where we wish to check the importation of those foreign goods which, because they are bounty-fed, or

gramme.[1] We must find some words to describe the two programmes without using names. We ought to be able to devise something which will not be personal, but will sufficiently describe them in general terms. It will be clearly understood that the decision is not binding on the leaders, or any of them, but is merely taken for information . . . a vote after discussion in a thoroughly representative Meeting would furnish all of us with a really valuable indication of what is practicable, as well as of what is desirable.

Here once more was the old difference of opinion between Mr. Chamberlain who since 1903 had been ready to challenge the issue on his tariff policy, and the Party Leader who put unity first. Neither had shifted from their positions, but the difficulty of reconciling these in practice was greatly increased, now that the Unionists were in Opposition, and Balfour no longer responsible for the carrying on of government. Formerly it had been comparatively easy to find agreement on the basis that Mr. Chamberlain should be free to go ahead of the main body of the Party. Now, if there was to be an advance guard, its Captain must become the leader of the whole army. Balfour saw what Mr. Chamberlain at first failed to see.

tariff protected abroad, are sold below cost price here. Such importations are ultimately as injurious to the British consumer as they are immediately disastrous to the British producer. *Secondly*, I desire closer commercial union with the Colonies, and I do so because I desire closer union in all its possible modes, and because this particular mode is intrinsically of great importance and has received much Colonial support. I also think it might produce great and growing commercial advantages both to the Colonies and the Mother Country by promoting freer trade between them. No doubt such commercial union is beset with many difficulties. These can best be dealt with by a Colonial Conference, provided its members are permitted to discuss them unhampered by limiting instructions. *Thirdly*, I recommend, therefore, that the subject should be referred to a conference on those terms. *Fourth*, and last, I do not desire to raise home prices for the purpose of aiding home productions.

[1] Mr. Chamberlain's programme.

BALFOUR AND CHAMBERLAIN

Private. 1906

4 CARLTON GARDENS.
Feb. 8th, 1906.

MY DEAR CHAMBERLAIN,

Though this is merely a business letter, I hope you will allow me to thank you for the very kind terms in which you have spoken of me in your communication to the public. I am sure that even were the differences between us much greater than they ever have been, or are ever likely to be, our friendship can suffer no diminution.

Now as to the Meeting. It is clear that the members of the Party must have an opportunity of " blowing off steam " on any subject they like, and the two subjects which they would most like are certain to be Fiscal Reform and Party Organisation. But is your idea of requiring them to choose between the Glasgow speech and the " half-sheet of notepaper " really practicable? If they choose the Glasgow speech, how can you refuse to become their Leader? If they regret the " half-sheet of notepaper " how can I continue to lead them? There is something amounting to absurdity in asking a Party to give an opinion upon an important question of policy, and, when it has given that opinion, perhaps against its titular leader, asking that leader to be good enough to continue his work on their behalf. This difficulty will not arise if the Meeting occupies itself merely in hearing and expressing various opinions, if the difference between the Glasgow speech and the " half-sheet of notepaper " is left an open question. But if, on the other hand, we take the course you propose, it seems to me that should the vote go against you, *your* position will not be made easier; should it go against me, *mine* will become impossible, and you will have to reconsider your decision to " refuse the leadership under all circumstances."

Mr. Chamberlain's answer to this was a request for " a few hours' delay " to consider " issues so important." His letter shows how the situation was affecting him.

Let me say at once how heartily I reciprocate the opening words of your letter of yesterday. The profession of

ARTHUR JAMES BALFOUR

politics has many disadvantages, but it becomes intolerable when it threatens such friendship as ours.

Next day, he wrote again, stressing the fact that there should be no insuperable difficulties in the way of agreement between them, since they both desired the same great objects, and were both ready to make sacrifices to secure them. But he thought that a suspicion of dual aims had contributed to the recent defeat, and that confusion must continue until some joint programme or declaration could be framed. He and Mr. Austen Chamberlain had drafted something:

> I do not think [the letter concludes] that there is anything in it which may not be found almost *verbatim* in your speeches and declarations: and, although it is not nearly as definite and does not go nearly as far as the Glasgow programme, it *does* officially deprecate any premature decision against either a general tariff or a small duty on foreign corn.
>
> If on examination you find in it anything which is inconsistent with any previous statement of yours, I should be very glad to reconsider the wording; while, if in substance you are able to assent to it, I see no reason why it should not constitute the charter of our co-operation during the existence of the present Parliament, and the basis of all instructions to our several organisations.
>
> I am,
> Yours very truly,
> J. CHAMBERLAIN.

Balfour's reply, written from Hatfield, is dated the 10th of February, which was a Saturday. On Monday the 12th he was due to make his first speech to his City constituents, and it seems that he was determined to be bound by no formula beforehand. It is at any rate hard to see what other motive could have inspired the *naïveté* with which, in the following letter, he alludes to his speech as to something which he and Mr. Chamberlain must both await with the same expectant interest.

Private.
HATFIELD.
Feb. 10*th*, 1906.

MY DEAR CHAMBERLAIN,

Thanks much for your letter.

Believe me, I fully recognise the cordial endeavour you have made in the draft Resolution to frame a formula which shall meet the difficulties of the case.

But I venture to think that we had better put off any decision as to the exact course to be pursued at the Party Meeting until we have had an opportunity of talking it over, and until you have seen what I say to-morrow in the City. What that will be I do not myself yet know, in the sense of having prepared a speech, but it will be my first important utterance after the adverse decision of the constituencies, and my last utterance, as far as I know, before the meeting of Parliament. It will therefore necessarily have tactical importance, if no other; and I think we ought to have it present in our minds before any final decision is taken. Could you see me on Tuesday afternoon at, say, 5 o'clock? And would it not be a good thing that I should ask Lansdowne and Gerald[1] to be present? By all means bring Austen, if he can come.

Yours ever,
ARTHUR JAMES BALFOUR.

Mr. Chamberlain accepted the proposed date for further conversation. In the meantime the City speech was made. In as far as it concerned tariffs it was Balfour's old plea for the open question, for not confounding expediency with principle. One passage shows how aware he was of the rising tides of economic nationalism. He had been speaking of Peel's fiscal policy.

> I have no quarrel with that. My quarrel has been with those who thought that the economic world, as they

---

[1] His brother, Gerald Balfour.

ARTHUR JAMES BALFOUR

conceived it, was going to be conducted henceforth, not upon national lines, but upon cosmopolitan lines. They thought the world was to be one economic community. . . . They were wrong. The world has, rightly or wrongly, insisted that, in the latter half of the nineteenth century, as in days gone by, industry shall run upon national lines, and not upon cosmopolitan lines. Personally I am old-fashioned, and I regret it; but is it not folly not to see facts as they are, as I have stated them?[1]

This speech was of the type which his contemporaries were apt to label "obscure." After he had made it, with only three days to run before the Party meeting, Mr. Chamberlain and he moved quickly towards the agreement which was embodied in the published correspondence known as the "Valentine Letters."

4 CARLTON GARDENS.
February 14th, 1906.

MY DEAR CHAMBERLAIN,

The controversy aroused by the Fiscal Question has produced, not unnaturally, an impression which I have constantly combatted, that the practical differences between fiscal reformers are much deeper than is in fact the case. The exchange of views which has recently taken place between us leads me to hope that this misconception may be removed, and with it much friction which has proved injurious to the Party.

My own opinion, which I believe is shared by the great majority of the Unionist Party, may be briefly summarised as follows:

I hold that Fiscal Reform is, and must remain, the first constructive work of the Unionist Party.

That the objects of such reform are to secure more equal terms of competition for British trade, and closer commercial union with the Colonies.

That, while it is at present unnecessary to prescribe the exact methods by which these objects are to be attained,

---

[1] See *The Times*, February 13th, 1906.

THE "VALENTINE LETTERS"

and inexpedient to permit differences of opinion as to those methods to divide the Party, though other means may be possible, the establishment of a moderate general tariff on manufactured goods, not imposed for the purpose of raising prices or giving artificial protection against legitimate competition, and the imposition of a small duty on foreign corn, are not in principle objectionable, and should be adopted if shown to be necessary for the attainment of the ends in view or for purposes of revenue.

Believe me, yours sincerely,
ARTHUR JAMES BALFOUR.

40 PRINCES GARDENS.
February 14th, 1906.

MY DEAR BALFOUR,

I cordially welcome your letter of to-day, in which you have summarised the conclusions that we have reached during our recent discussion.

I entirely agree with your description of the objects which we both have in view, and gladly accept the policy which you indicate as the wise and desirable one for the Unionist Party to adopt.

In endeavouring to give effect to this policy and in defending all Unionist principles, any services that I can render will be entirely at your disposal.

I am, yours very truly,
J. CHAMBERLAIN.

The "Valentine Letters" deprived the Party meeting of most of its anticipated spice. Parliament had opened on February 13th. For the next month the little phalanx on the Opposition benches was led by Mr. Chamberlain. Balfour was actually a member of the House from February 27th, when he was returned for the City of London by a majority of some eleven thousand over the four thousand polled by his (Free Trade Unionist) opponent, Mr. Gibson Bowles. The election, though its issue was never in doubt, had involved some fatigue,

ARTHUR JAMES BALFOUR

1906 including early morning visits to Smithfield and Billingsgate. When it was all over he had a bout of influenza, and did not take his seat till March 12th.

That day's business was a full-dress debate on the fiscal question. The House was packed. The friends who knew Balfour, and the foes, many of whom knew him not, were all equally eager to watch the manner of his return.

Here in a family letter is an eye-witness's account from the Ladies' Gallery of the scene, and of the first encounter between Balfour and the new Prime Minister, Sir Henry Campbell-Bannerman.

Balfour had gone down to the House in a fighting mood.

> Arthur . . . seemed to be snorting battle like a war-horse . . . his talk was all of the speeches he meant to make . . . and he told us some of the points he was going to make to-day. At 2.30 he and Alice[1] drove off in one brougham, and Evelyn[2] and I[3] followed in another. This was the first time I have seen the new House. Herbert Gladstone was answering a Question about the Aliens Bill. Joe and Austen and Wyndham on our Opposition Bench. . . . Mrs. Herbert Gladstone told us Asquith could not be there—thrown out of a cab yesterday, and feeling the effects of it to-day. . . . If he had been there I can't believe the scene that followed would have happened.
>
> About half an hour after the end of Questions Arthur appeared at the Bar. Clarke and Acland-Hood close to him. He put up his glasses and surveyed the House with an interested smile. Many shook hands with him and were cordially greeted. When Joe was up asking a question about the business of the House, Arthur looked at him with an amused face, and his finger on his lip. Questions over, the Speaker said any Member wishing to do so could take his seat. Then the three came forward. The cheers of our men

[1] Miss Balfour.   [2] Lady Rayleigh.
[3] Lady Betty Balfour, Mr. Gerald Balfour's wife. The letter is from her to Lady Frances Balfour.

"ENOUGH OF THIS FOOLERY"

were kept up a long time, but the volume of sound was not great, the rest of the House keeping silence. He sat himself down with his accustomed leisurely manner, still smiling, between Joe and Austen.

Then a speech from Kitson, and another. . . . When Arthur rose the whole House cheered him. It was odd to think how many had never seen or heard him before.

His manner and delivery were his very best—no hesitation, no looking for words. Point after point was made with perfect courtesy and never failing effect, as if he was thoroughly enjoying himself. His own men warmed behind him, the Government men jeering and laughing whenever he appealed for a plain and distinct answer to his questions, but they did not interrupt, and listened respectfully—or at any rate silently. Before sitting down he leaned far over the Table, and begged for an explanation or answer. When he sat down a man from the back Government benches sprang up, and the whole House called out: "Bannerman, Bannerman." Several speeches followed, and no Front Bench man rose. Then Joe got up. He simply repeated Arthur's questions, and once more begged for a reply, and when silence followed he moved the Adjournment. A tremendous noise at this. Arthur looked quite delighted. Some new men followed, urging their leader not to take advice from the Member for Birmingham. . . . Then A. J. B. rose again. This second speech brought Campbell-Bannerman to his feet, amidst roars of applause from all sides. He was obviously angry, stammered and was rude. . . . I shall be much astonished if the effect of the whole afternoon is not to put new heart and spirit into our men, and to make the Government side realise they have now a formidable opponent. . . .

"Enough of this foolery!" Sir Henry Campbell-Bannerman had exclaimed, alluding to the awkward questions about existing Indian cotton duties and the like, which were, he declared, too utterly futile, nonsensical and misleading to deserve an answer. "Enough of this foolery! It might have answered very well in

31

ARTHUR JAMES BALFOUR

1907 the last Parliament, but it is altogether out of place in this Parliament. The tone and temper of this Parliament will not permit it. Move your amendments and let us get to business."

The tariff debate had been intended primarily for a mocking salvo fired over a fallen foe; "the proper sequel to the Liberal triumph at the polls," as Sir Henry Campbell-Bannerman's biographer describes it.[1] The fight opened in earnest with an Education Bill, designed to reverse the settlement of Balfour's Act, by withdrawing rate aid from denominational teaching. The destruction of that Bill by the Peers' Amendments gave the signal for the struggle between the two Houses, which became the major political issue throughout the remaining years of Balfour's leadership of the Party.

Political animosities were mounting to a pitch rarely known in our modern politics. It was a period in which the national genius for compromise, and the inclination to achieve it, both seemed to have lost their power over the development of events. These all led up to the struggle between Lords and Commons, and it is not only in retrospect that the climax appears inevitable. From the moment when the Peers refused to pass the Education Bill of 1906 as it stood, till the final trial of wills over the Budget of 1909, the coming collision was the dominating fact towards which everything was tending. That seems to have been Balfour's conviction, and he never encouraged attempts to evade the challenge. Least of all did he desire to see the House of Lords preserve its powers by declining to exercise them. Nor was he an enthusiast for its reform. This was brought under serious consideration in the year 1907, in consequence of a Bill introduced by Lord Newton at the instigation

[1] See *Life of Sir Henry Campbell-Bannerman*, by J. A. Spender, Vol. II, p. 272.

THE HOUSE OF LORDS

of a section of the Unionists, who believed that by 1907 removing the obvious weaknesses in the constitution of the House of Lords, the Peers would be strengthened to resist the attack upon their powers.

The real position was frankly stated by the Liberal peers. They were not interested in the constitution of the Upper House, but only in the question of its relations with the Commons. They voted, therefore, with the minority against the proposal to refer the Bill to a Select Committee. The Committee sat throughout the year 1907, and reported finally in favour of certain reforms, including modification of the hereditary principle. The suggestion seemed to Balfour very dangerous. He put his beliefs about the Second Chamber, its duties, and its constitution into a speech delivered in his old Manchester constituency in October 1907.

> The power which the House of Lords has, and which it undoubtedly ought to exercise, is not to prevent the people of this country having the laws they wish to have, but to see that the laws are not . . . the hasty and ill-considered off-spring of one passionate election. Now supposing our Radical friends take in hand to reform the Second Chamber, is it not obvious that if you were to attempt to substitute for the House of Lords anything in the nature of the American Senate . . . instead of diminishing the power of the Second Chamber you will increase it, and increase it at the expense of the power of the House of Commons? . . . If you have got rid of what people are pleased to call the hereditary principle, a Chamber so elected would . . . insist, naturally, rightly and properly, on having their voice in the constitution or support of a Government, their voice in the general consideration of financial administration. . . . I am too much a member of the House of Commons to desire it for my part. . .

What he had said in the country he said to his colleagues in the Upper House. When the Committee

ARTHUR JAMES BALFOUR

on Reform was on the verge of reporting he wrote to Lord Lansdowne on February 22nd, 1908:

> If the subject were one which only concerned the domestic politics of the House of Lords, I should say nothing; it would be out of my province. But I gather that all the schemes which are before you would require legislation ... and that though there are at least two plans which find favour ... they both involve the admission that hereditary Members of the Upper House should have some qualification besides birth and solvency for exercising legislative functions. I hope you will think twice before you admit this innovation. The justification for the House of Lords is partly historical, partly practical. It is an original portion of the British Constitution, and it works well. It is only bad political theory that asks for anything more. But if the House of Lords ... admit that hereditary right is an insufficient qualification ... they inevitably raise the question why it is a qualification at all. ...
>
> Of course I do not mean by this that no change should be admitted. I have always been in favour of Life Peers. The principle is already admitted, and it has historical justifications.[1]

Nothing in point of fact came of the Report of the Committee on Reform. Events moved on during the years 1907 and 1908 much as Balfour had forecasted.

> The real point [he had written to Lord Lansdowne on April 13th, 1906] is to secure that the Party in the two Houses shall not work as separate armies. This is all-important. There has certainly never been a period in our history in which the House of Lords will be called upon to play a part at once so important, so delicate, and so difficult. I conjecture that the Government methods of carrying on their legislative work will be this: They will bring in Bills in a much more extreme form than the moderate members of their Cabinet probably approve; the moderate members will trust to the House of Lords cutting out or modifying the most outrageous pro-

[1] See *Life of Lord Lansdowne*, p. 363, for parts of this letter omitted here.

visions. The left wing of the Cabinet, on the other hand, while 1908 looking forward to the same result, will be consoled for the anticipated mutilation of their measures by the reflection that they will be gradually accumulating a case against the Upper House, and that they will be able to appeal at the next Election for a mandate to modify its constitution.

This scheme is an ingenious one, and it will be our business to defeat it as far as we can.

I do not think the House of Lords will be able to escape the duty of making serious modifications in important Government measures; but if this be done with caution and tact, I do not believe that they will do themselves any harm. On the contrary, as the rejection of the Home Rule Bill undoubtedly strengthened their position, I think it quite possible that your House may come out of the ordeal strengthened rather than weakened by the inevitable difficulties of the next few years.

It is, of course, impossible to foresee how each particular case is to be dealt with; but I incline to advise that we should fight all points of importance very stiffly in the Commons, and should make the House of Lords the theatre of compromise. It is evident that you can never fight for a position which we have surrendered; while, on the other hand, the fact that we have strenuously fought for the position, and been severely beaten, may afford adequate ground for your making a " graceful concession " to the Representative Chamber.

Yours ever,
A. J. B.

If Balfour's Parliamentary reputation was still capable of being enhanced, enhanced it was from the beginning of the 1906 Parliament. He was in his element in the opening fight over the Education Bill, knowing his subject from A to Z, and stirred to the depths of his political convictions by the attempt to upset the principles of freedom for religious teaching on which his own Act was founded. The hundred and fifty-seven Unionists were soon experiencing the joys of battle as only a small Opposition under an inspiring leader can. Most of

ARTHUR JAMES BALFOUR

1906 them were seasoned men, but some of the veterans were absent in the beginning. Lord Hugh Cecil had lost his seat at Greenwich, and his vitriolic oratory was badly missed, but on the other hand there was now his brother, Lord Robert, beginning at once to take advantage of unique opportunities, and among other formidable new recruits there was Mr. F. E. Smith.[1]

There was "bonny fighting," therefore, up till the middle of June, when the Government began to closure the Education debates by guillotine. The Third Reading took place on July 30th. Before then Balfour was doing all he could to prepare the Lords for their entry on to the field. He circulated a Memorandum for a suggested policy on July 4th.

> I assume that the House of Lords will read it (the Bill) a second time, and that they will amend it drastically in Committee. I assume the first because I think its rejection on Second Reading is a policy which so far commends itself to no responsible members of the Opposition, and I assume the second, because the strong feelings which the Bill has aroused in every part of the country would not, I think, be satisfied with merely surface amendments.

Then comes a technical examination of the Bill, which apparently entailed more knowledge of the subject than some of their Lordships possessed; for Balfour followed it up ten days later with another paper, longer and more simply stated, setting forth a scheme for Amendments, insisting, as his own Act had done, on the rights of the parents, who desired denominational teaching for their children. "This," he wrote, "should be the governing element in any scheme which the House of Lords may substitute for the plan of the Government."

[1] Afterwards Earl of Birkenhead.

THE LORDS INSIST

The debates in the Upper House ended on December 6th with the emergence of a transformed Bill. The Government refused to consider the Lords' Amendments in detail, and asked the Commons to reject them as a whole. This was an unprecedented challenge to the Peers, and the moderates in the Cabinet had perhaps persuaded themselves that it would lead to an immediate compromise, which would, as the Prime Minister wrote to the King, " save the Bill, and settle the conflict at least for a time."[1]

Negotiations were opened privately with Lord Lansdowne on the same day that the Cabinet's decision was announced in the House of Commons, where every effort was made to throw the whole responsibility for a breakdown upon Balfour. The Prime Minister appealed to him as " the man having authority over the two Houses " to say whether he wished to save the Bill. Balfour had no desire to " save the Bill." What he desired to save was the educational system of which he had himself been the chief architect.

How far he was from shirking the responsibility can be seen from a private letter written a year later, where he says : " What difference my continuing to lead the Opposition has made neither I nor anyone else can accurately gauge. But I strongly suspect that the Education Bill of last Session would have become law in what I think a very pernicious form had I been away." It was therefore with no feelings of regret or dismay that he greeted the passing of the motion whereby the Lords decided by a majority of 142 to 53, that " this House do insist on its Amendments."

When the Bill came down for the last time to the House of Commons on December 18th, he was laid up with influenza. Therefore he heard neither the Prime

[1] See *Life of Sir Henry Campbell-Bannerman*, Vol. II, p. 307.

ARTHUR JAMES BALFOUR

1906 Minister's indictment of himself, nor the threat which accompanied the withdrawal of the Bill:

> The resources of the House of Commons are not exhausted, and I say with conviction that a way must be found, and a way will be found, by which the will of the people, expressed through their elected representatives, will be made to prevail.

Reports from the country of Liberal audiences " at fever-pitch about the Lords" caused the Government to consider for a moment the idea of an immediate election. But those Unionists who had judged the indignation to be largely unreal were justified in their belief. It was decided that " the Education Bill was not big enough for the great issue which must be raised before the final battle was joined."[1] The House of Lords had rejected other Government Bills in 1906, but had not refused the Trades Disputes Bill, which relaxed the law of conspiracy in respect of peaceful picketing, and exempted Trade Union funds from liability in action for damages for torts. This was a question which roused in great sections of the community feelings far more powerful than any controversy over Education. The Trades Disputes Bill was, to begin with, the outcome of the Report of a Royal Commission set up in 1903 when Balfour was Prime Minister. It reversed the result of a judgment of the House of Lords on the Taff Vale Case, which made Trade Unions suable for their funds. Resentment against that judgment had been a contributing cause for the great increase of the support for organised Labour, which had struck Balfour as the really important fact disclosed by the Election of 1906. Undoubtedly both the Unionist and Liberal Parties shrank now from denying to the rising forces in

[1] See *Life of Sir Henry Campbell-Bannerman*, Vol. II, p. 312.

TACTICS OF THE LORDS

politics the privileged position they demanded. Undoubtedly also both Parties disliked the necessity. Lord Lansdowne frankly said so when advising the House of Lords to pass the Bill.[1] Balfour perhaps objected to it less than some of his colleagues. In a speech on its Third Reading in November 1906, he propounded a cardinal article of his faith—belief in the capacity of Englishmen to use exceptional powers with moderation. But he disliked the provision extending the exemption to Employers' Unions. He thought that combinations of employers might prove as dangerous in the future as combinations of workmen.[2]

The acquiescence of the House of Lords over the Trades Disputes Act had deprived the Government of a most advantageous opportunity of " accumulating the case." It had also legalised a claim to privilege on the part of organised Labour which was very repugnant to the lawyers who were so strongly represented in Sir Henry Campbell-Bannerman's Cabinet.[3] Thus the main legislative harvest of the Government's first year was not a particularly welcome crop to themselves. No measures as important as either the Education, or the Trades Disputes Bills, came up to the Lords in 1907, but they frustrated an attempt at Scottish land legislation which would have introduced the very principle of dual ownership that was in process of being abolished in Ireland.

The Liberal Party were by this time suffering from a sort of " persecution mania " on the subject of the House of Lords. Mr. Lloyd George put their sentiments into words when he called it " not the watch-dog of the constitution, but Mr. Balfour's poodle."

[1] See *Life of Lord Lansdowne*, p. 359.
[2] *Hansard*, November 1, 2, 3, 1906.
[3] *Life of Lord Oxford and Asquith*, Vol. II, p. 183.

ARTHUR JAMES BALFOUR

1907   There was a vehement demand that the Prime Minister should fulfil his pledge, and "find a way" to curb its power. The result was a Resolution, carried through the House of Commons in June 1907, by 432 to 147, which declared that "the power of the other House to alter or reject Bills must be so restricted by law as to secure that within the limits of a single Parliament the final decisions of the Commons shall prevail." But there the matter was left for the time being.

In April 1908 Sir Henry Campbell-Bannerman died. Of all the Front Bench men who ever sat opposite Balfour in the House of Commons Sir Henry was perhaps the one on whom the attraction of his personality produced the least effect. " C. B. always disliked me," Balfour said once, and Mr. Lloyd George has told me since that this was true, adding that he thought the feeling was mutual, for he had never, in twenty-five years' experience, seen Balfour take less pains to observe the amenities of debate than where Sir Henry was concerned.

Mr. Asquith became Prime Minister, and the Bill of the Session in 1908 was a Licensing Bill, which proposed to cut down the number of public houses in a rigid ratio to the population. For fourteen years some compensation would be paid for the licences extinguished, but would thereafter cease. This penalisation of a particular form of property roused intense indignation, and since the mere cutting down of the number of public houses had been shown statistically to be in itself not a remedy for drinking, the Bill contained no off-setting advantage in the way of reform. Like the Education Bill, this measure struck at the root of legislation passed by Balfour's Government which had for one main object the raising of the status of the Licensee. Balfour was furious about it. He thought it made neither for justice nor for temperance. By removing the security for legitimate profit the Government were making it impossible for any self-respecting or independent man to have dealings with the great and legitimate industry of the publican.[1] This was against every interest of public decency and morality. Such were his views, shared in this instance by most of the Unionist Peers, who decided by an overwhelming majority to reject the Bill.

This was the position in November 1908, on the verge of the constitutional struggle which opened with the action of the Peers in respect of Mr. Lloyd George's Budget in 1909. Before relating Balfour's part in that story there is another side of the picture of these years of Opposition leadership to be filled in. He has been sketched in attack upon the foes in front. What now of his own demeanour under criticisms from behind? These, at the end of 1906, were beginning to perturb the Whips and Party managers. The fiscal question was still at the bottom of it all, and the very energy that Balfour brought to his attacks on the Government was made by contrast a matter of reproach. The right wing could not endure to see such fighting quality spent in a campaign of pure destruction. The old maxim that the business of an Opposition is to oppose was held by them to be out of date. They demanded a programme. The whole experience of Balfour's Parliamentary life reinforced his conviction that they were wrong. On this point he was adamant, and would not have yielded, even if the programme demanded had been concerned with something other than tariffs. His response to appeals on this head leaves no doubt as to that. They were made to him from quarters where advice cannot be lightly disregarded by a Party leader, however autocratic.

[1] See Albert Hall Speech, June 25th, 1908.

ARTHUR JAMES BALFOUR

1907 Balfour was no autocrat by temperament, and he was intensely respectful of expert opinion. But in this question he felt himself the expert, and in his refusal of a positive policy to his handful of Parliamentary followers in the first flush of the Liberal triumph he saw no room for argument. The Party could destroy its own hopes in two ways—by internal splits, which he could not stop, but still hoped to modify by maintaining his middle position in the tariff controversy—or by making itself the target for criticism, an act of self-immolation which he was determined to prevent so long as he kept the command.

This was his attitude throughout the four years of the Parliament of 1906. It has been found fault with on two counts, both of them, if true, seriously damaging to a leader's reputation. It was said that constructive policies made no appeal to his frigid and critical intellect, and secondly that he was too much out of touch with his rank and file to realise the depressing effect of his tactics upon them.

The record of his own Government in domestic and foreign policy should dispose of the first of these accusations. The second was a myth. Some members even of his own " Shadow Cabinet " at this period seem to have been under the impression that his life, on its political side, was hedged in by people who told him only what was pleasant to hear. But in reality from the small beginnings of the revolt against his leadership, until the moment five years later when he judged that the Party interests would be best served by his resignation, he was fully informed. It appears that even the following letter contained little that he did not know, although it dates almost the first mutterings of the discontent. It was written to him during his holiday in Scotland in January 1907 by his confidential

CRITICISMS

Private Secretary, Mr. J. S. Sandars. It refers in the 1907 first place to correspondence with the Party Whips and others. It tells of fresh funds and support forthcoming for the Tariff Reformers, hints at intrigues against Balfour's authority, and then goes on:

> It is pointed out by the more ardent section that since your letter of Feb. 14th last year, nothing has been said, no public speeches have been made by you in furtherance of this—the first constructive test of the Unionist Party. They do not argue that you wish to go back on your words; they do say that the policy of Fiscal Reform does not fill your heart and mind; they argue that in a case where you are really and profoundly moved, as in the matter of Education, you will fight, and fight hard, and spend the last ounce of your strength over it. And they contrast the matter in which you are interested with that which does not earn a speech, or part of a speech. . . . The rank and file clamour for some broad line of policy above and beyond resisting and denouncing a Government no matter how pernicious it may be. . . . They thoroughly appreciate your great services to the Party, your ripe experience, and the extraordinary skill you exhibit in leading the Party in Parliament. But they are not proof against the blandishments of those who promise that they can sweep the country with a fiscal policy that will be of enormous national benefit, and they cannot be made to see that their chance will come the sooner if only they will concentrate on the iniquities of the most vulnerable Government of modern times. If you do not speak on the fiscal question, then the malcontents will declare that their contention is well founded and that you are indifferent to the Tariff issue. . . . The bulk of the Party do not for a moment desire that you should commit yourself to details . . . but they do want a statement on broad lines touching Fiscal Reform in its relation to finance both Imperial and local; they would like a sympathetic reference to closer commercial union with the Colonies; they would like a point made of the fact that schemes of social reform cannot be accomplished without the elasticity of revenue which alone can be obtained from a wider basis of taxation. . . .

ARTHUR JAMES BALFOUR

1907

A speech on these lines would, in Hood's[1] opinion, pull the Party together. The point is—are you disposed to make it? It may in your judgement be unwise to make it. Be it so—but then, says Hood, we shall practically lose our army—very likely not all at once, but by degrees, until anarchy is succeeded by a new authority. . . .

I may observe that Hood has never mentioned to me the question of food taxation. *Personally* I consider the case as hopeless, so long as we advocate a policy which embraces it. In writing thus frankly to you even as the mouthpiece of others, I do not fail to see . . . the egregious folly of those who . . . wish to sacrifice a proportion of their strength by making themselves responsible for a constructive policy, which is just the target that their opponents want. But you have to take men as you find them, and if they will choose the path of difficulty it still behoves you—their leader—to guide them, doesn't it? How best to do it is the question.

Yours affecly.,

J. S. SANDARS.

Balfour answered by return:

Jan. 24th, 1907.

MY DEAR JACK SANDARS,

Thanks much for your most lucid, interesting and excellent letters. As regards the one on the Party and Tariff Reform, I was well acquainted with almost all that it contains. . . .

I rather propose telling the Party the " truth in love " at Hull, and not waiting for the 15th, where however I could repeat the lesson if it were necessary. I shall of course have to touch on Tariff Reform, and say what I have so often said before, but what apparently our Tariff Reform friends are never tired of hearing. I am by no means sure that we shall not have to carry the war into the enemy's camp and make it quite clear that if the Party is to be destroyed—which can easily be done by either wing—the disloyal T.Rs. have at least as much to lose as anybody else. But this is a policy only to be adopted in the last resort.

[1] Sir Alexander Acland-Hood (afterwards Lord St. Audries) Chief Opposition Whip.

LOOKING AHEAD

Balfour accordingly expounded straight away his reasons for resisting "programmes" in Opposition, recalling the great object lesson of Mr. Gladstone's "Newcastle Programme" of Social Reform in 1891, a source of much subsequent embarrassment to his Party.

> I am sure [Balfour said] that no competent politician has ever done what I have been asked by some people to do except under duress, and no politician who has done it in duress has ever done so without repenting what he did for the rest of his natural life.

Then he passed to tariffs, observing that if in the past year of strenuous opposition in Parliament he had said little about them, it was not because his views on great matters were subject to variations. He could not quite understand why a monthly bulletin was required of his opinions on the fiscal question. He tried then to give his audience something like his own range of vision.

> Unless we have it in us to take a view of the commercial relations of the great States of the world which reaches forward not one or two years, but into the far future, we are not in a position to form a sane judgment upon the fiscal controversy.... What is our relation as a country dependent entirely upon its manufactures to our great trade rivals in the world? That is, our relation to the markets which are, and the markets which are to be? That is the real question. ... I think I see signs, even amongst members of the Government, of some weakening in that rather childish self-complacency as regards our position among the great commercial nations, which was in place, I dare say, two generations ago, or even one generation ago, but, believe me, is not in place now....
> Fiscal Reform remains in my view the main constructive plank in the Unionist programme. But do not let us become a party of one idea, for if we become a party of one idea, we shall fail to carry even that idea to a successful issue.

ARTHUR JAMES BALFOUR

1907 Balfour looked as it were through a powerful telescope at developments as yet barely visible to the naked eye. They fill the field, they obsess his attention. The marketing problems of our own day appeared as much " the real question " to him nearly thirty years ago as to a generation consciously launched upon the tide of economic nationalism. They can understand his point without his exceptional vision. But for the Tariff Reformers of his own day the difference of focus was baffling. And he was forced often enough to lay the telescope down and turn his attention to quarrels between the two wings of his Party which seemed, from his point of view, little else but suicidal folly. The reader who is spared the petty details of these contentions, and of Party reorganisation in those years of opposition, should remember how large they bulked in the daily life of the Chief. They were a constant strain on the patience of a man peculiarly ill at ease in an atmosphere of squabbling.

Just as the technique of leadership in the House of Commons is different on either side of the Speaker's Chair, so it may be that the qualities required of a great political leader are not the same in opposition as those which have inspired confidence when his Party was in power. In opposition his personal authority is inevitably weakened. If, like Balfour, he is a first-class Parliamentarian the Party may be as ready as ever to admit his supremacy in the conduct of debate; but outside the House of Commons his judgment is sure to be more freely questioned. In the first place the check imposed upon open criticism by reluctance to weaken the Government no longer works. The Olympian atmosphere that surrounds Cabinet Ministers vanishes, and with it some of the deference paid to those who are in possession of special inside knowledge. For these, and other causes,

IN THE WILDERNESS

the rank and file begin, perhaps subconsciously, to demand from their leader a degree of respect for their point of view greater than they might claim when his time and thoughts are visibly occupied by great affairs of State. And this demand may require from him qualities quite other than those which originally marked him out for the leader's place. He must not only understand the minds of his people, but it becomes essential now that his own processes of thought should not be too far beyond their comprehension. The obstacles that, in Balfour's case, made this difficult, were increased by the habit of mind which some twenty years of power had engendered in him and in his followers. They were now clearly doomed to abide in the wilderness for a considerable time—a sojourn to which even a people who had escaped from captivity in Egypt did not adjust themselves easily or without murmuring.

Any impression that the Hull speech may have made soon wore off, and eight months later—in October 1907 —Balfour received from Mr. Austen Chamberlain a long and serious letter about the state of politics.

The fight, he wrote, was no longer the old type of straight contest between Government and Opposition. The Liberals were losing ground, but Labour-Socialism was making enormous progress. This, he felt persuaded, was because it advocated an active and positive policy, with a united and decided voice. The only remedy for this state of things was for Unionism to do the same.

Next came the old plea for a fresh pronouncement on an Imperial Tariff policy. The Government had committed itself to a universal non-contributory scheme of Old Age Pensions. Could not Unionism declare itself in favour of one to be financed, one-third by the State, one-third by the workman, one-third by the employer? There should be a Conservative land

1907 policy of purchase and ownership. A housing policy should be considered too, and some definite line be taken on home industries with special reference to sweating. " Surely here we have the elements of a fine programme, Conservative in the best sense of the word." Would Balfour not organise and proclaim it in broad general outlines ?

Three weeks after this letter was written, the National Union of Conservative Associations held its annual meeting—this year in Birmingham. There Balfour's first task was to pay tribute to an absent figure. Mr. Joseph Chamberlain's place was empty, and the deep emotion with which the great audience responded to the first mention of his name testified to their knowledge that it might never be filled again. His public life had in fact ended with the seizure which had followed the celebrations of his seventieth birthday the year before.

The criticisms of the Unionist leadership were of course not unknown to the Government, and the Prime Minister had predicted that Birmingham would be Balfour's Canossa. He was wrong. At the end of the Birmingham speech it was clearer than ever that if the Unionists were to change their tactics, they would have to change their leader also. Within these limits Balfour did what he could. The points in Mr. Austen Chamberlain's letter were specifically mentioned as things to be worked for. He went further than ever before in the direction of Preference, attacking the Government for " wantonly and recklessly " throwing away opportunities at the Colonial Conference of that year. He showed the Tariff Reformers the mighty facts which were working for them, and undermining the Free Trade case in respect of corn.

> Wheat [he told them] is now subject not to the law of increasing cost, it is subject to the law of diminishing cost,

BYZANTINE FEUDS

and enormous strides in the growth of wheat in Canada, Argentina and elsewhere—the enormous improvements in transport—however unfortunate for the farming class to which I belong—absolutely destroy the whole basis of the economic argument familiar to our forefathers.

1909

Time was with them. The urgent thing was unity. Someone had put down a Resolution declaring war on the Free Trade Unionists. It was not even formally discussed. Had it been so the Delegates from Lancashire and Yorkshire would have been up in arms.[1] There was nothing here to persuade Balfour that his judgment was in fault. The Birmingham meeting reasserted his position.

It was about this time that he wrote to a friend:

> As regards the attacks on myself, I quite understand your point of view that they do harm to the Party, and therefore ought, if possible, to be put an end to. But you will admit, I think, that I can do nothing to put an end to them. I am certainly not going to go about the country explaining that I am "honest and industrious," like a second coachman out of place! If people cannot find it out for themselves, they must, so far as I can see, remain in ignorance.

This is the last selection that need be given from the vast correspondence on a controversy which had perforce absorbed the greater part of Balfour's energy ever since fiscal reform became a living question in 1903. In face of the constitutional issues which were dominating politics in 1909 the quarrels between Unionist Free Traders and Protectionists degenerated into the likeness of Byzantine feuds. But their very continuance was a justification of Balfour's Fabian attitude, and he was presently to reap some reward for the skill and patience with which he had maintained it all those years. For it

[1] See Annual Register for 1907, p. 251.

1909 was a united Party that he led into the General Election of January 1910.

The second phase of the conflict between the two Houses opened with the introduction of Mr. Lloyd George's Budget in May 1909. Thenceforward events moved in direct sequence to the passing of the Parliament Act, and the causes of Balfour's resignation of the Unionist leadership in 1911.

That story had a prelude, during which a split in the Liberal Cabinet on a vital issue seemed likely to change the face of politics. In the first quarter of the year 1909 some members of the Government awoke, or suddenly confessed themselves awake, to the danger threatening British supremacy at sea from the progressive increase in the German navy. The Board of Admiralty, through the mouth of Mr. McKenna, the First Lord, demanded immediate provision for six new Dreadnoughts in the Estimates. Dynamic forces in the Cabinet, represented by the Chancellor of the Exchequer and the President of the Board of Trade (Mr. Lloyd George and Mr. Winston Churchill) held out for four. Mr. Asquith, the Prime Minister, who is said to have favoured the six, devised a compromise by proposing that four should be laid down at once, and preparations made for another four in the same financial year if need be.[1] Eventually this was done, and " the curious and characteristic solution was reached," described by Mr. Winston Churchill in his *History of the World Crisis*. " The Admiralty had demanded six ships; the economists offered four, and we finally compromised on eight."[2]

It is doubtful whether this result would have been attained but for the agitation in the country, which had been awakened in good earnest to the fact that our

[1] See *Life of Lord Oxford and Asquith*, Vol. 1, p. 253.
[2] See *The World Crisis*, 1911–1914, pp. 136–138.

A. J. BALFOUR
1911

WE WANT EIGHT

command of the sea was challenged. The Government which had talked so much of "the will of the people" in respect of policies that only commanded the support of sections, discovered now what the phrase could mean. The feeling was of course a fresh asset to the Conservative Party, as the bye-elections of that spring showed. There happened to be a good many of them. Liberal majorities fell, and in Central Glasgow the first re-gain of a Scottish seat took place. From the Conservative stronghold at Croydon spread the slogan: " We want eight and we won't wait."

It was apparently Mr. George Wyndham who first presented the public with that invaluable expression of its sentiments, in a speech at Wigan.[1] The Conservatives made full use of the Government's hesitation in satisfying the demand for more ships, but it was a case where Party advantage ran second to conviction. In a Debate on March 29th Balfour indignantly rebutted Sir Edward Grey's insinuations of Party motive in the Vote of Censure on the naval policy of the Government. Three nights the Opposition had waited, Balfour said, hoping that the Debates on the Estimates would produce assurances that the Government was fully alive to the situation, but never had he said one single word that could weaken their hands. These were days when men who differ from the Government of the day should sink their differences lest they should weaken the nation in the eyes of their potential opponents.

For Balfour this matter had been far above faction from the moment of his awakening to his responsibilities for Imperial Defence during the South African War. A letter must be quoted, dated two years before the German Navy Law of 1908, and before the shipbuilding

[1] See *Annual Register*, 1909, p. 62.

ARTHUR JAMES BALFOUR

1909 programme bequeathed by his own Government had been cut down under Sir Henry Campbell-Bannerman and Mr. Asquith. Balfour wrote to a correspondent who desired a Parliamentary debate on our naval strength.

> You are mistaken in supposing that no notice has been taken of C. B.'s speech on the two-Power standard. I have referred to it more than once, and, indeed, I believe it is my references, and my references alone, which have brought it into notice. If I had thought that C. B. represented his Government in this matter, I should regard it as one of the gravest events in our history. I rather think, however, he does not.
>
> As regards the strength of the Fleet, the difficulty is this. So far as my information goes, our strength is now very far above the two-Power standard. Foreign nations are not building, and, according to the view of the Admiralty, neither now nor for some years, would Germany have even a " look in " if they went to war with us. Now if this account of the present state of things is true, we who regard the maintenance of a powerful Fleet as the first duty of a Government have much more to lose than to gain by a debate in which the Admiralty would be forced to avow our overwhelming superiority. The reckless economists on the other side, who are in a vast majority, would quote C. B.'s precious dictum about the two-Power standard, and would ask how on earth this squared with the Admiralty performance. On purely public grounds, therefore, I am, as at present advised, not encouraging a party fight over this matter. If we were animated by purely party feelings, of course I should take a different line ; and, if I became convinced that the Admiralty really are doing the reverse of what I am informed on good authority is their real policy, I should do my best to rouse the whole country. At present I keep an open mind. . . .

Soon after this the Government's policy began to alarm him, and he kept his word. Here is one extract from the speeches he delivered up and down the country in the spring of 1909.

SEA-POWER

> For three years I and my friends have pleaded for the cause of a greater Navy, especially in respect of Dreadnoughts. For three years we have pointed out the inevitable dangers that are ahead of us.... They (the Government) had their warning, they refused to take it. It has come upon them, but I believe upon them only—as a surprise that Germany now has a power of ship-building not second even to this country, and superior to every other country in the world.... Was it not their duty to forecast all these possibilities ... and to take adequate precautions? We left them with a settled programme of four battleships a year. In their first year of office they built but three. In their second year they built but three. In their third year, at the very moment when Germany was straining every nerve to increase its power of output, they added nothing to their plant, and only two Dreadnoughts to the power of the British Navy.

1909

The conditional promise of Mr. Asquith somewhat quieted the nation. Interest flowed back into other controversies, but Balfour's uneasiness was not submerged. At the end of the year he wrote in a private letter:

> The condition of our first line of defence gives me great anxiety, and I have the profoundest distrust of the policy of the present Government in respect of this all-important part of their administrative duties.... I do not think it is possible to say *exactly* what ought to be done to put the Navy right, until we have adequate knowledge of the points in which it is wrong, which it is not easy for an Opposition to obtain. One thing however is certain: if we fail in maintaining our sea-power, it does not matter in the least where we succeed. Tariff Reform, Social Reform, all reforms are perfectly useless. As a nation we shall have ceased to count.

Balfour hammered on this subject in the General Election campaign of January 1910, knowing well enough that the Board of Admiralty, and probably some of the Ministers, welcomed secretly every word he said.

ARTHUR JAMES BALFOUR

1909 No sign of this appeared however in the replies of Mr. Asquith and Sir Edward Grey. Their tone was of rebuke to the scare-monger, and the following passage in a speech of his at Hanley on January 5th, 1910, was specially picked out for condemnation.

> I am not a pessimist about the naval future, if the country rises to the height of its obligations and its necessities. But unless the country will face facts, how can you expect it to rise to that height? Go about at this moment, and consult the statesmen and diplomatists of the lesser Powers, and I am perfectly confident you will find an absolute unanimity of opinion that a struggle sooner or later between this country and Germany is inevitable. I don't agree with them, but that is their opinion. They have watched with the closest interest, but not, I believe, always with perfect comprehension, that (to foreigners) most mysterious thing, English public opinion, and they have come to the conclusion, I believe utterly wrongly, that we are not alive to a sense of our responsibilities . . . and therefore we are predestined to succumb in some great contest, the occasion of which nobody can foresee, to a country which does face facts, which is alive to its responsibility, and which talks little, and does much.

Chapter III

DIE-HARDS

The Budget of 1909. Pros and cons of resistance by the House of Lords. Death of King Edward VII. The Constitutional Conference. Balfour's Memorandum on its break-down. General Election of December 1910. Balfour's views on the request of Ministers for a pledge from the King to create Peers. The Conservative Shadow Cabinet of July 21st, 1911. The "Die-hards" arise. Balfour's suppressed Memorandum on the Constitutional Crisis.

On April 29th, 1909, Mr. Lloyd George called up the storm. He introduced the most polemic Budget in our history with a moderation of language that masked for the moment the real nature of some of its proposals. These were highly complicated, and the new money to be got from them all was only sixteen millions, required that year for the naval increases, and projected social reforms. Fresh revenue was to be raised from increased income and super-tax, heavier death duties, bigger duties on spirits and tobacco, and from an entirely new tax of 20 per cent on unearned increment in land, payable on sale or death. It took the Opposition a little while to realise the full effects of this. As soon as they did so, the Conservatives determined to resist the land tax at all costs. It was not alarm at the immediate burden which lay at the root of that momentous decision. It sprang from the irresistible instinct of self-preservation in the class from which the Party derived its tradition and much of its strength. The land taxes, and the land valuation clauses attached to them, were a death-blow to the landed gentry. They

1909

1909 opened the way to unlimited confiscation. There was not a squire in England who could not visualise the results upon his son's inheritance. The country gentlemen needed no instruction about this from the political leaders, and, in respect of the valuation proposals, they foresaw better than anybody the inevitable breakdown of a scheme that would in the meantime cost vast sums of public money. There were further reasons that appealed with force to some minds, among them Balfour's. The insertion of a Land Valuation Bill into a Bill for raising revenue was an outrageous proceeding, and he protested against it with all his might.

> I defy any constitutional lawyer in this House to say it is legitimate for the House of Commons to introduce into its Finance Bill great measures of valuation and compulsory registration. . . . How dare you describe it as a Finance Bill ? By your own admission it is not a Finance Bill. It is a compulsory Registration Bill.

The Conservatives fought it line by line, with only a ten days' recess between Whitsuntide and November 4th, when it passed the House of Commons. Before then the interest had been transferred to speculation about the action of the House of Lords. Balfour, in a speech at Bingley Hall, in September, had told the constituencies that he did not believe the verdict of the country would long be deferred. The tension was too great, the opposing forces were marshalling before their very eyes.

This speech evoked more enthusiasm and less criticism from the Party than he had lately been accustomed to. The reason was obvious. The Budget had changed the antitheses of current politics from Tariff Reform versus Free Trade, to Tariff Reform versus Socialist finance. Balfour was on firm ground again, and a General Election was at hand. The speech seems to show that

COMING EVENTS

he was in no doubt that the House of Lords would 1909 reject the Budget. It seems certain also that he was in no doubt they would be right.

There is no evidence, as far as Balfour is concerned, for a belief which seems to have been current in Liberal circles[1] that the rejection of the Budget by the Lords was forced on, against the judgment of the leaders, by certain powerful Peers, notably Lord Cawdor, Lord Milner and Lord Curzon. If the verdict of history is that the Unionist chiefs should have risked revolt in their ranks rather than face the issue which the Liberals were avowedly determined to force upon them sooner or later—then by that verdict Balfour must bear his share of blame. The moment of irrevocable decision is unmarked. No definite answer as to the intentions of the Peers was given to King Edward when (with the Prime Minister's consent) he talked with Lord Lansdowne and Balfour on October 12th,[2] but on the other hand nothing was said to give the Sovereign hope that the collision could be avoided. It seems possible that there was one responsibility which the two Conservative leaders might have hesitated to assume—the responsibility, namely, for the paralysis of the country's finance through the rejection of the Budget. But that anxiety was removed by a disclosure which Mr. Lloyd George made—by chance or otherwise—in private conversation with a friend of Balfour's before the Finance Bill left the Commons. The Government, so the Chancellor of the Exchequer confided, had been engaged for some time in drafting a "stop-gap Budget." This showed that chaos would not follow upon rejection.[3]

[1] See *Annual Register*, 1909, p. 246.
[2] See Sir Sidney Lee, *Life of King Edward VII*, Vol. II, p. 668.
[3] As a matter of fact the situation was met by a Treasury Borrowings Act which was passed early in March, 1910. See *Life of Lord Oxford and Asquith*, Vol. I, p. 275.

ARTHUR JAMES BALFOUR

1910   The Bill went to the Lords on November 16th, and that day Lord Lansdowne gave notice of a Motion which Balfour had taken his share in preparing, as alternative drafts in his handwriting remain to show. The wording had to be as short as possible, containing the one point which the Conservatives must keep before the electorate. Finally Lord Lansdowne's Motion ran: " That this House is not justified in giving its consent to the Bill until it has been submitted to the judgment of the country."

" Is he wrong ? " Balfour asked next day in the Manchester Free Trade Hall. " He is abundantly right, and there never was an occasion when this power, vested by the Constitution in the Second Chamber, was more abundantly justified."

So the cup was filled. On November 30th, after six days of debate, the Lords threw out the Finance Bill. On December 2nd Mr. Asquith declared them to have committed a breach of the Constitution, and a usurpation of the rights of the Commons. On December 3rd Parliament was dissolved. The wine was drawn. Followed the drinking.

The General Election of January 1910 was fought mainly on the abolition of the Veto of the House of Lords. The Unionists regained over a hundred seats, and Mr. Asquith found his Parliamentary majority at the mercy of the eighty-two Irish Nationalist votes.

Thenceforward the main current of politics was forced more and more into Irish affairs. In the first flush of recaptured power over the Parliamentary situation Mr. Redmond, the Irish leader, demanded that the Veto should be abolished in that very year, and with it, the last impediment to the immediate granting of Home Rule. No question of House of Lords Reform was to be allowed to confuse this issue, and he further insisted

REDMOND DISPLEASED

that the British Budget must wait upon the introduction of the Parliament Bill. On these last two points Mr. Asquith acquiesced. But he was not yet ready to pledge himself to an immediate crushing of the resistance by the Upper House to a constitutional diminution of its powers. For that might involve the creation of more Peers, and would require a guarantee from the Sovereign, which the Cabinet was not, in February 1910, as yet prepared to demand. The Prime Minister told the House of Commons that " to ask, in advance, for a blank authority for an indefinite exercise of the Royal Prerogative in regard to a measure which has never been submitted to, or approved by, the House of Commons is a request which, in my judgment, no constitutional statesman can possibly make, and it is a concession which the Sovereign cannot be expected to grant."

This attitude was highly displeasing to the Irishmen, and so long as it was maintained there was judged to be a possibility that they would vote against the Budget, and turn out the Government.[1] On February 15th, the day before Parliament met, Balfour was sounded on behalf of the King, but no doubt at the instigation of Ministers, to find out whether the Opposition would be willing to help in passing the Budget if Mr. Redmond turned against his friends. Balfour's answer was that it would be vain to ask the Unionist Party to vote black where it had before voted white. But he prophesied that Mr. Redmond's threats would prove more formidable than his actions, and that the Government would pass the Budget and survive.[2] He was right, although the quarrels between the allies were not formally settled even when the Government introduced their Veto

[1] See *Life of Lord Oxford and Asquith*, Vol. II, p. 274.
[2] For the full text of this Memorandum of Balfour's, see *Life of Lord Lansdowne*, p. 389.

ARTHUR JAMES BALFOUR

1910 Resolutions in the third week of March. Balfour was at Cannes throughout that month for the sake of his health, which had not been very good during the winter. He came home before the Veto Resolutions were passed and the way thus cleared for the introduction of a Parliament Bill. A Bill was drafted in April, and sent out to King Edward, then at Biarritz, and in the meantime the Budget of the previous year was passed by both Houses (April 28th). The great majority of the Irish Nationalists had voted for it in the Commons, in spite of the Government's refusal to meet their wishes for a reduction of the duties on spirits. But, on the other hand, the Prime Minister had made an immense stride towards the Irishmen's point of view in the final debate on the Veto Resolutions on April 14th, when he said: " If the Lords fail to accept our policy we shall feel it our duty immediately to tender advice to the Crown as to the steps which will have to be taken if that policy is to receive statutory effect in this Parliament."[1]

Although the " steps " were not defined, the tone of this statement was sufficiently different from that of Mr. Asquith's February speech to convince the Opposition leaders that guarantees would be asked for from the King. But their speculation upon the future course of events had not crystallised into decisions about their own action, when King Edward's sudden death in the first week of May transformed the situation for the time being. Balfour and Lord Lansdowne felt, with Mr. Asquith, that every effort must be made to spare King George, at the outset of his reign, the perplexing constitutional decisions which would confront him if the conflict continued on existing lines. An attempt was therefore made to reach agreement by means of a Conference between the Party leaders. They met for the

[1] See *Life of Lord Oxford and Asquith*, Vol. I, p. 279.

THE BREAKDOWN

first time on June 17th, and continued their discussions at intervals until November 10th, when hope of agreement on the basic issues had to be finally given up.

The immediate cause of the breakdown of the Conference was defined by Mr. Asquith to the King as due to divergence on the question of whether constitutional changes (such as Home Rule, or the Franchise) should be excepted from the procedure of joint sessions of the two Houses, which had been agreed upon as the way to deal with deadlocks in regard to ordinary legislation. Balfour and his colleagues insisted that such vital matters should be submitted to a popular referendum *ad hoc*. The Government refused this suggestion " not only on its merits, but because they know that it would be quite impossible to get the Liberal Party to agree to it."[1]

This statement no doubt covers the essential facts behind the breakdown, from the Liberal point of view. From the Unionist side there is however still something to add. The Memorandum which Balfour circulated to the Conference when all hope of agreement had been given up fixes more exactly the point of failure as arising when the proposed changes in the relations of the two Houses were considered in connection with a definite question of current political controversy. In other words—Home Rule.

Lord Oxford's biographer truly says that the Conference had been attempting " nothing less than to convert the immemorial unwritten into a written constitution—a task of enormous difficulty in any case, and not to be achieved by men deeply committed in the controversies of the hour."[2] But it is an over-simplification of the Unionist leaders' attitude merely to state that the

---
[1] See Mr. Asquith's letter to the King, *Life of Lord Oxford and Asquith*, Vol. I, p. 290.
[2] See *Life of Lord Oxford and Asquith*, Vol. I, p. 291.

ARTHUR JAMES BALFOUR

1910 Government representatives " desired to remove obstructions in the way of Home Rule, and the others to block the way."[1] Balfour's Memorandum reveals that the Unionists would have compromised about safeguards against hasty legislation, provided that these safeguards had been made permanent instead of temporary. Here came the breaking-point. The passage dealing with it in the Memorandum is preceded by a sketch of the Unionists' scheme for a plebiscite. Balfour then goes on :

> The organic change which supplied the main text of these discussions was Home Rule ; and on this important subject a counter-proposal was offered by the Government. Their proposal differed from our own partly in its character, but also (which is more important) in its duration. We brought in the electorate voting by plebiscite, to end the deadlock caused by an irreconcileable difference of opinion between the two Houses. The Government members of the Conference preferred a General Election to a Referendum ; they brought it into play after the first, instead of the second, rejection of the Bill by the Upper House ; and they proposed that if the General Election gave a majority to the Home Rule Government their original Home Rule Bill should then be treated as " ordinary " legislation.
>
> Though preferring our own scheme, we should have raised no very serious objection to this alternative method of dealing with Home Rule had it been applicable to all Home Rule Bills, whenever proposed. This however our Government colleagues felt unable to concede. It was only the next Home Rule scheme which they proposed to safeguard ; and to us it seemed impossible to accept a plan which required us to admit that the Union was a part of the Constitution which only required temporary defence. We fully recognise that the suggestion was offered as a compromise, and not as a logical solution of the problem. Nevertheless, we could not make ourselves responsible for a scheme which seemed to imply that, since the people had on three separate occasions expressed their hostility to

[1] See *Life of Lord Oxford and Asquith*, Vol. I, p. 291.

THE KING'S PLEDGE

Home Rule, it was high time to withdraw the subject from their cognisance and to hand it over to the unfettered discretion of the House of Commons and the Joint Sitting.

Thus came the inevitable failure. After the breakdown of the Conference the position reverted to where it had been at King Edward's death. The Prime Minister had then been aware of King Edward's decision to require a General Election, before using his prerogative to overcome the opposition of the House of Lords to the Parliament Bill by creation of Peers. Mr. Asquith had " taken it for granted that, if the result of the Election was decisive, the use of the Prerogative, if needed, would follow as a matter of course."[1] He now, on November 16th, 1910, went with Lord Crewe, Lord President of the Council, to ask from King George the same pledges which he held himself to have received from King Edward. At this interview the Sovereign satisfied Ministers that if the Election turned out sufficiently favourable to the Government, he would " use the constitutional last resort to prevent it being stultified in the subsequent Parliament." At the same time it was agreed that the King's decision should be kept strictly secret, and the utmost efforts made to keep his name out of the subsequent debates in Parliament.[2]

This proviso was so well respected that the Opposition leaders were not made aware of the King's pledge until the following July.[3]

After the General Election of December 1910 had returned a Parliament in which the balance of Parties was practically unchanged, Balfour and Lord Lansdowne discussed the steps that they thought the King should

[1] See *Life of Lord Oxford and Asquith*, Vol. I, p. 294.
[2] *Ibid.*, Vol. I, p. 298.
[3] My authority for this and other statements concerning this period is a documented Diary compiled by Mr. J. S. Sandars, Balfour's secretary, and preserved among Balfour's private papers.

ARTHUR JAMES BALFOUR

1911 now take. Balfour's letter on this subject has been epitomised in Lord Lansdowne's Life.[1] His views were also recorded in a Memorandum of a conversation which took place on January 10th, 1911, and of which the notes were preserved among his private papers. It must be remembered that, both here and in the letter to Lord Lansdowne, Balfour spoke in ignorance that the King had either been asked to, or had actually promised to create peers.

The main points of his recorded remarks centred round the governing consideration that no alternative Ministry was possible. A third General Election was out of the question, and if any action of the King caused Mr. Asquith to resign, and Balfour himself took office, he could not remain in power more than a few days. Mr. Asquith would be bound to resume office, there would be much hostile criticism of the King's action, and the Liberal Ministry would return with greater strength and security. Therefore "His Majesty could not well ultimately refuse to comply with Mr. Asquith's demand, should it be made, for a promise to create peers." Balfour here emphasised that the King's responsibility for the action of his Ministers ended at the moment when it became clear that he was unable to change his advisers.

Balfour then described the manner in which he thought the King's assent should be given.

> His Majesty should tell the Prime Minister that he considers it unconstitutional, and a breach of the understanding that has hitherto obtained between the Sovereign and Parliament that the King should be asked to promise to perform an act under circumstances which have not arisen, and under conditions which are not clearly defined. . . . No one can foresee at what stage it may become necessary

[1] See *Life of Lord Lansdowne*, p. 407.

by the creation of Peers to pass the Parliament Bill. It might occur on the Second Reading in the House of Lords, or on some Amendment which moderate men throughout the country might think the Government should adopt, but from the adopting of which they were precluded by Party exigencies. In short . . . considering the fact that, taking actual votes throughout the country, the nation is divided in the proportion of about 9 to 11, the action of the Government might, under circumstances easily imagined, be of a highly revolutionary character. Having said this much, the King might go on to say that he considered it his duty to protest against the action of his Ministers, who were using constitutional machinery to make him perform an unconstitutional act, although he was precluded by circumstances from giving an absolute refusal to their demand.

These are the important passages from a statement of opinion which circumstances had already deprived of practical value. In his letter to Lord Lansdowne Balfour defined his reasons for considering that the demand for guarantees was an unconstitutional act on the part of Ministers.[1]

> The demand for pledges is, in my view, unconstitutional —for two quite different reasons :
> (*a*) The coercion of the House of Lords by the creation of four or five hundred peers itself strains the Constitution to the breaking-point. It is itself a revolution—perhaps a necessary one—but certainly a revolution. . . . One simple consideration proves it up to the hilt. No action on the part of the Sovereign can be part of the accepted machinery of the Constitution unless it is capable of repetition under similar circumstances. Now I take it that even those who think it within the proper limits of the Constitution to turn an Assembly of six hundred into an Assembly of a thousand, would hardly think the same of a subsequent scheme for converting an Assembly of one thousand into an Assembly of (say) eighteen hundred.
> (*b*) But even if the creation of five hundred Peers be a

[1] This passage has been omitted in the epitome of the letter given in Lord Lansdowne's Life.

ARTHUR JAMES BALFOUR

1911 — proper exercise of the prerogative it seems to me utterly indefensible for any Ministry to ask for hypothetical pledges as to the occasion on which it should be put in motion. . . . No human being can tell in what mood the country will be a few months hence. The Parliament Bill is so clumsy a piece of constitution making that its credit will hardly be increased by a House of Commons discussion. Is the King to promise he will create Peers to pass any Bill, or only this Bill? If the promise is to refer to *any* Bill, even Redmond, I should think, could hardly defend an attempt to exact it. If it is only to refer to *this* Bill, then the Government practically deprive themselves of liberty to accept amendments, however powerfully these may be supported in the House, and however favourably they may be received in the country.

The Parliament Bill had been passed by the House of Commons, and its Second Reading in the House of Lords debated without a Division (May 23rd), before any intimation reached Balfour of what had actually passed between the King and the Prime Minister on the eve of the General Election of December 1910. It was on a day in the first week of July, when Amendments to the Bill were in course of discussion in the Upper House, that he heard privately how the passage of the Bill in the form in which it had left the Commons had already been secured by the King's pledge. Balfour at once summoned his Conservative colleagues to review the situation in the light of this knowledge. The Shadow Cabinet met on July 7th at his house in Carlton Gardens. There for the first time surrender by the House of Lords was discussed as practical politics. There for the first time appeared the crack in the unity of the Party, which very soon developed into the " Die-hard " revolt. Already at this preliminary meeting the Diarist notes that " there was a distinct division of opinion among those present, but the majority decided that it would be imprudent to resist the menace of the creation of peers."

The effect upon events produced by the withholding of the facts from the Opposition leaders can be measured by the following extracts from a letter of Balfour's to his colleague, Mr. Walter Long, written in September 1911.

> Had I been consulted in November with that knowledge of the issue which we were only permitted to have in July, there is not the slightest doubt that we should have taken office, dissolved in January, and, I believe, carried the country with us, though of course this last point is necessarily doubtful. The iniquity of the Government in (*a*) rushing the King into pledges to be fulfilled by a straining of the Constitution many months after; (*b*) forcing a dissolution on an old Register; and (*c*) thereby making it quite impossible to have a third dissolution before the Coronation, is really difficult to express in parliamentary language. The King was not well advised, he has certainly been most monstrously treated by Ministers from whom he had a right to claim loyal service.

On July 18th, Mr. Lloyd George was commissioned by the Prime Minister to communicate to the Unionist leaders the knowledge which they had already heard privately on July 7th. The only new fact was the determination of the Government to ask the King to create the Peers before the Lords had an opportunity of reconsidering the Bill subsequently to the rejection of their Amendments by the House of Commons. The Government was not prepared to risk the loss of the Bill, and were determined rather to deny all further opportunity for negotiation between the Houses.

On this information was based the significant qualification," so long as we remain free agents," added by Lord Lansdowne to the speech on the Third Reading, in which he declared that the Peers would insist on their Amendments. In this debate Lord Halsbury gave the

ARTHUR JAMES BALFOUR

1911 first open warning of the intention of a group of Peers never to submit to the passing of an unamended Bill. The Die-hard Peers, already numbering more than sixty, thus burned their boats. Next morning, July 21st, the Shadow Cabinet met again in Balfour's house to make its final decision. Opinion was divided: the Diarist gives the numbers thus:

For Resistance	Against Resistance
Lord Selborne	Mr. Balfour
Lord Halsbury	Lord Lansdowne
Lord Salisbury	Lord Curzon
Mr. Austen Chamberlain	Lord Midleton
Mr. George Wyndham	Lord Londonderry
Sir Edward Carson	Mr. Bonar Law
Mr. F. E. Smith	Mr. Akers-Douglas
Lord Balcarres	(who sympathised with the minority, but voted as he did out of loyalty to Balfour)
	Mr. Alfred Lyttelton
	Mr. Chaplin
	Mr. Long
	Lord Derby
	Lord Ashborne
	Mr. Steel-Maitland
	Sir Robert Finlay[1]

Although the weight of personality as well as of numbers was with Balfour and Lord Lansdowne for non-resistance, still the minority was anything but negligible. It included Lord Balcarres,[2] the Chief Party Whip, who was gravely concerned about the effect

[1] In Balfour's "Shadow Cabinets" there were no definite rules as to who should be summoned. Thus Mr. Chaplin continued to be invited, although he had left the Government before the reconstruction of 1903. Mr. F. E. Smith, who had never served in a Ministry, was usually present, as were the ex-Law Officers (e.g. Sir Robert Finlay); Lord Balcarres, and Mr. Steel-Maitland attended in their capacities as Chief Party Whip and Party Organiser. [2] Afterwards Earl of Crawfurd.

DIVIDED COUNSELS

which the majority's decision would have upon the Party as a whole. On the afternoon of the same day about 200 Peers assembled at Lansdowne House, and the Die-hards there appeared to be in a proportion of about one to three.

The next few days passed in an atmosphere of confusion, not to say demoralisation, in the Conservative camp. Balfour was due to address a City meeting in the following week. It was decided that unless he were prepared to advocate "No Surrender," the engagement had better be abandoned.

The demand for a definite public pronouncement from him was waxing strong in the Carlton Club and elsewhere. Three of his colleagues, Lord Curzon, Mr. Chaplin and Mr. Long, were pressing for a Party meeting. This he would not grant, being always convinced that such advertisements of difference of opinion during crises did more harm than good. The followers had to content themselves with a letter published on July 25th, in which he supported the advice that Lord Lansdowne had already given to the Unionist Peers. But there is another document, more revealing of his thoughts, putting the same arguments with greater freedom, because it was a paper intended only for his Shadow Cabinet. In the event it was not circulated even to them, for he consented reluctantly to suppress it, at the strong instance of one or two colleagues who declared it to be contrary to the views Balfour had expressed at the Shadow Cabinet of July 21st, and furthermore likely to encourage the temper towards resistance.

Confidential.   *July 22nd,* 1911.

MEMORANDUM

I am sorry to trouble my colleagues with any further observations on the Constitutional crisis; but I find that

ARTHUR JAMES BALFOUR

1911

some who were present at the meeting at my house on Friday last have formed a wrong impression of my position.

Put briefly, that position is as follows. I regard the policy which its advocates call "fighting to the last" as essentially theatrical, though not on that account necessarily wrong. It does nothing, it can do nothing; it is not even intended to do anything, except advertise the situation. The object of those who advocate it is to make people realise what (it is assumed) they will not realise otherwise, namely, the fact we are the victims of a revolution.

Their policy may be a wise one, but there is nothing heroic about it; and all military metaphors which liken the action of the "fighting" Peers to Leonidas at Thermopylæ seem to me purely for Music Hall consumption.

I grant that the Music Hall attitude of mind is too widespread to be negligible. By all means play up to it, if the performance is not too expensive. If the creation of X Peers pleases the multitude, and conveys the impression that the Lords are "game to the end," I raise no objection to it, *provided it does not swamp the House of Lords*. All my criticism yesterday was directed against the policy of so profoundly modifying the constitution of the Second Chamber that it would become, with regard to some important measures, a mere annexe to the present House of Commons.

From this point of view the creation of 50 or 100 new Peers is a matter of indifference.

Let me add two further observations. I regard the importance attached to the particular shape in which the House of Lords are to display their impotence in the face of the King's declaration, as a misfortune. The attention of the country should be directed not to these empty manœuvres, but to the absolute necessity of stemming the revolutionary tide, by making such abuse of Ministerial power impossible in the future.

A. J. B.

The suppression of this Memorandum was a sign and a portent of a divergence between Balfour's point of view and that of his Party which was before long to

BALFOUR'S SILENCE

convince him that he must relinquish their leadership into other hands. The objections to the Memorandum raised by Lord Lansdowne and Lord Curzon were concerned with the revelation that Balfour was not unalterably opposed to a limited creation of peers. He failed to impress his friends with his own sense of proportion, his own instinct of what was important or unimportant in the coming phase of the conflict. He yielded to advice, and refrained from pressing his opinions or circulating his paper. But a sense of isolation began to grow in him, which could only lead him to one inevitable conclusion. From the Shadow Cabinet of July 1911 to the date of Balfour's resignation of the Leadership only some three months elapsed. Before entering upon the developments of those twelve weeks the thread of the narrative must be broken in order to turn back to an episode of the year 1910, and Balfour's treatment of a proposal made to him by Mr. Lloyd George for the formation of a Coalition Government.

Chapter IV

MR. LLOYD GEORGE'S PROPOSAL
1910

Mr. Lloyd George approaches Balfour, October 1910, with scheme for Coalition Government. Balfour's refusal. "I cannot be a second Sir Robert Peel." Balfour's commentary in after years. Balfour's views on conscription.

1910 The "Ifs" of history are a fascinating, sometimes a tragic, always a controversial subject. Argument is implicit in the very selection of one event as a turning-point rather than another, and it is seldom possible to establish that in given circumstances men could have acted otherwise than as they did.

The story of how Mr. Lloyd George approached Balfour in the year 1910 with a view to preparing against the impending dangers of war through a truce to Party conflict at home has been told at first hand by Mr. Lloyd George himself.[1] In Balfour's rejection of his proposals he sees, looking back, a loss of opportunity incalculable in its consequences. Balfour, in retrospect, perceived no opportunity at all. It therefore behoves his biographer to re-tell the story from his point of view.

The date was October 1910. At that time, Mr. Lloyd George laid before the Prime Minister Mr. Asquith, and some of his colleagues in the Government, Lord

[1] See *War Memoirs*, Vol. I, by David Lloyd George, p. 36, *et seq.*

A TRUCE PROPOSED

Crewe, Sir Edward Grey, Lord Haldane and Mr. Winston Churchill, a Memorandum which urged

> that a truce should be declared between the Parties for the purpose of securing the co-operation of the leading party statesmen in a settlement of our national problems—Second Chamber, Home Rule, the development of our agricultural resources, national training for defence, the remedying of social evils and a fair and judicial enquiry into the working of our fiscal system.

These proposals were submitted to Balfour with the consent of the Liberal Ministers already named. " Balfour," Mr. Lloyd George writes, was " by no means hostile ; in fact he went a long way towards indicating that personally he regarded the proposal with a considerable measure of approval. He was not, however, certain of the reception which would be accorded to it by his Party."

That was bound to be his first consideration. Apart from his own sense of duty to the as yet unbroken army of Conservatives, it was necessary to sound the feeling of all ranks. It was not enough if some of his own friends and colleagues favoured the plan, he was bound also to listen for the voice of the constituencies.

It was, after all, in Balfour's capacity as leader of a great Party that Mr. Lloyd George sought his co-operation. Balfour's own acceptance of office in a Coalition Ministry without that Party's active approval would have been merely an entry into a captivity from whence he could have exerted no influence at all upon the Party strife which it was the object to bring to a close. The point would hardly need labouring if it were not that Mr. Lloyd George's retrospect almost belittles it. Mr. Lloyd George relates how he offered to remove the difficulty which his own presence in a Coalition Cabinet would present to some of the leading

ARTHUR JAMES BALFOUR

1910 Unionists—and how, after that, Balfour still told him "there was one other man he would have to consult."

The man was Mr. Akers-Douglas (afterwards Lord Chilston) Chief Whip of the Unionist Party under Lord Salisbury, and Home Secretary in Balfour's Government from 1902 to 1905. The confidence which Balfour and his Cabinet placed in the judgment of this colleague was perhaps not generally realised, but those who knew would not have been astonished to learn that when he wanted a pointer to Party feeling Balfour should have turned to him. Nevertheless Mr. Lloyd George curiously misunderstands the position when he throws on Mr. Akers-Douglas the responsibility for Balfour's decision. "Mr. Akers-Douglas turned down the project for co-operation in settling these momentous national issues, and there was an end to it." The narrative from which this is a quotation itself refutes the idea that the advice which Balfour was bound to seek did more than reinforce his own ultimate recoil from the proposal. If Mr. Lloyd George's sequence of events is right, it was before ever Mr. Akers-Douglas was consulted that Balfour made the remark which gives the real key to his thoughts.

"I cannot become another Robert Peel in my Party," he said to Mr. Lloyd George, putting his hand on his forehead and more or less soliloquizing.

These are extracts from an account published twenty-three years after the event. It happens however that in the year 1913 Mr. Lloyd George had recalled the circumstances in conversation with a friend,[1] who wrote it down in his private diary. In substance the story is here the same, the conditions of the offered settlement being however more elaborated than they are in

[1] The Rt. Hon. J. Hills, M.P.

THE "UNFORGIVABLE SIN"

the *War Memoirs*. The House of Lords was to keep all powers, including money bills : differences to be settled by a joint sitting. Preference was to be given to the Colonies on all existing duties ; an impartial Commission to investigate the fiscal question ; Winston Churchill to go to the War Office and initiate national training ; a reasonable federal solution to be found for the Irish difficulty ; a Coalition Government to be formed, and Balfour to lead the Commons, and Asquith to go to the Lords.

1910

I have obtained permission to quote from this unpublished Diary, because, in the year 1928, it was shown to Balfour, and led to two illuminating conversations about these events.

I seldom heard him bewail more bitterly his own shocking memory for detail than on this occasion, as his interest awakened, and he studied with more and more absorbed attention the story of the Coalition which failed to materialise in 1910. Since then he had been a member of three Coalition Governments. These, too, were of the past before he read the Diary, a Conservative Government was in power, and his own course was nearly run.

I showed him the Diary one day in April 1928, in his sitting-room in Carlton Gardens. When he had finished reading he laid the typescript down on his knee and looked long into the fire. At last I called his thoughts back from their far journey—and he said, slowly and very thoughtfully :

> A lot of this may very well be true. My own remark about Peel—that was the point. I should say it now, and may well have said it then. Peel twice committed what seems to me the unforgivable sin. He gave away a principle on which he had come into power—and mind you, neither time had an unforeseen factor come into the case. He simply betrayed his Party. I have at no time been possessed by any desire to emulate him in this. I did join Coalition Governments under the circumstances you know. They

were War Coalitions, and from first to last they were to deal with the War and its problems. And—so far as I know—nothing that we did was done except by whole-hearted agreement between the Parties who had come together under those conditions—with the exception possibly of the Irish settlement, but about that I cannot say, for I never went into it. I was in America at the time and had my hands full.[1] But to return to this Diary. Some of it seems fairly fantastic to me. It's just like one of those comprehensive dreams of which Lloyd George is so fond.

At this point Balfour waved his hands about, then he looked at the Diary again with a dawning smile.

"Let me see," he said, "what was to become of Asquith?"

Myself. "He was to go to the Lords."

A. J. B. "To the Lords, was he? Have we any reason to suppose that Asquith would have considered himself ripe for that fate? Dear me! And some of my colleagues are stated to have favoured this scheme?"

Myself. "It doesn't exactly say that they favoured it. They were sounded about it."

A. J. B. "Quite—quite. Of course there are infinite gradations in conversations of this sort."

Myself. "It might be that they said they would like to know what you thought."

A. J. B. "Anything like that is possible. But the idea doesn't seem to me to have been founded on any practical possibilities.—Very interesting to think about now though."

He continued thinking after our talk was here broken off; for on the next day he returned to the subject again.

A. J. B. "I must say some more to you about that Diary. What was it that Lloyd George said he had actually proposed? Ireland must have been the point—otherwise the remark I made about Peel would not apply."

Myself. "Yes—it says 'a reasonable federal solution of the Irish difficulty.'"

[1] Note, See below, Chapter XVII.

POLITICAL ETHIC

A. J. B. "Exactly! Now isn't that like Lloyd George. 1910 Principles mean nothing to him—never have. His mind doesn't work that way. It's both his strength and his weakness. He says to himself at any given moment: 'Come on now—we've all been squabbling too long, let's find a reasonable way out of the difficulty'—but such solutions are quite impossible for people who don't share his outlook on political principles—the great things."

The objections to making public such unpremeditated talk as this have been set aside, because here is a revelation of the bed-rock of Balfour's political ethic. "Peel committed what seems to me the unforgivable sin. He simply betrayed his Party." Here in a sentence is the explanation of why he could not back Mr. Lloyd George's glittering project with the moral conviction that alone could have given it life. But—it may be asked—why could he not? The Irish settlement was, from the Unionist point of view, far the most formidable difficulty in the way of a bargain such as was now proffered, and already in 1910 many thinking men in the Party were coming to the conclusion that the dead-lock must be broken. Balfour's private correspondence bristles with evidence of this feeling. Proof was given in a letter he got in the very week that the Liberal overtures were made, from his intimate friend and colleague, Alfred Lyttelton.

16th Oct., 1910.

My dear Arthur,

I have been making diligent enquiry, and find there is very great sympathy with Local Federation among the younger intellectuals. I mention F. S. Oliver, Brand, Kerr, and Milner's kindergarten, Milner himself, and Garvin. My views are unimportant, but they lean that way—but, as you know, are always and in all topics not of vital conscience, subject to yours. . . .

ARTHUR JAMES BALFOUR

1910   When letters like this were reaching him, were not his scruples about "betrayal" a little out of date? Must it not be admitted that the statesman's mind, at this crucial moment, was for once lagging behind the times, was still seeking the solution of the Irish question along the lines laid down in the great years of his own Irish administration?

Such a question, had it been put to him, would certainly have evoked an emphatic denial. And, in fact, his letters of this period show that he was well enough aware that the Ireland of 1910 was not the Ireland of 1890. His own constructive legislation had been largely responsible for a fundamental change in the problem of Home Rule. It would have been unlike him indeed not to notice that the cry for self-government could no longer be explained away by the feeling that Ireland was ill-governed by Imperial Parliament. It was now the unmistakeable expression of nationalism, and he knew that nationalism was a craving which would only be sharpened by the sops which the "younger intellectuals" of his Party would dole out to it in the form of Federalism or Devolution. No settlement of that kind could bring lasting peace, and therefore to make such a settlement for the sake of peace seemed to him a betrayal of his trust. Already in the correspondence of 1910 there are indications that he foresaw the only possible answer to the Irish question. The time was not ripe, and he did not stress it. Only now and again he puts such a question as this to a "Federalist" friend.

> Is Ireland to form one province, or two? If two, will any Nationalist of any type accept this administrative solution? And if not, why not?

Next to Ireland, the most important part of Mr. Lloyd George's plan designed to attract Conservative

COMPULSORY SERVICE

support was no doubt national training for defence, to which Lloyd George himself was a recent convert.[1] Lord Roberts was then in the midst of his great campaign for universal service—a campaign that he had begun while Balfour was still Prime Minister, and for which he had pleaded passionately for Balfour's sympathy especially at the time when Balfour himself was rousing the country in the years 1908 and 1909 to the inadequacy of our strength at sea.

Balfour's views on compulsory service are best epitomised from a letter he wrote as late as 1912.

> It seems that whatever else we have we must have a voluntary army. You cannot raise soldiers by conscription, and then send them to tropical countries on the other side of the world, and if ever we come to conscription one of the most serious dangers will be its effect on voluntary enlistment.
>
> There is another point which, obvious as it may seem, is too little considered by those who are interested in problems of defence—I mean the question of money. Now whatever money is required for our security must be found, at whatever sacrifice. But the burden of armaments is already enormous, and if we increase it, we are bound to increase it in a manner which will give us what we want at the least possible cost. . . .
>
> I have heard the annual cost of Lord Roberts' scheme put at any sum between six and twelve million sterling. This would only give us an improved Militia, and a conscript Army on the continental basis.
>
> Now would not this money be much better spent, from the point of view of national security, upon increasing the Navy ? . . . Remember that a sufficient Navy not only secures your shores, but secures your commerce. A sufficient Army only secures your shores. . . . Germany is said to want colonies. She can hardly want Britain; but British overseas possessions she could force us to give up with little trouble or bloodshed if she were once mistress

[1] See *War Memoirs*, Vol. I, by David Lloyd George, pp. 36 *et seq.*

1910 of the ocean. The finest conscript army in the world could not delay their surrender by an hour.

Of this at all events I am quite convinced—that no man is worth listening to on this vital subject unless and until he has considered the problem in its full circuit. Of its two great aspects, the naval and the military, both must be taken into account, but it is the naval aspect that is fundamental.

This was Balfour's view. It remains a question whether, had he thought otherwise, he could have carried the country with him. Had it been so, Germany (Mr. Lloyd George thinks) " might have hesitated before plunging the world into the disaster of the Great War."[1] Perhaps, and perhaps again she might have precipitated that action by four years. Certain things, Balfour did think in the light of after knowledge, had been within the power of British statesmen to attempt which might have averted the War. The introduction of compulsory service, while the nation was at peace, was not among them.

> There are times [says Mr. Lloyd George at the end of his account] when the Party system stands seriously in the way of the highest national interests. . . . I shall always regard the rejection of the proposals for co-operation in 1910 as a supreme example of this kind of damage.

Against this might be set the argument that it was better for the unity of the country in August 1914 that outside the distracted Cabinet there was a united Opposition free to give its prompt support for our entry into the War.

[1] See *War Memoirs*, p. 39.

Chapter V

"B. M. G."
BALFOUR MUST GO

Balfour advises the Peers to pass the Parliament Bill. Halsbury Club Dinner. Balfour departs for Bad Gastein. Determines to resign the leadership. Arguments and persuasions. Balfour tells his family. Announcement on November 8th, 1911.

The story comes back now to the Constitutional struggle over the House of Lords as it stood in July 1911. The question of resistance by the Peers to the passing of the Parliament Bill was tearing the Unionist Party asunder. Lord Lansdowne was for surrender, Balfour backing him energetically in his own way. His advice was given to the Party at large in a letter published in *The Times* of July 25th.

> Let us [it concludes] then, if we can, agree. Let the Unionists in the Upper House follow their trusted leader. But if this be impossible, if differ we must, if there be Peers who (on this occasion) are resolved to abandon Lord Lansdowne, if there be politicians outside who feel constrained to applaud them, let us all at least remember that the campaign for the restoration of constitutional liberty is but just begun, that this is but an episode in it, and that unless the forces conducting it possess unity and discipline, ultimate victory is impossible. It would in my opinion be a misfortune if the present crisis left the House of Lords weaker than the Parliament Bill by itself would make it, but it would be an irreparable tragedy if it left us a divided Party.

ARTHUR JAMES BALFOUR

1911   The comments of the Unionist Press upon this appeal were favourable on the whole. But from the quarters that mattered most the response was of another character. On July 26th six hundred Unionists, peers and commoners, attended a banquet at the Hotel Cecil in honour of Lord Halsbury, the veteran leader of the Die-hards.

Among them were Mr. Austen Chamberlain, and other colleagues in the Shadow Cabinet, who had voted there for resisting the Parliament Bill. No criticism of persons was made in the speeches at the Halsbury dinner. Thoughts however could not fail to be crystallised in Balfour's mind, as well as in the minds of those who met to identify themselves with the rejection of his advice. The banquet took place on July 26th. So far as Balfour was concerned the story of the closing scenes of the constitutional struggle is soon told. There was only one moment of great interest in the House of Commons before the supreme issue was transferred to the House of Lords. This was the debate on the Vote of Censure on August 7th, when all the skill of the Leader of the Opposition was needed to combine the strongest condemnation of Ministerial action with avoidance of anything like implied criticism of the Sovereign in the " cruel position " in which his advisers had placed him so soon after his accession. The feat was accomplished. But Unionists noted the saying of one of them: " Asquith has sacrificed the King to his Party, and Balfour has sacrificed his Party to the King."

Balfour left England for Bad Gastein on the very day before the Bill was returned to the House of Lords. His absence at such a juncture was criticised. It was certainly significant of things now stirring in his mind, and a letter to Lady Elcho, written from Paris on the first evening of his outward journey, furnishes a clue to his thoughts.

SERIOUS THOUGHTS

Hotel Ritz, Paris. 1911
Aug. 10, 1911.

Politics have been to me quite unusually odious. I am not going into the subject, but I have, as a matter of fact, felt the situation more acutely than any in my public life —I mean from the personal point of view.

As you know I am very easy-going, and not given to brooding over my wrongs. But last Friday and Saturday I could think of nothing else: a thing which has not happened to me since I was unjustly " complained of " at Eton more than forty years ago ! On Saturday the cloud lifted; yet it *has* not, and perhaps *will* not disappear till recent events are things barely remembered. . . .

I am really looking forward to the cataracts, the pines, and the precipices of my " cure-place." I hope to write a short article on *my* philosophy (does not this sound grand ?) for the decennial number of the Hibbert. But Heaven knows whether it will come off.

You must not ask me to tell you anything about the last ten days. I am trying to forget it all.

Nevertheless at Gastein Balfour must have done a great deal of thinking on matters not philosophical (although the projected article was written there, and appeared in the *Hibbert Journal* for October). The following letter to Lady Elcho is the sequel of the one just quoted. It is dated from Whittingehame, about a month after his return from Austria.

Oct. 8th, 1911.

I am thinking *most seriously* of resigning my leadership. No one knows this but Alice,[1] Bal,[2] Steel-Maitland[3] and Sandars.[4] Say nothing about it therefore to anyone. I will not attempt to give even a summary of my reasons by letter. It would be too long. The dominant one is that I have been continuously in difficult office, or leading the Party in the House of Commons and the country, for twenty years

[1] His sister, Miss Balfour.   [2] Lord Balcarres, Chief Whip.
[3] Afterwards Sir Arthur Steel-Maitland.
[4] Mr. J. S. Sandars, his Private Secretary.

1911 without a single break. I do not believe our Parliamentary history has any parallel to it in point of mere duration; and political work is far more exacting now than at any period of our history.

Subsidiary reasons may be found in recent events; in my increasing years; in the fact that if the surgical operation has to be performed this is the most convenient time for performing it. Bal has persuaded me not to do it *before* the Autumn Session, but I hope to do it soon after. More when we meet.

Yours,
A. J. B.

By this time the inward struggle was clearly over. Among the "cataracts, pines and precipices" at Bad Gastein he had fought for his peace of mind and won it back. No trace remains of the circumstances of that battle. Those nearest to him can only say that it ended in victory.

The same Diarist whose Notes have been quoted in Chapter III of this volume has recorded a conversation just before Balfour went to Gastein early in August, which shows something of the ferment and direction of his thoughts at that time. Balfour began by talking of the shock given to Party unity by Mr. Chamberlain's tariff pronouncement in 1903, and of how he had himself "strained every nerve" to prevent a split.

> In accents which showed how deeply he felt it [the Diary goes on] he referred to the abuse which had been poured upon him, and the imputations which had been made upon his sincerity during the years between 1906 and January, 1910. But he had seen the success of his Fabian methods, and it would be admitted that he had saved the Party from breaking up, and that we went into the General Election of January, 1910, a united Party. "Now observe," he said, "our men were entitled by tradition to call themselves Protectionists, they were equally entitled to hold fast to the creed of Free Trade, as that had been the Party tradition

for more than a generation. It was worth anything to try and reconcile these conflicting opinions. And, whatever it cost me, I was rewarded with practical success. But now, on a question which is not one of principle, but of mere Party tactics, I am confronted with a deep schism among my leading colleagues. In a Cabinet, if there is a division of opinion, the rule is that the majority must prevail; and if the view of the majority is not accepted, those who will not accept it have no alternative but to leave the Government. But here, after a full discussion, a minority decline to accept my advice, which commanded the majority of votes at the Shadow Cabinet, and the dissentient members have gone out into the world and have embarked upon a policy of active resistance. I confess to feeling that I have been badly treated. I have no wish to lead a Party under these humiliating conditions. It is no gratification to me to be their leader. If they think that someone else is better able to discharge the duties of leadership, I am quite willing to adopt that view.

Balfour's auditor had " rarely heard him speak with more vigour or more intensity of feeling." His words seemed " pregnant with meaning and foreshadowed the possibility of a decisive step."

This conversation took place in Balfour's own study at Number Four Carlton Gardens, a lofty, rather sombre room, panelled in mahogany. There, more than anywhere in the house, one seemed to notice the absence of noise, in those days characteristic of the houses in the most Olympian of London's streets. The contrast between its calm and the stridency of the world of politics often seemed strange that autumn. It was not greater than the differences in the mode of expression employed by the occupant of the room and some of his critics to express their respective opinions. Perhaps at the very moment when Balfour was delivering himself of the upshot of his reflections in the way just recorded, Mr. Leo Maxse, Editor of the *National Review*, was

1911 already devising the Die-hard motto that heads this chapter. At all events it appeared for the first time in the September number of the *Review*. It is worth while to say a word here about Balfour's attitude towards the attacks made upon him by that most gifted journalist, who remained all through his personal friend. I can vouch for the truth of the story that on the day his resignation was announced Balfour remarked with a chuckle of sincere amusement: " I really think I must ask Leo Maxse to dinner to-night, for we are probably the two happiest men in London."

If the assaults of the *National Review* had produced any real effect upon the political position, this remark might perhaps not have been made. But they had in fact as little to do with the progress of events as the barking of dogs upon a shore has to do with the ebb and flow of the tide. " Balfour Must Go." " B. M. G." is the kind of simple hammer-blow for which every good journalist strives. As a " slogan " it has seldom been bettered, and the proof is that it is still remembered by people who were in the nursery at the time of its invention. But it neither hastened nor retarded anything.

When Balfour came back to Whittingehame from Gastein early in September, the reports from the Party managers confirmed his feelings of dissatisfaction. At the end of the month he invited Lord Balcarres and Mr. Steel-Maitland to Whittingehame, and broached to them the idea of resignation, resting his case on the length of time he had been in harness, his age, and the argument that when the Party returned to office he would be too old to survive a long Ministry. This, he said, was the best moment to make a change. Home Rule and Disestablishment would be the Government's programme for next year. It was only fair that his successor

WHITTINGEHAME GARDEN AND OLD TOWER

COLD ANALYSIS

should have a few months in the saddle before a critical Session. His hearers asked him if his decision was final. He said "No," but they did not feel convinced. One of them asked him who could possibly succeed him, and got a somewhat oracular answer: 1911

> The faculty for readiness in debate is not one which the country demands in a leader. W. H. Smith lacked it. A slower brain would often be welcome to the Party as a whole. I see all the factors in the situation. Perhaps this entails want of decision. Some people do not like the qualifications in my speeches. They are not to save myself, but to protect my Party in the future, when statements of leaders are recalled to injure the Party. F. E. Smith[1] contradicts himself once a week. There will be a great thunder-storm followed by torrents of rain, but the atmosphere will be cleared in the process, and the Party will ultimately come to its own. A political reaction of a violent type is inevitable. My successor ought to be well installed before the formation of a new Ministry.

In answer to the repeated question he said:

> Austen[2] in the Commons, Curzon[3] in the Lords. Long[4] is too discursive, too quick-tempered, too changeable, and too complimentary. The compliments which he pays to his opponents are the only features of his speeches I ever recall.

When the conversation had got to this point it must have been patent to his hearers that the die was cast. They argued with him, of course, but "every objection was met with cold analysis."

On the next day he got a letter from Mr. Walter Long, severely critical of the Party management and of Balfour himself, demanding a radical change in policy, and

---

[1] Afterwards Lord Birkenhead.   [2] Mr. Austen Chamberlain.
[3] Lord Curzon of Kedleston.
[4] Mr. W. Long, afterwards Lord Long.

ARTHUR JAMES BALFOUR

1911 threatening his own retirement from the Front Opposition Bench.

> Now this [observed Balfour to Lord Balcarres] comes from my oldest colleague, my *professed* friend and upholder.
> ... The letter is a bold and brutal invitation to retire. But I do not think the writer can have thought of stepping into my shoes; otherwise he would not have proceeded by such methods.

Conversation then turned upon arrangements connected with resignation, and Balfour went on to say that he had no personal feelings in the matter.

> Whatever ambitions I have had were satisfied years ago. I know I cannot be evicted from the leadership, and if I resigned I could make trouble, which is of course absurd; but Long asks me to change, and I cannot change.

A few days after this—on October 7th—the Halsbury Club was inaugurated.

This could not be ignored, remarked Balfour. Members of the Club differed on all constructive questions, but were united in disapproval of their leader's advice.

It only remained now to inform the leader of the Unionist Party in the House of Lords of the irrevocable decision. Balfour went to London towards the end of October, and there saw Lord Lansdowne. Lord Lansdowne's arguments made no impression, for Balfour told his Private Secretary that he had brought none of any weight; a version of facts which Lord Lansdowne himself hotly denied. He had tried to resist Balfour's resignation with all his strength, and much persuasion had to be exercised upon him to prevent his retiring at the same time.

On October 30th Balfour informed Mr. Akers-Douglas of his decision, and between that date and November 8th, the day fixed for announcement, it was found necessary to let at least a dozen people, chiefly colleagues, into the secret; which however in spite of rumours, was so well kept, that not one of the Parlia-

DECISION

mentary correspondents of the leading newspapers even got so far as an inspired prophecy. Only two days before the end Balfour made a great fighting speech at a dinner at the Hotel Metropole, chiefly on Home Rule, which contained no valedictory note whatever. But walking home to Carlton Gardens afterwards with Mr. J. S. Sandars, he talked with relief of this being his last speech as Leader of the Party.

Some of the interviews of this final week were not unspiced with comedy. Certain of Balfour's Die-hard colleagues had, a little late in the day, been plunged into consternation at the outcome of a situation for which they were in part responsible. Fervid appeals for reconsideration emanated from men who had been in his own Shadow Cabinet, and were now members of the Halsbury Club. One of them came to see him, and to Balfour's amusement seemed wholly at a loss what to say. Balfour, describing the scene, added that he had found himself quite unable to help his visitor out with any expression appropriate to the occasion, and that the interview was therefore " embarrassing and purposeless, but brief."

After much consideration it had been settled that the occasion for the public announcement of the resignation should be at a special meeting of the City of London Conservative Association, summoned at shortest notice for four o'clock on the afternoon of Wednesday, November the 8th.

On the 7th Balfour informed the King of his intentions:

Secret

4 CARLTON GARDENS.

Nov. 7th, 1911.

Mr. Balfour with his humble duty to Your Majesty begs respectfully to inform Your Majesty that he proposes

ARTHUR JAMES BALFOUR

1911   immediately to resign his position of leader of the Unionist Party. That position has nothing formally to do with Your Majesty's service. Yet it is so intimately bound up with the political system of this country that Mr. Balfour would regret to think that Your Majesty received the first information of the change through the public prints.

       Mr. Balfour proposes to develop his reasons, which are mainly concerned with health, at a small meeting which will be held to-morrow in the City. He hopes the news of his decision will not leak out till he has the opportunity of himself explaining it.

On receipt of this letter, King George, who was within two days of setting out upon his journey to India, sent Lord Knollys to Carlton Gardens to express his extreme regret, and to arrange that Balfour should come to Buckingham Palace to say good-bye. That interview took place at six o'clock on the same day, the 8th, soon after the City speech.

It happened that two or three members of Balfour's own family were at luncheon that day in Carlton Gardens, none of whom had any suspicion that the impending change was within an hour or two of its accomplishment. Nothing in the conversation at the table gave the faintest idea of anything unusual in the wind. Afterwards they adjourned to his sitting-room, and his sister-in-law, Lady Frances, who was an ardent advocate of Female Suffrage, began to upbraid Balfour for what she considered his indifference to a piece of news which had filled the newspapers that morning—namely, the sudden announcement of the Government's decision to bring in an Adult Suffrage Bill in a form which might be extended to women. " The whole country is thinking of nothing else," she exclaimed, " and yet you remain wrapped in your Balfourian apathy ! "

Balfour was standing with one foot on the fender, and his arm stretched along the mantelshelf. A peculiar

RESIGNATION

smile came over his face, he drew himself up, and 1911 surveying his relatives taking their ease in the arm-chairs, he replied to Lady Frances' remark: "Perhaps I may be giving the country something else to think about. In fact, my dears, I am resigning this afternoon, but it's a secret till four o'clock."

Then rapidly, as if to expel from the situation any touch of drama, he ran over the points of the speech he was about to make. He was clearly in excellent spirits. If in after years he had ever recalled the scene to his mind, he would have thought it a striking justification of his practice of discouraging unnecessary emotion. For who could have guessed that afternoon that the beginning of the second, and possibly the greatest, period of his public career still lay four years ahead? Yet had he known it, the City speech might nevertheless have stood as it stands recorded to-day, even including the passage that dwells on the danger of petrifaction in old courses which may assail a man even in the prime of his days. Not, he added, that he thought it had come upon himself as yet, but he did not feel possessed of the vigour necessary to conduct a Ministry again.

Every word of this was sincere. Balfour was very much alive to the kind of danger to which he was alluding. A joking remark quoted earlier in this book about "elder soldiers who are even more dangerous than elder statesmen" is only an example of how the idea would crop up in his thoughts and in his conversation. Possibly thus he earned his own immunity to the end from an ageing mind. But, although in 1911 he was still only sixty-three, with many years of good physical health before him, he had perhaps reached the point where unlimited hard work told on a constitution never robust, and all through life requiring the rational care

1911 with which he invariably treated it. Short breakdowns had lately been increasingly frequent. Without the three years' comparative rest which were now to follow, it may well be that the strain of the War period would have proved too great, and that the history of the services he was then able to render to his country would have had to be written, if written at all, in a minor, not in a major key.

Chapter VI

OUT OF HARNESS
1911-1914

Balfour and Bonar Law. " Nationality and Home Rule." The Unionists desire an election. Passions aroused by Home Rule Bill. Contrast with unity in face of danger from Continental war. Balfour's memorandum on Anglo-French relations. New Year's Eve 1913-14. The Gifford Lectures.

Three days after Balfour retired, two men who had worked with him in daily contact during the political life of the last few years speculated in casual conversation about his future, and one of them jotted down notes of their respective forecasts. One took the view that his appearances in the House of Commons would henceforth be limited to occasions of exceptional importance, and that very soon his re-entry into active politics would have become quite impossible. Newspaper reading not being numbered among the various tastes which would shortly absorb his leisure, he would get out of touch with affairs, and hesitate before reappearing in the arena where he had once been so much at home.

The other friend had doubts about this. He thought Balfour was looking forward with pleasure to excursions into debate in the House of Commons, but meant to forswear platform speeches. Nevertheless it might happen that if things went well with the Party, he (whom they still called "the Chief") would keep away for

1912 fear of embarrassing his successor. If things went ill, he might feel that his adventitious support would do more harm than good.

Neither prophecy came true, but the instincts of the second speaker were sounder than those of the first. Balfour had no intention of giving himself up entirely to a combination of metaphysics, outdoor exercise, and social life. The dust of battle had by no means lost its savour, and once the conflict round Mr. Asquith's Home Rule Bill had developed he took his share as much on the platform as in debate. He had abstained from taking any part in the discussions that preceded the choice of Mr. Bonar Law as his successor, and his reappearance at Westminster was delayed for more than a month after the reassembly of Parliament on February 14th, 1912. It was not till March 19th that he came down to the House of Commons and took his place on the Treasury Bench amid a roar of welcome from the Unionists. Two days later he spoke—not, as it happened, on Home Rule, for a coal strike over the minimum wage question had created a crisis that postponed the introduction of the Irish Bill. Balfour's first intervention in debate was to move, at Mr. Bonar Law's request, the rejection of a Bill to fix a minimum wage by districts.

He did so in his most vigorous style, and some people who had keen ears for lobby gossip were apparently disturbed for a moment lest he did in fact carry too much Parliamentary weight for his new position. One friend wrote to another:

> Of course there were always difficulties in *Arthurus Redux;* and he has made many of them by his speech. I have said that he would do one of two things: either he would damage himself, or damage Bonar Law. So far he has distinctly damaged Bonar Law. We were walking together this week, and his observation was, " Oh, that

THE ULSTER COVENANT

will all pass off. My intervention will be forgotten very quickly." I did not agree. Bonar Law does *not* stand where he did after A. J. B.'s speech, and as long as A. J. B. hovers and is liable to swoop down on that Bench there will be comparisons drawn not necessarily by House of Commons men, but by the general body of readers and observers. . . .

In politics you ought not to flirt; and certainly not at such a time as this. I mean when a Party is circumstanced as ours is.

This shows the sort of atmosphere that might have been created round Mr. Bonar Law and Balfour in the early days after the reversal of their positions. But in the total absence of personal preoccupations on the part of either of them no harm could arise. Bonar Law could count upon Balfour's weight being thrown wherever and whenever it was wanted, in debate, on the platform, or in private council. The new leader made full and ungrudging use of his powerful auxiliary, especially in the central struggle round the Home Rule Bill.

For the next two and a quarter years the Irish question passed through three stages, which Balfour himself described as beginning like the flow of a river outwardly smooth, leading to the rapids, and to the cataract beyond. The Bill was introduced in April 1912, and was still being fought when, in September of that same year, the Ulster Covenant was signed, and some half-million Irish men and women solemnly swore to resist " by every means that may be found necessary " the setting up of a Home Rule Parliament.

Within the next ten months the Bill twice passed the Commons (the second time under the Parliament Act), and twice was rejected by the Lords. So matters stood at the end of July 1913. Then followed the declaration by the English Unionists of support for Ulster in

1914 resistance, if an attempt were made to coerce her without an appeal to the electorate of Great Britain. The Government refused to advise a Dissolution, and in the spring of 1914 came the landing of arms on the shores of Belfast Lough.

The influence of reason, argument, and statesmanship upon the passions thus aroused was almost nil, but these were the only contributions which the Unionist leaders on this side of St. George's Channel could bring to bear upon the situation. In June 1912, three months before the Covenant was signed, both Mr. Bonar Law and Balfour had spoken in the House of Commons in support of the principle of an Amendment based on exclusion of part of Ulster from the Bill, but this was repudiated by the Irishmen of both Parties, and the Government still clung to its belief in the possibility of an undivided Ireland under a Dublin Parliament. More than a year had still to pass before Mr. Asquith and Mr. Bonar Law met to explore the possibilities of the separation of North and South.[1]

Apart from many platform speeches, Balfour made one public contribution to the controversy in a pamphlet called *Nationality and Home Rule*, which retains interest not to be measured by its effect upon the immediate question. It is an exposition, compressed into less than twenty pages, of the true nature of the demand of the Southern Irish—a demand which, he foresaw, no Home Rule of the sort dreamed of by English Liberalism could ever satisfy. The kind of Irish self-government proposed in the Bill would never be tolerated by any one of the self-governing Dominions. How then could it be permanently accepted by those whose policy was based on the indefeasible claims of nationality which

[1] See *Life of Lord Oxford and Asquith*, Vol. II, p. 34.

NO SOLUTION

would not stop short on the road to complete independence. If, he concluded, the Bill were really to put an end to the Nationalist agitation, it would be conclusive proof that the agitation was factitious, and the cause of Irish patriotism already lost.

1913

The truth of this diagnosis is evident now. No other living English politician was in a position to make it so confidently at the time. No Minister in 1913 could speak with a fraction of his authority on Irish questions. Mr. Asquith (like Mr. Gladstone) had never passed an appreciable length of time in Ireland, even if he had ever set foot there when he brought in his Home Rule Bill. Mr. Birrell, his Chief Secretary, was accustomed to reduce his visits to Dublin to a minimum. But not only did Balfour know the country and the people; he had been, as Chief Secretary, and afterwards as Prime Minister, more responsible than any other single man for the policy which had removed from Ireland all her removable grievances against English rule. He knew what he was saying therefore when he warned the Government that their Bill provided no solution for any Irish problem, or any British problem either. It was not a constitutional remedy; it was a parliamentary device.

The pamphlet, *Nationality and Home Rule*, was the polished and expanded version of a speech that Balfour made at Nottingham in January 1913. It was published first in October of that year in the University Magazine of Montreal, and printed once again in 1928, in a collection of Balfour's speeches.[1] He desired its inclusion there, less as a record of the old controversy than because in it is set forth his own beliefs about the place that nationalist sentiment should hold among the group

[1] *Opinions and Arguments* from Speeches and Addresses by the Earl of Balfour.

ARTHUR JAMES BALFOUR

1913 of loyalties which he held to be ennobling to human society.

> If I consider the case I know best [he wrote], namely, my own, I find that within a general regard for mankind which I hope is not absent or weak, I am moved by a feeling especially patriotic in its character, for the group of nations who are the authors and guardians of western civilization, for the sub-group who speak the English language, for the communities which compose the British Empire, for the United Kingdom of which I am a citizen, and for Scotland where I was born, and where my fathers lived before me. Where patriotisms such as these are not forced into conflict, they are not only consistent with each other, but they may mutually reinforce each other, and statesmanship can have no greater object than to make conflict between them impossible.

Nationalism, he knew, could draw its strength from many sources. A real or supposed community of race, of language, religion, culture, common memories, common hopes, geographical conditions, could all feed it.

> Only of this we may be sure, that whatever its real origin . . . it will be specially apt to justify its existence by a version of history which at the best is one-sided, at the worst is purely mythical. Therefore beware!

These opinions, formed before the Great War, were strengthened after the forces of national sentiment were everywhere unchained. In 1913, however, abstract reflections on national loyalties had little chance of influencing events. The efforts of English Unionists became concentrated on impressing upon the British public that Ulster would continue to treat Home Rule as a "matter of life and death." Balfour used these words in a speech at Haddington on September 6th, and declared that he did not believe the Government could proceed to the coercion of Northern Ireland without a new mandate from the country. But Mr.

BALFOUR'S SCHEME

Asquith was not to be moved. It would, he thought, 1913 be a misuse of terms to describe as "civil war" the "organised disorder" of the four counties of Ulster that might follow the passage of the Bill. Whereas, if the Bill were rejected or postponed, Ireland would become ungovernable. A victory for the present Government would not reconcile Ulster, a defeat (so he argued) would not be accepted anywhere as a verdict adverse to Home Rule.[1] Not sharing the Prime Minister's optimism about the nature of Ulster's resistance, Unionists canvassed among themselves every possibility for forcing an Election before the last and worst catastrophe should happen. It was in connection with these discussions that Balfour put on paper a scheme of his own, by means of which the King might achieve a Dissolution without incurring the evils that would normally attend such action taken by the Crown against the advice of Ministers. Things were moving rapidly, and at about the same date in September when Balfour was committing these tentative ideas to paper, a Conference was being arranged between British Party leaders on the basis of separate treatment for Ulster. Balfour's plan was therefore never, as far as I know, brought forward in any quarter where it might have influenced events. It remains among the "might-have-beens" of our constitutional history.

It is cast in the form of an answer to the question of what the King might do, if events should bring home to the country the true facts of Ulster's determination, and the Government still preferred to risk civil war rather than "break with their Nationalist friends."

> Is he (i.e. the King) or is he not, to become, however unwillingly, the accomplice of a policy whose consequences

[1] See *Life of Lord Oxford and Asquith*, Vol. II, pp. 31, 32 *et seq.*, for full exposition of his reasons for refusing to advise the King to dissolve Parliament.

may shake the Empire, and shatter the discipline of the armed forces of the Crown?

The decision will be a very difficult one, but if the King came to the conclusion that, except in obedience to a clear mandate from the country, he ought not to allow Ulster to be coerced, his best course, as it seems to me, would be to force a Dissolution.

How is this to be done? Not, I think, by refusing his assent to the Home Rule Bill, but by changing his advisers.

The first of these courses might be represented as unconstitutional. Not so the second. This at least is my view, which I should be prepared to argue on the proper occasion. The question arises—whom shall he send for? If he sends for Lansdowne or Bonar Law, he will, however unjustly, be accused of favouring one particular Party in the State. What then is he to do?

Were I in his place, I should be disposed to consider the propriety of sending for Rosebery or myself, not to form a Government in the ordinary sense, but to dissolve and act as his advisers until the new Parliament was returned, but no longer. There would be no difficulty in carrying on the routine work of the Offices during these few weeks without any paraphernalia of Parliamentary Secretaries and Under-Secretaries.

There are, of course, endless objections to this plan; but its advantages are manifest. Neither of the two Ministers suggested could be accused of straining the Constitution in their own personal interests, for, by hypothesis, neither of them is to retain office after the new Elections. No Party programme would, or could, be issued by them under such circumstances, and the exceptional character of the crisis would be emphasised by the exceptional character of the temporary Ministry. They would, by speech or address, make only one appeal to the country, the appeal, namely, that the country should take upon itself the full responsibility for all the consequences which Home Rule must bring with it.

I am not sure that it would not be better for Rosebery, if he would consent, to act alone, for I am still closely

FOREBODINGS

identified with the Party of which I was once the Leader, and this cannot be said of R. His " lonely furrow " would, after all, enable him to play an important rôle in public affairs. But I do not know whether he would look upon the matter in exactly the same light. If he refused to act, either alone or with me, I should not hesitate, in the circumstances I have indicated, to become sole Minister.

It is worth noticing that Balfour's foreboding of the effect of the Government's Irish policy upon the Army was recorded here fully six months before the " Curragh incident " of March 1914. In the previous September the strength of feeling on the Ulster question was still underrated by the Government. Balfour wrote in October that he suspected that they were only now beginning to understand it. It was in fact in that month of 1913 that the Prime Minister wrote from Balmoral to Mr. Bonar Law suggesting a private conversation. This was followed by another on November 6th,[1] and after both these talks Mr. Bonar Law wrote fully to Balfour. The answer he received on November 8th is an exposition of Balfour's private opinion about the whole situation. Among other things it shows how the demand for a General Election was no mere tactical manœuvre of the Unionists. Balfour at any rate thought that from the Government's own point of view Dissolution would be wise as well as right.

There can be no doubt that the bulk of the English Unionists were intensely sincere in their demand for an appeal to the country in the winter of 1913–1914. Whatever the verdict, it would have strengthened the hand of all those who were seeking for a reasonable compromise.

But it was not to be. The months passed in futile

[1] See *Life of Lord Oxford and Asquith*, Vol. II, pp. 35 *et seq.*

1914 efforts at agreement in London, while in Ireland Orangemen and Nationalists drilled. On February 19th, 1914, Balfour warned the Government that the "tinkering expedients" they had proffered would not save the situation.[1] The separation of Northern Ireland must be by " the clean cut " and nothing less. Then, reverting to the metaphor he had first used more than a year before, he said :

"We are in the rapids now, and even to the dullest hearing the mutterings of the cataract must surely be audible."

Some two months later thirty-five thousand rifles and three million rounds of ammunition were landed at Larne. Faced with this development of "organised disorder," Mr. Asquith entered on a final effort at negotiation, and on May 21st announced the introduction of an Amending Bill to the Home Rule Bill, which was then on the verge of passing into law. The Amending Bill was to be presented in the first place in the House of Lords. This procedure stirred Balfour to wrath.

> Personally I think it outrageous [he wrote in a Memorandum to his old colleagues]. Under the Parliament Act the Government propose to force through the main Bill. At the very moment they are pursuing this high-handed course, of which the Lords are the victims, they come to these same Lords and say. " We admit that our Bill requires vital amendment, and though as a partisan and incompetent body you are not fit to reject it, we rely upon you to make it workable. . . . Please help us re-draft it."

Balfour's strong advice was that the Opposition in both Houses should refuse any responsibility for the Amending Bill. The question at issue was now one of drawing the boundary of separation. How could the Lords take upon themselves the responsibility for

[1] Speech at Cannon Street Hotel.

making such a delimitation as Ulster would accept? And further, if they did make proposals which the Government would not concede, and the Bill dropped, how could they escape the charge of having by their wanton obstinacy brought on the country all the horrors of civil war?

Balfour's advice was not followed. The Lords so amended the Bill as to exclude all the six Ulster counties permanently from Home Rule. In that form it was due to return to the Commons on July 17th. But it was postponed for a last effort at an acceptable settlement, and on July 20th the Party leaders met, by the King's invitation, to confer in Buckingham Palace. Balfour was of course not of their number. On July 24th it was announced that the discussions had been fruitless. They had turned mainly on the frontier line, especially in Tyrone and Fermanagh. And after the World War had been fought, it was still (to quote Mr. Winston Churchill's incomparable phrase) "the dreary steeples of Tyrone and Fermanagh" that emerged above the receding floods, and obstructed the way to settlement of the Irish question.

There is no stranger comparison in all the history of British politics than appears between the tone and temper in which Parliament discussed Home Rule, and the deepening sense of unity in face of danger, which inspired debates on foreign affairs and national defence in the last years before the War.

Even the columns of *Hansard* revive the emotional contrasts called forth by a debate on the Irish, or on the European, situations. These changes of temper were not confined to the House of Commons, they were experienced in every dinner table conversation which turned on politics, and in those days conversations turned on little else. Among such I remember one

ARTHUR JAMES BALFOUR

1914 scene in Balfour's London dining-room, which must have taken place in the early summer of 1914. Sir Edward Carson[1] was one of the five or six people present at luncheon, and the talk was about some sneer at Ulster in some Minister's speech. Banging the table till the glasses rang, Sir Edward declared that social relations with Home Rulers had become impossible. Balfour did not dissent, but said in a tone of extreme depression that he had never expected to have to admit that such a thing could be true in this country. The mere admission of its possibility, by him, brought into consciousness the unexampled passions which were rending our familiar world. Nevertheless there was no moment when Balfour would have withheld from his opponents anything that could strengthen their hand in foreign policy. As a matter of fact, he had, at the Prime Minister's request, become a member of a Sub-committee of the Committee of Imperial Defence, which sat from March 1913, till February 1914, to consider the subject of invasion of these islands.

The constitution he had himself framed for the Committee made his presence no anomaly. But during these years of independence from Party obligations another invitation reached him informally from Government quarters. He was asked in June 1912, by Mr. Winston Churchill, then First Lord of the Admiralty, to put on paper, for Sir Edward Grey's benefit, some views on Anglo-French relations which he had expressed in conversation. The result was a Memorandum of much interest, especially as coming from the ex-Prime Minister under whom the *Entente Cordiale* was originally concluded.

It begins by noting that force of circumstances had by this time given the *Entente* a wider scope than the

[1] Afterwards Lord Carson.

A. J. BALFOUR
1917

strict letter of the Agreement had contemplated, and 1912 had created a public sentiment which would make it impossible for either Power to remain indifferent to any serious attack upon the other. Thus we were bearing the risks and burdens of an Alliance without the advantages. This was clearly illustrated by the existing naval position in the Mediterranean. The substitution of an Alliance for the *Entente* should be given serious consideration. Its advantages were evidently great from both the military and diplomatic points of view. The General Staffs would know accurately upon what character and amount of assistance they could rely, and " no longer feel themselves at the mercy of passing political moods and fancies." The diplomatic gain would hardly be less.

> An " Entente " is the natural prey of every diplomatic intriguer, . . . and it could hardly be doubted that the immediate effect of an Anglo-French Alliance would be to relieve international strain rather than to aggravate it.

On the adverse side a defensive Treaty had but one drawback, but that one was formidable.

Here follows a passage foreshadowing difficulties and even suggested solutions that later became familiar to successive relays of Delegates at Geneva wearily seeking a formula for " security."

> The line between offence and defence [wrote Balfour in 1912] is sometimes hard to draw. The Power that fires the first shot, that first crosses a frontier, may not be the real aggressor. . . . There are many people in this country (I am one of them) who would do everything in their power to save France from destruction, but have no mind to be dragged at her heels into a war for the recovery of Alsace and Lorraine. Such persons want to be assured that the France for which they are asked to fight is France defending her own independence, and the independence of Europe, not the France of Louis XIV, of Napoleon, or

even of the Second Empire. How then are we to allay their fears, and obtain both for France and ourselves the advantages that can be conferred by a Treaty, but never by an *Entente* ?

Balfour's suggested answer to this question was to require the Power who called on its ally for assistance to express its readiness to submit the points in dispute to arbitration. He thought some test of this kind must be brought to bear even on a case of sudden aggression, and in fact his suggested form of Treaty would have taken account of the moral judgment of the world as to its defensive character. He sums up in a way which shows that if he had been responsible for the foreign policy of this country in 1912 there would have been no moment of doubt about Britain's commitments to France in August 1914.

> I submit therefore (1) that the capacities of the much tried Entente are now almost exhausted. (2) That the advantages, military and diplomatic, of a Treaty are great, and are growing. (3) That its dangers, though real, are not unavoidable and (4) that in a judicious use of the modern machinery of arbitration may perhaps be found the best way of avoiding them.

This method of facing the facts of the situation did not commend itself to the Cabinet. In the chapter of the first volume of this book dealing with the making of the *Entente* a letter of Balfour's is quoted (written in 1912), in which he says he is struck—though not with disapproval—by the extent to which the military conversations between the General Staffs, begun in 1906, had already developed the Agreement in the direction of an Alliance. It may be that he learned this in conversations with individual Ministers at the time when he wrote his Memorandum. It was composed in June 1912, and it was at about this date, according to Mr.

APPEAL TO GERMANY

Lloyd George, that the bulk of the Cabinet which had been six years in office realised for the first time how far they were committed by the military conversations. They were "aghast; hostility barely represents the strength of the sentiment which the revelation aroused."[1]

Thus Balfour's realistic proposals fell at an unpropitious moment. Sir Edward Grey and the Prime Minister were occupied in emphatically assuring their colleagues that they remained " quite free, in the event of war, to decide whether we should, or should not, participate in the conflict."

The possibility of avoiding that conflict altogether was believed in by the majority of Englishmen with varying degrees of conviction, and ups and downs of hope, till the very end. Balfour spent much time and trouble in the summer of 1912 on an article on Anglo-German relations, which he contributed to a German periodical *Nord und Sud*.[2] In it he probed the causes of the uneasiness with which Great Britain saw " that marvellous instrument of warfare, the German Army and Navy " co-existing with an organised advocacy of German territorial expansion. The article ends with an appeal to Germany to teach the world that military power can be used in the interests of peace. If she would not, could it be a matter of surprise to her if other countries considered schemes for meeting what they were driven to regard as a common danger?

Balfour was no pessimist about the inevitability of war, yet the impression of one trifling incident of family life remains. It was during a walk through the woods at Whittingehame in the frosty sunset of the last day of the year 1913. Balfour was surrounded as usual by a

---

[1] See *War Memories*, Vol. I, p. 50.
[2] The essay is reprinted in Balfour's *Essays Speculative and Political*. (Hodder & Stoughton, 1920.)

number of the younger members of his family. Suddenly the booming of distant guns broke through the chatter and laughter and set the roosting pheasants talking. There was nothing odd in this, for in the clear air of such an evening the sound of firing practice from ships in the Firth of Forth was easily heard. But this time it struck somebody to say: " Perhaps it's the Germans," and the notion was eagerly pursued by the youngest in the party. Some of us however noticed a change in Balfour's expression, a momentary alertness of listening, and then a curious gravity as he gazed at the excited children, without making any comment on the subject of their joke.

During the holidays Balfour turned to his own best refuge from the anxieties of the outer world, and absorbed himself in the preparation of the third of his serious contributions to philosophic thought. Soon after he left office he had accepted the invitation of the University of Glasgow to be the Gifford Lecturer of the years 1913 and 1914. He worked at every interval of leisure in 1912, and in the autumn of 1913, upon the first ten lectures, which were published in book form in 1915 with the title of *Theism and Humanism*. The second half of the series, which in normal times would have been delivered in the winter of 1914, were delayed until after the War, and were published in 1923 as a book, called *Theism and Thought*.

The terms of the Trust under which Lord Gifford founded the Lectureship in 1887 are very wide. Natural theology must be the subject, and that theme is defined simply in the donor's will as " the knowledge of God." It could thus be approached from the historical, the psychological, and many other angles besides the metaphysical, and had indeed been treated in a great variety of ways by a succession of distinguished thinkers.

THE GIFFORD LECTURES

Balfour determined to deal with it from the plain man's point of view. He took certain beliefs, which he classified as "inevitable beliefs," beliefs, that is to say, which we all live by in practice, however much they may be criticised in theory. He put them into three categories: those that concern the material world, those which relate to the ends of human action and include morals, and those that have to do with beauty and other subjects of contemplative interest. Belief in God he did not include among the "inevitables" of the plain man's creed; but he proceeded to examine them one by one, as part of a developing and improving system, and to enquire how they would appear, if belief in God were excluded from them; or, to use his own words,[1] "to determine on what theory of the universe the highest values of ... the good, the beautiful and the true could be the most effectively maintained."

That was the scheme of the Lectures. The conclusion of the argument was, "for those who would accept it, to link up a belief in God with all that is, or seems, most assured in knowledge, all that is, or seems, most beautiful in art or nature, and all that is, or seems, most noble in morality."[2]

This is a very explicit statement of Balfour's own theological position, a thing essential to understanding of his character. His reserve about deep matters was great, and some friends who justly claimed to know some sides of him very well have declared that they remained in doubt about such a fundamental thing as the nature of his belief in God. Such a perplexity would have been dispelled if they had ever read his written words upon the subject. The passage just

[1] See Preface to *Theism and Thought*.
[2] See Introductory Lecture: *Theism and Humanism*.

quoted might not indeed be enough in itself. Men have thought of God in many ways. In what way did Balfour think of Him? He answers the question thus:

> When in the course of these lectures I speak of God, I mean something other than an Identity wherein all differences vanish, or a Unity which includes but does not transcend the differences which it somehow holds in solution. I mean a God whom men can love, a God to whom men can pray, who takes sides, who has purposes and preferences, whose attributes, howsoever conceived, leave unimpaired the possibility of a personal relation between Himself and those whom He has created.[1]

This was the faith that lay at the root of his being. The Gifford Lectures were in fact the final and most constructive expression of thoughts aroused in his youth by the so-called conflict between science and religion, the existence of which conflict he had set forth to disprove in his earlier books.

His belief in the existence of a personal God was no slow evolution, though in none of his writings is it so stripped of metaphysical expression as in the Gifford Lectures.

Once, near the end of his life, he remarked upon the continuity of his thinking on these matters.

> As to my philosophy, [he said] it has been continually in my mind—I've worked at it off and on—well! since I was at Eton. No! Really *before* Eton I believe I began muddling about these ideas. You know—when I look back at myself I'm appalled by how little I have changed in eighty years.

The autumn and winter of 1913–1914, when the Gifford Lectures were being finished and delivered, were a very intensive period in the family history. I have mentioned already how he would discuss the

[1] See *Theism and Humanism*, p. 21.

THE "GIFFORD GATES"

Lectures with his family, and encourage the impression, which readily took root, that they were a sort of communal achievement. His relatives certainly took a communal pride in the astonishment which his method of delivering them aroused in everyone capable of appreciating the feat involved by his discarding of almost all notes. For the sustained effort of an hour of close philosophical reasoning he still used nothing but the same kind of long envelope with some half-dozen single words jotted down it, which used to be his only visible preparation for a political speech. With this in his pocket he would set forth from Whittingehame, lunching in the train between Edinburgh and Glasgow, deliver the lecture in the afternoon, and return home the same night. This he did ten times in the last winter before the War.

There stand to-day, in the wall surrounding the garden at Whittingehame, a pair of wrought-iron gates. Balfour erected them in the spring of 1914 with the money that accrues to the Gifford Lecturer.

Sometimes during the War he would look at the date "1914" interwoven with the scroll-work of the gates and wonder whether posterity would ask why on earth he had chosen that year for this particular form of commemoration.

Chapter VII

THE FIRST NINE MONTHS OF WAR

AUGUST 1914 TO MAY 1915

The first days of August. Balfour in London. Promise of Unionist support for the Government. Correspondence with Lord Haldane. Balfour's views of Sir Edward Grey and Lord Kitchener. The Passing of the Home Rule Bill. Balfour's visit to his nephew at Blackdown Camp. Dinner at the Automobile Club. Disquiet abour war preparations. Balfour joins the " War Council." Visit to the Battle-cruisers. Letter from Lord Fisher. Balfour's views of war strategy. Balfour consults Mr. Bonar Law on his position in " War Council." Difficulties of the Unionists.

1914 Balfour remained in London through the days before the August Bank Holiday, held there against every normal habit by interest in the swiftly developing European crisis. His house in Carlton Gardens was close to the great Offices of State. He was accessible to those who sat in conclave there, and his personal position, his wide experience, gave him more insight into the hourly changes in the situation during the days before we entered the War than almost any man in England, except those on whom responsibility rested. Yet he was at leisure to think in his own arm-chair, or to wander musingly about the streets as he was always fond of doing. He could mingle with the multitudes that surged up and down Whitehall and clustered about Downing Street. He could retreat from them up the Duke of York's Steps, and in his own

THE FLEET UP CHANNEL

study listen to Mr. Winston Churchill and others who 1914 brought him the latest telegrams from abroad, or the latest orientation of opinion in the Cabinet Room. "He was a veritable rock in times like these," Mr. Churchill records.[1]

But it was not from Mr. Churchill, with whom he was in the most constant touch, that he heard the greatest secret of the moment. During one of his afternoon strolls he met by chance Admiral Lord Fisher. They stood and talked on the pavement, undisturbed though no doubt identified by many passers-by. When they parted Balfour's last doubt of the inevitability of war was gone. He told me about it later, thus:

> One thing I knew before the Cabinet knew it. I met old Jackie Fisher in Cockspur Street,—it was on the Wednesday before the Monday, I think (July 29th), and he told me that Winston had ordered the Fleet up the Channel. Yes—I heard that from old Fisher, who was sometimes my dearest friend and sometimes my bitterest enemy; but at that moment he happened to be my dearest friend. It wasn't quite such an outrageous breach of confidence as it sounds perhaps,—for if the Cabinet didn't know I have no doubt Asquith did.
>
> I was quite sure after my talk with Fisher that day that we should have war, and I remember I dined that day with Almroth Wright.[2] It was a medical dinner—nothing specially interesting—only I happened to remember walking home from Park Crescent where he lived, and looking at all the people in the street going along happily, and saying to myself that I knew that war was coming upon them. I just happen to remember that walk.

This was on "the Wednesday before the Monday"—the Bank Holiday Monday when the old world ended. Balfour's conviction of the inevitability of war was

[1] *The World Crisis*, Vol. I, p. 218.
[2] Sir Almroth Wright, K.B.E.

113

ARTHUR JAMES BALFOUR

1914 not due to the information about the Fleet movements, but to his estimate of the situation which made that movement right. From that day on, his growing anxiety was the hesitation of the Government, which prevented the French from knowing how far they could count upon our aid. He was kept abreast of the struggle that was taking place in the Cabinet Room. After the morning Cabinet on Sunday, August 2nd—the day on which it was known that the Germans were marching on Belgium—Mr. Churchill paid him a hurried visit, and told him that he thought half the Cabinet would resign when war was declared. Balfour at once said he was certain that if so, the Unionist leaders would be quite prepared to join a Coalition Government, although such a necessity would be a very great misfortune.[1] The thought in his mind was that a Coalition at that moment might hasten the formation of an anti-War Party.

When he proffered Unionist support on his own initiative Balfour had probably already got into touch with Mr. Bonar Law and Lord Lansdowne, who was out of London. At some time on Saturday or Sunday Balfour sent them word that the Unionist attitude should be made clear to the Government without delay. He had heard, again from Mr. Churchill, of a rumour going round the clubs that the division of opinion in the Cabinet had its counterpart in the Conservative Party. Much of his time on the Saturday was spent (as he wrote to his sister) in " conveying to the French and Russian Ambassadors that this idea was totally unfounded."

He did it with the more energy because he had just heard that a misunderstanding of his own attitude had

[1] My authority for this is my own notes of his conversation on August 11th, the first time I saw him after the Declaration of War.

arisen in the highest quarters, partly perhaps through his own fault. He had met Sir Arthur Nicolson[1] (the Permanent Under-Secretary of State at the Foreign Office) at dinner earlier in the week. Sir Arthur had talked of Britain immediately joining with France and Russia, as if this were a matter of course, and Balfour, although entirely agreeing, had, characteristically, put the other side of the case. Sir Arthur had apparently reported this to Sir Edward Grey as if it were Balfour's real opinion, and it further came round to the Unionist leaders that Sir Edward had cited their attitude to the French Ambassador as an excuse for the Government's inaction. Balfour had sought an interview with the Foreign Secretary to put the matter right, but, failing to see him on Saturday, could only send a message through the Private Secretary to explain that he had been entirely misunderstood. This, and other circumstances, made him urgent to consult his colleagues. Messages from other quarters also reached the Unionist leaders on Saturday. That evening some of them met at Lansdowne House. Lord Lansdowne, Mr. Bonar Law and Balfour were present, also General Sir Henry Wilson, Mr. George Lloyd and possibly others. The Unionists decided that evening to send a message to the Prime Minister offering to see him if he so desired. They met again on Sunday morning at Mr. Bonar Law's house, Mr. Austen Chamberlain being now arrived from the country and added to their consultation. No answer had come from Mr. Asquith, and it was decided to write to him. Mr. Bonar Law therefore signed a letter which had the agreement of them all, declaring that " any hesitation in supporting France and Russia would be fatal to the honour and future security of the United Kingdom," and offering unhesitating support to the

[1] Afterwards Lord Carnock.   [2] Afterwards Lord Lloyd.

ARTHUR JAMES BALFOUR

1914 Government "in all measures required by England's intervention in the War."[1]

By the Monday morning the situation on the Belgian frontier had put an end to hypothetical discussions in Cabinet. When Mr. Lloyd George had made up his mind—as he did on this day[2]—the die was cast. The Unionist leaders felt that the circumstances of the time justified them in pressing that there should be no more delay over the most vital of the next steps, the despatch of the Expeditionary Force. Probably Lord Lansdowne and Balfour discussed the propriety of putting forward their views, for on Tuesday, August 4th, both of them approached Lord Haldane, who was temporarily in charge of the War Office. Lord Lansdowne's conversation with him is recorded in his Life.[3] Balfour's views were written in a letter, in which he reminded Lord Haldane of their recent work together on the "Invasion" Sub-Committee, and went on:

> As you are aware, I was altogether opposed, as a matter of general policy, to completely denuding these Islands of regular troops, . . . but surely there are almost overwhelming reasons at this moment for giving all the aid we can to France by land and sea.
> (1) As regards Germany we have burnt our boats. We have chosen our side and must abide by the results.
> (2) The sort of British Force that we could send, after leaving 2 Divisions at home, is no doubt a very small fraction of any Continental army, but it is *not* a very small fraction of the troops immediately available for field operations in the North-east of France.
> (3) If Germany could be stalemated in her advance through Belgium and North-east France, her position

[1] These facts are taken from Sir Austen Chamberlain's *Down the Years*, pp. 92 *et seq.*, where he corrects the statements made in Lord Newton's *Life of Lord Lansdowne*, that the Unionists' letter was sent to Mr. Asquith only on Monday, August 3rd.
[2] See *War Memories*, by David Lloyd George, Vol. I, p. 71.
[3] See *Life of Lord Lansdowne*, p. 440.

becomes very perilous with the menace of Russia on her Eastern frontier. If, on the other hand, the Germans are in sufficiently overwhelming numbers to inflict on France a crushing defeat, the whole future of Europe might be changed in a direction we should regard as disastrous.

(4) Is it not a fundamental principle of strategy of this particular kind either to keep out of the conflict altogether, or to strike quickly and to strike with your whole strength?

This letter brought from Lord Haldane a request for a talk, and at eleven o'clock on the night of the fourth of August, the hour that saw us at war with the greatest military Power in the world, these two metaphysicians discussed in no metaphysical spirit the destination of England's Army.

I gathered [Balfour wrote in a Memorandum which he made next day of their conversation] that the Government were still hesitating—on military not on political grounds. The arguments in favour of sending the Force at once were those in my letter; the arguments against it were, as I understood him, (1) that if the Force were kept for the present at home, it would form the nucleus of a much more formidable Army. . . . If they were sent now they would form a comparatively trifling addition to the forces at the disposal of the French, and if they were destroyed we should be weaker at the most decisive moment of the War. (2) That if we deprived ourselves of regular troops now, the free action of the Fleet might be hampered.

As regards the second argument I was disappointed to hear him use it. He repeated it more than once, and each time I reminded him that the Sub-Committee of Imperial Defence . . . was of opinion that a mobile column consisting of two really effective Divisions of regular troops, in addition to all the other Regulars and Irregulars in the country would be sufficient to secure us from raids. . . .

On the whole I was rather depressed by a certain woolliness of thought, and indecision of purpose, which seemed to mark his conversation—otherwise very interesting.

ARTHUR JAMES BALFOUR

1914 It seems, from Lord Haldane's own evidence,[1] that this impression may have been due to his effort to convey the state of mind of the Cabinet rather than his own. For himself, he says, he was desirous " from the outset " of sending off all six Divisions of the Expeditionary Force. On August 5th a Council was held, and a decision taken. Lord Haldane wrote it instantly to Balfour.

HOUSE OF LORDS.
August 6th, 1914.

MY DEAR BALFOUR,

After War Council this evening we sanctioned the immediate despatch of an Exped. Force of 4 Divisions and the Cavalry Division. There has not been much delay, as mobilisation could not take place early—they should be on the transports by Sunday. All this is of course very private. We have telegraphed to Belgium that this force is starting.

Yours very sincerely,
HALDANE.

Balfour, greatly relieved, still criticised the delay. On August 7th he wrote to Lady Elcho, saying:

I cannot doubt the decision was a right one, but it might with advantage have been taken earlier. I do not the least blame the Government for refusing to make up their minds about the Expedition till Sunday or Monday (August 2nd and 3rd); but after that every hour's delay seems to me to have been an unnecessary waste of priceless time.

This is a contemporary comment, but here is the place to record Balfour's later opinions about the handling of the situation in the Foreign Office during the last week of peace, as he expressed them when the publication of Sir Edward Grey's own *Memoirs* in 1925 gave him material for judgment. Then his criticism was extremely cautious. The most I ever heard him say was in the course of a family discussion as to whether war could have been prevented if the Foreign Secretary

[1] See *Autobiography*, R. B. Haldane, p. 277.

had warned the Cabinet that he would resign unless more were done than to protect the northern coasts of France with the Navy. Balfour expressed no opinion on that point, but he said :

> I think if I had been Foreign Minister I should have talked to Lichnowsky.[1] I should have said, " I speak for myself alone, but I speak with a full sense of my own responsibility. Take it from me that if Germany attacks France, England will come in." I should not have said to him that she would come in *at once*, but I should have made perfectly clear my conviction that sooner or later she would do so. I think that would have been the action that a strong Foreign Minister would have taken. I think it might have had an effect on Germany. But Grey did not attempt it.

Nevertheless Balfour had a very high opinion of Sir Edward Grey. One day the conversation was about great Foreign Ministers of English history, and to a list including Castlereagh, Grenville, Canning, Palmerston and Salisbury, Balfour added " Grey," and when reminded of the criticism quoted above, he said : " That's a very moot point. I think Grey was a great Foreign Secretary."

At the War Council held on August 5th Lord Kitchener was present. Rightly or wrongly Balfour attributed to him the credit of forcing the decision to despatch the Expeditionary Force at once, and he never failed to weigh this on the favourable side of a judgment of Lord Kitchener which became more and more critical as time went on. This topic must recur; enough for the present to say that Balfour might have condemned many of Lord Kitchener's weak points far less harshly than Mr. Lloyd George and other Ministers have publicly done, had it not been for one which he held Lord Kitchener to suffer from, and

[1] Prince Lichnowsky, German Ambassador in London.

1914 which for him was the unforgivable sin: the reluctance, namely, to assume responsibility. It was an opinion formed from observation before the War, and Balfour would never admit that it was unjust. When the accuracy of Lord Kitchener's instinct about the length of the War became apparent, Balfour would only say that if he had really been convinced about his own estimate, he should have insisted upon immediate preparations for an adequate supply of guns and shells as well as of men. He gave full value however to Lord Kitchener's immense prestige, and thought his appointment as War Minister right in August 1914.

Between the date of the decision to despatch the Expeditionary Force and its departure round the 12th of August, the Unionist leaders were forced again into a bout of Party controversy by the Government's revival of the question of Irish Home Rule. Only ten days had passed since, on the initiative of the Unionists, an agreement had been reached—or so they believed— to postpone controversial discussion at home lest it should weaken our influence abroad. The Prime Minister's own testimony shows the spirit in which the suggestion had been made; he wrote on July 30th, 1914, that Mr. Bonar Law and Sir Edward Carson had proposed in the interests of the international situation that we should postpone for the time being the Second Reading of the Amending Bill, lest advertising our own domestic dissensions should weaken our influence in the world for peace. Carson had said that at first he thought it impossible to agree, as it would strain still further the well-known and much tried patience of his Ulstermen, but he had come to see that it was now a patriotic duty.[1]

When Mr. Asquith agreed to the Unionists' proposal,

[1] See *Memories and Reflections*, by Lord Oxford and Asquith, II, pp. 5–9.

A BROKEN PROMISE

peace was still in the balance, but within a day or two 1914 Northern and Southern Irishmen were alike flocking to the colours, and the Ulster Volunteers were scattered through the length and breadth of the realm in the training camps of " Kitchener's Army." But Irishmen on neither side abated one jot of the determination that had brought them to the brink of civil war, and the Unionists were deeply resentful of the advantage they felt had been taken of their suggestion for a Party truce.

On August 8th Balfour wrote to his sister, Miss Balfour:

> The Government are contemplating a monstrous iniquity. They actually propose, after adjourning for a fortnight, to go on with the Home Rule policy ! ! I spent all yesterday afternoon in writing a Memorandum exposing the wickedness and folly of such a plan, and if they cannot be brought to reason this will probably be published in Monday's papers over the signatures of Lansdowne and Bonar Law. The scheme of the Government seems at first sight unbelievable, but apparently they are terrorised not merely by the Irish, but by the Radical tail.

To this letter there is a postscript:

> I hear by telephone from Bonar Law that after reading my Memorandum they have postponed their decision till Monday morning's Cabinet. I have some hopes now that a way will be found, and that no dirty linen will be washed in public.

The hope was not altogether fulfilled. The Government insisted on placing the Home Rule Bill on the Statute Book, though deferring its operation to a date to be fixed after the end of the War. Parliament was also to have an opportunity of passing an Amending Bill, and Ulster was not to be coerced by force. These were new pledges, but they replaced promises only a few days old, that no controversial legislation should be

1914 undertaken till the discussion of the Amending Bill could be resumed, and that no Party should be put in a worse position by its postponement.

Apart from these understandings, bitterly cited by Mr. Bonar Law before he led the Unionists out of the House when the Home Rule Bill was brought in on September 15th, there were other circumstances which might have made the Government pause. On August 7th, nearly ninety Members of Parliament had already been called away on military service. Sixty-three of them were Unionists, twenty were Liberals. The House no longer represented the real balance of Parties. Moreover, meetings of a Party character had been stopped all over the country by mutual consent.

> How was it possible [wrote Balfour in his Memorandum] to let political warfare run riot within the House of Commons, and proclaim a truce everywhere else? Such a policy is unthinkable.

Having registered their protest, the Unionists continued, in all matters concerning the prosecution of the War, to give the Government the steady support that in those early months was not always forthcoming from the Liberal and Labour benches.[1]

Before the end of August two of Balfour's nephews were already on active service, for one went to France with the Expeditionary Force,[2] and another was with the Battle-cruisers in the North Sea.[3]

Balfour drove down with me to Blackdown on August 11th to say good-bye to Oswald, who had passed out of Sandhurst a few weeks before the outbreak of war and had joined the 60th Rifles. Everything

[1] See *War Memories*, I, by David Lloyd George, p. 216.
[2] Oswald Balfour, youngest son of Balfour's brother Eustace.
[3] Captain the Hon. Arthur Strutt, afterwards Admiral Strutt, second son of Lord and Lady Rayleigh.

in the camp was ready for departure. We wandered among lines of picketed horses and field guns, a swarm of aeroplanes roaring and swooping overhead. Two staff officers presently recognised Balfour, and he drew apart with them for a low-voiced conversation, returning with the certain news that the Division was to embark for France that same night. Then we had tea at a small table on a lawn in front of some hotel, surrounded by other groups like our own. As we drove off after saying good-bye Balfour leaned forward till his nephew could no longer be seen, and then threw himself back and gave way to an uncontrollable burst of tears. He recovered his composure quickly, but he was silent the whole way back to London, whereas, on the journey down, contrary to his habits in a motor-car, he had talked with animation, relating many of the things which have formed the basis of the earlier part of this chapter. That night some of his family and friends dined with him at the Automobile Club (his own household staff having migrated to Whittingehame). The dining-room was crowded, and his entry attracted attention, some people whom he knew, and more whom he did not, coming up, shaking hands, talking of the war news. As usual on such occasions Balfour looked vaguely and amiably mystified. He never got used to being known by strangers; never himself recognising his nearest and dearest in any unexpected place, he thought this the most extraordinary of gifts. The wine waiter came for orders. " Have you still got any German beer ? " Balfour asked, and when he received a rather shocked affirmative, said : " Then let's have it while we still can." The talk at dinner was of strategy, mainly between Captain William Balfour,[1] who had come from Aldershot on the eve of departure with the

---

[1] Now Colonel Balfour of Balbirnie.

ARTHUR JAMES BALFOUR

1914 Cavalry Division, and Sir Foster Cunliffe,[1] whose special subject was Military History. Balfour listened, drawing them on by questions which betrayed, as usual, how near his professed ignorance came to expert knowledge.

For the first month or two of the War Balfour was busy with work on the administrative Committee of the Fund—which reached more than a million pounds in the first few days—raised by the Prince of Wales for the relief of distress. It was by the King's express wish that Mr. Asquith asked Balfour to undertake this business. On September 8th he wrote to his sister after having dined at Number 10 Downing Street:

> for the first time since I left office, except only the official Dinner to meet the King. No man there except the Prime Minister, Winston, and Baker (the Parliamentary Under Secretary at the War Office) . . . Winston was in his most characteristic mood. He talks airily of a British Army of a million men, and tells me he is making siege mortars at Woolwich as big, or bigger, than the German ones, in order to crush the Rhine fortresses! I have been begging him to do all he can to diminish the strain on the personnel of the Navy. It is what the Germans are counting on. No doubt he is right in saying that if *we* suffer by keeping the sea, the Germans will *also* suffer by staying in port. It is not good either for the efficiency or the morale of a Fleet to be bottled up as they appear to be at this moment.

Inside knowledge without power to influence events except by criticism is a galling thing, and as the defects in our improvised war machine became apparent, Balfour's position began to fret him, especially when in September the friction over Home Rule cut him off temporarily from contact with Ministers. By then the shortcomings in the equipment and camps for Kitchener's Army were beginning to be realised.

[1] Sir Foster Cunliffe, Bart. Killed in Flanders, July 13th, 1916.

HARNESS AGAIN

It was with alacrity, therefore, that Balfour accepted 1914 the invitation of the Prime Minister to become once more a member of the Committee of Imperial Defence. He attended his first meeting on October 7th, and from that day may date the end of the one important interval in his life passed without either office or responsibility; for although membership of the Defence Committee did not technically involve either, its functions in wartime were in fact those of the War Council, by which name it was known from November 1914 onwards. Thus, three years exactly from his resignation of the Party leadership in 1911 Balfour began the second period of his official life. He served on the War Council for six months before the formation of the first Coalition Government, in May 1915, brought him into a Cabinet again as First Lord of the Admiralty. How much in the inner ring he was by that time can be seen from a letter of Mr. Asquith's dated November 24th, 1914. The first battle of Ypres had not yet closed, and the last notable incident at sea had been the naval defeat off Coronel.

> My dear Balfour,
> The existing situation, both military and naval, is critical. I propose to have at noon to-morrow a consultation at 10 Downing Street . . . to take a full survey of all its aspects. I should be greatly obliged if you could make it convenient to attend. The only Ministers summoned are E. Grey, Lord K., Winston and Lloyd George. They may bring with them one or two experts. Naturally I don't wish this to be known.
> Yours always, H. H. A.

In the early months of the winter 1914 Balfour was furthermore occupied by an elaborate and detailed piece of work connected with organisation of the civil population of the South and East coasts in case of a German

1914 raid. He undertook this in conjunction with Colonel Hankey,[1] and it involved many meetings with the Lord-Lieutenants and other County officials in England and Scotland.

He came home to Whittingehame for the first war Christmas, where most of the family were collected, including his nephew Oswald, recovering from a wound received in the Aisne battle of September. Just before the short holiday ended Balfour paid a visit to the Battle Cruiser Squadron in the Firth of Forth. A telephoned invitation to luncheon from Lady Beatty,[2] whose private yacht was lying off Rosyth, was interpreted to mean that the great ships were in the Firth. Their movements were, of course, shrouded in mystery. They moved in darkness, but the country-side was always agog with rumours about the presence or absence of the battle cruisers from their refuge above the boom that was slung between the arches of the Forth Bridge. They had come in to their anchorage at the dead of the night on December 28th, 1914—it was a year almost to the day since the walk in the woods when the sound of gun-practice from the Forth had made us laugh. We sailed round about them in a motor-launch after Balfour and Sir David Beatty had finished the private conversation which succeeded lunch on the yacht. There was *Lion*, the Flagship, and *Indomitable*, just back from the Mediterranean, painted in two shades of grey like a tabby-cat. There was *Tiger*, newly commissioned, and we turned round about her so that Balfour could see her four mighty guns aft, which had never yet spoken in action. Next her lay *Queen Mary*, fated to perish at Jutland, and beyond these were others, and beyond

[1] Secretary to the War Council; afterwards Sir Maurice Hankey.
[2] The wife of Admiral Sir David Beatty, afterwards Earl Beatty, then in command of the battle cruisers.

EVERYONE'S CONFIDANT

them again, higher up the estuary, some of the light cruisers were dimly visible. It was an elating, an awe-inspiring spectacle.

These upper waters of the Forth, where the monster ships could lie in safety, were not so familiar to East Lothian folk as the widening stretches below the Bridge, where the Firth merges with the sea. There, so to speak, our own series of views began, views associated with every joyful expedition of past years to golf-links or picnics on the shore. It seemed intolerable that there, of all places, German submarines should lie in wait. Yet there, on that very day, their presence was suspected. So Admiral Beatty had told Balfour, and so he told us on the way home. Curiously we peered at the inscrutable waters.

So ended the first war year. People were used by that time to unbelievable changes taking place in their private lives and in the life of the nation. The faculty of astonishment was dulled. Yet it might even so have stirred if we had known that in a few months the chief responsibility for the British Navy and the keeping of the seas would be in Balfour's hands.

At the turn of the year 1914–1915, however, the necessity for Unionist co-operation in the Ministry was not yet foreseen. Nevertheless cracks in the structure of Mr. Asquith's Government might already be appearing to those in a position to observe them. Balfour was everyone's confidant, and was, for instance, early aware of the friction developing between Mr. Churchill and Lord Fisher. This culminated in May 1915 with the resignation of the First Sea Lord, which hastened the break-up of a Ministry no longer capable of carrying the whole strain of the times. One immediate cause of the temperamental explosion at the Admiralty was differences over the conduct of the Dardanelles campaign.

ARTHUR JAMES BALFOUR

1915   The Dardanelles campaign itself had been undertaken as the result of a change in the policy of the conduct of the War, imposed by the stalemate on the Western Front, which was the most salient fact of the military position at Christmas 1914. The question of new objectives, and fresh theatres of war, came before the War Council early in January. Then it was that Mr. Lloyd George and Mr. Churchill put in Memoranda, in which they respectively urged for undertaking military operations in Southern Europe, and for an attack on the northern coasts of Germany.[1] Before either of these cogently argued plans was circulated to Members of the War Council, Balfour, while still in Scotland, had received from Colonel Hankey[2] a review of the war situation in all theatres, including the outline of a policy for striking a blow at Turkey. This was somewhat on the same lines as Mr. Lloyd George's plan. It aimed at enlisting the Balkan States on the Allied side, by helping them to the one common object that could overcome their mutual jealousies—the ejection of Turkey from Europe. It was backed up by a highly characteristic letter from Lord Fisher, a sample of many that poured in upon Balfour during this period, which was emphatically one in which the Admiral counted him among his "dearest friends."

ADMIRALTY,
WHITEHALL.
Jan. 4th, 1915.

Strictly Private and Confidential and Personal.

DEAR MR. BALFOUR,

    . . . We have a War Council, and we are going to meet

---

[1] See Mr. Asquith's *Memories and Reflections*, Vol. II, p. 54; also *War Memoirs*, by David Lloyd George, pp. 367 *et seq.*; also *The War Crisis*, by Winston Churchill.

[2] See *The World Crisis*, by Winston Churchill, Vol. I, beginning of Chapter V.

LORD FISHER'S LETTER

next Thursday, and our proceedings remind me of a game of ninepins! The ninepin in falling knocks over its neighbour and so on! Plans " ad infinitum " (and I'll back my Winston against the field!)—We also have a " Junta " at the Admiralty, and I've been within an ace of leaving, but this is absolutely between ourselves. . . . I really don't contemplate a long stay where I am! (*As I said before this is absolutely personal to yourself.*) . . . But all this is not to the purpose of my letter which really was solely begun to urge on you the peculiar merit of Hankey's Turkey Plan. *I do hope you will give it all your support*, but it is vital that Sir William Robertson, now Quartermaster General in France, should command it, and that his Turkish Expeditionary Force *should embark at Marseilles* (ostensibly for the defence of Egypt) and that it should consist of at least 100,000 seasoned troops from Sir John French's Army, to be replaced by Territorials from England now ready. . . . CELERITY. It was SOLELY celerity that sent the German Squadron to the bottom at the Falklands! Anything done in a great hurry is ALWAYS done the best. . . . So please carry this plan next Thursday or tell them you will resign from the War Council, and I will humbly follow you!

I have said over and over again . . . that you really are the ONE man to direct the War. As it is I don't find anywhere the courage of a louse or the backbone of a slug!

       Yours truly, FISHER.

In much of its phraseology this letter is identical with one written by Lord Fisher to Mr. Churchill the day before.[1] But in writing to the First Lord he refrains from naming the " One Man " who, in his view, was alone fit to conduct the War, and the references to his own discontent are likewise only to be found in the letter to Balfour.

The production of the Ministers' plans, together with

[1] See *The World Crisis*, by Winston Churchill, Vol. I, p. 95.

ARTHUR JAMES BALFOUR

1915 a request from Sir John French for large reinforcements, put the issue of " Westerners " against " Easterners " in the forefront at the January War Councils. Balfour was not a great believer in the theory that the War could be won elsewhere than in its main theatre. In a letter dated January 2nd, 1915, he wrote:

> I fear everybody must agree that the notion of driving the Germans back from the West of Belgium to the Rhine by successfully assaulting one line of trenches after another seems a very hopeless affair. . . . If the Russians are as strong as they profess to be (of which so far I have seen no signs), they ought not to have the same difficulty in an offensive on the Eastern frontier as we are experiencing on the Western, for when they have satisfactorily disposed of the Austrians they might be able to do what the Allies cannot do in Flanders and in France, namely turn the right flank of the enemy's line, and invade his country. Put the matter, however, as we like, no dramatic *dénouement* of the present situation seems to be in sight. . . .
> But I am not sure that I see in proposals for attacking the enemy elsewhere than in the North of Europe any solution of our difficulties. It is not that I deny the advantages of inducing the Balkan States, with the assistance of the Allies, to make a combined attack on Turkey. . . . But I fear that months of preliminary negotiations would be required to allay passions due to events in the past, and to arrange such a division of the spoils as would satisfy these jealous little States. And in addition . . . there looms before us the menacing question of Constantinople. Who is to own it? . . .
> Moreover it must be remembered that Germany is perfectly indifferent to the fate of her allies, except in so far as her own fate is bound up with it. . . . I agree, however that from the political and diplomatic point of view it would be desirable to deprive Germany of everything she has to bargain with, and to hit Turkey as hard as we can. But, I fear, operations like these, however successful must be regarded as merely subsidiary.

THE WAR COUNCIL

Nevertheless Balfour must have become impressed by the advantages to be reaped from the Dardanelles enterprise, for when the discussions of it by the War Council during January culminated on the 28th with the decision to undertake a purely naval attack upon the Straits, he summed up his enumeration of points in its favour by saying " it was difficult to imagine a more helpful operation." This is the more remarkable because in the earlier stages he seems to have felt some necessity for reserve in expressing his views upon major questions of policy or strategy. The development of the Sub-Committee of Imperial Defence into the " War Council" had begun to make him uneasy about his own responsibility as a member of the Opposition. This development took place within two months of the time when he was invited to join the Committee early in November, but the moment of definite change cannot be precisely fixed.

Colonel Hankey, summoning Balfour to the Meeting on January 7th, 1915, still refers to it as the " War Council " between quotation marks, and Balfour, writing to Lord Lansdowne on January 9th, says : " Already some of its members occasionally describe it among themselves as a ' Council of War.' " In this letter, Balfour discusses his own future course, perceiving by this time that the body in question was by its very personnel becoming the deciding factor in the conduct of the War.

> The members besides myself [he wrote] are the P.M., Kitchener, Grey, Churchill, Lloyd George, Crewe and Haldane among Cabinet Ministers—Lord Fisher, General Wolfe-Murray of the War Office, and Hankey. I am a rather curious addition to this collection; and the question arises, ought I, or ought I not, to say to Asquith that my presence on it puts me in a position so delicate and difficult

that I am reluctant to continue my services? . . . If one can imagine a Debate arising upon military or naval policy I might—and almost certainly should—have to keep silence. But this seems a small matter. On the other hand, it is very easily conceivable that I might in Council give an opinion in favour of some course of action, which in the event would lead to disaster more or less serious. Such chances are inevitable. Would that seriously embarrass my friends? It is hard to say beforehand.

My personal ease and comfort would of course be much consoled by declining any further share in the work. At the same time, if I can be of any use, I do not see how I can refuse my services. I am too old to fight, and this is all I can do for the general cause. I do not like to shelter myself behind objections which seem rather Parliamentary than national.

His friends approved of his staying on, and thus arose the anomalous situation of a leading member of the Opposition taking part, though the idea of Coalition was not yet accepted, in the deliberations of a body that was virtually an Inner Cabinet. The very rapid development of the War Council into something of this kind during the last months of the Liberal Government is attested by letters that passed between Balfour and Mr. Bonar Law at the end of January. The correspondence was called forth by manifestations of Unionist restiveness at the lack of information about the Government's proceedings. The Party truce had survived the episode of the Home Rule Bill, but the Opposition were beginning to feel that they could not indefinitely be debarred both from responsibility and from criticism.

Balfour's personal problems were great in the four months during which he was the sole representative of his Party in a position to know the most secret facts about the prosecution of the War, in the field and in the factories. How much he knew and how much he thought

A UNIQUE POSITION

right to impart, remain to some extent guesswork. Mr. Lloyd George has stated in his *War Memoirs* that essential knowledge was withheld even from Ministers, and the War Council did not even meet between the 6th of April and the 14th of May, when Lord Fisher's resignation precipitated the political crisis. Writing to Lord Lansdowne in January 1915, Balfour says:

1915

> I won't put down on paper anything about the proceedings—partly because some of them at least are of the kind about which the least written, or even said, the better.

It appears that in the view of the Unionist leaders Balfour's membership of the War Council added nothing to their responsibility for affairs, or even to their knowledge of them. Ministers for their part probably desired his presence at their deliberations, as much for its own sake as a symbol of Unionist support. It was a curious situation, showing the beginnings of the unique position he was to acquire among " elder statesmen " even outside the bounds of his own country. He took it with the straightforward calm with which he accepted all the strange diversities of tasks that were allotted to him during the War and its aftermath.

One thing however which came to his knowledge during this first period he did not take calmly. His letter of March 5th, 1915, to Mr. Lloyd George on the subject of shortage of rifles and shortage of shells has been published in full elsewhere.[1]

> I most earnestly trust [it begins] that you are not letting slide the matter about which we talked the day before yesterday.

A letter from Mr. Lloyd George crossed this, telling Balfour about an informal meeting at which the Prime

[1] See *War Memoirs*, by David Lloyd George, Vol. I, p. 172.

Minister and Lord Kitchener were present, when munitions had been discussed. A deplorable shortage had been revealed, the failure of the War Office to foresee and provide had been admitted, and Government control over all armament factories and workers was to be established.

> I sincerely wish you had been present [Mr. Lloyd George wrote]. These views have to be pressed on the War Office, . . . and I am sorry to say I had very little support. It is essential that your influence and position should be behind this pressure. There will be an adjourned meeting for Kitchener to produce further figures. I hope . . . it will be possible for you to attend.[1]

When the Bill giving the Government fresh powers had passed, a special Committee for mobilising industry was set up on April 12th, after nearly a month's delay owing mainly to Lord Kitchener's objections to giving it full executive powers. Balfour and Mr. Lloyd George were its two principal members. The work of the Committee was, however, much hampered by the refusal of the War Office to give it proper cooperation. Before that difficulty could be overcome the Government had been changed and the chief importance of the Committee remains as marking the recognition that the supply of munitions must be considered a task in itself, not to be left for the other great War Departments to carry out according to their own ideas and capacities.

The moment was approaching when Balfour's energies were to be all absorbed in the gruelling work that falls upon the First Lord of the Admiralty in war-time. This chapter may end with a letter in which he describes his thoughts and occupations in the final weeks of

[1] See *War Memoirs*, by David Lloyd George, Vol. I, pp. 176, 177.

WORK IN HAND

comparative freedom before departmental work overwhelmed his remnants of leisure. At Easter 1915, he wrote to Lady Wemyss :[1]

> I would have written to you some time ago had I not waited day after day for the proofs of my nine lectures. ... I have not finished the tenth.[2] I sometimes think that if I lived to the day of Judgment in London under present conditions I never *should* finish it. The interruptions are endless and unforeseeable—sometimes tragic. Yesterday morning, for instance, I promised myself unbroken quiet. Whoever heard of business on Good Friday? Not at all. Poor Natty's[3] funeral took me off to Willesden: and so another forenoon passed and saw nothing accomplished. To me Natty's death is a greater blow than most people would suppose. I was really fond of him; and really admired that self-contained and somewhat joyless character. He had a high ideal of public duty and was utterly indifferent to worldly pomps and vanities. Moreover he was perfectly simple.
>
> . . . . . .
>
> I have had a good deal of public work of one sort and another. The F. Office people got me to write for American consumption a defence of our recent blockading operations. Technically we were wrong. Morally we were justified. I am not sure that we will win. However I did my best; and I think I made a fairly good job of it. At the same time I was writing a Memorandum for Winston on the naval supply of cordite, and attending all Lloyd George's conferences with Trade Union leaders.
>
> Now beginning next Monday I am going to work on a Committee of which Ll. G. and I are the non-expert, and therefore the most important, members, in order to increase our output of munitions of war. Something of the kind should have been done seven months ago. The delay

---

[1] Lord Elcho had recently succeeded his father in the Earldom of Wemyss and March.
[2] The first series of his Gifford Lectures which appeared in book form under the title of *Theism and Humanism*.
[3] Lord Rothschild.

1915   was deplorable and fraught with peril—but better late than never.

To-day I go to Windsor for a few days, after that I think to Terling.[1] I am looking forward with amusement to seeing whether I shall be served with ginger beer at the royal table,—or whether "total prohibition" is to be deferred. I understand that Rosebery is to be of the party. *He* will not like his champagne being cut off. Asquith, who would like it still less, is not to be there.

[1] The house of his brother-in-law, Lord Rayleigh.

Chapter VIII

FIRST LORD OF THE ADMIRALTY

MAY 1915 TO DECEMBER 1916

Lord Fisher resigns. First Coalition Government formed. Mr. Asquith offers Balfour the Admiralty. Critics of Balfour's appointment. Admiralty problems. Appointment of Sir Henry Jackson as First Sea Lord. Departmental organisation. Sir John Jellicoe. Rise of the submarine menace. Balfour's view of Mr. Asquith and Lord Kitchener. Balfour's Memorandum on the Air Board. The Battle of Jutland. The Admiralty communique. Sir Edward Grey and Mr. Asquith insist on replacement of First Sea Lord. Sir John Jellicoe appointed.

Mr. Bonar Law had discussed with Balfour in January 1915 the increasing difficulty of supporting the Government without the power of either criticising or influencing its conduct of the War, but he had found no way out of the unsatisfactory position except by a Coalition, which he was still unprepared to make. Nevertheless, as the spring went on, and the first disillusionments of that year began to be felt through the failure of the Allied offensive in France, the success of the first German gas attack, and the breakdown of the naval attempt upon the Dardanelles, it became impossible for the Unionist leaders to hold their followers on the original line of unqualified support of the Administration. Moreover, with the knowledge they had of the full facts about shell shortage and its causes, they became increasingly doubtful

1915

1915 whether abstinence from criticism was the right thing in the national interests. They had already given notice of their intention to demand a debate on munitions, when Lord Fisher's resignation from the post of First Sea Lord came to their knowledge. Mr. Churchill told Balfour on the morning of May 17th.[1] Balfour did not give the slightest sign that, as far as he was concerned, the departmental crisis must be made the signal for a greater upheaval. Although he said at once that his Unionist friends would be greatly perturbed, he "undertook to go and prepare them for it, and steady their opinion." "Nothing (Mr. Churchill adds) could exceed the kindness and firmness of his attitude." As a matter of fact, Balfour neither proffered, nor had been asked, his opinion about the formation of the First Coalition Government. He told me a few days later that he had never heard a word of it until eleven o'clock in the morning of May 17th. It was probably then that he sought out his Unionist colleagues to fulfil his promise to Mr. Churchill. Mr. Bonar Law must already have been in conclave with Mr. Lloyd George, or on the point of it. In that interview they agreed that Coalition was the only way to preserve the national front.[2] Mr. Lloyd George instantly flew on the wings of fulfilled desire from the Treasury to No. 10 Downing Street, presented his blunderbuss to the Prime Minister (the expression is borrowed from Mr. Asquith's biographer[3]) in the shape of a statement of the position, coupled with the threat of his own resignation, and was back again to bring Mr. Bonar Law to Downing Street. Within a quarter of an hour the thing was there settled, and when Mr. Churchill, all unsuspecting,

---

[1] See *The World Crisis*, Vol. II, p. 365.
[2] See *War Memoirs*, by David Lloyd George, Vol. I, p. 228.
[3] See *Life of Lord Oxford and Asquith*, Vol. II, p. 166.

reached the Prime Minister's room in the House of Commons after luncheon with the list of his proposed new Board of Admiralty in his hand, Mr. Asquith received it with " No ; this will not do. I have decided to form a national Government by a coalition with the Unionists, and a very much larger reconstruction will be required." A few minutes later it had dawned on Mr. Churchill that the reconstruction involved his own resignation, he had been asked his advice about his own successor, he had answered that Balfour could succeed him with the least break in continuity, and he had perceived that the Prime Minister was deeply gratified by the suggestion.[1]

Hollywood would surely have slowed down such timing in the scenario of a British political crisis. But this was the pace at which it was actually taken, or, more accurately, ran itself through. For so soon as Mr. Bonar Law and Mr. Lloyd George had set things in motion, pressure of events shaped the First Coalition Ministry. Nevertheless the appointment of the most important newcomer to the most important of the vacant posts was not made with quite the universal consent which Mr. Churchill's narrative implies. That Balfour should be offered the Admiralty was virtually decided when the Prime Minister and the outgoing First Lord found themselves in agreement on the point. But doubts were expressed at the time about the wisdom of the choice, and it is important to note the first quarter wherein these doubts arose. So soon as Mr. Lloyd George heard what place it was that Mr. Asquith proposed Balfour should fill, he went to the Prime Minister and expostulated. The Admiralty in war-time, he said, was an 8 a.m. to 10 p.m. job, seven days in the week, with overtime added. It would tax the physique

[1] See *World Crisis*, Vol. II, p. 366.

ARTHUR JAMES BALFOUR

1915 of any man in his prime, and Balfour was sixty-seven. It was a department whose chief was inevitably snowed under with routine, and Balfour would adapt himself hardly to pressure of desk-work such as he had not suffered since he left the Irish Office twenty-five years before. He would have no time to think about great issues of policy or strategy except those where the Navy was concerned, whereas it was on the broad political questions raised by the War that Balfour's genius should above all things be employed. Mr. Lloyd George begged the Prime Minister to put him in a less arduous office. Arguments of the same kind were also brought before Mr. Asquith by Colonel Hankey. The views of the Secretary to the War Council might have impressed the Prime Minister even more than the protests of Mr. Lloyd George. As Secretary of the Defence Committee he had watched Balfour at work closely, and for years. Already perhaps he knew that side of him better than anybody alive. Mr. Lloyd George and Colonel Hankey went quite independently to Mr. Asquith. In fact, I believe that neither of them knew of what the other had done until, in 1933, they separately told me their own part in the story.

The Prime Minister declined to change his mind. "He is tougher than you think," he told Colonel Hankey, and as a matter of fact in this he was right. Balfour's physical strength stood the next nineteen months very well, and although he had to leave a sick-room to play his part in the political crisis of December 1916, this was his only real illness during the War.

It is easy enough to guess why the Prime Minister refused to reconsider the choice which met his immediate difficulties so completely. The Admiralty, with its disrupted Board, was the political storm centre, and it was essential to put a Minister of great weight and

ADMIRALTY PROBLEMS

experience in charge of its reconstruction. Mr. Asquith did not contest the claim of the Unionists to the post. It could not be filled by a Peer while Lord Kitchener was Secretary of State for War, because it would have been impossible for the heads of both the Service Ministries to be in the House of Lords. The choice lay therefore between five Ministers, namely, Mr. Bonar Law, Mr. Austen Chamberlain, Mr. Walter Long, Sir Edward Carson and Balfour himself. The Admiralty was not the post for the official leader of the Unionist Party; Mr. Long had not the right qualifications for it. Of the others, Sir Edward Carson was still an untried man. Mr. Lloyd George did in fact put him in the Admiralty as Balfour's successor in 1916, and found that administration was not his strongest point.[1] Mr. Austen Chamberlain might have been considered, but had not the vital argument in his favour which came from Balfour's seven months' service in the War Council. It is therefore difficult to criticise Mr. Asquith's choice. It is impossible to maintain that it proved unquestionably right.

The problems of the British Admiralty, when Balfour took charge, were unique and unprecedented. Perhaps no statesman has ever combined in himself all the qualities demanded of a First Lord during this crucial year of the War at sea—the period that saw the Battle of Jutland, the withdrawal from Gallipoli, and the intensifying of the submarine menace which followed upon the disappearance from the waters of the German raiding squadrons. Only the technical expert could fully appreciate the profound changes wrought by these events in the situation. No administrative genius, no wisdom about men and affairs, however ripened, could give a civilian Minister complete confidence in his own

[1] *War Memoirs*, by David Lloyd George, Vol. II, p. 1020.

ARTHUR JAMES BALFOUR

1915 judgment, when it came to adapting naval policy to the new developments. Moreover the constitutional relationship between the First Lord and his Board precluded the former from initiative on technical matters. Mr. Churchill's overriding of that division of functions had partly caused the ferment which the Prime Minister relied on Balfour to soothe. He did so almost instantly, and while he ruled no unnecessary nervous strain added to the terrific burdens of the Board. That was an invaluable service. Yet even among those who can best appreciate it, a certain sense of shortcoming has lingered. Balfour would be the first to demand its analysis, the first to recognise the importance of a correct appreciation of the Admiralty's direction at this period of our national history. But the extreme difficulty of the task is not diminished by the fact that criticisms have seldom fastened on what was done, but rather on what was not done, while he was responsible for naval policy.

Nothing perhaps reveals more strikingly how thorough a professional Balfour was in the art of government than his invariable readiness to serve wherever his services were thought appropriate by the captain of the team. He went to the Admiralty with the same equable alacrity with which he accepted all the many parts which he filled in his half-century of public life. On May 19th he wrote to the Prime Minister:

MY DEAR ASQUITH,

A propos of our conversation yesterday evening, I hope you understand that if, as Bonar Law tells me, my accepting office in any Coalition Government is in his view desirable, and even necessary, I am quite indifferent as to what office I take, except that I do not think I could usefully be responsible for any heavy administrative office, except the Admiralty. On the other hand, I am perfectly ready to join the new Government without a portfolio, or to accept

ALTERNATIVES

any office (Chancellor of the Duchy, etc.) which would carry with it no heavy office work. Indeed personally I should prefer it.

        Yours ever,
                ARTHUR JAMES BALFOUR.

Duchy of Lancaster—or—the Admiralty! Few other men could have written of these as alternatives with the perfect sincerity that distils from this letter. If Mr. Lloyd George had seen it, he might have renewed his protests on the ground that Balfour clearly did not know the fierceness of the slavery awaiting him. The world has learnt, since the publication of Mr. Winston Churchill's *World Crisis*, what methods were in vogue at the Admiralty in the Churchill-Fisher period. This dæmonic couple had worked practically the clock round.

> Lord Fisher . . . usually retired to rest shortly after 8 o'clock, awaking refreshed between four and five or even earlier. . . . I altered my work somewhat, . . . being called at eight instead of at seven. . . . This enabled me to work continuously till one or two in the morning. We thus constituted an almost unsleeping watch throughout the day and night.[1]

Such, even in war-time, was not the practice of the Chancellory of the Duchy of Lancaster. By the irony of fate it was to this office that Mr. Churchill, at the height of his powers, now found himself transferred.

The history of the War is very largely a history of personal combinations. No more instructive illustration of this is to be found than at the Board of Admiralty. What might have been the effect if, while Balfour was at the helm, the First Sea Lord had been a man with the energy and fertile imagination of Lord Fisher, or if,

[1] See *World Crisis*, Vol. I, p. 405.

1915 when Mr. Churchill's daring and initiative were at work in policy, the expert authority had been a sailor with the calm, slow-kindling mind of a scientist? Sir Henry Jackson, whose appointment as First Sea Lord was made almost immediately after Balfour's, was above all things a scientific officer. He had worked with Signor Marconi in the early days of wireless telegraphy. He had a great technical knowledge of ships and gunnery.

His appointment was not made with enthusiasm, nor until alternatives had been considered. These were in fact only two, since popular prejudice against the German birth of Prince Louis of Battenberg was still held to preclude his return to the post he had filled at the opening of the War. There remained Sir Arthur Wilson, who was holding the office of First Sea Lord in the interregnum, and Sir John Jellicoe, who was in command of the Grand Fleet. A letter to Balfour from the Prime Minister of May 20th suggests that Sir Arthur Wilson should be confirmed in his post, with Sir Henry Jackson as additional Lord and "possible successor." This idea probably originated with Colonel Hankey and Mr. (afterwards Sir James) Masterton Smith, Principal Private Secretary to the First Lord. No men were more capable of judging what of the available combinations would be the best. But even if Balfour would have agreed to Sir Arthur Wilson, the old Admiral would apparently have declined to serve under anyone but Mr. Churchill.[1] Sir John Jellicoe's transference from the Grand Fleet does not seem to have occurred seriously to anyone. Indeed at that time probably not even his critics would have been prepared to suggest the name of any other Admiral as his successor. A letter to Balfour from a member of the Board dated May 21st, 1915, throws a little light on some conditions

[1] See *World Crisis*, II, p. 371.

among the Admiralty staff, as they stood when Balfour 1915 picked up Mr. Churchill's legacy.

The writer suggests a " nice" letter from the new First Lord to the Commander-in-Chief.

> There has been a good deal of pulling the black cat through the hedge backward, and it will be no waste of time to smooth things out.

Balfour did more than write. On May 27th he went up to Whittingehame for one night in order to see Sir John Jellicoe, who came down from Scapa to the Forth in the *Iron Duke*. They must have discussed Sir Henry Jackson's appointment then, for my diary notes:

> There was really no one else and A. J. B. said the one fear *all* the Admirals seemed to have in common was that of being put under someone who did not grasp the full danger of mines and submarines.

This remark is interesting in view of criticisms of Admiralty apathy as the submarine menace grew in 1916.

Possibly none even among the high departmental chiefs left behind after the collapse of the Churchill-Fisher combination realised at first the drop in pressure which had suddenly taken place within the Admiralty building. It was not only that the system of " unsleeping watch" practised by the First Lord and the First Sea Lord had kept the machine vibrating all round the clock, but also the fact that the organisation of the Office at that time permitted executive decision to be taken either by the First Lord or the First Sea Lord.

This was a part of Mr. Churchill's " working arrangement" which was never formally rescinded under Balfour, but was altered as soon as he and Sir Henry Jackson were succeeded in 1917 by Sir Edward Carson and Sir John Jellicoe. The latter has severely criticised

1915 the organisation which made it possible,[1] and Lord Fisher's biographer has done the same.[2] The system had in fact been responsible for Lord Fisher's resignation. A Minute about the despatch of cruisers to the Mediterranean had reached him, marked by Mr. Churchill, "First Sea Lord to see after action."

It must at first sight seem that very dangerous potentialities lay here. It is certainly necessary to look at the reasons why Balfour, after such a warning, was content to leave the Departmental organisation unchanged. The thing turned on the war-time development of the functions of the Chief of the Admiralty Staff. This officer theoretically acted under the First Sea Lord and possessed only advisory functions, but as the pressure of executive work grew, his services in Mr. Churchill's time were called on by the civilian First Lord as well as by the First Sea Lord.

> The fault [wrote Lord Jellicoe] appeared to lie in non-recognition of the fact that the First Sea Lord was in reality the Chief of the Naval Staff, since he was charged with the responsibility for the preparation and readiness of the Fleet in war, and for all movements.

For this reason the two offices were later on combined in one man.

It may well be that changes of this kind were right and desirable. The Admiralty, unlike the War Office, had not at this date had any opportunity of working out its Staff organisation by years of trial and experience. The whole creation was new. But here were problems in which Balfour at all events was no tyro. Organisation had preoccupied his mind when he set up the Committee of Imperial Defence. The crisis in Indian administration that had led to the quarrel between Lord Curzon and

[1] See *The Crisis of the Naval War*, by Viscount Jellicoe, p. 9.
[2] See *Life of Lord Fisher*, by Admiral Bacon, Vol. II, pp. 161 and 167.

HUMAN RELATIONSHIPS

Lord Kitchener had centred round the allocation of power between a civilian and a service chief. It is clear that he gave his whole attention to the position at the Admiralty, and came to the conclusion that more depended on the human relationships than on any reorganisation on paper. He wrote in a private paper at the end of his service as First Lord:

> Personally I am inclined to think that the present system, if properly worked, is the best. The Navy, especially in time of war, cannot, and ought not, to be regarded as a self-contained and separate entity. The part it plays depends on its relations to other Departments at home, and to allied Governments. The ordinary training of a sailor is an admirable one, but it is hardly suited to supply all the qualifications which such a situation requires. No doubt the difficulty of drawing a line between the matters which are within the province of the First Sea Lord and his Staff, and those on which the First Lord should have an important say, is considerable. It requires tact and judgment in all concerned. But I think the sailors themselves who know the inside workings of the Admiralty would be the first to admit that a civilian Chief, wholly unconnected with the feuds which unfortunately have done so much harm in recent years in the Navy, may be of great value, though all would acknowledge that a First Lord who insisted on running the Admiralty without regard to naval opinion would be a serious danger.

The effect of Balfour's personality at the Admiralty was exactly that which the Prime Minister had no doubt reckoned upon when he sent him there as Mr. Churchill's successor. His imperturbable calm and cheerfulness was as soothing to frayed nerves as was his invariable consideration for the time and convenience of his subordinates. His insatiable appetite for technical information was perhaps never a greater asset than in his work at the Admiralty. He drew out the knowledge and opinions of his experts with unwearying and respectful attention. He never alarmed them by dazzling excursions on to their own ground. In short he was entirely successful in dispelling the distrust that so often separates the Service from the civilian mind.

Mutual confidence and reliance between Balfour and his Board were maintained to the end. It happened that his principal advisers, Sir Henry Jackson and Sir Henry Oliver, were both deeply imbued with a sense of the importance of taking no risks where British command of the sea was at stake. Balfour's own temperament inclined him the same way, and it does not appear that he was ever particularly desirous of forcing on the day of a decisive fleet action. It seems that in the war at sea he was content, before as after the Jutland Battle, to pursue the policy of attrition which he also advocated for the war on land, and to devote his energies to tightening the blockade.

Critics of this point of view there may always be. In 1916 Germany began to adopt a more aggressive policy in the North Sea area. During that period no change was made in the instructions under which the Grand Fleet had been working ever since war began, nor in the Commander to whose influence the extreme caution of those instructions was very largely due. Before and after Jutland Admiral Jellicoe's strategy was ruled by the determination to preserve the capital ships from torpedo attack. Whether this was right or wrong in the period in question remains a matter of controversy.

Only one thing is agreed even now, at the conclusion of all that has been said and written on the subject, namely, that had Sir George Callaghan still been in command, or had Admiral Jellicoe been replaced before the Battle of Jutland by Admiral Beatty, greater risks would have been taken both in the strategic dispositions of the Grand Fleet in the North Sea and in the

CONFIDENCE IN JELLICOE

tactics of the battle. The possible results upon the fortunes of the War still remain a matter of discussion. Those who hold that British naval history in the year 1916 is a history of a great opportunity missed of inflicting crushing damage on the German High Seas Fleet will continue to criticise the First Lord who left the supreme command at sea to a man who, as he well knew, was by temperament and conviction ultra-cautious. Those, on the other hand, who are more impressed with the truth of the saying that Lord Jellicoe was "the only man who could have lost us the War in an afternoon," may say that Balfour was justified in making no change.

Positive evidence of the continued confidence reposed by the Board in Admiral Jellicoe's management of the Fleet is afforded by a Report written by Balfour for the Cabinet in October 1916.

> Probably the German policy . . . is to avoid a general action in the North Sea, while doing everything possible gradually to whittle down the strength of the Grand Fleet till something approaching equality is attained. The most hopeful method . . . is to tempt the British into the southern portion of the North Sea, which is crowded with mines and haunted by submarines, by holding out hopes of a general action. The general action would be refused, but in the meanwhile some very unpleasant accidents might happen to our fighting ships. . . . The Commander-in-Chief and Admiral Beatty are therefore of opinion (and the Admiralty agree with them) that the proper way of dealing with this situation is to retain the Grand Fleet in the North, unless and until the Germans have so far committed themselves to a forward movement that they cannot retire without trying conclusions with the British. . . .
> Probably most of us would prefer that the part played by the fleet should in appearance be more vigorous and aggressive; but there can be no doubt that the policy recommended by the War Staff and Commander-in-Chief is the one most embarrassing to the Germans. What the

enemy would like to see would be a series of small and inconclusive operations in which by a timely retirement their own battle fleet would avoid disaster, while by mines and submarines we should lose a ship here and a ship there, till the cumulative effect became serious.[1]

In this same Memorandum of October 14th, 1916, Balfour deals with the submarine menace, as it stood near the end of his term of office. Mr. Lloyd George has sketched his impression of Balfour's attitude towards this most formidable naval problem of the War, in sentences where admiration and criticism are blended. "Fearless but irresolute" he calls him, and describes how

> even the woeful tale of increasing sinkings of our ships by German submarines, and the apparent impotence of the Admirals to stop the disastrous process did not daunt him. . . . He had no notion of how the German attack upon our shipping could be circumvented. He only assumed that sooner or later it would be done. . . . Clearly he was not the man to stimulate or organise the activity of the Navy in a crisis. But he was the ideal man for the Foreign Office, or to assist the Cabinet in big issues.[2]

Mr. Lloyd George was evidently hardening in the opinion he had expressed to the Prime Minister the year before. The treatment of submarine warfare under Balfour is however a doubtful illustration of his judgment. For in assuming that sooner or later the enemy would be circumvented Balfour turned out to

---

[1] In the summer of 1934 I talked over this Report with the late Admiral of the Fleet Lord Beatty. He suggested that I should put a footnote to the effect that it was significant that, shortly after his own succession to the post of Commander-in-Chief, the Battle Fleet was transferred from Scapa to Rosyth.

It was agreed that Lord Beatty should see my proposed footnote before this book was published. His death unfortunately prevented this, but I have thought it right to give my recollection of his desire. He seemed to attach importance to the point, and I understood him to say that in October 1916, Rosyth was not ready to receive the Battle Fleet.

[2] See *War Memoirs*, by D. Lloyd George, Vol. II, p. 1017.

A. J. BALFOUR AND D. LLOYD GEORGE VIEWING THE WRECK OF A ZEPPELIN, SEPTEMBER 1916

be right. One measure that did much to save the situation was the escorting of merchant vessels in convoys by destroyers and other small armed craft. This system was first adopted in May 1917, five months after Balfour left the Admiralty. Even then it required all the strength and determination of the new Prime Minister, Mr. Lloyd George, to overcome the objections of naval opinion. It could not have been done earlier on the main trade routes by reason of lack of vessels of the required type. It could not have been done so soon, had not the United States shipping resources become available when America entered the War in March.[1] As late as the end of February 1917, it was estimated that only forty ships were available for convoying Atlantic traders, whereas for the homeward-bound portion alone eighty destroyers or sloops were required.[2] Thus convoy was not included in Balfour's Report on protective measures. In the circumstances of the time it was surely not merely a facile optimism that prompted him to write in October:

> We must for the present be content with palliation. Nevertheless we are not wholly helpless, and I will endeavour to describe what has been, and is being, done to diminish an evil which unfortunately we cannot wholly cure.

This Report, coupled with grave warnings from Admirals Jellicoe and Beatty about the spread of the submarine danger, led to a Conference on November 2nd of all the highest naval experts, who only agreed unanimously on one point: the need for co-ordinating our submarine effort under a single Commander.[3]

[1] See *The Crisis of the Naval War*, by Viscount Jellicoe, Chapter IV: " The Introduction of the Convoy System."
[2] *Ibid*, p. 111.
[3] See *Naval Operations*, Vol. IV, Newbolt, p. 325.

1915 Such was the undecided condition of naval opinion on submarine policy up to the end of Balfour's period of responsibility. Fortunately however there had been no division of opinion about the need for pressing forward with the technical devices against submarines, begun under Mr. Churchill. To these were added in 1916 the invention of the first really effective mine used in the British Navy. The credit of it belongs to Sir Henry Jackson. But it was not until he and Balfour had left the Admiralty that it was manufactured and used in sufficient quantities. Delay also attended some of the inventions recommended by the new Board of Invention and Research that Balfour set up within two months of coming into office, and of which he persuaded Lord Fisher to be Chairman.[1]

The submarine question overshadowed most others for every First Lord throughout the War. Balfour's first six months of office saw the climax and conclusion of the Gallipoli enterprise, and a word must be said about his attitude as Head of a Department which had vast powers of Yea or Nay in this matter. Twice at least after the failure of the military attacks on the Turkish positions in August 1915, the Board of Admiralty might have weighted the scales in favour of one more attempt to rush the Narrows and reduce the forts, by ships alone. The first time was at the end of October 1915, when Commodore Keyes, Chief of Staff in the Mediterranean Command, came to London to urge a new scheme for doing this which had the backing not indeed of the Commander-in-Chief in the Mediterranean, but of Admiral Wemyss, the Second-in-Command. The next occasion was in December, when abandonment of Gallipoli had been almost universally recommended by the military advisers, and was on the point of being

[1] See *Life of Lord Fisher*, Vol. II, p. 286

reluctantly agreed to by the Cabinet. Admiral Wemyss, now himself Commander-in-Chief in the Mediterranean, once more declared himself confident that the Navy could force the Dardanelles, and thus save the whole military situation. This time the Board of Admiralty definitely refused to support the project. Previously they had deferred an opinion. It does not appear that on either occasion Balfour influenced the decision of the Sea Lords. His own view of the policy to be pursued at Gallipoli is contained in a Memorandum of November 19th, 1915, which may in some degree explain why he, objecting as he did to evacuation, was yet unprepared to advocate an immediate attempt to wrest victory out of the circumstances of the moment.

Secret.
19*th November*, 1915.

I am aware that many of my colleagues, both in the War Committee and the Cabinet, are strongly in favour of the abandonment of the Gallipoli Peninsula. Though I was not at the moment in favour of its occupation, I venture in this paper to give some reasons against leaving it now.

For the sake of argument (though only for the sake of argument) I am prepared to admit that neither the Army alone nor the Navy alone, nor the two in combination, can either drive the Turks from the Peninsula or compel them to surrender. The question before us is therefore, reduced to this: Ought we to cling to Gallipoli until it becomes (if it ever does become) untenable, or ought we to leave it at once?

Our position on the Peninsula resembles a beleaguered fortress, and I am as reluctant to abandon it as I should be to abandon any other fortress which is well garrisoned, well provisioned, and has no practicable breach in its defences. By such an abandonment we should lose credit in our own eyes, and in those of our friends. Quite apart from its effect on our prestige in the East (about which so much has been said in the Cabinet) we have a character to lose in the

ARTHUR JAMES BALFOUR

1915   West. To Russia the blow would be staggering. Even those who rate at the lowest our military organisation and training have never denied us the qualities of tenacity and courage. What will they say when they see us deserting a position so important and so hardly won?

It will be said in answer that we have no right to sacrifice valuable lives on a point of honour. This may be so; but more than a point of honour is involved. I have likened Gallipoli to a fortress, and the resemblance is very close. One object of a fortress is to compel the enemy to divert an important portion of his forces to the task of capturing or masking it. This function is certainly performed by our Gallipoli entrenchments. Another function of a fortress is to block some line of communication which might otherwise be of military advantage to the enemy. This function also is performed by our Gallipoli entrenchments; and the Admiralty is of opinion that the task of closing the Dardanelles to enemy ships would be harder to perform were our position at Helles to be abandoned to the Turks. It may even be doubted whether, so long as we maintain this threat to Constantinople, any serious attempt will be made to divert large forces for an attack on Egypt.

It is urged by those who are in favour of abandonment that since this is ultimately inevitable, we had better do it at our own time, before bad weather and German artillery make the operation compulsory.

I do not deny that there is force (even very great force) in this argument; but there are also arguments on the other side. *Can* the operation be made compulsory? The difficulty of transporting heavy artillery and vast quantities of shells from Sofia or Constantinople to Bulair or Chanak is very serious. On the Asiatic side the distances are enormous. They are not enormous on the European route, but that route, though well under 100 miles, is very far from being easy. There is but one good road, commanded by the fleet for many miles, and in winter no other road seems practicable. Only a comparatively unimportant trickle of supply can go through the Sea of Marmora. In these circumstances it does not seem to me very likely that for a long time to come (if ever) the Turks will be able to use

EVACUATION

against our defences the overwhelming power of high explosives which have been found in France the only method of dealing with well constructed trenches. Indeed I believe that, if it was not for the vulnerability of our landing stations, nobody would suggest that our position could be made untenable.

If it be replied that supplies of German ammunition, though slow in coming, will surely come at last, my answer is that some risks must be run and some possibilities must be faced. It is not wisdom but folly to assume that all the chances are going to favour the enemy. Many things may happen in the next few months. We might even find a use for the troops released from Salonika, which would relieve the pressure on Anzac and Helles. But these are possibilities outside the scope of this paper. My point is a smaller one. It is admitted on all hands that the losses which would accompany voluntary retirement would be very heavy; I admit also that the losses which would accompany an involuntary retirement would be heavier still. But I suggest that, if we succeed in staying on, we shall suffer neither kind of loss, and that in any case it may be worth while to risk the difference between the two, rather than desert, in the sight of East and West, an important strategic position, which has been gloriously captured, is gloriously held, and may perhaps never be dangerously threatened.

A. J. B.

November 19th, 1915.

These arguments failed to convince. The veto of the Admiralty on Admiral Wemyss' project was followed by the decision to evacuate Gallipoli. I recall going into Balfour's sitting-room on December 20th, and being struck by the look of unspeakable relief on his face as he looked up from the official telegram he was reading. It contained news of the withdrawal of the troops from Suvla and Anzac without the loss of a single life. At the time I knew too little of the issues that hung so long in the balance, or of the dangers so marvellously escaped, fully to understand his emotion. The story has since become the material for great literature, but no written words have ever deepened my impression of what must have been the strain on all those who shared responsibility for the Gallipoli Expedition. It was enough to have seen the anxiety lift from the countenance of one.

To the unusual mood of relaxed tension produced by the Gallipoli news a conversation noted in my diary that same evening is very likely due. Its importance is enhanced by the date—a twelvemonth, namely, before the First Coalition Government was broken up by Mr. Lloyd George with Balfour's active assistance. Some writers (I will only cite here Mr. Asquith's own biographer[1]) hold the view that this was done at the cost of failure of personal loyalty. I shall not anticipate what has to be said on that score as regards Balfour. But since the insinuation has been made, it must be recorded for how long some of Mr. Asquith's colleagues suppressed the gravest criticisms rather than take the step that led to a change of Prime Minister in December 1916.

The extract from my diary is given without change or omission. Balfour and I were dining alone.

Dec. 21st, 1915.

Suddenly we were in the midst of a discussion of all his colleagues and the Government position.

A. J. B. No one tells me, and I see no one of the kind who could, but I know that the Government is hated, discredited, distrusted. They hate Asquith. Well—he has his faults, and they are the worst kind for the present crisis. He is an arbitrator, an eminently fair-minded judge—the best-tempered man I ever knew—a splendid chairman of a

---

[1] See *Life of Lord Oxford and Asquith*, by J. K. Spender, Vol. II, Chapter L: " Arts and Stratagems."

ASQUITH. KITCHENER.

committee, and after all a Cabinet is only a committee; but I never heard him originate or suggest. If he were in this room now and heard us talk, he would still be incapable of understanding that more is required of him than the admirable balance he can give. But these are admirable qualities.

Myself. But—is he the very best man we could have in the place?

A. J. B. I tell you, my dear—he would have been all right if he had had a decent War Minister. The public (and perhaps it is as well) lays the blame in the wrong place. K. knows nothing—he does nothing right.

Myself. In fact, he [i.e. Lord Kitchener] is a stupid man?

A. J. B. That's it; he is. He is not a great organiser —he is not a great administrator, nor a great soldier,— and what is more, he knows it. He is not vain. He is only great when he has little things to accomplish.

Myself. And yet—I feel as if he were rather a great man.

A. J. B. You are not wrong. He is in a way. But our language has no word for the subtleties I would like to express about K. I must call his greatness *personality*. He has that in the highest sense.

We ought to have had a civilian at the War Office—for instance, some one like Runciman, some one who could not override his experts and his colleagues on technical points. All this the public can never understand—nor perhaps should they; but they blame Asquith. Now—who could succeed Asquith?

Myself. Many people say you could.

A. J. B. They are wrong. I am open to the same fatal objection as George Curzon, whom you know many others want. We belong to the minority. It must be a Liberal.

Myself. But many good judges say *you* could carry both the House and the country with you.

A. J. B. I don't think I could. Of course I don't know this House. I never go near it. I could pick it up again very soon, but my instinct tells me I could not lead it, even if I would.

Whatever these last remarks may have implied (he did not develop them) it was no hint of waning

ARTHUR JAMES BALFOUR

1916 parliamentary skill. But he knew that his power over the House of Commons had been won, and held, by his pre-eminence in debate, and that for debate the war-time Parliament gave no scope.

A controversy which went forward in 1916 shows Balfour defending his point of view outside the House of Commons. The question at issue was that of setting up a Department for Air, with executive authority over production, on which the Admiralty should be dependent for its supplies. There is no doubt that Balfour would have resisted this to the point of resignation so long as he held the post of First Lord. He had only reluctantly agreed in May 1916 to the setting up of an Air Board under the Presidency of Lord Curzon to co-ordinate the air activities of the Navy and Army. Balfour never expected it to do much more than aggravate friction between the Services, and disappointment was not perhaps uppermost in his mind when the Board issued a Report which he described as " a document of formidable proportions, consisting of thirty folio pages mostly filled with attacks on the Admiralty." He set himself to demolish it in a Memorandum that raised a smile on the faces of some of his colleagues when they opened their Cabinet boxes one morning in November 1916, and perhaps pictured Lord Curzon doing the same.

> Of the Air Board's performances [wrote Balfour], as summarised in the Report, I have little to say—and they have not much to say themselves. . . . But I must take some exception to the language in which it is expressed. One would really suppose that in order to transfer the sixty aeroplanes, the four guns, the engines, the machines, from their old to their new owners, treasures of industry, knowledge and diplomatic dexterity had to be expended. " We succeeded," say the Air Board, " in doing this or securing that." So they did. But were the difficulties so very formid-

THE AIR BOARD

able? Did the Army or the Navy resist any reasonable 1916 request? I have heard nothing to suggest it. . . .

To do the Air Board justice however, they are far more interested in abusing the Admiralty than in praising themselves. I do not suppose that in the whole history of the country any Government Department has ever indulged so recklessly in the luxury of inter-Departmental criticism. The temptation no doubt has often existed but hitherto it has been more or less successfully resisted. In the case of the Air Board however, the ardour of youth and the consciousness of superior abilities have completely broken through the ordinary barriers of official self-control.

The Army also is mentioned, but only for the purpose of artistic contrast. It is the virtuous apprentice, the lustre of whose shining merits serves but to darken the shadows in the character of his wicked rival.

. . . . . .

The relation between a fighting Department and a supply Department should resemble that which exists between the War Office and the Munitions Department. The Department which supplies should do nothing but supply; it should neither determine the amount nor the character of the things supplied. The Air Board are not likely to content themselves with so modest a rôle. . . . The Admiralty . . . would view with the greatest misgiving a system under which they would have to use aeroplanes and sea-planes whose number and design were determined for them by an independent and (I suppose I must now add) hostile Department,—which would have the right to criticise, the power to embarrass, but no direct responsibility for military or naval action.

This was Balfour's last word on a question that was still unsettled when he left the Admiralty in December 1916. The narrative turns back to the summer, and to the climax of the War at sea.

On the morning of May 13th the Admiralty became convinced that the German High Seas Fleet was putting out in full strength at last. By nightfall every section of the British Battle Fleet had left its bases and was steaming eastwards to meet the enemy. By the afternoon of the next day the Commander-in-Chief's message came through : " Fleet action is imminent."

After that (it was 4.50 p.m. on Wednesday, May 31st) no message from Admiral Jellicoe reached the Admiralty until the evening of Friday, June 2nd. Yet there could be no doubt that battle had been joined. Intercepted telegrams proved it, and by Friday disabled ships were beginning to reach home.

During these two long days the First Lord, and he alone, could decide how much the nation should be told. Balfour issued no statement, even to the Cabinet. He judged that it could only cause unnecessary anxiety. The Prime Minister and Sir Edward Grey were the only colleagues who shared with the Board of Admiralty the suspense of the forty-eight hours between Admiral Jellicoe's first message and the second. There was some criticism of this, but it was lost in the storm which arose over the *communiqué* that was issued immediately upon receipt of the first news of the Battle of Jutland. This unvarnished statement of the facts as far as they were known on that Friday evening was quoted at the time as a supreme example of Balfour's faulty understanding of the psychology of the plain man. He was far from dismissing these criticisms, but the more he considered them, the more certain he became that in essentials the *communiqué* was rightly drafted. It ran thus :

> On the afternoon of Wednesday May 31st a naval engagement took place off the coast of Jutland. The British ships on which the brunt of the fighting fell were the Battle Cruiser Fleet, and some cruisers and light cruisers supported by four fast battleships. Among those the losses were heavy. The German Battle Fleet, aided by low visibility, avoided prolonged action with our main forces,

and soon after these appeared on the scene, the enemy returned to port, though not before receiving severe damage from our battleships. The Battle Cruisers, *Queen Mary, Indefatigable, Invincible,* and the Cruisers *Defence* and *Black Prince* were sunk. The *Warrior* was disabled, and after being towed for some time had to be abandoned by her crew. It is also known that the destroyers *Tipperary, Turbulent, Fortune, Sparrowhawk* and *Ardent* were lost, and six others are not yet accounted for. No British battleships or light cruisers were sunk. The enemy's losses were serious. At least one battle cruiser was destroyed, and one severely damaged; one battleship reported sunk by our destroyers during a night attack, two light cruisers were disabled and probably sunk. The exact number of enemy destroyers disposed of during the action cannot be ascertained with any certainty, but it must have been large.

Balfour, with the First Sea Lord and one or two others, sat in the First Lord's room drafting this document. He was urged to telegraph to the Commander-in-Chief for more information before issuing it. He refused, reminding his companions of what the pressure must be on Sir John Jellicoe at that moment, when the Fleet had just come back to Scapa Flow, and declaring that he would do nothing to add to his burdens. Then someone suggested adding some reassuring note to the *communiqué* on Balfour's own responsibility. This he absolutely declined to do. The *communiqué* went out.

The evening papers dealt with it each after their own manner. The nation got its first impressions from the headlines, and many people may never have read the full text until the next morning, by which time a further message had been received correcting the list of destroyer casualties, and raising the German losses in capital ships from two to three. But meanwhile consternation and anger had spread through the country.

Balfour has been criticised for not holding up all details for the morning papers, issuing that night only

1916 some general statement of a heavy engagement in progress. But he thought himself bound to withhold nothing that he knew, and still more bound to add nothing that he did not know for certain.

The Germans pursued the opposite policy, and he used to point to its results as the vindication for his own. For when at last the enemy admitted that their loss of the battle-cruiser *Lützow* and the light-cruiser *Rostock* was justly claimed by the British, though concealed by themselves for military reasons, a revulsion of feeling followed among the neutrals, who had been perplexed and alarmed by the tone of the English statements.[1] Confidence in British war reports was henceforth unshakeable, at home and abroad. That seemed worth a few hours of undue despondency. Balfour thought it necessary all the same to defend himself at considerable length in a speech a week after the battle. The people he was most sorry for, he said, were the Fleet. The Fleet had come in bitterly disappointed that the Germans had in the main succeeded in evading an engagement. But knowing that they had inflicted a blow of the severest character on the enemy, they considered the tragic note struck in the newspapers quite unnecessary, and very undeserved.

> If my candour, if my desire immediately to let the people know the best and the worst that I knew, was in any way responsible for that result, I can only express my regret. But confidence in the desire of the Admiralty to deal straightly and fairly with the British public will be increased by what has occurred, and if that be so there is nothing to regret.

What was Balfour's own view of Jutland? He expressed it once in conversation with Admiral Beatty as "a missed opportunity." But it was not a topic which he

[1] See *Naval Operations*, Vol. IV, p. 11.

THE SUBMARINE DANGER

often referred to. Much more readily he would point out that after the battle, as before, the command of the sea remained with the British Navy. When Balfour left the Admiralty in December, strategy was already basing itself fully on that vital fact.

The last of Balfour's acts as First Lord was not the least important. Early in November Sir John Jellicoe had paid a brief visit to London to impress upon the Board the appalling increase in submarine activity, and the necessity of concentrating on counter-measures. A special Department was thereupon set up for that single purpose, but the feeling grew that this was not enough. A manifestation of uneasiness came in the shape of a letter from the Foreign Secretary, remarkable because Sir Edward Grey was notorious for his reluctance to express opinions on matters outside his own Department. The note is undated, but almost certainly written in November 1916.

Private.

The submarine danger seems to me to be increasing so rapidly that unless in the next two months or so we can do something about it, the Germans will see their way to victory.

My impression is that the Germans, who would have closed with a proposal for peace in terms of a draw in September or even October, are now out again for victory. Under these circumstances we must make every effort to cope with submarines, and there is no time to be lost.

Your present Board may be the best possible. I am not in a position to say that they are not; but I have an impression that people get stale in one job, and I cannot help thinking that Jellicoe at the Admiralty, with adequate power and scope to deal with the submarine question, would be worth trying. It is impertinent of me to make a suggestion, especially as I know you are already considering it, but I feel the situation to be so serious and critical that I don't like to leave any stone unturned.

ARTHUR JAMES BALFOUR

1916 The deplorable habit of not dating letters, which Sir Edward Grey shared with too many others of Balfour's colleagues, makes it impossible to know whether he had discussed the matter with Mr. Asquith before writing, or whether Balfour had talked to the Prime Minister about the possible retirement of Sir Henry Jackson before he heard from Sir Edward Grey. It is clear that the need for a change in the First Sea Lord was already in Balfour's mind about the middle of November, for on the 20th Mr. Asquith wrote:

Secret.

MY DEAR BALFOUR,

You told me the other day that Sir Henry Jackson had placed himself and his office at your disposal. He is an excellent man of very special attainments, and in difficult circumstances has shown great tenacity and staying power.

Nor have I anything to say in the way of criticism, or otherwise than of hearty appreciation, of the technical side of naval administration since he has been First Sea Lord. Newspaper clamours—as you know well—I totally disregard.

But not only in view of the increasing seriousness of the submarine situation, but of other prospects hardly less grave, I have brought myself very clearly to the conclusion that the time has come for a change, and that Jackson should be replaced by the best naval expert that we can find. Obviously Jellicoe is the only alternative.

I quite realise the difficulty of taking him at this moment from the Grand Fleet, especially as his only possible successor in the command (I am sure you would agree) from the combatant point of view is Beatty, who, with all his fine fighting qualities, is yet comparatively untried in the domain of fleet administration on a large scale.

Among the necessary risks of war, none are more hazardous than the changes and chances of personnel.

But, not without much reflection and consideration, I feel bound to submit to you that his substitution is called for as a matter of promptitude and even of urgency.

CHANGES IN THE BOARD

I need hardly add the assurance of my perfect confidence, 1916 which is shared by all our colleagues, in your supreme control in all that concerns the Navy. I regard it as one of our principal assets in the conduct of the war.

Yours always,
H. H. Asquith.

Neither of these letters makes it quite clear whether Balfour decided for himself that the retirement of Sir Henry Jackson had become necessary, or whether he, to some extent, yielded to opinion. It may be that he would have preferred to bring Admiral Jellicoe to the Admiralty without dispensing with the services of the First Lord whose scientific temperament had fitted so well with his own, for when Sir John Jellicoe visited London early in November, Balfour suggested to him that he should take charge of the new Department supervising anti-submarine measures. The idea was not acceptable, and before the end of the month the chief command at sea passed to Sir David Beatty, and Admiral Jellicoe was appointed First Sea Lord. He and Balfour never actually worked together in Whitehall, for still greater changes were in progress there in the first week of December 1916.

Chapter IX

CRISIS AND RECONSTRUCTION
DECEMBER 1916

> Signs of break-up of the First Coalition. Lloyd George and Bonar Law present scheme of War Council Reform. Balfour falls ill. Balfour backs Lloyd George. His reasons. Coesrrpondence with Asquith. Bonar Law and Lloyd George visit Balfour. They discuss alternatives. Balfour's account of Buckingham Palace Conference. Balfour accepts the Foreign Office. Balfour and Lloyd George.

1916

The conversation quoted in the last chapter, which shows Balfour's consciousness of some defects in Mr. Asquith's leadership of a nation at war, took place in December 1915, some twelve months before the break-up of the first Coalition. As the year 1916 went on signs of approaching political upheaval multiplied. One of the most significant followed upon the catastrophe of Lord Kitchener's death at sea, early in June, when the cruiser *Hampshire*, on which he was proceeding to Russia, went down through enemy action, and all on board were drowned.

The new Secretary for War was Mr. Lloyd George. His was not the appointment that Mr. Asquith would have recommended if left to himself. He had thought of Mr. Bonar Law. But Mr. Bonar Law's mind, like that of others, was troubled about the conduct of the war in the field and in council, and he was being driven into " an unwilling alliance of discontent "[1] with the

[1] See Lord Beaverbrook, *Politicians and the War*, Vol. II, p. 23.

colleague who had earliest, and most persistently sounded the alarm. Mr. Lloyd George's transference to the War Office was made at the instance of Mr. Bonar Law.[1] The significance of this combination was great. In the first place it was a successful challenge to the authority of Mr. Asquith, on a point where a Prime Minister cannot afford to be defeated—the appointment to key posts in his Government. Power was passing— had in fact passed. Nothing but the disadvantage to the Allied cause of a political crisis in Great Britain could have kept the forms of the First Coalition intact for the next five months.

The break-up of Mr. Asquith's Cabinet was due to pressure from within far more than from without, although confidence in the Government was ebbing in the country, and criticism becoming more and more outspoken in the Press. The opening move was made on November 25th, when Mr. Lloyd George, backed up by Mr. Bonar Law and Sir Edward Carson, presented Mr. Asquith with a scheme for reform of the War Council, involving a reduction of its number to four, and the retirement of the Prime Minister from its Chairmanship. His place—and here was the crux of the matter—was to be filled by Mr. Lloyd George. The revolt against Mr. Asquith's leadership was far advanced by the time the two Unionist leaders were prepared to set their hand to such a scheme, and Mr. Bonar Law at all events had come to the point reluctantly and with much searching of heart. The story of how his alliance with Mr. Lloyd George was at last cemented has been told by Lord Beaverbrook in his book, *Politicians and the War*. Balfour had no hand in

[1] Lord Riddell in his *War Diary* (see p. 198) states that Mr. Lloyd George's appointment to the War Office was made " in direct opposition to Balfour's views, as well as to the Prime Minister's." No evidence at my disposal supports this.

bringing it about. He does not at this stage seem to have been behind the scenes at all. He was not consulted when the War Council scheme was being drafted. Nor was this unnatural, for Mr. Lloyd George was determined to press the Prime Minister to make a change at the Admiralty, which would involve Balfour's exclusion from the War Council, where his place would be taken by the new First Lord. Sir Edward Carson was cast for this office in Mr. Lloyd George's mind, and it may well be that a certain awkwardness was felt in seeking Balfour's approval of the new scheme while these changes were under discussion. His colleagues had yet to learn how unimportant the personal side of the question seemed to him. Moreover it may not have been evident to them at the outset how vital his support would be. It seems that when Mr. Bonar Law entered into negotiation with Mr. Asquith he had not realised how deeply rooted in his Unionist colleagues was the distrust of Mr. Lloyd George, which he had himself only recently shaken off. Mr. Bonar Law did not take the Conservative Ministers into his confidence until November 30th, when he found the bulk of them hostile to the scheme of reconstruction, especially to the change in the Chairmanship of the War Council. That at any rate is the impression given of the meeting by Lord Beaverbrook, who states that Balfour was not present. It seems, however, that he was, for he made a Memorandum of the events of the next ten days, dated December 7th, which opens with a reference to this first conference.

> *Thursday, Nov. 30th.* There was a meeting of the Unionist Members of the Government in B. L.'s room at the House of Commons. So far as I remember, very little was determined upon except that the existing state of things as regards the management of business in the War Committee should not be allowed to continue. That night I fell ill

and could transact no business, except a few formal signatures, or discuss the political situation further with colleagues, till Saturday evening. On Sunday evening I saw R. Cecil in my bedroom and heard something of what the Unionists have been doing in the meanwhile.

The story cannot have altogether pleased him. In the three days of his absence from their conclaves most of the Unionist Ministers had hardened in their feelings against Mr. Lloyd George, on account of a newspaper article which seemed to have been inspired by him to influence the course of the negotiations by premature publicity. They had come to the conclusion that reconstruction from within was not possible after this, and had urged Mr. Asquith to tender the resignation of the Government to the King. The effect of this would be an open trial of strength between the Prime Minister and Mr. Lloyd George.

Balfour's comments on this fashion of breaking up the National Government are not recorded. When he first heard of it on the evening of Sunday, December 3rd, there were still hopes of agreement between Mr. Asquith and Mr. Lloyd George. Balfour was still feeling very unwell, and he does not seem to have said much to Lord Robert Cecil about his own opinion. But there can be little doubt that he had already made up his mind to back Mr. Lloyd George by every means at his command. He did not know yet that the struggle for power on the War Council question was centred in part round his own person, but once that struggle had begun he was clear about how it should end. Mr. Asquith's retirement from the Government must be averted if possible, but the loss of Mr. Lloyd George would be the greater disaster. From this point of view, suspicion of motives, and indignation about methods, were mere waste of time. Balfour in arriving at this

1916 conclusion was spared the doubts and mistrusts which prolonged and embittered the crisis, and was thus enabled to play his decisive part in bringing it to an end with the least possible disturbance to national unity.

Some family correspondence, about the end of December 1916, shows something of what he thought. One letter relates how somebody had said that Mr. Lloyd George wanted to be a dictator. "Let him be," said A. J. B. "If he thinks he can win the war, I'm all for his having a try."

Another letter gives a luncheon table scene in Carlton Gardens.

> Rocking back in his chair, and pressing his knee against the table, with that peculiar flash of the eye he sometimes has when eager, A. J. B. said, "Personally I am sorry Asquith is not still P.M. That is what *I* wanted. But I was all for Lloyd George being given a free hand. Since the war began he has done two big things—far the biggest things that have been done—and he alone could do them. The first was the creation of that Department for Munitions—a vast thing—a vitally important thing—we couldn't win without it. You may say *he* didn't run it, that such and such a great business director undertook *this* part; such and such a manufacturer undertook *that* part. But who chose those men and overrode routine, and gave them the chance of working? Lloyd George, and Lloyd George alone. The second great thing he has done is the Transport. He went to the War Office—in many ways he was probably a very bad War Minister. But *he* saw that we were in such a position that we *couldn't* make a great advance even if we tried. And against the opposition of all the soldiers at the War Office he put in Geddes to manage the Transport, and it is being *done*. As you may imagine, I have no prejudices in favour of Lloyd George. I have opposed every political principle he holds—but I think he is the only man who can at this moment break down that wall of military red tape, and see that the brains of the country are made use of."

THE CENTRE OF DISPUTE

These were the considerations that Balfour was 1916 turning over in his mind as he lay in bed at the beginning of the political crisis, echoes of the battle coming up to him continually after Lord Robert Cecil's first visit on Sunday evening, December 3rd. Balfour's own Memorandum describes what he heard.

> On Monday Lord Lansdowne, who had been at Bowood, came to lunch; but he knew little or nothing as he had been away.
>
> I heard more of what the Prime Minister and the Liberal wing of the Government were doing from Masterton Smith;[1] and from these various sources I gathered that on Friday L. G. had put a pistol to the head of the P.M., and demanded that the War Council should be reduced in size, and that he (L. G.) should be made its Chairman; also that on Sunday the Prime Minister in writing agreed to these terms, but did not assent to the list of the names of the three colleagues who were to constitute the new War Council. The formula then employed was that the Prime Minister agreed to the machinery, but disputed the personnel.
>
> On Monday afternoon the Prime Minister saw his Liberal colleagues and they persuaded him that the new arrangement, however it might appear in form to safeguard his power and dignity, in reality destroyed both, and on Monday night he therefore wrote to L. G. receding from the position he had been willing to take up on Sunday. L. G. therefore resigned.
>
> In the meanwhile I was still confined by illness, but realised that the dispute about personnel (to which I refer above) really centred round me; L. G. wanted a change at the Admiralty, which was being resisted by the Prime Minister. I thereupon wrote the following letter explaining my views, and offering my resignation.

[1] Afterwards Sir James Masterton Smith, then Private Secretary to the First Lord of the Admiralty.

171

ARTHUR JAMES BALFOUR

Private.

Dec. 5*th*, 1916

MY DEAR ASQUITH,

I have been in bed since the political crisis became acute, and can collect no very complete idea of what has been going on. But one thing seems clear: that there is to be a new War Council of which Lloyd George is to be the working Chairman, and that, according to his ideas, this Council would work more satisfactorily if the Admiralty were not represented by me. In these circumstances I cannot consent to retain my office, and must ask you to accept my resignation.

I am quite well aware that you do not personally share Lloyd George's view in this connection. But I am quite clear that the new system should have a trial under the most favourable possible circumstances; and the mere fact that the new Chairman of the War Council *did* prefer and, as far as I know, *still* prefers a different arrangement is, to my mind, quite conclusive, and leaves me no doubt as to the manner in which I can best assist the Government which I desire to support. The fact that the first days of the reconstructed Administration find me more than half an invalid, is an additional reason (if additional reason were required) for adopting the course on which, after much consideration, I have determined.

Yours very sincerely,
ARTHUR JAMES BALFOUR.

(Despatched *via* Mr. Masterton Smith about noon.)

Balfour's Memorandum continues:

The Prime Minister replied by sending me a copy of his letter to L. G.

Letter from Mr. Asquith to Mr. Lloyd George.

December 4*th*, 1916.

MY DEAR LLOYD GEORGE,

Thank you for your letter of this morning.

The King gave me to-day authority to ask and accept the resignations of all my colleagues, and to form a new

ASQUITH'S LETTER

Government on such lines as I should submit to him. I start therefore with a clean slate.

The first question which I have to consider is the constitution of the new War Committee.

After full consideration of the matter in all its aspects, I have come decidedly to the conclusion that it is not possible that such a Committee could be made workable and effective without the Prime Minister as its Chairman. I quite agree that it will be necessary for him, in view of the other calls upon his time and energy, to delegate from time to time the Chairmanship to another Minister as his representative and *locum tenens*; but if he is to retain the authority, which corresponds to his responsibility, as Prime Minister he must continue to be, as he always has been, its permanent President. I am satisfied, on reflection, that any other arrangement (such, for instance, as the one which I indicated to you in my letter to-day) would be found in experience impracticable, and incompatible with the retention of the Prime Minister's final and supreme control.

The other question which you have raised relates to the personnel of the Committee. Here again, after deliberate consideration, I find myself unable to agree with some of your suggestions.

I think we both agree that the First Lord of the Admiralty must, of necessity, be a member of the Committee.

I cannot (as I told you yesterday) be a party to any suggestion that Mr. Balfour should be displaced. The technical side of the Board of Admiralty has been reconstituted, with Sir John Jellicoe as First Sea Lord. I believe Mr. Balfour to be, under existing conditions, the necessary head of the Board.

I must add that Sir Edward Carson (for whom, personally, and in every other way, I have the greatest regard) is not, from the only point of view which is significant to me (namely, the most effective prosecution of the War), the man best qualified among my colleagues, past and present, to be a member of the War Committee.

I have only to say, in conclusion, that I am strongly of opinion that the War Committee (without any disparagement of the existing Committee, which, in my judgment, is a most efficient body, and has done, and is doing, invaluable work) ought to be reduced in number; so that it can sit more frequently, and overtake more easily the daily problems with which it has to deal. But in any reconstruction of the Committee, such as I have, and have for some time past had, in view, the governing consideration, to my mind, is the special capacity of the men who are to sit on it for the work it has to do.

That is a question which I must reserve for myself to decide.

Yours very sincerely,
H. H. ASQUITH.

Balfour's Memorandum continues:

I replied at four o'clock with a letter in which I reiterated the grounds on which I desired to resign (Copies of both my letters were sent at the same time to B. L.) When the second was written I was ignorant that L. G. had already resigned and that the P.M.'s resignation was to follow.

Second letter from Balfour to Mr. Asquith.

Dec. 5th, 1916.
4 p.m.

MY DEAR ASQUITH,

I feel very grateful for your note and its enclosure. I value very highly your appreciation.

I do not, however, feel much inclined to change my views. I still think (*a*) that the break-up of the Government by the retirement of Lloyd George would be a misfortune, (*b*) that the experiment of giving him a free hand with the day-to-day work of the War Committee is still worth trying, and (*c*) that there is no use trying it except on terms which enable him to work under the conditions which, in his own opinion, promise the best results. We cannot, I think, go on in the old way.[1] An open breach with Lloyd George will not improve matters, and attempts to compel co-operation between him and his fellow-workers with

---

[1] This important sentence has inadvertently been omitted from the letter as printed in Mr. Spender's *Life of Lord Oxford and Asquith*, Vol. II, p. 278.

whom he is in but imperfect sympathy will only produce fresh trouble.

I am therefore still of opinion that my resignation should be accepted, and that a fair trial should be given to the War Council à la George.

Yours very sincerely,
ARTHUR JAMES BALFOUR.

Balfour's Memorandum continues:

> On Wednesday morning B. L. and L. G. came to see me in bed. Various alternatives were discussed. It was agreed that if the Sunday arrangement was to be regarded as finally abandoned, the best thing would be to form a Government in which L. G. should be Chairman of the War Committee, and in which Asquith should be included. To me it seemed clear that, if such a Government were possible, it was only possible with B. L. as Prime Minister, and it was in the highest degree improbable that Asquith would consent to serve L. G. [*sic*. The sentence should probably end " under L. G."]. B. L. explained that he had been sent for by the King, and had suggested a meeting at B. P., at which both he and L. G. were very anxious that I should be present.

Before quoting Balfour's account of what passed at Buckingham Palace some comment must be made upon the earlier part of the story, firstly in respect of his resignation on Tuesday, December 5th.

The step was entirely without emotional content for him, but could hardly be equally so for the Prime Minister. Mr. Asquith had resisted Mr. Lloyd George's demand for a change at the Admiralty, and here his view of the national interest no doubt coincided with the chivalrous standards of personal loyalty between colleagues which he had conspicuously upheld throughout his political life. Balfour's calm rejection of his championship now forced him back upon the defence of his own claim as Prime Minister to the Presidency

ARTHUR JAMES BALFOUR

1916 of the War Council. Balfour himself did not feel that the efficiency of the Government demanded the combination of the two offices in the same person; rather the contrary. He never had the opportunity of discussing the question with Mr. Asquith in private, for the Prime Minister was not among the visitors who sought to see Balfour as soon as he was able to receive them. Mr. Lloyd George, however, was. He came with Mr. Bonar Law on the morning of December 6th. It was a crucial moment. Mr. Asquith had tendered the resignation of the Government the night before, and the King had summoned the leaders to Buckingham Palace for that afternoon. Mr. Bonar Law, Sir Edward Carson, Mr. Lloyd George and Lord Beaverbrook had met early to discuss where first to turn for support for the new Administration. Balfour's separate resignation was still unknown to them, and they were unaware of the views he had expressed in his letters to Mr. Asquith of the day before.[1] They felt certain, however, that Mr. Lloyd George's intentions with regard to him had been communicated, and an approach to him under these conditions did not seem very hopeful.[2]

> I confess [Mr. Lloyd George writes], I underrated the passionate attachment to his country which burnt under that calm, indifferent, and apparently frigid exterior.

It was, therefore, with some misgivings that Balfour's aid was sought at last. Together Mr. Bonar Law and Mr. Lloyd George had compelled the fall of the First Coalition. But Mr. Bonar Law could not guarantee the needful Conservative support for the Second. It lay with Balfour now to make or mar it.

[1] See *Politicians and the War*, II, p. 292; also *War Memoirs*, II, p. 998.
[2] See *War Memoirs*, II, p. 999.

VARIOUS ALTERNATIVES

Lord Beaverbrook states that Balfour did not at this 1916 interview commit himself definitely in any way to the new Ministry, but simply said that nothing could be decided until there had been " an all-round talk at Buckingham Palace."

Balfour's own brief account, given above, leaves an impression of more active co-operation. There was discussion and agreement about the best way to keep Mr. Asquith in the Government under another Prime Minister. Such a conversation must surely have proceeded on the hypothesis that all who took part in it were prepared to serve, whoever that other Prime Minister might be. In this connection one sentence in Balfour's record must be especially noted: " Various alternatives were discussed," he says. Probably one of these alternatives was that Balfour himself should be Prime Minister. Mr. Lloyd George, writing of the Buckingham Palace Conference held in the afternoon, has stated:

> It is now a matter of history how we expressed our readiness to serve under Mr. Balfour—all of us except Mr. Asquith, who asked indignantly, " What is the proposal? That I, who have held first place for eight years should be asked to take a secondary position? " This broke up the conference.[1]

Balfour's contemporary account, continued below, gives no corroboration to this dramatic conclusion, and does not suggest that the idea of his taking Mr. Asquith's place was discussed at the Conference. Neither does Lord Crewe, who wrote down what Mr. Asquith told his Liberal colleagues on his return from the Palace.[2] It seems possible therefore that Mr. Lloyd George's memory has here played him false and that

[1] See *War Memoirs*, II, p. 997.
[2] See *Life of Lord Oxford and Asquith*, Vol. II, p. 274.

ARTHUR JAMES BALFOUR

1916 his own willingness and Mr. Bonar Law's to serve under Balfour were expressed in Carlton Gardens, not at the Palace, where Mr. Asquith never had an opportunity of agreeing or refusing to accept a place in a Balfour Administration.

Balfour himself never for a moment entertained the suggestion that he was the man to form a Government. He did however mention to some members of his family that the idea had been mooted, but without going into particulars.

The thread of his own Memorandum is now resumed, on the afternoon of December 6th.

> The Meeting was fixed by the King for 3 o'clock, and I was commanded to come half an hour earlier. I explained my view of the situation to the best of my ability, insisting that, as far as my opinion was worth anything it was quite impossible for the same man effectively to carry out the ordinary duties of a Prime Minister and Leader of the House of Commons, in addition to those of Chairman of the War Committee. The King asked me to be ready to start the discussion at the Meeting after he had bid the Members (i.e. Asquith, B. L., L. G., Henderson and myself) welcome. Accordingly I said a few words upon the double necessity of altering our accustomed machinery, and of maintaining, if possible, a National or Coalition, Government. A general conversation ensued, very moderate in form, but, so far as Asquith and L. G. were concerned, with a sub-acid flavour. Asquith insisted that he could give more effective support to the Government outside it than if he were a Member. He claimed that his hold over his Party in the House of Commons and in the country was undiminished, and that he would therefore be able to prevent anything in the nature of either factious or pacifist intrigue.
>
> Henderson, for his part, dwelt upon the difficulty he anticipated in inducing organised Labour to associate itself with any Government of which Asquith was not a member. Asquith denounced the action of the press, which he said had played a most pernicious part both before and during

CONSULTATION

the crisis, and which ought to be controlled in Britain as it was controlled in France. There seemed to be a general consensus of opinion on the part of the three members principally concerned that a return to the Sunday arrangement was now impracticable.[1]

When the King, at the end, asked me my opinion, I observed that there were only three persons from among whom a Prime Minister could be chosen, and they were all present at the table, but that I gathered that if either B. L. or L. G. were selected to fill the place, A. would refuse to serve under them, while H. believed that organised Labour would stand aloof. Both these gentlemen thereupon interrupted me and said that they had not gone quite so far as I seemed to suppose. A. in particular said that he must consult his friends before offering a final opinion.

Shortly afterwards the King brought the meeting to a conclusion, it being understood that B. L. was to form a Government, which should, if possible, include A., and A. was to consider whether such inclusion was practicable or not from the point of view of his immediate friends.

I brought back B. L. at his own request to my house, as he wished to consult me upon a particular point. The point was this. He himself was most reluctant to be the head of the new Government because, by whatever name it might be described, L. G. would undoubtedly be its most powerful member, and he (B. L.) would much prefer that the forms of power and its substance should go together. I told him that while I agreed with him in thinking that L. G. ought to be the dominant spirit on the War Committee, his [*sic.* the pronoun clearly refers to Mr. Bonar Law] functions as Leader of the House and Prime Minister were of such vital importance to the success of the Administration that it was waste of time to define as to whether the Head of the War Committee or the Head of the Government was its real Leader. I did not convince him, and he then asked me whether, if A. showed any readiness to serve under him, it was wise to push him a little further, and try to get

---

[1] The reference is to Sunday, December 3rd, when it seemed that Mr. Asquith might come to an accommodation with Mr. Lloyd George. See *Life of Lord Oxford and Asquith*, Vol. II, p. 261.

him to serve under L. G. I replied in the negative. This is only of interest in showing B. L.'s point of view. The situation which he contemplated never arose. A. met his friends after the B. P. meeting, and they agreed to decline to take part in the new Coalition.

The conversation shows how strongly Balfour held the opinion which he had expressed to the King, about the desirability of separating the functions of Prime Minister and Leader of the House from those of the Chairman of the War Council. Balfour seems to have been alone in holding the view that it was impossible for the same man to carry out the double duties effectively. Mr. Asquith was precluded from weighing this point by his conception of the Prime Minister's status. Mr. Bonar Law brushed the argument aside for theoretical considerations about the forms and substance of leadership. In consequence almost unlimited power over every field of British politics was thrust into Mr. Lloyd George's hands.

Balfour's Memorandum goes on to deal with the formation of the Second Coalition, and his own acceptance of office. The date is still December 6th, in the evening of the day. Balfour dictated the whole Memorandum on December 7th, and the single existing copy is marked "Not revised," a fact which shows itself here and there in the wording. He was still far from well when he dictated it. He had gone to Buckingham Palace at some risk, and he went back to his bedroom immediately on his return.

> At half-past nine Bonar Law and Edmund Talbot came to see him. [*sic*. It should surely be "came to see me."] The former explained that since the only reason why he, rather than L. G., should attempt to form a Government was that A. might serve under him; he would certainly not serve under L. G., and since A. had refused to serve

BALFOUR TO THE FOREIGN OFFICE

under either, there was no further reason why he should attempt to form a Government. He therefore handed the responsibility over to L. G., and he now brought me a formal request that I would undertake the position of Minister for Foreign Affairs. If I consented, it would, in the view both of L. G. and himself, greatly help with the rest of our Unionist colleagues. I agreed to the proposal provided it was understood that I might have a reasonable time to recuperate from the sharp attack from which I was still suffering. To this he very gladly agreed.

We had some casual conversation about the Admiralty, and he seemed pleased, and I rather think surprised, when I said there was no objection to Carson succeeding me.

Lord Beaverbrook gives a somewhat different account of the conversation:

> Bonar Law went to Balfour and found him sitting in a chair in his bedroom wearing a dressing gown. He offered him the Foreign Secretaryship. Lord Balfour jumped up instantly and replied: "Well, you hold a pistol at my head —I must accept."[1]

The dressing-gown is the most certainly accurate item in this description. Balfour's way of getting out of an arm-chair could not be called "jumping," even when he was well. When he was ill it is hard to imagine the "pistol" which would have hurried him. It is doubtful whether in fact the offer of the Foreign Secretaryship was a "pistol" at all that evening. More than once in after years Balfour pointed out to me, and to others, the spot near Buckingham Palace where Mr. Bonar Law suggested to him, as they left the Conference together, that he should be Foreign Minister in a new Administration. However the offer may first have been made, its formal acceptance in the evening had a sensational effect, for it put beyond doubt the ability of Mr. Lloyd George to form a Government. It may be that Mr. Asquith and the group of Liberal Ministers

[1] See *Politicians and the War*, II, p. 300.

1916 who now followed him into Opposition were taken by surprise, for they had been entirely out of touch with Balfour through the week. It appears that Mr. Bonar Law himself had not entirely expected the course of action which, to Balfour, was merely the consistent outcome of the views that had dictated his resignation a few days earlier. Writing to Lord Beaverbrook, Mr. Bonar Law observed:

> Under all the circumstances I think that the part played by him (Balfour) was the biggest part played by anyone in the whole crisis. It was quite plain to me that he would have given anything, apart from the sense of duty, to be free from the responsibility of being a member of the Government. He knew that Lloyd George had been trying to have him removed from the Admiralty, and at that time it was at least doubtful whether Lloyd George could form a strong Government. Yet he took his decision without a moment's hesitation, and he did it, as he explained to me afterwards, for this reason—that unless the new Government succeeded, then the only alternative was to return to the old situation with the conditions, if possible, even worse than before.[1]

One question Balfour put to Mr. Bonar Law after his acceptance of office was settled. " Would you mind telling me," he said, " why Lloyd George was so anxious to get me out of the Admiralty ? "

" You had better ask him yourself," was the answer.[2]

But Balfour never did so, although in the next six years of intimate association with the Prime Minister in two Coalition Governments many opportunities for satisfying his curiosity must have occurred. It continued mildly to assail him whenever these events were the topic of conversation. He would then say: " I really must remember to ask the Little Man about that

---

[1] See *Politicians and the War*, II, p. 301.
[2] See *War Memories*, II, p. 1000.

some time or other." In the end, however, it was not 1916 he who put the question to Mr. Lloyd George, and he was not alive to hear the answer, given with vehemence :

> Did A. J. B. never know that I always thought he was wasted there ? It was never the right place for him. I was determined to use that vast sagacity of his on the things he could do best. And was I not justified ? Think of him in America ! Think of him in Paris !

Mr. Lloyd George, thus speaking, slightly telescoped history. When he demanded Balfour's removal from the Admiralty the Foreign Office was not vacant. It only became so when Sir Edward Grey and the other Liberal Ministers went into Opposition with Mr. Asquith. But in any process of reconstruction other Cabinet posts must have become available, and everything in Mr. Lloyd George's relations with Balfour in the First Coalition supports the belief that he would have wished to keep him as a member of his Government. The desire was probably increased on personal grounds by the end of the week of crisis. A family letter written soon after alludes to A. J. B. and Lloyd George as having " fallen in love with one another at the Buckingham Palace Conference." This little joke serves to show that the personal relationship withstood every strain in the week of crisis, and came out strengthened at the end. The terms on which the Prime Minister and the Foreign Secretary stand to one another is as important to the historian as to the biographer, and particularly so in the period on which this story is about to enter. Looking at the matter from the point of view of Balfour's own life, he was now, at the age of sixty-eight, required to work out the technique of collaboration with a Chief twenty years his junior, wielding almost a Dictator's powers, and whose genius and outlook were in nearly every respect the opposite of his own. It was not the

ARTHUR JAMES BALFOUR

1916 first, nor yet the second time that Balfour's personal relations with another great political figure had smoothed and eased the course for both, and left its stamp on British political history. The twenty years' collaboration with Lord Salisbury was unique of its kind. Later on mutual loyalties spared the Unionist Party the consequences of disputed leadership between him and Mr. Chamberlain. And now he worked again, this time under the next heir to the great Radical tradition.

Salisbury, Chamberlain, Lloyd George. The three names measure the span and variety of Balfour's experience when he took the Foreign Office in December 1916. This chapter may close with extracts from a letter, written a few months later, to his cousin, Lord Robert Cecil. The date is September 12th, 1917. The quotations begin with a comment upon the new Prime Minister's character.

> He is impulsive; he had never given a thought before the War to military matters; he does not perhaps adequately gauge the depths of his own ignorance; and he has certain peculiarities which no doubt make him, now and then, difficult to work with. But I am clearly of opinion that military matters are much better managed now than they were in the time of his predecessor. You mention the case of the Dardanelles, and draw from it the moral— a very good moral in its way—that civilians ought not to ask soldiers and sailors to carry out operations in which they disbelieve. But there is another moral to be drawn. In the Dardanelles affair the principal actors at home were a soldier without strategical genius, who controlled the military machine, a sailor equally without strategical genius, who ought to have controlled, but did not, the naval machine, and a brilliant amateur who attempted, but failed, to dominate both. If ever there was an operation which required the hearty co-operation of Army and Navy, it was Gallipoli. If ever there were two men between whom hearty co-operation was impossible, it was Kitchener and

"THE LITTLE MAN"

Winston. There was the opportunity for the Prime Minister 1916 to do what a Prime Minister alone can do, which is to compel subordinate Departments to work together. Asquith did nothing. He never seriously attempted to co-ordinate in one homogeneous whole the efforts of soldiers, sailors, and diplomatists, and the result was disaster. Now I have not the slightest doubt that Lloyd George would have endeavoured to be master in his own Government. He would have *tried* at all events to harmonise the jarring elements, and though I admit that with Winston, K. and Fisher the task was almost hopeless, I cannot help thinking that, had he been P.M., this particular page of military history would have been very differently written. . . .

Is there any one of his colleagues in the present War Cabinet you would like to see in his place? Is there any member of the late Government you would like to see in his place? Do you believe there is in the House of Commons any genius on the back benches fit for the place? Do you think there is somewhere in the undistinguished mass of the general public some unknown genius to whom, if we could but find him, we might entrust the most difficult, and the most important task with which British statesmanship has ever been confronted?

For myself I am inclined to answer all these questions in the negative, and that being so, the most patriotic course appears to me to provide the man whom we do not wish to replace with all the guidance and help in our power.

Chapter X

ENTER THE UNITED STATES
1917

Balfour's views on Peace Terms, December 1916. Balfour and Lord Robert Cecil. American misunderstanding of Allied aims. The Zimmermann Telegram. The U.S.A. enters the War. The "Balfour Mission" embarks for America. Balfour and President Wilson. The "Secret Treaties." Balfour addresses Congress. New York welcomes Balfour. Return of "Balfour Mission" to England. British need for money and ships. Balfour and the United States.

1917 When Balfour became Foreign Minister in Mr. Lloyd George's Government he had already given some consideration to the problems of his new Office. Only a month or two had passed since he had written a long and reasoned Memorandum upon the Peace Settlement, in response to a request which Mr. Asquith had made to all the members of the War Committee in the autumn of 1916. This Paper has been published already by Mr. Lloyd George.[1] It is reproduced as an Appendix to this volume[2] for reference purposes, because as the history of Balfour's tenure of the Foreign Office proceeds it is interesting to see how much of his first rough draft of a new Europe was capable of being translated in the end into terms of Treaties and frontier lines. Even in November 1916, when nearly all Belgium and some of the richest provinces of Northern France were in German occupation,

[1] See *War Memoirs*, Vol. II, p. 877 *et seq.*
[2] See below, Appendix A.

when Russia's armies were broken, when Roumania's oil and corn were about to replenish the enemy's stores, and when above all other anxieties, the mounting total of submarine sinkings of British ships had reached more than a hundred thousand tons a month, the First Lord of the Admiralty nevertheless based his Peace Settlement upon the hypothesis that the Central Powers would have to accept any terms which the Allies might impose.

Such was the position, and such his attitude, when he went to the Foreign Office on December 6th, 1916.

His first act was to hand over the guidance of affairs for the time being to Lord Robert Cecil. Balfour had stipulated for " reasonable time to recuperate " after his attack of influenza and in the Second Coalition his cousin had doubled his former office of Minister of Blockade with the Under-Secretaryship for Foreign Affairs. Often in the next two years he acted as Balfour's deputy, much as, twenty years back, Balfour himself had done for Lord Robert's father. The association was equally happy, although Lord Robert's views of the relative importance of things were founded on a political philosophy more easily ruffled than Balfour's. Bouts of indignation were apt to assail him over the doings of the various Governments in which he served, and that of Mr. Lloyd George was by no means an exception. In it he markedly developed what Balfour once described as " the resigning mind, which is as bad as the resigned mind." More than once Balfour paused in the flow of business to soothe and to reason. But the final argument was not entirely addressed to reason. " You realise that your resignation will almost certainly involve my own? I certainly could not remain at the F.O. without you." This was written in September 1917.

Balfour spent most of December 1916 at Eastbourne.

1917 The turn of the year was black. Bucharest fell on December 6th, and with that Roumania collapsed. The news of Russia's internal condition was grave, and on January 8th Germany declared for unrestricted submarine warfare. Worst of all, to Balfour's mind, was the state of Allied finances. Therefore when a set-back occurred to the hopes of speedy American intervention, for which all England was longing, Balfour's convalescence became unexhilarating indeed.

On December 18th Mr. Page, the United States Ambassador in London, handed to Lord Robert Cecil a so-called " Offer of Peace " from the Central to the Allied Powers. Next day he brought another Note, this time from President Wilson to the belligerent and neutral Powers. It was an appeal for a statement of war aims, and it gave out, as the President's belief, that the objects of both sides were " virtually the same as stated in general terms to their own peoples and to the world."

This implication that their war aims were on the same plane as Germany's deeply angered the Allied countries. " That one sentence will enrage them," wrote Colonel House when he saw the President's draft.[1] But all his influence could not prevail to change it. British resentment was brought home to the American Ambassador by Lord Robert Cecil's manner, when he saw him a few days after the Note was presented,[2] the more impressively because Lord Robert was as eager a friend of the United States as Balfour himself. But whatever their feelings, the British Ministers were determined to prevent public expression of indignation. The Foreign Office cautioned the newspapers, and hostile comment was subdued as far as possible. The

[1] See *Intimate Papers of Colonel House*, II, p. 407.
[2] See *Life and Letters of Walter Page*, II, pp. 209 et seq.

LORD ROBERT CECIL AND A. J. BALFOUR
1914

WAR AIMS

official answer of the Allies was delayed until January 10th, 1917. Drafted in conjunction with the French, it was largely concerned with redrawing the map of Europe. Balfour felt it must be supplemented, if the Allied war aims were to make their full appeal to the American mind. On January 18th, therefore, he drafted his own Despatch upon the Allied Note to Sir Cecil Spring Rice, our Ambassador in Washington. This was his first important piece of individual work as Foreign Minister. The effect of the two documents was described to him by Sir Cecil on January 19th :

> So far as diplomacy is concerned, things are going well for the Allies here. It was expected that we would refuse to reply to the President's enquiry as to our terms in the same way that Germany did. Now that we have accepted, and Germany refused we hold the first place in the popular respect. . . . Then came your Note. It is impossible to describe the effect on the minds of those whom you would regard as of your make. There seems to be a universal feeling in a certain class that here at last is found the true and full expression of what made the war, and of what alone can end it.[1]

The final paragraphs of Balfour's Despatch were intended to dispel the idea of peace before victory.

> Though the people of this country share to the full the desire of the President for peace, they do not believe that peace can be durable if it be not based on the success of the Allied cause. For a durable peace can hardly be expected unless three conditions are fulfilled. The first is that the existing causes of international unrest should be as far as possible removed or weakened. The second is that the aggressive aims and the unscrupulous methods of the Central Powers should fall into disrepute among their own peoples. The third is that behind international law and . . . treaty arrangements . . . some form of international sanction

[1] See *Letters and Friendships of Cecil Spring Rice*, Vol. II, p. 370.

should be devised which would give pause to the hardiest aggressor.

Balfour had long thought the question of will and power to coerce an aggressor a vital one for an international League. He had touched a chord, for Sir Cecil Spring Rice's letter went on :

> Your Note strikes a theme that has been deep in the President's thoughts for many months, namely, the plan of a Court of International Sanction, which would have the force of preventing wars. . . . It is believed . . . that your Note offers a distinct possibility of action along the lines indicated. . . . The President says the Democratic Party is pledged to some such action.

Not so, however, the Republican Party, and the Senate. Sir Cecil never left the British Government in the dark about their resistance to the idea of a " League of Peace." President Wilson may have welcomed parts of Balfour's Despatch, but as a whole it made small impression upon his mind, and it was followed on January 22nd by his last appeal to the belligerents, made in a speech to the Senate, where he called for a " Peace without Victory." When that unhappy phrase came across the Atlantic the hopes of all workers for mutual understanding between America and the Allies reached their lowest point. It was Germany who revived them, and that shortly, by the declaration of unrestricted submarine warfare on January 31st, 1917. Two days later the United States Government sent Count Bernstorff, the German Ambassador, his passports. But for the moment that was all.

Ever since the middle of January, however, a piece of information had been in the possession of the British Government, which would move, if anything could, the vast populations behind the Atlantic seaboard States, who still read of the European War with as much

THE ZIMMERMANN TELEGRAM

detachment as if it had been raging in the moon. This was the famous telegram from Zimmermann, the German Foreign Minister, to the German Minister in Mexico, instructing him, if and when the United States should enter the War on the Allied side, to propose to Mexico an alliance which would restore to her, when peace came, her "lost territories in Texas, Arizona and New Mexico."

1917

The method by which this information had reached the British Intelligence Service made it impossible for some time to communicate it to the United States Government. Therefore for over a month Balfour read in his despatches from Washington of the slow wakening of the American will to war, but could do nothing to hasten the process. Till—at last—information about the Mexican plot reached London through channels which enabled the Intelligence Service to cover up the traces of how it had first been got.

Joy was unbounded in Whitehall, and the Foreign Secretary himself was unusually excited. "As dramatic a moment as I remember in all my life," he once said, referring to the scene in his room at the Foreign Office on February 24th, 1917, when he handed to the American Ambassador the sheet of paper containing the decoded message. By the ceremony of this act the British Government gave its pledge that the communication was authentic. Nevertheless the American nation not unnaturally took a little while to satisfy itself that the telegram was not part of some gigantic hoax. It might have taken longer, had not the German Foreign Office, within a few days of the publication, admitted the message to be genuine.

On February 26th, two days after the telegram had been given to the United States Government, but before its publication, the President asked Congress for power

1917 to arm American merchant ships. The Bill had an overwhelming majority in its favour, but twelve obstructors were able to block its passage until the Session automatically closed on March 4th. Feeling inside and outside the Senate rose very high, and the President, convinced that he had the country behind him, used his own executive authority to arm the ships. America saw him now in the light of a leader.[1] On March 9th he delivered his Message to the new Congress.

> It is [wrote Sir Cecil Spring Rice to Balfour] the first time that a President has publicly declared that the United States must play a part in the community of Nations.

But still the "overt act" that might bring America into war was lacking. It came on March 15th, when the *Algonquin* was sunk without warning, and a few days later three more American merchantmen, with the loss of a number of American lives. At that the Embassy in Washington reported again to the Foreign Office: "Although . . . public feeling in the West still remained tranquil, a wave of deep indignation swept the East."

But the President was still cautious—and determined to share responsibility for every step as widely as possible. Nevertheless, things were moving. As early as March 2nd the American Ambassador in London wrote in his diary:

> Mr. Balfour, Mr. Bonar Law and I to-day had a conference of an hour or more about exchange with the United States, and the possibility of more loans there to pay for munitions and food bought there. Could a great popular loan be got in the United States (like the great Victory Loan here) ? . . . Balfour has always held in the Cabinet that

[1] See *Intimate Papers of Colonel House*, II, p. 461.

A GREAT DAY FOR THE WORLD

the problem of exchange is the great problem—not the 1917 submarine.[1]

Balfour, aware as he was of the desperate need for American help in every sphere of the War, yet never joined in the criticisms of delay that were the talk of nearly every London dinner-table during the last weeks of the time of waiting. Mr. Page wrote on February 8th:

> Mr. Balfour said that never for a moment had he doubted the President's wisdom in the course he was pursuing. . . . Nor had he ever entertained the slightest doubt of the American people's ready loyalty to their Government or to their high ideals. One of his intellectual pleasures, he added, had long been contemplation of the United States as it is, and even more, as its influence in the world will broaden.[2]

At last the hour struck. On April 2nd the President asked Congress for a Declaration of War on Germany.

The Ambassador of the United States in London felt as great a weight lifted off him as Englishmen themselves. Mr. Page hastened to the Foreign Office. "It's a great day for the world," said Balfour, shaking him warmly by the hand. With that they settled down to the practical questions which surged in through the opened flood-gates of feeling between the English-speaking peoples.

> Nearly the whole afternoon was spent with Balfour and Lord Robert Cecil [wrote Mr. Page]. Mr. Balfour had a long list of subjects: Could we help in (1)—(2)—(3)—. Every once in a while he stopped, . . . long enough to tell me how the action of the United States had moved him.[3]

---

[1] See *Life and Letters of Walter Page*, III, p. 325.
[2] *Ibid.*, II, p. 251.
[3] See *Life and Letters of Walter Page*, II, p. 229.

ARTHUR JAMES BALFOUR

1917   Probably it was on this same afternoon that Balfour asked Mr. Page why the British were so unpopular in the United States.

> Among other reasons [the Ambassador answered] our official people on both sides steadfastly refuse to visit one another and become acquainted. Neither he, nor Lord Grey, nor Mr. Asquith, nor Mr. Lloyd George, had ever been to the United States, . . . and not a single member of the Administration was personally known to a single member of the British Government. "I'll go," said Balfour, " if you are perfectly sure my going will be agreeable to the President."[1]

Thus the proposal was made which in its outcome had so much to do with setting the relations between the Allied countries and the great Associate Power upon a basis of right understanding. The world owes much to the two Americans, Mr. Page and Colonel House, who had prepared the foundations for the all-important contacts. The delicate ground was probed by the Foreign Office. On April 5th Colonel House wrote to President Wilson:

> I enclose a cable which has just come from Eric Drummond.[2] Of course it is really Balfour speaking. . . . Balfour is the most liberal Member of the present Cabinet, and it would be of great service to the relations of the two countries to have him here, and to talk with him in person.[3]

The President agreed, though he told Colonel House that he visualised certain dangers, and feared that some Americans might suspect " an attempt in some degree to take charge of us as an assistant to Great Britain." These slight misgivings are worth recording only

---

[1] See *Life and Letters of Walter Page*, II, p. 253.

[2] Sir Eric Drummond, then Private Secretary to the Foreign Secretary, afterwards Secretary-General of the League of Nations, 1920–1932.

[3] See *Intimate Papers of Colonel House*, III, p. 36.

THE BALFOUR MISSION EMBARKS

because the success of Balfour's visit was so apparently spontaneous, that the care with which pitfalls were avoided is apt to be forgotten.

On April 9th the President's welcome was cabled to London, together with the suggestion that the British Mission should be announced as diplomatic rather than military.

I well remember the sparkle in Balfour's eye, when he told his family where he was going. From the tone of his voice one might have judged him setting off for the golf-links for some eagerly anticipated match, and I recall none of the customary groans that preceded embarkation on a boat of any kind. Submarines—for once—we did not mention; such allusions would have seemed singularly out of place. But no secret of the War was more carefully kept than the route and the date of departure of the Balfour Mission to America. Or would so have been kept, but for the indiscretion of the Chief of the Mission himself. The story of the lift-boy is true.[1] It happened in the Station Hotel at Dumfries, where the twenty-five members of the party waited, until some activities of the U-boats off the north coast of Ireland should subside. After twenty-four hours word came to entrain once more, and as their " special " moved off Sir Eric Drummond said to Balfour: " Thank goodness we are off without anyone finding out that you were there." " Except the lift-boy," said Balfour. " But how on earth——? " " Well, he brought me his autograph book, and of course I signed it."

They boarded the *Olympic* at Greenock at dead of night, and as they were being escorted to their cabins, faces peered at them from every doorway. Small wonder, for the ship had been waiting for them for

[1] See *Lord Balfour: a Memory*, by Sir Ian Malcolm, p. 44.

1917 days, and the tamest of the rumours current among the passengers had been that the Shah of Persia was expected, or, perhaps, the Czar of Russia. Balfour stalked along, unconscious of being an object of interest. They had still another twenty-four hours to wait before they left the Clyde, owing to the presence of enemy submarines being reported in the Irish Sea. When at length they sailed they encountered a storm that forced the escort of destroyers to turn back almost as soon as the liner came out of the Firth. A life-preserving suit of india-rubber was placed in Balfour's cabin, but after inspecting it for a moment he said that on the whole he would rather drown in his night-shirt.[1]

Once the sea went down he enjoyed the voyage. It was not a holiday for any of the twenty-five members of the British Mission, which included, besides the Foreign Office people, soldiers, sailors, economists, and experts in the new war sciences such as munitions. America's entry into the War disposed of some problems, but created plenty more, which there had been little time to consider before leaving home. The Mission led by Balfour was essentially a technical Mission, but it required for success the creation of an atmosphere which was the diplomatic achievement of its leader. In that atmosphere machinery of international co-operation was set up, the value of which might have outlived the War had it not been indiscriminately thrown on the scrap-heap at the end. At the very moment when President Wilson set the Allied nations planning the structure of the League in 1919, the great inter-Allied War Commissions were allowed to dissolve under pressure from the United States, bequeathing nothing of their experience to the post-war world. This however is by the way.

[1] See *Lord Balfour : a Memory*, by Sir Ian Malcolm, p. 44.

A MISSION HYMN

Balfour's life on board ship was a mixture of work, 1917 exercise and social intercourse, carefully regulated by a personal Private Secretary whose tact and power of divination were quickened by a deep affection for his Chief. From the date of the American journey to the end of the Peace Conference in Paris, Sir Ian Malcolm took the burden of the important small things which make so much difference in the daily life of a public man. Sir Ian was the author of some *Mission Hymns*,[1] which delighted no one more than the Mission's Chief. One of them reproduces very faithfully the instructions that Balfour impressed upon all his following as soon as the *Olympic* stopped rolling.

CIRCULAR NOTES

In your hours of ease, I beg you
    Missionaries, one and all,
Read, mark, learn, digest and pass on
    This concise Encyclical.
You will find its interest chaining
    —Sometimes even entertaining.

First of all you must remember
    That you go to U.S.A.,
To a land of candied critics;
    So be careful what you say.
I shan't mind the least if some
    People think you're deaf and dumb.

If with questions you are pestered
    By the Press for news athirst,
Do not risk replying till you've
    Wired home for instructions first.
Heaven knows what might occur
    If you answered " on the spur."

[1] Printed in 1917 for private circulation only.

ARTHUR JAMES BALFOUR

1917

E.G.: " Why bring re-made soldiers
  On your diplomatic stunt ? "
Should the ready lie elude you
  Give a non-committal grunt,
Or remark with pungent wit
  " *Miles nascitur non fit.*"

(*Note for General T. Bridges*—
  Please observe a strict disguise ;
Don't appear in medalled khaki
  Or regard their martial cries.
If they cap you, don't salute ;
  If they challenge you, don't shoot.)

Should they ask if England's starving,
  You may answer " Look at me,
Do I seem emaciated
  Or in need of sympathy ? "
If you have the indigestion
  Ask for notice of the question.

(*Note :* for everyone connected
  With the mysteries of Trade.
Never soil your lips by uttering
  That suspicious word " Blockade."
If *they* mention it to you,
  I don't know what you're to do.)

Very possibly they'll ask you
  " What is happening in Greece ? "
" What about the Spring Offensive ? "
  Or what day the war will cease.
You should say " I've no idea,"
  And manœuvre for the rear.

(*Note :* for Admirals and others
  Who pursue the path Marine ;
The Department would prefer you
  To be neither heard nor seen

THE "BALFOUR MISSION" ARRIVES, APRIL 20TH, 1917

ARRIVAL

<blockquote>

In your sailor suits by day;
  It might grieve the U.S.A.)

There is just one other matter
  Which diplomacy dictates
Should be handled with discretion
  In non-alcoholic States:
'Twould be well received, I think,
  If the Mission didn't drink.

That completes the list of topics
  I would have you bear in mind;
To sum up: I urge my colleagues
  To be deaf and dumb—not " blind."
Please observe punctiliously
  These injunctions.—A.J.B.

</blockquote>

1917

S.S. *Olympic*.

On the morning of April 20th in bright sunshine, the *Olympic* berthed in Halifax harbour, and Balfour, for the second time in his life, after an interval of forty years, set foot on the American Continent. But the lapse of time was as nothing compared with the change between the languid young man of thirty who had once complained of the discomfort of Pullman cars,[1] and the septuagenarian who, before the Mission had crossed the Canadian frontier, was delivering to the Associated Power the first Message from its British Ally. Newspaper correspondents were of course on the special train, and Balfour had got his statement ready before he left the *Olympic*. The original manuscript in his own hand is now in the Library of Princeton University.

Not much could be said on this " first page of a new chapter in the history of mankind." So Balfour described it, adding that no opinion on policy would be even tolerable until he had had the honour of conferring with the President.

[1] See Vol. I, p. 37.

ARTHUR JAMES BALFOUR

1917   The Mission reached Washington on the afternoon of Sunday, April 22nd, and the motors, with a cavalry escort, drove among cheering crowds and through streets fluttering with Stars and Stripes and Union Jacks, to the house of Mr. Breckenridge Long, put at their disposal by the United States Government, whose guests the British were throughout.

Next morning Balfour called at the White House.

The exact degree of sympathy engendered at any time between him and President Wilson is hard to measure. On Balfour's side there could not fail to be appreciation of immense gifts of culture; and on the intellectual plane the two men were bound to enjoy each other's company and to get on well together, as was conspicuously the case during the American visit. Balfour's opinion of the President as a statesman was undoubtedly modified in Paris, but I never heard him really " let himself go " on the character of the President, a fact in itself significant. I never heard anything but praise, genuine certainly, but always expressed in carefully chosen phrases.

They met of course a number of times during the month that Balfour remained in the United States, before his departure for Canada on May 22nd, when Mr. Wilson broke all precedents by visiting him in person to say good-bye. The most important of these occasions was the evening of April 30th, when, after a family dinner at the White House, the President and Balfour entered upon an informal conversation about War Aims, Colonel House acting as steersman in the conversation.[1] Then it was that Balfour disclosed to the President the existence and the character of certain " Secret Treaties " concluded between the Allied

---

[1] See *Intimate Papers of Colonel House*, II, p. 51 *et seq*, for full details.

THE SECRET TREATIES

Powers. All doubt as to the British Foreign Minister's entire openness on this subject has been removed by the publication of Colonel House's *Papers*. It was raised for a time after the President, speaking to the Senate Foreign Relations Committee in 1919, almost on the eve of his final physical collapse, asserted that he had no knowledge of the Treaties as a whole, before he went to Europe for the Peace Conference. The allegation of concealment, when repeated by Mr. Ray Stannard Baker, was acutely resented by Balfour,[1] but he never attributed to President Wilson more than a lapse of memory, which he himself would be the last to consider surprising, or to condemn.

1917

Talking to me on the subject in 1928, without having read Colonel House's *Papers*, which had recently been published, he said :

> House tells me he has blown to pieces that story that I never told Wilson about the Secret Treaties when I went over in '17.
> *Myself.* " But did you tell him ? Was it his business ? "
> *A. J. B.* " Oh, yes. I was bound to tell him. But it was a very delicate business, for of course they *were* secret. The way I got over it was to tell him about them *as* a secret,— as man to man. I told him personally."
> *Myself.* " Then did he forget all about it afterwards ? "
> *A. J. B.* " I think he said he had never been informed. I don't think he said he did not know. But quite likely he did forget. I can quite understand that. You see when Wilson had made up his mind about coming into the war, it was the *present* and the future that interested him, not the past. I felt the same—those Treaties had no importance by that time."

It certainly would have been futile for Balfour and President Wilson, sitting in the library at the White

[1] See Letter from Balfour to Colonel House in the *Intimate Papers*, III, p. 64.

ARTHUR JAMES BALFOUR

1917 House in April 1917, to spend time in trying to straighten out the tangled inheritance which Mr. Asquith and Sir Edward Grey had bequeathed to their successors through the "Secret Treaties." One of these, the Constantinople Agreement of May 1915, which gave the Straits to Russia, was denounced in due course by the Soviet Government. There remained the "Treaty of London," which had bribed Italy into the War in 1915 by promises of territory in Europe, and her "just share" of the spoils of the Ottoman Empire in Asia Minor. This last provision had been cut across before Balfour went to America, by the "Sykes-Picot Agreement" of May 1916, between the British and the French. And at the very moment when Balfour was crossing the Atlantic, Mr. Lloyd George was endeavouring to appease the Italians by recognising their claims to Adalia and Smyrna in the Agreement of St. Jean de Maurienne of April 17th, 1917. The efforts of the British to combine "peace with honour" in 1919 were greatly complicated by these various incompatible arrangements. The American President however was never called upon to endorse them.

The different branches of the Mission settled to their work. Balfour kept general touch, alert for any point where a word from him might lessen difficulties, but never attempting to interfere with the course of technical negotiations. The benefits of the contacts then set up were mutual. Britain had sent of her best in the personnel of the Mission, and they brought with them the experience gained through three terrible years of "trial and error" in the vital problems of war production; for example, in the questions of "dilution," of "priority," and so forth. All that they knew they gave, and in return they learned something about their new Associate.

WE ARE ALL ONE

The Mission had been forty-eight hours in Washington, when one of its members wrote to a friend at home: 1917

> Everything here is going on splendidly; A. J. B. is winning over everyone he meets. . . . It does seem hard to understand out here why there should be any animosity between the two countries. You have only to dig down one inch, and we are all one. I think they feel that here too. This may be the feeling of the Eastern States as opposed to the others, but there are plenty of serious men here! To-day we have an awful trip with the French to Mount Vernon. Top hats and a yacht!

In spite of the top-hats, the Englishmen found the expedition to George Washington's tomb anything but an " awful trip." Balfour's historical sense was deeply stirred, and his speech made a great impression, all the more by its contrast in style with that of M. Viviani, one of the most eloquent orators of his day. This was almost the only great public occasion when the French Mission, which was in the United States at the same time, appeared together with the British, the piquancy of the ceremony being thereby much enhanced.

> The whole thing has made a great impression [wrote the same Englishman]. People here still feel that England is the England of the War of Independence and such animosity as there is is based more on old history than on—say—the Irish question, or our supposed airs. . . . You hear a terrific amount of the Irish question discussed, and we get shoals of letters about it.

Ireland was, in fact, the one subject that roused a shadow of anxiety in the minds of those concerned with staging an event, which was to be not merely the climax of America's welcome to the British, but a landmark in the history of the English-speaking peoples, the invitation, namely, to Balfour to address Congress. It would never do for this to be marred by the faintest hostile

ARTHUR JAMES BALFOUR

1917 demonstration. What would the Irish-Americans do? The Englishman's letter to his friend goes on:

> Congress was, I hear, rather hesitating about asking Mr. Balfour down, but the Irish members went *en bloc* to the Speaker, and told him they all very much hoped to see Mr. B. address Congress from the floor of the House. . . .

No Briton, however faintly conscious of his political heritage, could fail to be moved when singled out as the recipient of the highest honour that one great Democracy can bestow upon another. By tradition and by training, Balfour was before all things a Parliamentarian. Who better able than he to appreciate the significance of the gesture of Congress? It is not often made. The last occasion had been in 1880, when Mr. Parnell addressed the House. Now Balfour succeeded his adversary of days bygone. The Official Record gives the best idea of the proceedings.

> The SPEAKER. The Chair appoints as a Committee to escort the British Commissioners to the floor of the House the gentleman from Virginia, Mr. Flood; the gentleman from Maryland, Mr. Linthicum; the gentleman from Arkansas, Mr. Goodwin; the gentleman from Wisconsin, Mr. Cooper; and in the absence of the gentleman from Pennsylvania, Mr. Porter, and the gentleman from Massachusetts, Mr. Rogers, the next ranking members of the Committee of Foreign Affairs, he appoints the gentleman from Pennsylvania, Mr. Temple. The Committee will proceed to the Speaker's room, and, in accordance with the previous order, the House will stand in recess for 30 minutes.
>
> Accordingly (at 12 o'clock and 30 minutes p.m.) the House stood in recess.
>
> The President of the United States entered the Executive Gallery of the House and was greeted with prolonged applause and cheers.
>
> The Chief Justice and Associated Justices of the Supreme Court of the United States were seated in front of the Speaker's rostrum.

A MARVELLOUS SCENE

At 12 o'clock and 35 minutes p.m., the Commissioners of the Government of Great Britain to the Government of the United States, the Right Hon. Arthur James Balfour, Principal British Secretary of State for Foreign Affairs; Gen. G. T. M. Bridges, of the British Army; Admiral Sir Dudley R. S. de Chair, K.C.B., of the British Navy; Fleet Paymaster V. A. Lawford, D.S.O., R.N.; Lord Cunliffe, Governor of the Bank of England; Sir Ian Malcolm, M.P. and Major Spender-Clay, M.P., British General Staff, escorted by Mr. Flood, Mr. Linthicum, Mr. Goodwin of Arkansas, Mr. Cooper of Wisconsin, and Mr. Temple, entered the Hall of the House, accompanied by Sir Cecil Arthur Spring Rice, the British Ambassador Extraordinary and Plenipotentiary accredited to the United States, Mr. Phillips, and Mr. Hugh Gibson, of the Department of State. The distinguished visitors were escorted to the Speaker's rostrum amid prolonged applause and cheers.

The SPEAKER. Gentlemen of the House of Representatives, I present to you the Right Hon. Arthur James Balfour, Principal British Secretary of State for Foreign Affairs. Prolonged applause.

Three days later followed the reception by the Senate. But it was the House of Representatives that most impressed the Englishmen. Sir Ian Malcolm wrote home to Miss Balfour:

> It was a marvellous scene, crammed, jammed full, the floor with deputies, diplomats and judges, the galleries with ladies and press-men. He made a splendid speech, and then stood on the floor of the House, and shook hands with every member as the procession passed him, and with as many children as the Congressmen cared to bring with them. He was in excellent voice, and the whole show was a triumphant success. But *the* emotion was when the President of the United States appeared among the Congressmen to shake his hand ! ! History contains no record of a President ever before appearing on the floor of the House, or even of his appearing in his box to listen to a speech. Both these things he did yesterday out of compliment to our Chief.

ARTHUR JAMES BALFOUR

1917

In the afternoon A. J. B. played tennis; he never played better in his life; and to-day he has motored out to the country to talk Foreign Affairs with Mr. Lansing. Next Friday we go to New York for two days.

Outdoors and indoors, New York gave him a giant's welcome. Its echo in England brought an indescribable feeling of reassurance, helping us to realise the spirit in which the United States was moving up. It was with far more than a mere personal emotion that Balfour's family read the story, as told in a private letter from an American friend, of his reception in the Carnegie Hall, at a benefit performance for the British Red Cross.

> When there was shown the moving pictures of the Battle of the Ancre we cheered the Tommies as if they had been actually present, the Highlanders—the Welshmen. . . . We had worked ourselves—the six thousand of us—to a pitch of enthusiasm which knew no bounds. Then there was a momentary hush, and all eyes turned to the hitherto unoccupied box; then there came shouts from all over the house, repeated over and over again: " Balfour ! "
> It was Balfour, standing by Choate, bowing, bowing. Balfour, who had won our minds and hearts by his first speech he made in Washington, and " Joe " Choate, the best beloved citizen of our City, if not indeed of the whole country. We New Yorkers were not going to let any of the audiences . . . outdo us in heartiness of welcome. And we did not ! We just stood up and roared at him, and roared and cheered again and again. And then the orchestra struck up Rule Britannia, and we sang it with all our might, and defiantly. . . .
> The performance was over, but the audience lingered; and there arose another mighty shouting, " Balfour, Balfour ! " And bye and bye, when Choate waved his hand for silence, Balfour spoke to us, as we stood stock still, hardly breathing,—spoke as a friend to friends. . . . We all of us, every one, came away satisfied and content in mind and heart, resolved, determined more absolutely than ever that " this world must be made safer for Democracy."

HOPE AND CONFIDENCE

This was what people felt and thought and looked forward to in the spring of 1917, at the beginning of the sternest period of the War by sea and land. Only in the atmosphere of that period of hope and confidence in the world's future can the achievement of the Balfour Mission be appraised.

Balfour's appearances in company with his old friend, Mr. Joseph Choate, formerly American Ambassador in London, were soon to be recalled with an unexpectedly solemn significance. On the last day of the New York visit they drove together to service in the Anglican Cathedral.

> As I parted from him on the steps [wrote Balfour] we took a tender farewell of one another. As we shook hands he said, "We probably shall not meet again till Peace is reached." He was right. He died within a few hours from heart failure.[1]

This was on the 22nd of May. Before the British Mission recrossed the Canadian border they had gone down to Virginia, where pro-Ally feeling was no new growth. In Ottawa, Toronto and Quebec the enthusiasm began all over again. At last, on June 9th, the *Olympic* entered the Mersey, and Sir Ian Malcolm composed the last of the *Mission Hymns*.

He called this one " Recessional " :

> Now the Mission's over,
> Home is drawing nigh ;
> Shadows of real warfare
> Creep across the sky.
>
> Flag-days without number,
> Cripples in the street,
> Weary war-stained heroes,
> Once again we greet.

[1] See *Chapters of Autobiography*, by Arthur James Balfour, First Earl of Balfour, p. 241.

ARTHUR JAMES BALFOUR

1917

>Gone the Balls and Banquets,
>Junkettings no more;
>These we left behind us
>On the further shore.
>
>But that far-flung welcome
>We shall ne'er forget,
>Proof that ancient striving
>Leaves us brothers yet.

> It is quite impossible [wrote the British Ambassador in Washington] to exaggerate the importance of the work done here, and an enumeration of the details would give a very poor impression of what has actually been done. It is more in the nature of a new light and a new atmosphere. It is rather rain and sunshine than seed, although good seed has been sown.

So it proved in the months of that summer of 1917, when submarine sinkings were at their worst, the financial needs of the Allies at their most desperate, and the lag between promise and performance in the United States apparently widening not closing. The Administration there would not, or could not, believe the awful truth of the figures, reported back from their own representatives in London, of the rate at which the U-boats were destroying merchant tonnage. Suspicions grew out of ignorance.

> Unfortunately [wrote Balfour] you must frighten Englishmen if you want them to eat less food, and you must frighten Americans if you want them to build more ships, while you cannot frighten either without encouraging Huns.

It almost seemed as if the Navy Department thought that Great Britain was trying to get America to protect her commerce, while her own fleet stayed safe in harbour. Mr. Page in despair turned to Balfour to reinforce his protests. "Whatever else they think of the British in

A. J. BALFOUR AND JOSEPH CHOATE IN NEW YORK, MAY 22ND, 1917

AMERICAN HELP

Washington," he said, " they know one thing—and that is that a British statesman like Mr. Balfour cannot lie."[1] On June 30th therefore Balfour sent a personal letter to the President, drafted in consultation with his own successor at the Admiralty, Sir Edward Carson, and the First Sea Lord. It put the food situation bluntly; it begged for armed small craft of every kind from the only Allied country able to supply them, and it spoke of the convoy system as the best hope for the future, provided only that enough destroyers could be spared for the duty. The balance as between capital ships and light craft in the United States shipbuilding programme therefore became a matter which the President himself discussed with Sir William Wiseman, the British adviser whose presence in the United States was one of the best results of the Balfour Mission.

Mr. Wilson's own instincts were that the days of the monster battleship were over. The discretion left by Congress to the Navy Department was used, during the remainder of the War, for the building of the smaller vessels which the Allies so urgently needed. Even more important, from the historical point of view, was the proposal for a naval agreement that Balfour cabled to Colonel House early in December 1917, which might assist the United States in concentrating upon light craft at this crisis. The draft in Balfour's own handwriting runs thus:

> That in view of the diversion of Government shipbuilding in the Naval Yards of the U.S.A. from the construction of capital ships to that of vessels suitable for anti-submarine warfare, the Governments of the U.S.A., Great Britain, France, Italy, Russia and Japan engage singly and severally to assist each other against any maritime attack for a period of four years after the conclusion of the present war.

[1] See *Life and Letters of Walter Page*, II, p. 284.

ARTHUR JAMES BALFOUR

1917 It is of some interest, in view of subsequent events, to note the reasons why Balfour proposed this General Treaty, rather than one of mutual maritime defence between Great Britain and the United States alone.

> This [he wrote in a Memorandum to the War Cabinet of June 22nd, 1917] would have the immense advantage of being both simple and adequate, and I confess for reasons of high policy, there is nothing I should like more than a defensive alliance with America, even for four years, that would be capable of extension and development should circumstances prove suspicious. The objection to it arises out of our existing Treaty with Japan. It is quite true that there is no logical incompatibility between our actual Treaty with Japan and this suggested Treaty with America. Both are defensive. . . . All the same I fear that any such simple Treaty with America . . . would be regarded, as far as Anglo-Japanese relations are concerned, as the beginning of the end of an Alliance which has already lasted twenty years, and which has on the whole conduced to stability in international relations in the Far East. This is a danger not to be lightly run, and probably the best way of avoiding it—indeed the only way that occurs to me—is to try to associate Japan from the beginning with the new arrangement.

This however was the very aspect of the matter that alarmed President Wilson, who rejected the Treaty of Mutual Assistance on the ground that it looked too much like an Alliance with the great European States and Japan.

The United States Government was persuaded to concentrate its shipbuilding energies mainly on destroyer construction. This strengthened the hands of all those at the Admiralty who were pressing for the adoption of the convoy system on a big scale—and with the convoy system began the decline of the submarine sinkings—the brightest spot of the year 1917.

Insistent as was the call for ships, the appeals for

STAGGERING FIGURES

money were more urgent still. Before Balfour had been 1917 three weeks at home a financial crisis developed, owing partly to a misunderstanding about United States help to Great Britain in respect of Russian obligations. Not all Colonel House's acquaintance with Balfour's character prevented him from describing the following telegram in his Diary as " panicky " :[1]

July 29*th,* 1917.

> For reasons fully explained to Page here and to Spring Rice in Washington, we seem on the verge of a financial disaster that would be worse than defeat in the field. If we cannot keep up exchange, neither we nor our Allies can pay our dollar debts. We should be driven off the gold basis, purchases from U.S.A. would immediately cease, and the Allies' credit would be shattered. A consequence which would be of incalculable gravity may be upon us on Monday next if nothing effective is done in the meantime. You know I am not an alarmist, but this is really serious. I hope you will do what you can in proper quarters to avert calamity.
>
> BALFOUR.

Serious it was. Thirty-five million dollars on Monday, a hundred million dollars on Thursday, and a hundred and eighty-five million a month for two months after, was the British requirement.

> This is a staggering amount [wrote Colonel House to the President] and indicates the load Great Britain has been carrying for her Allies. It seems to me that we should have some definite understanding with England as to what money she will need in the future and how far she can count upon us.

On July 5th the Foreign Office cabled again : " Balfour is most grateful to House for his intervention ; the results are already apparent."

[1] See *Intimate Papers of Colonel House,* III, p. 10.

ARTHUR JAMES BALFOUR

1917   Personal correspondence could not settle everything, and had it not been for the contacts made by the Mission to Washington some difficulties might hardly have been overcome before it was too late. The greater part of Balfour's work at the Foreign Office was directly concerned with the United States, and much of the rest of it indirectly so, for the thing most to be avoided was any suspicion on the part of American statesmen that they were being kept in the dark about Allied diplomacy. Balfour saw to it that there should be neither shadow nor substance behind such fears. He kept a vigilant watch over all matters affecting Anglo-American relations which came within the Foreign Minister's scope. When all the world is at war that scope is greatly restricted, for the main object of diplomacy is peace, and when peace has once been broken the Foreign Office becomes the handmaid of the Departments whose business is the conduct of war. Many of the tests fail by which the achievements of a Foreign Minister are normally judged. But in this matter of preserving a good understanding with the great Associated Power, Balfour had a comparatively free hand, and in his eyes there was no task of more paramount importance.

Chapter XI

THE CONTACT WITH JEWRY

Opposition of Jewish non-Zionists to Zionist idea. Sir Mark Sykes interprets Zionism to British Government. Balfour champions Zionist cause in Cabinet. Balfour's faith in Zionism. His attitude to Arab claims. His speeches to Zionist audiences. Zionists approach the British Government in 1914. Dr. Weizmann's conversations with Balfour. Zionist diplomacy in 1916. Balfour as Foreign Secretary discusses future with American Zionists. "Balfour Declaration" before the Cabinet. Weizmann and Trotsky. "Balfour Declaration" issued in November 1917.

Balfour's return from America in May 1917 is a convenient point at which to review the part he took in the previous and subsequent negotiations between the British Government and the Zionists, which led in November 1917 to the pledge of British support for a Jewish National Home in Palestine. The promise was given in the form of a letter to the President of the English Zionist Federation, Lord Rothschild, and signed by Balfour as Foreign Secretary. Hence it became known as the "Balfour Declaration," and the name survived even after the text of it was incorporated in 1922 in the Mandate of the League of Nations whereby Great Britain administers Palestine. This has led to a certain amount of misunderstanding of Balfour's personal responsibility for a pronouncement which was essentially a Cabinet decision, arrived at after the most thorough consideration.

To say this is by no means to minimise the effect of his influence upon the policy of Mr. Lloyd George's

1917

ARTHUR JAMES BALFOUR

1917 Cabinet. From the first he threw his whole weight on to the side of the Zionists, and without it they might not have prevailed. They fought their case under heavy handicaps by comparison with united peoples, such as the Czechs, who were also struggling for recognition of their claims during the Great War. In England the most formidable foes of Jewish nationalism were themselves Jews. In social and political circles especially, the indifference or hostility of the Jewish aristocracy of wealth worked actively against the Zionists. The nationalist leaders, most of them born and bred among the oppressed masses in the Russian Empire, had few contacts with this sheltered class. Among British politicians the Zionists had indeed gained one active sympathiser of their own race in Mr. Herbert Samuel, but he was not a member of Mr. Lloyd George's Ministry; whereas the Cabinet contained the very spear-head of Anglo-Jewish opposition to the Zionist movement, in the person of Mr. Edwin Montagu, Secretary of State for India. Mr. Montagu could not extend to his own people the sympathy he evinced later for nationalism in India. He saw the spectre of anti-Semitism in every country if its Jews permitted themselves to dream of a territorial centre or a national political existence outside their present citizenships. Such aspirations in English Jews he looked upon as traitorous disloyalty to their native land. In the case of Jews living under less happy conditions he believed their relations with the countries of their birth would only be worsened.

This was not a point of view which ever appealed with great force to the non-Jewish populations of the British Empire, many of whom as, for example, the Scotch, are perfectly accustomed to combining strong separate racial consciousness with a wider loyalty.

ZIONISTS AND ANTI-ZIONISTS

Nevertheless, among all the pros and cons of granting special rights to the Jews in Palestine, the division of opinion among Jews themselves was bound to weigh with British Ministers, although, apart from Balfour, Mr. Lloyd George, General Smuts, and the Secretary for War, Lord Milner, were all in sympathy with the Zionists. Moreover by the autumn of 1917 there was a body of opinion on their side among the expert advisers of the Government, due in great measure to the influence of Sir Mark Sykes, who acted as connecting link between the War Office, the Foreign Office, and the War Cabinet, in respect of Middle Eastern affairs. When the Zionists obtained the sympathy of this Englishman they gained an ally hardly less valuable than Balfour himself, in that stage of their struggle when they were striving to get promises of support from individuals translated into a public statement by the British Government as a whole.

In August 1917 a draft Declaration, approved by the Foreign Secretary, came before the Cabinet. The end of three years' negotiation then seemed in sight; but there was delay, accountable enough at first, less so as the weeks ran on. Rumours of opposition in the Cabinet became certainties. Outside, the anti-Zionist Jews opened the attack against the recognition of Jewish nationhood. It was a tragic moment, even judged by the standards of Jewish history. An internal bitterness was engendered which only began to pass away fifteen years later when the persecution of German Jews under Hitler struck a mortal blow to the dreams of Jewish assimilationists everywhere. There are now few Jews in any country who hold that the British acknowledgment of their historic right on Palestinian soil was against the interests of Jewry. This would not be relevant to the story of the Balfour Declaration of

ARTHUR JAMES BALFOUR

1917, but for the fact that, owing to the opposition of Mr. Montagu, the victory of the Jewish nationalists was ultimately fought and won in the British Cabinet, not mainly on the ground of British interests, or of Allied interests (for these aspects of the matter had been considered at an earlier stage), but on the more far-reaching question of the effect upon the Jewish problem as a whole. It was precisely here that Balfour could argue with the greatest conviction. He had given deep consideration to that side of the subject. Readers of the first volume of this book will remember his conversation with the Zionist leader, Dr. Weizmann, in Manchester in the middle of the General Election of 1906.[1] He had been profoundly interested at that time in the connection of the Jewish national movement with a return to Palestine. He had discerned a determination behind the Zionist ideology which appealed to him as a philosopher, and impressed him as a student of history. He became convinced that the revival of the sentiment of Jewish unity was no less worthy of respect than other national movements of the modern world, which were better understood because they sprang from geographically united peoples. His view of the expediency of acknowledging the historic right of the Jews to a special position in Palestine was a long range view, stretching further into the past and the future than was perhaps the case with some of his colleagues. He thought of the Zionists as guardians of a continuity of religious and racial tradition that made the unassimilated Jew a great conservative force in world politics, and he felt strongly about the way in which the Jewish contribution to culture and to religion had for the most part been requited by the Christian world. This moral indignation existed in him before he ever heard of Zionism. I cannot

[1] See Vol. I, Chapter XIX.

THE JEWISH PROBLEM

remember a time that he did not express it strongly whenever anti-Semitism was a subject of conversation, and it avowedly counted for much in his Palestinian policy. He never put it more clearly than to the House of Lords in 1922, when Lord Islington attacked the acceptance of the Mandate by Great Britain.

> I hold [Balfour said] that from a purely material point of view the policy that we initiated is likely to prove a successful policy. But we have never pretended—certainly I have never pretended—that it was purely from these materialistic considerations that the Declaration of November 1917 originally sprung. I regard this not as a solution, but as a partial solution, of the great and abiding Jewish problem. . . .
>
> I do not deny that this is an adventure. Are we never to have adventures? Are we never to try new experiments? . . . Surely, it is in order that we may send a message to every land where the Jewish race has been scattered, a message that will tell them that Christendom is not oblivious of their faith, is not unmindful of the service they have rendered to the great religions of the world, and most of all to the religion that the majority of Your Lordships' house profess, and that we desire to the best of our ability to give them that opportunity of developing, in peace and quietness under British rule, those great gifts which hitherto they have been compelled to bring to fruition in countries that know not their language and belong not to their race? That is the ideal which I desire to see accomplished, that is the aim which lay at the root of the policy I am trying to defend; and though it be defensible indeed on every ground, that is the ground which chiefly moves me.[1]

This passage is essential to an understanding of Balfour's consistent advocacy of British support for the Zionist endeavour, but it should never be inferred that the Foreign Secretary urged the establishment of the National Home in Palestine irrespective of British

[1] See *Hansard*. House of Lords, June 21st, 1922.

ARTHUR JAMES BALFOUR

policy in the Middle East, or without considering the difficulties and risks of large-scale Jewish immigration into the midst of an established Arab population. In Balfour's opinion, the type of Jew likely to be attracted by the agricultural life of the Zionist settlements was also likely to be an element which would help to rescue Palestine from the desolation bequeathed by Ottoman rule. Here his vision of the future was keener than that of the majority of his contemporaries. A speech he delivered to a Zionist audience in London in 1920 may have been thought optimistic at that date even by some of his hearers.

> Men ask themselves [he said] how in these narrow limits [of Palestine], to be traversed in an automobile in an easy day's journey, were there good roads, from Dan to Beersheba—they ask themselves how that country can be made physically adequate to be the home for the self-development of the Jewish people. The problem presents difficulties which I myself should regard as overwhelming were we dealing with another people and with different conditions. . . . What are the two necessities? One is skill, knowledge, perseverance, enterprise; the other is capital; and I am perfectly convinced that when you are talking of the Jews you will find no want of any one of these requisites. Of skill, of knowledge, of all that the most modern methods can teach in the way of engineering or of agriculture, the Jewish race, who have themselves contributed to the result, can easily make themselves the master. And when I consider capital I am not thinking of the great millionaires. . . . I doubt not they will do their duty; but I am thinking of the innumerable Jews in the poorest circumstances who out of their poverty are prepared to contribute to the success of this enterprise.

All this has become almost a commonplace since Palestine, out of her own tax-payers' money, has built first-class roads, passing through orange groves, orchards and crops, in tracts of land which were tree-

ARAB FEELING

less swamp or arid desert when Balfour was speaking. It is clear to-day that his confidence was well founded on the economic side, but the further question will be rightly asked, whether he under-estimated the political objections to Jewish settlement. His speeches to Jewish audiences prove that he saw, more clearly than did some of their own leaders at that time, the danger to themselves from their political inexperience in the task of accommodating their new life to its Arab environment and to British ideas of administration. These speeches, it may be said in passing, are a remarkable illustration of the position Balfour held among Jews, which enabled advice or warning from a statesman of alien race to be so given or so received. It is from another point of view however that his attitude to Arab feeling must be examined.

For some time after the Balfour Declaration he was never called upon to express an opinion about the Arab attitude, for the simple reason that no hostility had been evinced by Sherif Hussein, Emir of Mecca, and his sons —then the acknowledged representatives of Arab nationalism—when they became aware of the promise of a National Home in Palestine for the Jews. They had no objection in fact to the policy in itself, as was proved by the attitude of the Emir Feisal at the Peace Conference, nor did they claim that it was a breach of any promise to themselves, for Palestine had been excluded from the area where the Arab right to independence had been admitted in the correspondence between the Sherif of Mecca and Sir Henry MacMahon, which preceded the entry of the Arabs into the War on the Allied side.[1]

Most of Syria on the other hand fell within these boundaries, and it was the refusal of the French to admit

1917

---

[1] These letters, never yet officially published in full, appeared in the French newspaper *Le Temps* on September 18th, 1919.

ARTHUR JAMES BALFOUR

1922 Arab claims there which forced the British Government to acquiesce in an arrangement at the expense of Arab aspirations in that region. The thing was already done in 1916, through the so-called " Sykes-Picot " Agreement, before Balfour became Foreign Secretary. This was in fact one of the " Secret Treaties " of which it was his duty to inform President Wilson, as narrated in the last chapter. The Agreement was altered again when he was no longer in charge of the Foreign Office, but the changes in its final form made no difference to the breach of faith with the Arabs, in so far as breach of faith there was. On that matter Balfour was always inclined to take a broad view.

> Of all the charges made against this country [he said in the House of Lords in June 1922], I must say that the charge that we have been unjust to the Arab race seems to me the strangest. It is through the expenditure, largely of British blood, by the exercise of British skill and valour . . . that the freeing of the Arab race from Turkish rule has been effected. And that we . . . who have just established a King in Mesopotamia, who had before that established an Arab king in the Hedjaz, and who have done more than has been done for centuries past to put the Arab race in the position to which they have attained—that we should be charged with being their enemies, with having taken a mean advantage of the course of international negotiations, seems to me not only unjust to the policy of this country, but almost fantastic in its extravagance.

This was all true. Nevertheless the withdrawal of the British from Syria had not a little to do with the beginnings of political agitation among the Palestinian Arabs against organised Jewish settlement in their midst. The prospect of a French Mandate over Syria was as unwelcome to the Syrian Arabs as to the Sherifian family at Mecca. The desire for independence grew, and inevitably the movement did not stop short at the

THE ARAB QUESTION

Syrian border. Arab politicians found that the Christian and Moslem Arabs of Palestine could most easily be united in a common cause by working up on their fears of Jewish domination and of eventual dispossession from the soil. The opportunity was exploited, and in those early years the work of fomenting discord was aided by the extravagant and provocative utterances of a small section of Zionists. The responsible Zionist leaders soon saw why Balfour always insisted on the need of discipline in the ranks, and on the difficulties that a politically inexperienced people would find in maintaining it.

1920

> You come [he said to a Jewish audience overflowing the Albert Hall in July 1920] from every nation under heaven, with ideas absorbed from the populations wherein you have sojourned. . . . You come with many different theories as to the method by which your common object may be carried out. . . . There is no harm in that; it only becomes dangerous when these different sections insist not merely that the object shall be carried out, but that it should be carried out precisely in the fashion that commends itself to them. Beware of that danger; I am not sure it is not the greatest danger which may beset you in the future.

The warning was uttered in connection with his estimate of their greatest difficulty—the Arab question.

> It will require tact, it will require judgment, it will require above all sympathetic good-will on the part both of Jew and Arab. So far as the Arabs are concerned —a great, an interesting, an attractive race—I hope they will remember that . . . among all the Great Powers, most especially Great Britain has freed them from the tyranny of their brutal conqueror, who had kept them under his heel for these many centuries. . . . I hope that, remembering all that, they will not grudge that small notch, for it is not more geographically, whatever it may be historically—that small notch in what are now Arab territories being given to the people who for all these hundreds of years have been separated from it.

ARTHUR JAMES BALFOUR

1914   The relations of Jews and Arabs in Palestine have passed through several crises in the years since Balfour said this. He lived to hear of the Arab outbreak against the Jews in August 1929, an event which reinforced the sceptics about the wisdom of the policy of 1917. His own confidence was not shaken. The Land League methods in old days in Ireland had inured him against being unduly impressed by organised agitation, and his own experiences in Palestine and Syria in 1925 (to be described in a later chapter) had proved to him again how easily the political agitator could turn the tap on and off.

So much for Balfour's attitude towards Zionist enterprise. It gave him a leading part in the drama of the Zionists' approach to the great Allied Powers during the War. The entry of Turkey into the conflict made the future of Palestine a practical question for the first time in living memory, for if the Allies were victorious the Ottoman Empire would surely break up. The autumn of 1914 was therefore the moment in history when Zionist Jews throughout the world were most desirous to meet and consult one another. It was also the moment when the international machinery of their organisation was paralysed by the division of Europe into opposing camps. The Executive body could not make contact; and the centre of gravity shifted in the first place to the handful of Zionist leaders in England. England had the strongest tradition of friendship for Jewry. England moreover was the country most likely to concern herself with the future of Palestine. Later on, the Zionist Committees of the United States enter into the story, but the first practical steps towards gaining the ear of powerful men were taken in Manchester. In that city there was a little group of ardent Zionists, most of them British Jews,

BRITISH SUPPORT

disciples of Dr. Chaim Weizmann, himself a Russian subject by birth, British by naturalisation before the War, and in 1914 still holding the post of Lecturer in Chemistry at Manchester University which he had filled at the time of his memorable meeting with Balfour in 1906. Round him gathered the others; some with names later familiar to wider circles, but most of them young, and all without personal influence in Whitehall. Yet, not without confidence, they set about to scale Olympus. In October 1914, Dr. Weizmann wrote to Dr. Schmarya Levin in America:

1914

> As soon as the situation is somewhat cleared up we could talk plainly to England and to France with regard to the abnormal situation of the Jews, having combatants in all armies, fighting everywhere, and being nowhere recognized. . . . Now is the time when the peoples of Great Britain, France and America will understand us. . . . The moral force of our claims will prove irresistible; the political considerations will be favourable. . . . But we must be ready for this moment when it comes. We must unite the great body of conscious Jews in Great Britain, America, Italy and France. The German and Austrian Jews will understand us later on.

Two of the Continental leaders came over to England, Mr. Sokolow and Mr. Tchlenow, and Dr. Weizmann went with them to London, furnished by Mr. C. P. Scott, of the *Manchester Guardian* (one of the earliest Englishmen to give open support to Zionism), with an introduction to the Chancellor of the Exchequer. Mr. Lloyd George's imagination was kindled. In the first place (Balfour always averred), because he knew his Bible. Dan and Beersheba meant more to him than Teschen. He sent the Zionists on to Mr. Herbert Samuel.[1] In this English Jew they discovered a friend. On December 14th, 1914, Dr. Weizmann had an

[1] President of the Local Government Board in Mr. Asquith's Ministry.

223

ARTHUR JAMES BALFOUR

1914 appointment to see Balfour, although Balfour was not as yet a member of Mr. Asquith's Government. Dr. Weizmann approached him by the advice of Professor Alexander of Manchester, himself a Jew, acquainted with Balfour as a brother philosopher. Dr. Weizmann found the conversation of eight years back still fresh in Balfour's memory. They went on with it, on abstract lines.

Balfour repeated some talk he had had with Frau Wagner in Bayreuth, two years before, on the position of German Jews. Frau Wagner had complained how Jews had captured the stage, the press, the Universities and commerce, and she expressed the resentment of Germany at being obliged to receive all culture at Jewish hands. Dr. Weizmann observed to Balfour that here was the very crux of the Jewish tragedy. The Jews who were giving their energy and brains to Germany were doing it as Germans, not as Jews. They were enriching Germany, not Jewry, and must sink their Judaism to put their brains at Germany's disposal. The Zionists could not accept them as Jews, yet the Germans did not recognise them as Germans. Thus the Jews stood the most exploited and most misunderstood of peoples.

Balfour was greatly struck, saying that he regretted having hitherto only come into personal contact with British Jews. Could he help Dr. Weizmann in any practical way? " Not while the guns are roaring," the other answered. " When the military situation becomes clearer I will come again."

" Mind you come again," said Balfour. " It is a great cause you are working for; I would like you to come again and again."[1]

[1] See Report to the Zionist Organisation Executive of January 7th, 1915, for Dr. Weizmann's account of this interview.

TENTATIVE IDEAS

The year 1915 passed before Dr. Weizmann took him at his word. The following was the year of the correspondence between the Sherif of Mecca and Sir Henry MacMahon, the year also of the secret Sykes-Picot Agreement between Great Britain and the French. The Zionists had not as yet access even to the corridors of the Government offices, though occasionally they met various Ministers in their homes. Thus, through Mr. Samuel, Sir Edward Grey's personal attitude was discovered. He was in full sympathy with the Zionist ideal, but afraid lest mention of a British Protectorate over Palestine might offend the French, and also some English Liberal opinion. The Liberal Cabinet would not be likely to commit themselves to any responsibility for Palestine. At the same time they did not want to see it in the hands of any other Great Power. They might favour the organisation of a Jewish Commonwealth there as an independent political unit. These views were not officially expressed, but the Zionists sensed them, and whenever a chance occurred they pressed the arguments for a British Protectorate.

> If Great Britain [wrote Dr. Weizmann] does not wish anybody else to have Palestine, this means that it will have to watch it and stop any penetration of another Power. Such a course involves as much responsibility as would be involved by a British Protectorate over Palestine, with the sole difference that watching is a much less efficient preventive than an actual Protectorate. I therefore thought that the middle course could be adopted: viz. the Jews take over the country; the whole burden of organisation falls on them, but for the next ten or fifteen years they work under a temporary British Protectorate.

These tentative ideas belong to a period before the Mandate system had been thought of. In 1915 the future of all enemy territory was hidden in the uncertainties of ultimate victory.

ARTHUR JAMES BALFOUR

1916 Therefore the Zionists did not yet press for official pronouncements, but spent most of their energy in trying to form a united front in all the Allied countries, and not least in the United States. They succeeded so well in this difficult task that when Balfour went to America in 1917 the ground was prepared for important talks there. In the meanwhile he saw Dr. Weizmann once or twice in 1916. The Zionist leader, who was also a brilliant scientist, had just put at the disposal of the British Government his discovery of a process for the manufacture of acetone upon which the supply of cordite for the battle-front depended.[1]

Dr. Weizmann was therefore working by now under the Admiralty. Balfour was First Lord, and Dr. Weizmann went one day to his room on official business. As the interview ended Balfour introduced the other subject. " You know, Dr. Weizmann, if the Allies win the War you may get your Jerusalem." He bade him call again, he wanted to discuss the Russian and English Jews. How could the Russian Jews be whole-hearted in the Allied cause, considering the treatment they had received? Dr. Weizmann explained how, to the Eastern Jew, who had preserved the tradition intact, Palestine was a hope, an article of faith. For many Western Jews the meaning had been lost. " But why should they oppose it? " Balfour asked. " Why can I afford to be a Zionist, and not they? " The Jew answered that nobody would challenge Balfour's position, but that anti-Semitism lurked even in England.

---

[1] See *War Memoirs*, by David Lloyd George, Vol. II, p. 584 *et seq.* for account of Dr. Weizmann's services to Great Britain in the matter. Mr. Lloyd George is not quite accurate in describing British policy in Palestine as a kind of *quid pro quo* for the patriotic action of the Zionist leader. The Balfour Declaration was not part of a bargain, nor a reward for services rendered.

NON-ZIONIST OPPOSITION

However good an Englishman a Jew might be, he was constantly challenged.[1] 1916

In the spring of this year, 1916, the Zionists began to make a little contact with the great Departments, whose goodwill would be at least as necessary as the sympathy of Ministers when the moment really came for them to step into the arena of Allied politics.

The spokesmen of certain bodies of non-Zionist Jews were beforehand with them at the Foreign Office, throwing all their weight into other plans for helping the Jews in the Russian Empire and elsewhere. They pressed upon the Foreign Office a formula for a Palestine policy acknowledging nothing more than " the historic interest " taken in that country by their " community." The word " race " was not used. The Zionists were in ignorance of the existence of this formula for some time after it had been submitted to the Foreign Office, and it is probable that the anti-Zionists were not fully aware of the interest in Zionism taken by some Ministers. There were honest efforts nevertheless to find a common ground for united appeal; but the gulf was too wide, and there was a breach in the summer of 1917, after which the British non-Zionist Committee worked openly to hinder the granting of the Balfour Declaration. But once the policy was settled, the bulk of Anglo-Jewry supported it, at any rate in theory. The non-Zionist standpoint never particularly impressed the Foreign Office, which in 1916 began some investigations of its own into the views of the Governments of France and Russia. The French were found doubtful at that stage, the Russians sympathetic.

Zionism was now on the brink of being launched into

[1] See *The New Judæa*, March-April, 1930, for Dr. Weizmann's account of this interview.

ARTHUR JAMES BALFOUR

1916 the current. "Before long politicians will be unable to brush it aside as the fantastic dream of a few idealists." So wrote the first Lord Cromer in July 1916.[1]

By October events forced the Zionist leaders to begin testing the sympathy they had been garnering in the past two years. Palestine was still a Turkish province, but vast transformations were taking place outside. Russia was drifting out of the War. There were signs that the United States would soon be pulled in. More than half the Jews in the world lived in those two countries. Never again would Jewish opinion be a matter of more concern to all the belligerent States. In fact, before many months were past the Foreign Office were noting with interest hints in the German Press of the possibility of a Jewish State in Palestine, of course under Turkish supremacy.

In October 1916, therefore, the Zionists submitted their first formal programme to the Foreign Office (still ruled over by Sir Edward Grey). Something hardly less significant happened in the same month. Dr. Weizmann and Mr. Sokolow were allowed to communicate with each other and with other Zionist leaders abroad, by sending telegrams through the Foreign Office, which transmitted them in code.

At the end of 1916 Mr. Lloyd George formed the Second Coalition Government, and Balfour as Foreign Secretary became the Minister most directly concerned with these affairs. He had only just taken charge when, on February 2nd, 1917, serious negotiations were really started. On that day Sir Mark Sykes came to a meeting of Zionist leaders to hear and discuss their desires. It is a pity that Mark Sykes's Life tells so little of how he became a convert to the Zionist idea early in the War. It seems that his first approach

[1] See the *Spectator*, July 1917.

GREAT VISIONS

was along parallel lines with Balfour's. "It was his Catholicism," Mr. Shane Leslie says, "that assisted Mark to understand the Jewish tragedy. He was interested in the ethos of the real Hebrew, not of the Anglicised Jew."[1]

1916

When it came to practical politics, Sykes brought a knowledge of the Middle East and its peoples which Balfour could not supply. "The connection of the Arab State with a liberated Caliphate in the Moslem world, and the realisation of Zionism for the Jews, seemed to assure a new future."[2]

> It might be the destiny of the Jewish race [Sir Mark Sykes said to a Jewish audience] to be the bridge between Asia and Europe, to bring the spirituality of Asia to Europe, and the vitality of Europe to Asia. . . . No British Jew will be less British because he can look at the cradle of his race with pride. You know the Semite sleeps but never dies. To-day the Arabs are seven or eight millions. There is a combination of man-power, virgin soil, petroleum, and brains. In 1950 Baghdad, Damascus and Aleppo will be each as big as Manchester. Therefore I warn Jews to look through Arab glasses.[3]

These were wise words, and great visions. Sykes the Zionist was the same man who designed the flag of Arab liberation: "Black fess for the Abbasids of Baghdad, white for the Ommayads of Damascus, green for the Alids of Kerbela, and red chevron for Mudhar heredity."[4] He wore himself to death, interpreting Arab and Zionist aspirations to each other and to the politicians of the West. His influence was enormous. If he had survived to assist the working out of his dreams, nationalities on both sides of the Jordan might be nearer towards harmony to-day.

[1] See *Mark Sykes: His Life and Letters*, by Shane Leslie, p. 269.
[2] *Ibid.*, p. 270.   [3] *Ibid.*, p. 272.   [4] *Ibid.*, p. 280.

ARTHUR JAMES BALFOUR

1917   The Zionists soon heard, in the tone of their best friends, the hard note of reality. Dr. Weizmann's first interview with Balfour at the Foreign Office in March 1917, was concerned with difficulties arising from French and Italian claims in Palestine. Balfour suggested that, failing agreement with France, it might be best to aim at a joint Anglo-American Protectorate. Dr. Weizmann felt doubtful of the prospects of working under two masters, whose general principles of administration might be far apart. But he and his friends were much more perturbed by rumours of a Franco-British division of Palestine, leaving Tiberias and part of Galilee in French hands. This was in fact the line of the Sykes-Picot Agreement, news of which had leaked out. Alarmed by this, and more so by stories of decisions to internationalise the rest of the country, the Zionists determined to present their case to the critical spirits at the Quai d'Orsay, as they had already done in London. How they prevailed does not come into this story; but the upshot was cabled across the Atlantic by Mr. Sokolow from Paris to the American Zionists on April 24th, 1917. The French Foreign Office had agreed that an Allied victory in the Middle East would mean recognition of Zionism.

Dr. Weizmann and his group were now making superhuman efforts to mobilise the scattered nation in every Allied country for a united demand for a British Protectorate over a Jewish Commonwealth in Palestine. American support was essential. The Zionists there had for leader Mr. Justice Brandeis, an American-born Jew, a Judge of the Supreme Court, a great figure in the world of law and politics, to whom President Wilson himself was readily accessible, a man who could meet a British Secretary of State on equal terms. This was important, for Balfour was in America for a month during this decisive period in Jewish affairs.

In the United States as elsewhere, the Jewish magnates were still hostile to the national movement. As late as January 1918, our Ambassador in Washington reported,[1] on the authority of Mr. Justice Brandeis himself, that the Zionists " were violently opposed by the great capitalists, and by the Socialists, for different reasons." This in itself shows how baseless was the idea, once very prevalent, that the Balfour Declaration was in part a bargain with American financiers.

Palestinian policy was however one of the subjects on which Balfour definitely intended to explore American feeling. He was introduced to Mr. Justice Brandeis at a party at the White House almost immediately after his arrival in Washington. " You are one of the Americans I had wanted to meet," he said, and a day or two later they had the first of one or two talks. Balfour remarked to Lord Eustace Percy, a member of his Mission, that Brandeis was in some ways the most remarkable man he had met in the United States. It seems from such notes of these conversations as survive, that Balfour pledged his own personal support to Zionism. He had done it before to Dr. Weizmann, but now he was British Foreign Secretary.

Mr. Justice Brandeis seems to have become increasingly emphatic, during the course of the British Mission's visit, about the desire of American Zionists to see a British Administration in Palestine. He gave no great encouragement to the idea of United States participation, observing that the bulk of American citizens were still opposed to the War, and would not wish to undertake responsibilities outside it. Dr. Weizmann's letters and

[1] Letter to Mr. Balfour. See *Letters and Friendships of Cecil Spring Rice*, Vol. II, p. 421.

1917 telegrams were keeping him shrewdly informed of the British point of view. England, Dr. Weizmann said, was not yearning to annex Palestine, and would hardly care to oppose the internationalisation which would be fatal to Zionist hopes, except for the attraction that the idea of large-scale Jewish settlement was beginning to have for her. Hence, Zionist policy must be to keep to that simple demand for a British Protectorate, rejecting all other schemes which would tend to raise fresh jealousies, and bring about some joint control. The American Zionists grasped the point. A Jewish national diplomacy was in being.

In Balfour's absence the Foreign Office had been left in charge of Lord Robert Cecil, with whom Dr. Weizmann had a long interview, expounding the objections to an Anglo-French division of Palestine, which he called "a Solomon's judgment of the worst kind." Lord Robert, already almost as convinced a Zionist as Balfour, was impressed. By the end of April, the Foreign Office recognised, with some slight dismay, that the British Government was virtually committed. Early in June Balfour was home from America, assured by his conversations with Mr. Justice Brandeis, and by what he had learned from him of the President's attitude, that there would be active sympathy there. (There is no evidence that he discussed Palestine with Mr. Wilson himself.) The idea of United States co-operation still lingered a little in his mind.

> Personally [he wrote, in a Foreign Office Minute of June 13th], I should still prefer to associate the U.S.A. in the Protectorate should we succeed in securing it.

Before the end of June 1917, negotiations entered their final phase. Dr. Weizmann, now accompanied by Lord Rothschild, called upon Balfour at the Foreign

THE BALFOUR DECLARATION

Office and put it to him that the time for a definite **1917**
Declaration of support and encouragement was come.
Balfour asked them for a draft which he would put
before the War Cabinet for sanction. By August it
was in a form he was prepared to sponsor. Here is the
final text of the Charter of Jewish national rights—the
" Balfour Declaration."

> His Majesty's Government view with favour the establishment in Palestine of a national home for the Jewish people, and will use their best endeavours to facilitate the achievement of this object, it being clearly understood that nothing shall be done which may prejudice the civil and religious rights of the existing non-Jewish communities in Palestine or the rights and political status enjoyed by Jews in any other country.

The struggle in the War Cabinet was not over till
early in November. Mr. Montagu opened his offensive
late in August with a Memorandum of passionate
protest. The Cabinet was more than shaken, for on
September 24th Balfour replied to a grumble over the
continued delay, made by one of his own Foreign
Office people.

" Yes. But as this question was (in my absence)
decided by the Cabinet against the Zionists I cannot
do anything till the decision is reversed."

He wrote " *till* "—not " *unless.*"

The difficulties with France having been cleared up,
the Foreign Office was in fact now anxious to reap all
the immediate advantage there might be in the Declaration. It was apparently expected to have some direct
result on the Russian Revolution, then passing out of
its Menshevik phase. Lenin and Trotsky took power
in the same week of November 1917 that Jewish
nationalism won its recognition. Years before in
Geneva, Trotsky and Weizmann had night after night

ARTHUR JAMES BALFOUR

1917 expounded from rival cafés in the University quarter their opposite political philosophies. Both of them Russian born, both of them orators, both of them geniuses, they had swayed the crowds of Jewish students from one side of the street to the other. Round the marble-topped tables, often garnished only with the cruet-stand, the carafe of water, and the tooth-picks that the management provided free, they argued till the dawn with their generation. Leon Trotsky, apostle of Red Revolution—Chaim Weizmann, apostle of a tradition unbroken through two thousand years. Now by a most strange coincidence in the same week each of them accomplished the fulfilment of his dream.

Elemental forces were at work here which might destroy, but not influence one another. The English departmental mind hardly took the measure of either. " A pity our Declaration did not come four months earlier," one high official wrote. " It might have made all the difference in Russia." This remark was evoked by a description sent by the British Consul at Odessa, of a two-miles long procession of Jews marching past the Consulate, their bands alternately playing " God Save the King " and the Hatikvah, the Jewish National Anthem. A crowd of over a hundred thousand Russians watched them, with how much comprehension it is hard to say.

In other Allied countries, and in the United States, the Declaration caused demonstrations of the wildest enthusiasm among the Jewish masses. A great wave of friendliness flowed towards Britain and its effect was none the less great for being imponderable.

Before the end of the year 1917 Lord Allenby dismounted from his horse outside the Damascus Gate of Jerusalem, to enter the Holy City on foot. Palestine was in British military occupation, and so remained

BELIEF IN IDEALISM

until the final approval of the Mandate by the League of Nations in 1922. [1917]

Three years later in April 1925, Balfour himself went to Palestine as the guest of the Zionist Organisation, to open the Hebrew University at Jerusalem, and to see the beginnings of the National Home in the new towns and colonies in the northern plains. That visit will be described in a later chapter. Otherwise, his interest in the Zionist enterprise remained too continuous to be told here in detail, without at the same time describing all the vicissitudes of contemporary Palestinian history.

Balfour's Zionism displays a facet of his character which stands out in this, because the circumstances that produced it were unique. The Jewish question served to bring to the surface a never dormant belief in the force of idealism, and a courage in backing his belief. He looked upon Zionism as having provided one of his two greatest opportunities in life, his work as Chief Secretary for Ireland being the other. Near the end of his days he said to me that on the whole he felt that what he had been able to do for the Jews had been the thing he looked back upon as the most worth his doing.

Chapter XII

FOREIGN MINISTER IN WAR-TIME

Balfour's view of political bearing of military problems. Relations with Lloyd George. Sir Maurice Hankey. Balfour defends Lord Hardinge. Balfour's Memorandum on proposals of General Staff. Peace proposals of 1917. Balfour's view of them. The " Lansdowne Peace Letter." War Aims. Policy towards the Bolsheviks.

1917 When Balfour seated himself for the first time at the big writing-table in the Secretary of State's room at the Foreign Office, certain associations must have stirred within him. How often he had opened that door, and seen Lord Salisbury's massive form filling that chair. How much of his own training in international affairs had been acquired within those very walls, from the lips of one of the most autocratic and secretive Foreign Secretaries in our history. And how much of the great Salisburian tradition must now be jettisoned if the Foreign Secretary in Mr. Lloyd George's Government was to play the part he had determined upon when he accepted office in the Second Coalition. Under such a Prime Minister, and at such a moment, it was useless to try to apply the old rules, or to stand upon the old dignities. Lord Curzon's efforts to maintain them, later on, only led him to alternating paroxysms of anger and mortification. Balfour avoided these paralysing emotions, not only by temperament but because he recognised that the exigencies of the times demanded the single command

THE DOUBLE PROBLEM

in the council room as much as in the field. Something of his attitude to this, and to the situation in general, is revealed in a letter to Lord Robert Cecil dated September 12th, 1917. It was called forth by a French proposal for the diversion of a number of big guns to the Italian front.

> I do not think [Balfour wrote] that any neat or clear-cut principles can be laid down by which hard cases can be solved by rule. Each must, I fear, be taken separately, and dealt with, as far as may be, on its merits. One of the fundamental difficulties of the situation is that the distinctions between what are respectively political reasons and military reasons for any given policy are practically arbitrary, . . . and those who have ultimately to decide must take both sets of reasons into account.
>
> Now in many of the great wars in which the country has been engaged we have had men who were experts in both branches of policy :—Marlborough for example, and Wellington. In the case of the two Pitts the political side of military operations was better understood than the purely military or naval side. But the elder Pitt was assisted by men of genius like Hawke, Clive and Wolfe; and the younger Pitt had Nelson. I do not know that the historian is likely to admit that we have produced either Chathams or Nelsons. We have certainly got neither Marlboroughs nor Wellingtons.
>
> Moreover, it must be remembered that among the most important political considerations which have a direct military value is co-operation with the Allies. In the Seven Years War and the Napoleonic wars this co-operation . . . was far easier to manage. The division of effort between the Allied Powers was well marked. We provided money, and we dominated the ocean; they did their best to provide armies for the Continent. . . .
>
> Things are very different now, and the result is a complication of the problem, which makes it quite impossible to treat it as " military " in the narrow sense of the word, and impossible therefore to leave it to the management of soldiers and sailors. I am by no means sure that the War

1917 Committee have taken the right course about sending guns to Italy. . . . But can we regard Haig, or even Robertson, as impartial judges in such a controversy? Both of them have staked their last shilling on the theory that the war must be decided on the Western Front; both of them have the profoundest distrust of the military capacity of our Allies. . . . Neither of them is specially qualified to deal with either Anglo-French, or Anglo-Italian problems. We cannot, in such a case as this, hand over the final decision to them on the ground that they are military experts and that we are not.

Balfour was not a main protagonist in the controversies between the Cabinet and the Higher Command, which were among the most unsatisfactory features of the winter of 1917–1918. In November Mr. Lloyd George made up his mind about the necessity for establishing a Supreme War Council composed of representatives of the Governments of Great Britain, France and Italy, to meet at Versailles once a month, without executive power, but with the aim of improving Allied co-ordination in military effort. In a speech which he made in Paris Mr. Lloyd George used very plain language about the waste of life and resources due to the lack of real unity. The new War Council was accepted unwillingly by the Army Council, and with suspicion in many quarters. Balfour however wrote to Lord Robert Cecil on November 19th:

> As regards the new Paris machinery, he would be a rash man who would say it was going to succeed. It certainly will not succeed if the personages concerned—military and political—try not to make it work. But I cannot believe the present system is satisfactory; and the only other alternative . . . is the one towards which the French are evidently going to press us,—namely a single Commander-in-Chief for *all* the Armies, and that a Frenchman. Of such a solution I confess myself profoundly distrustful.
>
> In the meantime it seems to me that with Russia in

A. J. BALFOUR AND LORD HAIG
1918

dissolution, Italy in defeat, and France just emerging from a political crisis, there can be few greater calamities . . . than a break-up of the Government—however agreeable from a personal point of view such a consummation might be!

Let me add I do not see the theoretical difficulty . . . of the Government under the new system having two sets of military advisers instead of one. If the responsibility for general policy rests really, and not merely nominally, with the Government, it seems to me absurd to lay it down, as an inviolable principle, that they should only get their technical advice from a single source—though no doubt this might save them a great deal of trouble.

To anybody who sought his advice Balfour steadfastly expounded his own point of view about the form of public duty required in war-time. In February 1918, he was asked by the War Cabinet to use personal persuasion on General Robertson either to accept the post of British Military Representative on the Supreme War Council as successor to Sir Henry Wilson or to retain his post of Chief of the Imperial General Staff with somewhat reduced powers. He made note of their talk:

> I did my best to persuade him (General Robertson) that the responsibility of refusing a great position at the most critical moment of the war was one which he was hardly justified in taking. Extreme cases might be conceived in which the machine to be worked was so obviously fated to break down that no man could be required to undertake the duty of working it. But it seemed to me, . . . though I had nothing to do with the contrivance of the Versailles plan, that with a little good will it could be made to work smoothly and efficiently; and that, if this were so, I thought he should consider it his duty to work the plan. We discussed the subject on these lines for over half an hour; I regret to say with no result at all.
>
> General Robertson was very anxious that the scheme should be so modified that the Military Member at Versailles should be subordinate and representative of the C.I.G.S.

1918   In that case he would be quite ready either to retain the position of Chief of the Staff, or to go to Versailles.

I had however no commission from the Cabinet to discuss a scheme, which had, I gathered, already been rejected at the late Conference, nor indeed was I qualified to do so.

These letters show the spirit which animated Balfour's co-operation in Mr. Lloyd George's first Cabinet; the spirit of consistent loyalty not so much to the trusted leader as to the irreplaceable person. The attitude was probably not maintained entirely and always without effort, but signs of effort were fleeting and slight. Only in the private correspondence with old friends whose attitude was less philosophical, some such remark as this is occasionally to be found :

> We all unfortunately suffer from the P.M.'s method—or lack of method—of doing business, and must keep our tempers as best we can.

One of Mr. Lloyd George's "methods of doing business" which gave rise to a good deal of contemporary criticism, does not appear to have caused Balfour any perturbation at all. The Prime Minister established a private Secretariat, working in huts erected in the garden of No. 10 Downing Street, supplying him with information and advice on various aspects of his vast range of responsibilities, and notably on Foreign Affairs. The influence of this "Garden Suburb" was inevitably suspect in the Foreign Office across the way, and resentment may sometimes have been fed by real cases of confusion, very upsetting to Departmental routine.[1] But there is no evidence that while Balfour

[1] The Foreign Office itself had brought in from various quarters experts on the territorial and other problems raised by the War, notably in its Political Intelligence Department, which reached its maximum in numbers and efficiency under Balfour, and included such authorities as the late Sir James Headlam-Morley, Mr. L. B. Namier and Messrs. R. and A. Leeper, etc.

BALFOUR FOREIGN SECRETARY

was Foreign Secretary any important step in foreign policy was undertaken without his knowledge, at any rate after his return from the United States.

His successor, Lord Curzon, may or may not have had cause for the suspicions which tortured him in this respect.[1] Certain, however, it is that Balfour would never have submitted for an instant to mental torment of that kind. Deliberate as was his policy of "a free hand for the Little Man," it would not have stretched to toleration of anything really impairing to the work of his own Office. But on the other hand, he suffered from no taboos about official routine. Many a time in the great years gone by he had listened to the wailings of the Foreign Office when Lord Salisbury carried off his papers to Hatfield, dealt with them there in the solitude of his study, and preserved no record of the process. And yet the prestige of Britain had not declined in those days. The cases were not parallel, but it is more than probable that Balfour was confident in his own power to prevent any echo of two voices in British foreign policy reaching the sharpest ears abroad. His own easy relations with Mr. Lloyd George were a safeguard. In the terrific pressure of the war years access to the Prime Minister was not always immediately possible even to his colleagues. But Balfour had only to turn the handle of the door and saunter in. There is no record of these interviews, not less important than the War Cabinet meetings. The Foreign Secretary was not a member of the War Cabinet, but alone among the Departmental Ministers was given the right to attend whenever he thought fit. The extent to which he exercised that privilege is shown by the fact that out of more than five hundred meetings held under the Second Coalition Government, he was present in

[1] See *Curzon: The Last Phase*, by H. Nicolson, pp. 59 *et seq.*

1917 person at more than three hundred, and represented by Lord Robert Cecil at over a hundred more. This without counting his attendance at fifty-five special meetings convened to consider super-secret subjects.

The risks of sudden decisions being taken without consultation were thus reduced to a minimum. Moreover through the personality and position of Sir Maurice Hankey, the Secretary to the War Cabinet, Mr. Lloyd George and Balfour could both be certain that no break in the chain of vital communications would be allowed. Sir Maurice had their complete confidence—in Balfour's case I know that he had it in superlative degree. He saw them both daily, often hourly. It was rare during this period not to find him any day at the luncheon table in Carlton Gardens. Balfour speaking about this present book, during the last year of his own life, charged me to try to bring out the immense value to Ministers, and particularly to himself, of Sir Maurice's qualities of loyalty, wisdom, and absolute discretion during the Coalition Government and later at the Peace Conference.

I remembered how one day soon after Balfour's return from Paris he had stopped when out walking and, striking his stick upon the road, had exclaimed: "I tell you that without Hankey we should not have won the War!" Reminded of this he said: "Well! I don't think I exaggerated!"

Almost as soon as Balfour came back from America, he was called upon to defend his own Permanent Under Secretary against attack in the House of Commons. The Debate upon the Report of the Commission appointed to enquire into the conduct of the campaign in Mesopotamia would normally not have concerned the Foreign Secretary, but only the India Office, and the Indian Government. It happened however that Lord Hardinge, who had been Viceroy

LORD HARDINGE

when the Mesopotamian Expedition was equipped, had now returned to England as permanent head of the Foreign Office. His responsibility for mismanagement which had led to ghastly suffering for our troops was really as nominal as that of the Secretary of State for India, Sir Austen Chamberlain. But when the Report was published in July 1917, Sir Austen Chamberlain insisted on resigning, and Lord Hardinge pressed to be allowed to do the same. Three times, while the Report was under discussion by Parliament, Balfour refused his request, and on July 18th took upon himself the sole responsibility, not only for the refusal, but for encouraging Lord Hardinge to take part in the Debate on the Report in the House of Lords. This Lord Hardinge had done, and thereby had swelled the murmurings of the public inside and outside the House of Commons, which was in a mood to look for a scapegoat. Efforts by the Government to constitute a judicial tribunal, before which both officers and civilians could be heard, had failed to satisfy the House. Finally it was decided to let the soldiers appear before the Army Council and to take no further steps, since the War was still raging, and it was no time for "witch hunting." Parliament however demanded a Debate.

The return of a Viceroy to resume the position of a civil servant was without precedent; the intervention of a civil servant in debate hardly less so. But Balfour felt entirely at his ease in defending it. He laid it down that Lord Hardinge's speech in the House of Lords was correct, because the subject of discussion did not concern the Foreign Office. As for permitting his resignation, the House had refused to constitute a tribunal which could have judged not only his responsibility for Mesopotamia, but that of every Minister in the Coalition Government.

ARTHUR JAMES BALFOUR

1918

All are equally responsible [Balfour said]. And it makes my blood boil to think . . . that only one man whom you suppose you can attack with impunity, should be sacrificed, when, if he was guilty, multitudes are no less guilty than he.

After this debate Balfour received a number of letters.

> The whole Civil Service ought to be grateful to you [wrote one great Permanent Official] for the gallant stand you made on Hardinge's behalf. Nobody else could, or would, play the part.

Balfour was fortunate in his staff. With Lord Robert Cecil at his side, and such permanent officials as Lord Hardinge, Sir Eric Drummond, and not least, Sir Eyre Crowe, for whose mind and methods he had the greatest admiration, he could, and did, leave a good deal of a Foreign Minister's routine work to others. But although now in his seventieth year, his natural force was in no way abated. His power and will to defend his Department is illustrated by a paper addressed to the General Staff, which had rashly proffered criticism of British diplomatic action in a country remote from the theatre of war. To appreciate fully the sharpness of a pen that never inflicted the slightest hurt unintentionally, it should be remembered that the following Memorandum was written in the midst of the great advance of the German armies upon the Marne.

May 13th, 1918.

The General Staff has taken advantage of the leisure provided for them by the German offensive, to circulate a paper telling the Cabinet how the State Department at Washington and the Foreign Office in London are mismanaging our relations with the Republic of Mexico. I am grateful to the General Staff for their assistance, but would respectfully point out that their method of rendering it is not very convenient. If one Office finds subject of

A MEMORANDUM

comment or criticism in the policy of another, it should discuss it in private, and only bring it up for decision by the Cabinet if the differences between the Departments prove to be both impossible or irreconcilable.

I do not for a moment suggest that the General Staff have no interest in Mexican affairs. Though they cannot themselves land a corporal's guard to protect the oil-fields, it is true that Mexico, like every other country in the world, may influence for good or evil our military fortunes. But personally I think that their fears in this particular case are very greatly exaggerated. They are seemingly of opinion that unless we can scold President Wilson into a policy of conjoint action with France and Britain, involving an immediate revolution in Mexico, America will divert half a million men from the French to the Mexican frontier, and that for months to come American reinforcements will be kept on the wrong side of the Atlantic. Believing all this they are naturally anxious, but their anxiety affords no justification for their procedure. Let them consider the converse case. Let them remember that while diplomatic failures may hamper the Army, military failures make the Foreign Office helpless. But what then? Because the General Staff have not been fortunate enough to oil the wheels of diplomacy with a few dramatic victories, am I to ask the members of my Department to draw up alternative plans of military operations for immediate consideration by the Cabinet? No Cabinet could work under such conditions. Every Government Department has its shortcomings, and all the other Government Departments are very sensible of them. But to suppose that things would be improved by each Department usurping the functions of its neighbour, and without previous consultation attempting to impose its particular nostrum by the sheer weight of Cabinet authority, would ruin any system of Government, and paralyse the energies of even the most patient and hard-working Administration.

A. J. B.

The reactions of the War Office to this rebuke are not recorded. What would they have been in Germany

1918 if any politician had addressed a similar reproof to the Great General Staff? What might have been the effect upon history if the German Foreign Office had, at any time during the War, been under a Minister as capable as Balfour of defending the citadel of political action against irruptions from the military authorities?

When the ice-pack thaws, the danger to navigation begins. Balfour prepared a Memorandum for the War Cabinet on September 20th, 1917, which opens:

> From the Foreign Office point of view we have now reached the most critical and difficult stage of the War . . . the middle stage, when fighting has lost none of its violence, when all the natural channels of diplomacy are still choked, but when, nevertheless, some at least of the belligerents are endeavouring to start informal conversations about terms of peace.

Advances, hesitating and inconclusive though they were, had actually come from Bulgaria, Turkey and Austria; and the Foreign Office had heard through our Ambassador in Spain that the Berlin Foreign Office, where von Kühlmann now presided, wanted to enter into conversations with the British Government. The Spanish Government was an orthodox channel, and Balfour felt that the proposal must not be ignored; the war spirit would be strengthened in Germany, but weakened in England, if we seemed to be fighting on for fighting's sake.

> I have little doubt [Balfour went on] that Kühlmann would greatly prefer that the conversations with the British Government that he desires, should be kept secret. . . . If his object is to make mischief among the Allied Powers his best course is to carry on negotiations secretly until they have reached a stage that lends itself to misrepresentation, and then betray them. If, . . . as I am inclined to believe, he is genuinely anxious to find a basis for settlement, this end might well seem to him easier of attainment

if he begins . . . with a dialogue rather than a general debate.

. . . . . .

I suggest that the Cabinet should authorise me to call together the Allied Ambassadors, and tell them that a neutral Power had informed us that Germany was desirous of entering into conversations with us, . . . and that in our opinion it would be wise to listen to any proposals that she might have to make, it being clearly understood that we should at once communicate them to our Allies.

. . . . . .

I doubt whether (the Germans) would ever consent even to our communicating their purpose to the Great Powers of the Entente; but this we must risk. Indeed, if I am to speak my whole mind, I am by no means sure that a refusal on their part to proceed further in the matter —and on such a ground—would not, *at the moment*, be the best thing that could happen to us.

Mr. Lloyd George went to Paris and talked the matter over with the French. He discovered, as Balfour had suspected, that tempting approaches had been made to them, and that they were highly suspicious of a trap. Balfour's way of handling the situation was agreed to, and after he had met the Allied Ambassadors on October 8th, he telegraphed to Madrid the British willingness "to receive any communication that the German Government may desire to make to them relating to peace, and to discuss it with their Allies." No answer to this telegram ever came from Berlin.

The Memorandum of September 20th sets beyond doubt Balfour's views about peace negotiation in the autumn of 1917. He clearly did not judge the time to be ripe, but would not have refused to enter into serious conversations with Germany. The Conference between the Central Powers and the Bolsheviks at Brest-Litovsk was soon to show that Germany was in fact nowhere

1917 near ready for negotiations on terms that the Allies would accept. The true mind of Austria was less understood in England. Balfour's diplomacy has been criticised in this regard. "I am sure that we could have detached Austria," wrote Lord Esher to Lord Lansdowne in December 1917, "if we had had the skill to make her definite peace offers six months ago."[1] But the matter did not in practice turn out to be so easy. In the same month General Smuts, representing the British Government, held secret and unofficial conversations in Geneva with Count Mensdorff. Nothing came of them, for the Austrian could hold out no hope whatever of his country separating herself from Germany during the War. And indeed, although Austria was already hysterically anxious for peace, it had to be a peace arranged with both the Central Empires, if Hapsburg domination was to survive. The Germanic elements in Austria in control then, and in control till the end, must cling to Germany, as cling they did until the final crash in October 1918. When Germany accepted President Wilson's terms, Austria joined in with her in pathetic agreement.

Some of Balfour's comments upon General Smuts' efforts explain the coolness with which he viewed the "peace-feelers" of that date.

> This brings out clearly [he wrote, for the War Cabinet on December 15th] the main danger incident to negotiations at the present moment. If we make proposals fully satisfactory to all our Allies they will be regarded as utterly unreasonable by all our enemies. If on the other hand we make tentative qualifications in their extreme demands, and the negotiations nevertheless break down, (as I rather think they will) then we shall have given a most powerful instrument into the hands of our foes, for making mischief between us and our friends.

[1] See *Life of Lord Lansdowne*, p. 471.

PEACE TALK

The public could not of course be told anything about the receptivity of the Government towards such overtures as that of Kühlmann in September, and the Austrian overtures which sent General Smuts to Geneva in December. It may be that Balfour did not feel himself at liberty to speak of these matters even to Lord Lansdowne, who consulted him orally some time in the first half of November about his own desire to elicit a fresh statement of War Aims from the British Government by means of a parliamentary question. It seems that in this conversation Balfour either asked or agreed that Lord Lansdowne should formulate for him, in writing, his views on the situation, framing the kind of statement he would like to see made in Parliament. Balfour received a Memorandum, together with a covering letter from Lord Lansdowne on November 16th.[1] His reply begins: " I do not know that this is a very suitable time for discussing peace matters. I rather think not." The letter goes on to define Balfour's own views on certain war aims. He did not desire any dismemberment of Germany, "if by Germany is meant that part of Central Europe that properly belongs to the German people." Neither Alsace-Lorraine nor " historic Poland " could thus be claimed. These observations would apply *mutatis mutandis* to Austria also. He did not desire to see the destruction of Germany and Austria as " trading communities." As for the " Freedom of the Seas " it concerned the whole world, and could not be decided at a Conference between belligerents alone.[2]

Lord Lansdowne gave up the idea of a parliamentary

[1] Both documents were published in the *Nineteenth Century* in March 1934. A copy of the Memorandum exists among Balfour's papers, but the original of the covering letter has not been found.
[2] This letter has been published in the *Life of Lord Lansdowne*, by Lord Newton (p. 464), and also in the *Nineteenth Century* article.

1917 statement, but told Balfour that he proposed to put his own views before the public in the form of a letter. This was in fact the celebrated letter published in the *Daily Telegraph* of November 29th under the title of " Co-ordination of Allied War Aims." Lord Lansdowne spoke to Balfour of his intention to send it, on November 26th. They had met outside St. Margaret's, Westminster, and Balfour was going to Paris for a Council that night. A note found among Lord Lansdowne's papers after his death gives his recollection of what passed.

> I agreed [he wrote] to abandon action in Parliament, and admitted that it might be undesirable to press the Government. I therefore proposed to put my view before the public in the form of a letter. He [i.e. Balfour] did not dissuade me. I said I was anxious not to publish anything misleading, or which might seem unfair to the F.O., that I would gladly have shown him my draft, but that was impossible, as he was leaving at 8.30 that evening. Did he object to my showing the draft to Hardinge, in order that he might tell me if the letter contained any inaccuracies? He assented, adding: " Hardinge knows my thoughts." I showed my letter to Hardinge. He made one or two suggestions not touching questions of principle. He observed that it was " statesmanlike " and " would do good."[1]

This so far has been the only published first-hand account of the hurried conversation between Balfour and Lord Lansdowne in the street. But five days after the publication of the " Lansdowne Letter," Balfour, in a Memorandum circulated to the War Cabinet, wrote his own impressions of how the matter had been left. In respect of Lord Lansdowne's intention to write a letter he says:

> I agreed to this procedure, assuming, as I was surely entitled to do, that the Letter would contain those parts of

[1] See *Nineteenth Century*, March 1934, for full text of this Note.

his proposed Question (i.e. in the House of Lords) to which I had raised no objection, and would contain nothing else of moment. It was of course only in reference to the subject thus restricted that I authorised any appeal to Lord Hardinge while I was absent in Paris. Lord Hardinge was quite qualified to represent my views on these points, and it was only with regard to them that I authorised his being consulted.

Here was a very serious mutual misunderstanding. It explains why Balfour was content to leave so important a matter to Lord Hardinge without giving him any instructions. Lord Hardinge was not wrong in believing that the Foreign Secretary had desired him to be consulted as a technical expert. On leaving the Foreign Office Lord Lansdowne took his letter in the first place to Mr. Geoffrey Dawson, Editor of *The Times*, who endeavoured to persuade him to hold it up, partly because he thought that Lord Lansdowne's statement that Balfour had approved the letter, might be founded on misunderstanding, and also because he considered that its publication would be inopportune at a moment when the leading members of the Government were all in Paris. Mr. Dawson believed that he had succeeded in persuading Lord Lansdowne to withhold publication. On November 29th, however, the morning following their second discussion of the matter, the letter appeared in the *Daily Telegraph*, for which it had been accepted by Lord Burnham.

On December 1st, Reuter's[1] issued a *communiqué* which was published in *The Times* saying:

> It is authentically stated that the following is the view of His Majesty's Government with regard to Lord Lansdowne's Letter:—Lord Lansdowne in his Letter only spoke for himself. Before writing it he did not consult, nor has he been in communication with any member of the

[1] I have been unable to trace its origin further.

ARTHUR JAMES BALFOUR

Government, His Majesty's Ministers reading it with as much surprise as did everyone else.

Balfour was in Paris when this *communiqué* was issued, and it is safe to assert that he did not read it while there. Nor can he have discussed it with Mr. Lloyd George, who returned to London with him on December 2nd, and next day was apparently wondering whether he knew about the letter beforehand or not.[1] It must be presumed that nobody drew Balfour's attention to the two-days-old newspaper when he returned to the Foreign Office, and Lord Lansdowne himself made no public correction, or private protest, about a statement which was hardly fair to himself. The chances are that Balfour never did know about it. All his instincts urged him to forget the episode of the letter as quickly as possible. He had thought it a mistake, and a mistake committed by a dearly loved and greatly respected friend. But it was done and could not be undone. A family record of conversation on December 11th mentions that he said he had not even read Lord Lansdowne's letter. There was no need, for Lord Lansdowne's Memorandum to himself covered it all. Yet, I believe, if he had realised that Lord Lansdowne might be silently suffering some injustice through the *communiqué*, Balfour would have made the complete facts public at once. Therefore it has seemed right to give them fully here. The story may be wound up with part of a letter to Lord Robert Cecil, which shows why the War Aims question seemed to Balfour at the moment flat and unprofitable. The date is December 29th. He was writing about a War Cabinet.

> There was the usual endless talk about "defining War Aims," a problem in which I take no very great interest,

[1] See *Lord Riddell's War Diary*, p. 295.

WAR AIMS

because, as it seems to me, there is not the slightest difficulty in defining what ends we want to gain by the war. The real difficulty is to find out how far we shall be able to attain them, and how far the Allies are prepared to fight till they are attained;—and no amount of defining will help us to solve either of these problems. . . .

Ll. G. has called for a military Report from G.H.Q. on the possibility of obtaining a decisive victory over Germany in the field. And the Cabinet appears to think that everything turns upon the answer. I do not take this view myself. I know exactly what answer they will give. They will say that now Russia is out of the War, you have no right whatever to expect decisive military successes. But this seems to me to settle nothing. What we really want to know is whether, under the new circumstances, the combined military, economic and political " squeeze " which the Allies will be able to exercise upon the Central Powers is greater than the " squeeze " which the Central Powers can exercise upon the Allies. If so, we have a clear motive for going on. If not, not . . .

Some Members of the Cabinet seemed to think that something would be gained if, instead of discussing war aims at large, we attempted to define the " minimum " war aims. Personally I think such a course would have every disadvantage. It would involve the open declaration that there were a certain number of objects to which this or that Ally attached great importance, but for which, for our part, we did not mean to fight for ever to obtain. This, if it got known, would certainly discourage our friends and encourage our enemies.

But I have a further objection to it. The only clear meaning I can attach to the phrase " minimum war aim " is the aim for which we should still be prepared to fight even if we had to fight single-handed. That there are such aims I do not doubt. But we have not got—and probably never shall get—to the stage in this War of having to consider what they are.

When Balfour wrote this letter at the very end of 1917, the event had happened which might well seem

253

ARTHUR JAMES BALFOUR

1917 to postpone the prospect of decisive victory indefinitely. In November the Bolsheviks had gained control of the Russian Revolution, and already they had concluded an armistice with Germany. The Russian armies were no longer in being. Although for some months past they had represented no power of offensive, still they had opposed inert masses of men between the Germans and the inexhaustible resources in food and raw material which lay behind them. When the armies melted away it was not only the strategic balance of advantage that was altered. It was not only the release of fresh Divisions for Germany's western battle, but it was also the whole question of the " squeeze " which Balfour refers to in his letter. The siege of Germany was over. The Central Powers were no longer hemmed in. The " Eastern Front " had become a hinterland that was almost a world in itself. Moreover it was a world which had been thrown into chaos by the fall of the Russian Empire, and now presented a fresh set of political and economic problems for all belligerents. No European really knew what forces might be gathering in the vast territories where Bolshevik rule was not established—in the Ukraine—in the Caucasus—in Siberia—nor what influence they might have upon the War in Europe. It was vital to discover, but at the turn of the year the searchers at Whitehall had not delivered very precise information, as the following letter from Lord Robert Cecil shows. Balfour had gone to Whittingehame for a short New Year holiday.

FOREIGN OFFICE.
January 8th, 1918.

MY DEAR ARTHUR,

Since I saw you last a good many things have happened. We have been trying, not very successfully, to

BALFOUR'S SITTING-ROOM AT WHITTINGEHAME

RUSSIA MYSTERIOUS

get in touch with our organisations in South Russia. The 1918 Russians appear to be determined not to fight with anyone except one another. Even that they do in a half-hearted way.... As for the Caucasus, the position is absolutely chaotic, or at least the accounts of it that reach us are of that description. In South Caucasus the difficulty is that the Tartars, and possibly the Georgians, think that they have now an unrivalled opportunity for exterminating the Armenians.... We are engaged in trying to find money to help the Armenians to organise an Army, and at the same time to persuade the Georgians and Tartars to reserve their massacring temper for the Turks....

I have had to agree to a Committee called the Russia Committee, as the only means of unifying our action with that of the War Office in those parts. This Committee meets I believe every day; but I have declined to be a member of it, and I insist that no urgent decisions are to await its consideration. On the whole it does not seem to be doing much harm at present; and so far as it has spurred on the Treasury to find money for all these people it may have done good.

The position north of Tiflis is even more mysterious. About 50% of our telegrams describe Kaledin as hopeless and useless with an infinitesimal following. The other 50% represent Kaledin and Alexieff as being at the head of a large organisation embodying all the Cossack tribes from Siberia to the Black Sea, in a Federation of growing importance and power....

Quite at the other end of the world, Vladivostock is another mystery. No one seems to know for certain whether it is in the hands of the Bolshevists or of the Moderates, though the balance of evidence inclines to the latter.

The Japanese will not tell us what they intend to do, and are very angry if anyone else proposes to do anything. If they were not too unreasonable, the proper plan would undoubtedly be to land a force at Vladivostock to protect our stores there, the force being in substance Japanese, with a few French, Americans and British added for the sake of appearances.

ARTHUR JAMES BALFOUR

1918   It was a Report from the "Russia Committee," fortified by a Memorandum of Balfour's, which decided the War Cabinet, towards the end of January, to broach the subject of intervention through Vladivostock to President Wilson and the principal Allies. This was the beginning of a Russian policy for which its chief protagonists would scarcely put up a whole-hearted defence to-day. Its apologists might indeed say that the Allied Powers had no choice, when Germany was girding herself for her last gigantic effort, but to do anything and everything to checkmate her exploitation of the Russian situation. All the great European belligerents did in fact treat the crumbling Empire of the Czar like a chess-board, and every move they made upon it was with an eye to their own life and death struggle. Thus preoccupied, they never fully understood the entirely different interests which prompted the movements of the contending Russian elements now to one side, now to the other. As late as April someone in the Foreign Office solemnly commented on a telegram from Russia: "This is a confession that if the Bolshevists are out for war at all, it is for war on a 'class' and not on a 'national' basis." Beneath which appears the red pencilling of the Foreign Secretary: "What we must if possible get them to do is to postpone the anti-bourgeois millennium until they and we have beaten the Germans."

Balfour might flippantly mock the belated discovery of his Department, but some of his own considered views exhibit a miscalculation of the possible outcome of the class struggle in Russia, surprising even from a man sheltered as he had been by the times in which he had lived, by the country that he belonged to, and by the circumstances of his private life, from any personal observation of the issues of class warfare. Cabling

MISTAKES BREED

to Lord Reading in Washington on April 19th he wrote:

> If we could bring about a national revival such as freed Russia from the despotism of Napoleon, very great results might ensue. . . . If the necessary national spirit could be generated it would be possible to create an army armed and supplied from stores now at Archangel and Vladivostock. . . .
>
> It seems to us that if this national revival is to take place, the Allies must actively help to bring it about, and that they ought therefore to unite upon a policy which has for its object allied intervention in order to free Russia from all forms of foreign control. It is of course essential that the Allies should avoid taking sides in Russia itself, for local politics are now so bitter that whichever side we took we should make its opponents our enemies. . . .

He saw no paradox in this last point, upon which he was continuously insistent. Mistakes breed, in other things besides sums of arithmetic. The errors of British diplomacy in Russia in the early days of Lenin and Trotsky came from the naïve belief that their realistic minds would be more inclined to accept the *bona fides* of the great capitalist States than these States had shown themselves to be in respect of Bolshevik intentions. Assurances were conveyed by Balfour to Mr. Lockhart, then our Representative in Moscow, as follows:

> In so far as they (the Bolsheviks) are opposing or embarrassing our enemies, their cause is our cause. In so far as they endeavour to foment revolution in this or any other Allied country, we shall thwart them to the best of our ability. In so far as they are dealing with the internal politics of those parts of the country where they are *de facto* rulers, we have no desire to interfere. The very principles which induce us to co-operate with the Bolsheviks urge us to support any forces in Russia which seem likely to offer resistance to our enemies, or aid to our friends.

1918 But we cannot pledge ourselves to abstain from such action in other parts of Russia as may in our opinion help to win the war: though we have not the slightest intention of indulging in any anti-revolutionary propaganda.

This telegram was dated February 21st. On the 29th Mr. Lockhart saw Lenin.

> Our ways [said the Russian] are not your ways. We can afford to compromise temporarily with capital. It is even necessary, for if capital were to unite, we should be crushed at this stage of our development. . . . So long as the German danger exists I am prepared to risk a co-operation with the Allies. . . . At the same time I am quite convinced that your Government will never see things in this light. It is a reactionary Government. It will co-operate with the Russian reactionaries.[1]

Had it not been for the objections of President Wilson, which had delayed for months the Vladivostock landing, Lenin's prophecy would by that time have come true. The Bolsheviks' suspicions were aroused by rumours from the Far East, and on March 10th Mr. Lockhart sent a telegram deserving of more attention than the Foreign Office gave it.

> By sheer logic of events [he explained] the working classes are the only force in Russia which does not welcome German intervention. Already, as in the Ukraine, there are several bourgeois combinations which are plotting to form a Government under the Germans. If by permitting Japanese intervention at the present moment we destroy the only force in Russia which will oppose Germany, we must take the consequences.

Thus Mr. Lockhart—in close touch with Trotsky, too obviously close for the prejudices of some people at the Foreign Office. " He treats him (Trotsky) as if he were a Bismarck or a Talleyrand," observed one

[1] See *Memoirs of a British Agent*, by Bruce Lockhart, p. 238.

THE RUSSIAN KALEIDOSCOPE

of them. Not however Balfour. He was interested by clear opinions, however violently expressed. But Mr. Lockhart was a civilian, and the advisers of the British War Office in Russia were insistent opponents of his views. They urged the powerlessness of Russia to make any sort of resistance to a German advance into the rich regions of Western Siberia. The situation was lost, they reported, unless Japan acted, and acted soon. The distinction which British Ministers continued to cherish in their own minds between military operations and political interference reinforced the arguments of the soldiers. Balfour spoke in the House of Commons about Japanese assistance for the Russians, and there is a note of genuine annoyance in his minute on Mr. Lockhart's subsequent expostulation from Moscow:

> I have constantly impressed on Mr. Lockhart that it is *not* our desire to interfere in Russian internal affairs. He appears to be very unsuccessful in conveying this view to the Bolshevik Government.

Two or three days later however—on March 25th—Mr. Lockhart reported hopefully on the prospects of the Moscow Government themselves asking for Allied help against the Germans, who at that particular turn of the kaleidoscope were supporting the reactionaries in Finland and in the Ukraine, where a bloody peasant revolt was in progress. But the moment for co-operation passed amidst all the conflicting information which filtered through to London from agents and missions to Russia, military, economic, or unlabelled, many of them so isolated by the collapse of communications, and local fighting, that they did not even know of each other's presence in the country. The same conditions made it doubtful how far the Bolsheviks could control their own people in Asiatic Russia. The

ARTHUR JAMES BALFOUR

1918 Foreign Secretary was not much impressed by Bolshevik overtures, for when Mr. Lockhart asked if intervention in Siberia could be suspended in return for an undertaking from Lenin and Trotsky to declare war on Germany within six weeks Balfour minuted: "What we want is the reality of anti-German hostilities, not a formal and quite impotent declaration on the subject."

Nevertheless at the end of April an instruction on Allied policy for our Consul in Vladivostock says:

"The intervention must have Bolshevik consent, as they represented the *de facto* Government, with whom it was impossible not to reckon."

In June the situation was entirely altered by the appearance in Siberia of great bodies of war prisoners, all taken by the Czar's troops from the German and Austrian armies, but now resuming military formation on different sides; for some thirty thousand of them were Czecho-Slovaks, whose only desire was to fight for the Allies against the Central Empires. British Ministers were eager that they should do so where they were. German forces (also largely recruited from war prisoners) were reported to be about to ascend the Volga, and so capture the corn-lands of West and Central Siberia. The French however were eager for the appearance of the Czechs on the Western Front, urging the disintegrating effect this would produce on what remained of Austrian *morale*. The French Foreign Minister came over to London and argued his case for a whole day with Mr. Lloyd George, Balfour and General Sir Henry Wilson. Reluctantly the British compromised, undertaking to find transport for five thousand men, although shipping at that time was so scarce that every Czech embarked at a Russian port meant so many fewer American soldiers brought across the Atlantic. This was hardly settled when there came

THE RUSSIAN MUDDLE

a telegram from the British Consul at Vladivostock, 1918 reporting that the local Soviet had "thrown off the mask," that orders had come from Moscow to attack the Czechs on their way to the coast, that German war prisoners were in possession of Irkutsk, that the Czechs (who had repelled their assailants) were in control of part of the railway, and that further delay in Allied intervention would entail the definite loss of Siberia.

This message arrived full of indecipherable groups of words. When it was put before Balfour it bore the departmental instruction: "Repeat to Washington when corrupt passages have been elucidated." Once more the Chief's red pencil flicked over the page: "Quite right, but do not linger over textual revision till text becomes out of date. It is better (for a document!) to be corrupt than useless."

The wire was sped to Washington. President Wilson was already yielding a little on the question of intervention, which had been the subject of incessant pressure from London ever since Balfour had made a first effort at persuasion in January. On July 3rd American Generals in Paris attended a meeting of the Supreme War Council, where the forthcoming Allied operations in Russia were discussed.

It is possible that but for the crisis created by the appearance of the Czechs in Siberia, and the sudden attack upon them on their way to the coast, that President Wilson would have maintained his objections to intervention, which had better have been kept up to the end, or else withdrawn when the policy was first urged upon him by the British. It was partly due to the long wrangle with the United States Government that the Allied troops landed at Archangel and Murmansk only in August, when the German power was

ARTHUR JAMES BALFOUR

1918 already cracking in the West and the original arguments for sending them were ceasing to be valid. The contingents, when they came, were moreover ludicrously small for any purpose except that of giving encouragement to the Whites in the Russian civil war. But that unfortunate story need not be pursued here since, the policy once decided, the responsibility of the Foreign Office fades out of the military arrangements of 1918.

With the Armistice the last shadow of the original objectives of the Expeditions vanished, but the question of withdrawal was nearly as much governed by political considerations as the landings had been. When the decision was taken in 1919, however, the Foreign Office was in Lord Curzon's charge, and Balfour in Paris does not seem to have taken much part in the discussions. His hands were otherwise full. British public opinion was by that time deeply stirred by a moral indignation at Bolshevik methods, which was a comparatively small factor in the policy of the spring of 1918—partly because most people had then neither the leisure nor the information for pronouncing judgments.

The murders of the Imperial family produced a profound change in the attitude of the civilised world, but when these crimes were committed in the middle of July 1918, the despatch of Allied troops to Russia was already a settled affair. Thereafter the "Terror" intensified, and by the summer of 1919 the idea of co-operation with the Bolsheviks, which had been hoped for as lately as the spring of the previous year, would not have seemed tolerable to any civilised Government.

Chapter XIII

TREATY MAKING

Balfour's conception of responsibility. His attempt to deal separately with the Military Clauses. Departure of Signor Orlando. The " Council of Four." Work on the British Empire Delegation. Balfour's Memorandum on France and Germany. Balfour defends the Treaty of Versailles. Balfour becomes head of the British Delegation. The Treaty of Trianon. The " Anschluss." The Tyrol. Balfour's letter to Lord Curzon. Balfour leaves the Foreign Office. Lord Curzon and Mr. Lloyd George. Balfour at the Peace Conference.

The night before Balfour left England to attend 1918 the Peace Conference of Paris in January 1919, he dined with Lord and Lady Wemyss, and said to his hostess : " As I have always told you, it was not so much the War as the Peace that I have always dreaded." No more is recorded—perhaps no more was said. But it is certain that he went to France with his hopes pitched low.

Balfour had done no platform speaking during the Election campaign of December 1918. He was quite in accord with the Prime Minister in thinking an appeal to the country right. " Our General Election was, I think, a necessity, but a very inconvenient necessity," he wrote on December 17th to Colonel House. His own Address to his City of London constituents argued for continuity of administration in the momentous transition from war to peace. It treats mainly of the restoration of normal life in an industrial country. It says nothing about the terms of peace. Almost his

ARTHUR JAMES BALFOUR

1919 only recent public utterance on that subject had been made two weeks before the Armistice, at an Australian and New Zealand luncheon. Then he had said that it was not consistent with the security of the unity of the British Empire that the German colonies should be returned to Germany.[1]

Another of Balfour's observations in private talk was noted about this time. " This Peace Conference is going to be a rough and tumble affair," he said. The casual prophecy stuck in memory after its accuracy was proved, perhaps because of the incongruity of its author's participation in any " affair " that could be so described.

There are some curious differences of opinion among historians who came into personal contact with Balfour during the Peace Conference, about the part he played there. In the view of the American, Mr. Stannard Baker, he stood for the " philosophy of doubt " as opposed to President Wilson's " philosophy of faith." " Sure like the English Hamlet of the disadvantages of every course of action."[2] For Mr. Winston Churchill, on the other hand, he was the model of swift and firm decision during the brief period when the absence of the other Conference Chiefs put the leadership into his hands for two or three weeks. Other writers have introduced his figure with a less definite touch, stressing his air of detachment, the epigrammatic quality of his remarks, the charm of his dinner-table conversation, the boyishness of his enjoyment of the lawn-tennis without which he could never have held out through nine months of the Conference atmosphere. All these traits are genuine pieces of the Balfourian make-up, familiar to the British

[1] See *The Times*, October 24th, 1918.
[2] See *Woodrow Wilson and World Settlement*, by R. Stannard Baker, Vol. I, p. 302.

THE FOREIGN SECRETARY IN PARIS
1919

OFF TO PARIS

public through forty years. Conference circles discovered them with delight.

On the very eve of his departure from London, in the second week of January 1919, I met him coming out of the Secretary of State's room in the Foreign Office. I was myself at that time inhabiting a corner of one of the temporary huts in the court-yard, where I was employed in painting an ethnic map of East Galicia with speckles of blue to represent Poles, red for Ruthenians, yellow for Jews. Balfour never failed to enquire into the progress of this work, though he did not always exhibit a proper sense of the importance which I then felt to be its due. He asked after it now, and as we left the Foreign Office together I imparted my fears lest the boundaries of the new Poland might after all be settled before the result of my labours could follow him to Paris. "I wish I thought so," he said, with no banter in his voice. We walked on across the Horse Guards Parade, stopping for a moment in the middle, as he often did, to look at the surrounding scene.

He began talking earnestly about the damage now being done to the hope of the world's recovery by every day's delay in return to normal conditions. We parted at the top of the Duke of York's Steps, and I watched him sauntering down Carlton House Terrace, a profound impatience, as I now knew, filling his mind. There can be little doubt that among the aims of statesmanship at the Paris Conference Balfour put speed first, or nearly so.

The picture of him at work in Paris has to be drawn in relation to two very distinct backgrounds. During the first four or five months of the Conference, between January and June, the Treaty with Germany was the main business for the plenipotentiaries of the Great

ARTHUR JAMES BALFOUR

1919 Powers. Between June and September (the date when Balfour returned home) the settlements with the Succession States of the Austrian Empire took precedence, broadly speaking. In the first period the initiative in British policy was with the Prime Minister, during the second with the Foreign Secretary, who became head of the Delegation when Mr. Lloyd George went back to England.

In Balfour's case it was to be expected that the difference in his attitude during these two stages would be very marked. His attitude towards responsibility was always extremely clean cut. No man was ever more courageous in accepting it, and this once done, the acceptance was complete. On the other hand he always showed himself very loath to assume it at all in circumstances that he could not control. This characteristic showed itself in the smallest incidents of life, such as the guidance of an expedition. Either the map was in his pocket, or in somebody else's. In the latter case he never asked for it, and proffered neither criticism nor aid.

In the later period of his public life he often made the distinction between what he considered to be his business and what he did not, more emphatically and openly than Cabinet Ministers usually do. In the conditions of emergency which had led him to put Mr. Lloyd George's Government into power—his principle had been " a free hand for the Little Man." Balfour's interpretation of a " free hand," whether for himself or for other people, was so literal as to be sometimes startling to more timid minds. I will once more illustrate it with an anecdote of family life. In the days of horse-drawn carriages he was driving with his sister to a dinner party. They were immersed in conversation, which she interrupted by remarking that she thought

THE TIME FACTOR

the coachman had taken the wrong turning. "Well," said Balfour, "that is his business, not ours." History does not relate how far the principle of non-interference was carried into practice on this occasion. The point rather is that there was a principle behind this apparent passivity, and it would be rash to assume that it was ever otherwise with him.

But let it not be supposed that Balfour assigned to himself, or would have permitted himself to be relegated to, the post of a detached onlooker while the Treaty of Versailles was in the making. There was seldom a day when some of the British experts from the wonderful organisation presided over by Lord Hardinge at the Hotel Astoria were not sent for to the Foreign Secretary's flat in the Rue Nitot, there to discuss innumerable points of detail in preparation for the next meeting of the Conference. So that when he defended in Council the recommendations of his own experts on the territorial changes, he did so with knowledge and conviction born of study and thought on his own part, and there was nothing in these chapters of the finished Treaty that he was not prepared afterwards to defend. "No one," he was wont to say, when frontiers were criticised, "has ever made a practical suggestion as to how they could be bettered." His judgment on the economic and financial provisions was formed less on their intrinsic soundness, and more in relation to the time factor which seemed to him most worth consideration as regards those parts of the German settlement which time itself might be expected to adjust. This is clear from some undated notes found among his papers, which throw some light upon his view of the Reparations clauses, and upon other things as well. The following fragment is evidently part of a projected answer to some critic. Its first and last pages have disappeared.

1919 > Let me remind you [it begins] of the circumstances in which the decisions were taken to which you so strongly object. From the general tone and temper of your narrative it might almost be supposed that the problem of German Reparations was dealt with in the leisurely atmosphere say of a Hague Conference. The judicial weighing of precedents, the legal interpretation of documents, a careful survey of financial conditions, the embodiment of results in protocols that should have completely satisfied the Allied Powers, and left no room for German chicane—these should have been the main preoccupation of the Allied negotiations. Had this been done you suggest all subsequent trouble would have been avoided, and Peace when it came would have been Peace indeed. But when would it have come? Is it not clear that at the end of October, 1918, the victory of the Allied and Associated Powers was assured, and that every day's delay was the occasion of irreparable loss to every belligerent and many neutrals? In no previous wars was this the case——

Here, in the middle of a sentence at the foot of a page, the argument breaks off. No doubt it was written after Balfour's return from Paris. He had sat there through nine months feeling the power slipping away from the Council of the Allies. In the spring of the year they had imposed their own terms upon the Germans. Before the leaf fell their writ had almost ceased to run among the small fry in Eastern Europe. On the 26th of July, the affairs of Hungary being under discussion, Balfour delivered himself thus:

> If it were known that all the Powers had demobilised so fast under the stress of domestic necessity, it would be regarded as absurd that the Powers who eight months ago were conquerors of the world could not impose their will upon an army of 120,000. That inglorious situation he (Balfour) did not particularly mind, but he wondered how the Conference would be able to terminate its work successfully.

URGE TO HURRY

This is only typical of many of his observations at the Council table during the second period of the Conference when he was himself leading the British Delegation, and the evils due to earlier delays began to make themselves felt in an ignominious loss of authority. The records show how soon he himself had begun to try to avert the danger. As early as February 20th he told the Dominion Delegations how "some weeks previously" he had circulated a Paper on the subject of the dilatory procedure of the Conference.

The second half of February and the first week of March covered a period when, Mr. Lloyd George and President Wilson having left Paris for a time, and M. Clemenceau recovering from a bullet wound, Balfour was in charge. Historians of the Conference have all noted the Resolution of the Supreme Council dated February 22nd, ordering that the Reports of the expert Committees on frontiers, finance, and economic relations with Germany should be in readiness by March 8th. This urge to hurry is rightly attributed to Balfour. It represented in reality less of a triumph than a compromise, for his first suggestion had been defeated. This was to isolate the Military, Naval and Air clauses of the German Treaty from the political and economic provisions, and present them to the Germans for immediate signature, thus obtaining an important instalment of the Preliminary Peace. The proposal was made on the hypothesis (which afterwards turned out to be optimistic) that the drafts of the military terms were ripe for approval by the Council.[1] Its rejection may have made little difference, but its putting forward is of some importance in a study of Balfour's attitude towards the Treaty of Versailles.

The military clauses once out of the way, the pressure

[1] See Colonel House, *Intimate Papers*, Vol. IV, p. 353.

of " domestic necessity " in the matter of the postponement of demobilisation would have relaxed, and the scope and opportunity for statesmanship in respect of the economic and territorial provisions been increased. But Balfour's only strong support in the Council of Ten came from our Delegation in the person of Lord Milner.[1] M. Clemenceau was in favour of nothing that might in the long run advantage the Germans. Mr. Lansing, the American Secretary of State, was not prepared to agree to the division of the Treaty into parts before the Covenant of the League of Nations was safely inserted into the text. The Italians objected to the German settlement running ahead of the Austrian. Balfour did not insist upon his proposal. The question of a preliminary peace was however left nominally open, while the " speeding up " Resolution of Balfour's was agreed and put into effect. At the same time, with Colonel House and M. Clemenceau, he began to consider in private, matters incapable of being decided by the expert Committees.[2]

On March 8th Mr. Lloyd George was back from London, and President Wilson landed again in France on March 14th. The general lines of the Draft Treaty were complete enough for the stage of decision to be opened. The real " rough and tumble " of Balfour's prediction had begun. It was at this period that the Foreign Ministers of the Allied and Associated Powers withdrew from the conclaves of the Delegation Chiefs,

---

[1] Then Secretary of State for War.

[2] Mr. Stannard Baker, in his *Woodrow Wilson and World Settlement*, has accused the British representatives, and Balfour in particular, of lending themselves to an intrigue to side-track the Covenant of the League of Nations, and to carry through, in President Wilson's absence, decisions contrary to his wishes. This indictment has been so completely disproved by documentary evidence in Vol. IV of Colonel House's *Intimate Papers* (pp. 373 *et seq.*) that nothing more need be said on the subject here.

THE COUNCIL OF FOUR

and the "Council of Ten" became the "Council of Four," and at one time a Council of Three, when the indignation of the Italians over the denial of their claims upon the Adriatic coast caused the temporary retirement of Signor Orlando to Rome. This departure was the occasion of considerable display of the Latin temperament. On the evening that it was to take place Balfour rose from the dinner-table in his own flat in the Rue Nitot saying: "I must go now and put on my wading boots." His companions looked at him startled. Was the strain of the Allied disagreements proving too great for him also? His next words reassured them. "To say good-bye to Orlando," he explained. "He was in tears when I left him, and I have no reason to suppose that he has stopped crying since."

Balfour was entirely in agreement with the exclusion of the Foreign Ministers from the Supreme Council when the Treaty was being cast into final form. The practice was only a formal extension of the private talks that he and Colonel House had begun with M. Clemenceau, and he associated himself with Mr. Lloyd George in the protests against leakages of information, which was one of the chief arguments for reduction in size of the deciding body. His own exclusion did not weigh with him against the increase of efficiency. He was careful however not to lose touch. His flat was under the same roof as the Prime Minister's, immediately above. This arrangement had been made at the beginning of the Conference at Mr. Lloyd George's own desire. In Paris, as in London, Sir Maurice Hankey was at hand to fill up any gaps in their communications. The Foreign Secretary left less to chance in this respect than the casual observer might have supposed. Once Balfour asked a very trusted member of the Prime Minister's staff whether Mr. Lloyd George had read

1919 a certain Memorandum. " I don't think so," was the answer, " but I have." " Not quite the same thing is it, Philip—yet ? " said Balfour mildly.

Then there arose a question about the Minutes. At first the Four had dispensed even with a Secretary, but that was soon found impracticable, and Sir Maurice Hankey recorded decisions, which at first were circulated only to the Four themselves. It was Balfour who insisted that he must have the written records, which were thenceforth available in duplicate for each Chief Delegate for such distribution as they might think fit.

On occasion Balfour himself was present at the Council of Four. He came, for example, whenever the business included the claims of Italy to Fiume. At another period of the crowded weeks of April he came to report the progress of the negotiations with the Japanese over the future of Shantung, which had been left in his hands to conduct.

Not infrequently he was called in on other occasions when discussion seemed to be reaching a deadlock— and would (so Colonel House told me in 1930)

> give his opinions at that stage with perfect good humour. He was practically the only man at the Conference [Colonel House went on] who never suffered from hurt feelings. He gave the impression of being above all those small things.

Colonel House told me further how he used to be struck by the unruffled simplicity with which Balfour would sometimes say to him : " I never was told that." If there were things that he should have been consulted about, but was not, this shrewdest of observers never believed that the omission was conscious on the part of Mr. Lloyd George, with whom he saw that Balfour could get on as few others could.

THE BRITISH EMPIRE

> Men can only act according to their natures [said Colonel 1919 House]. When A. J. B. worked alone he was always at his best, and always right,—it did not suit him to be hampered by instructions.

Division of labour became more and more essential as the settlement with Germany was hustled towards a conclusion. Every Delegation had its own problems in this, as in all other respects, and dealt with them in its own way. British Ministers had a set of considerations peculiar to themselves, of which they could never afford to lose sight, however great the pressure from other directions might be upon their time and thoughts.

Inter-Imperial relationships were in a state of transition at the precise moment when the several members of the British Commonwealth of Nations met together to bear their share in remodelling the world. The new status which the self-governing Dominions had won for themselves by their contribution to the Allied victory was acknowledged in the invitation to their plenipotentiaries to attend the Conference. It had been recognised, but from the domestic point of view it had still to be regularised.

The British Empire had outgrown its constitution, but Paris was not the place, even if it had provided the opportunity, for entering upon the delicate business of framing a new one. This was a matter to be pondered at leisure, and discussed in the privacy of the family. Seven years in fact were to pass before the Imperial Conference met in London for the purpose. In 1919 not even a British mind could forecast the lines along which the British peoples would eventually preserve the unity of the Commonwealth as a whole, through the independence of the parts. In the meantime it was highly undesirable to put any pull on the chain which bound the Dominions to the Mother Country. No one

ARTHUR JAMES BALFOUR

1919 could doubt that some of its links had been strengthened by common effort in the World War. But others might have been dissolved. A tactless speech, an ill-judged effort to exert authority, might do immeasurable harm.

Nevertheless the British Empire Delegation,[1] though it might not be driven, must be guided through the channels of international diplomacy, unfamiliar to every individual among the Overseas representatives, with the notable exception of General Smuts, now no longer a member of the British War Cabinet, but second South African Delegate under General Botha, Premier of the South African Republics.

The Executive power at the Peace Conference lay only with the Supreme Council. Everything that was decided by them was open to previous expression of opinion by the British Empire Delegation, and in the case of some of the fundamental questions in the settlement with Germany, the views of the Dominions were of vital importance. The allocation, and the terms, of the Mandates over ex-German colonies in Africa and in the Pacific are one obvious example, but there was not a chapter in the Treaty of Versailles, from Disarmament to Reparations, on which the Empire Delegation could not claim a right to be heard.

The potentialities of such a body for strengthening the hand of Great Britain were only equalled by the injury that would be done to British influence in the Conference if the Empire spoke with a divided or uncertain voice. The continuous attendance of the British Ministers at the Meetings with the Dominions was nearly as important for the future of international settlement as of Imperial policy.

[1] This was the term used to describe the Committee of Delegates from the Mother Country, the Dominions and India.

IMPERIAL UNITY

Accordingly Mr. Lloyd George and Balfour were 1919 commonly both of them present, and if the Prime Minister were absent Balfour usually took the Chair. But wherever he sat, his interpolations in discussion show him alive to every consideration here mentioned, and doubtless to a hundred others less obvious. The very first Meeting of the Empire Delegation provides an illustration. It took place on January 13th, a few days before the Conference actually opened. The British Prime Minister was in the Chair, supported by his Foreign Secretary, by Mr. Bonar Law, and Mr. Montagu, Secretary of State for India. Sir Henry Wilson, Chief of the Imperial General Staff, was also present. The Premier of Australia, Mr. Hughes, was there with Sir Joseph Cook, Minister for the Australian Navy. South Africa had her two Generals, Botha and Smuts. There were Sir Robert Borden, Prime Minister of Canada, and from India Sir S. P. Sinha and the Maharajah of Bikanir.

The first question on the Agenda was precisely one of those thorny ones that must not be mishandled—the representation of the British Empire in the Allied Councils. The technique of the main Conference was not yet worked out, and the Dominion Delegations showed some natural jealousy for their separate rights. Balfour listened, finally spoke—a few short sentences. He quite understood, he said, the strong sense of nationhood that animated the various fractions. The problem before them was how to reconcile this intense patriotism with Imperial unity. He thought that if each time we met the other nations in Conference we said that the British Empire was to be represented as a whole, and also separately, it would be asking too much.

At this there was no demur. The first step towards

1919 making the British Empire Delegation into a team was taken. The creation of team work cannot fall to the credit of any one man, still less the sustaining of team spirit. But it may be possible to say that the influence of a single man was decisive. A day has only twenty-four hours, and a man at the height of his strength can only give so many of them to his labour. Balfour's seventy-first birthday was passed in Paris, where he came, like all his colleagues, without a break after the four years of strain. From January to June Balfour gave to his colleagues from the British Empire the best of the ripened fruits of his long and varied experience.

There might be no consensus of opinion as to what was the best or the most valuable gift that individual statesmen brought to the Councils of the Allies. One of Balfour's particular contributions was a sense of historical perspective developed through his lifelong habit of using the lessons of the past to feed his insatiable interest in the future. Long ago the schoolmaster had observed that the ten-year-old child took " no interest in antiquity as such," although he " cared most for history, and this most in its political, social and economic aspects."[1] Sixty years after, this was still true, and now the critical, richly stored mind projected on to the screen of the coming time, not repetitions, but deductions drawn from the past.

Some of Balfour's remarks, notes and memoranda in Paris produce the impression that he thought of the Conference less as a beginning of a new order or the end of an old one, than as a point in time, whose realities would be no more static than time itself. If this definition of his attitude be a true one, it may account for an apparent indifference to some of the compromises, and to some of the defects which caused consternation as

[1] See Vol. I, Chapter I, p. 22.

FRANCE'S FEARS

the drafting of the Treaty brought them to light. On the other hand it sometimes gave his arguments a peculiar strength, and an interest which passage of time has certainly not destroyed.

There is no better example of this quality than in some notes he prepared at a moment when British and French policy came into sharp conflict over the question of Germany's western frontiers. The date was March 18th, 1919.

France's Fear of German Aggression.

The case which the French present to us with regard to the Left Bank of the Rhine is very forcible, but very one-sided. They draw a lurid picture of future Franco-German relations. They assume that the German population will always far outnumber the French; that as soon as the first shock of defeat has passed away, Germany will organise herself for revenge; that all our attempts to limit armaments will be unsuccessful; that the League of Nations will be impotent; and, consequently, that the invasion of France, which was fully accomplished in 1870, and partially accomplished in the recent War, will be renewed with every prospect of success.

I do not wish to deny the importance of these prophesyings; but I desire to point out that, in the first place, if there is a renewal of German world politics, it is towards the East rather than towards the West that her ambitions will probably be directed. Her great successes in the War were Eastern successes; and her great failures were Western failures; and, so far as anybody can forecast the fate of Europe, it would seem that in the West the forces that will in future make for effective defence are far stronger than in 1914. On the other hand, the collapse of Russia, and the substitution for it of a number of small and jealous States, will increase the opportunities for German diplomatic intrigue, and diminish the resisting power of the anti-German forces in the East.

I conceive therefore that if international relations and international methods are, as the French assume, going to remain in the future what they have been in the past; and if what civilisation has to fear is the renewal without substantial modification of German ambition, it is in the East rather than in the West that the storm will first break; and no attempt to guard against the dangers of the future can be deemed other than narrow and incomplete which concentrates its whole attention upon bridge-heads and strategic frontiers upon the Rhine and the Treaty of 1814, and draws all its inspiration from Generals and Statesmen absorbed in the military memories of 1870 and 1914. If Germany is going again to be a great armed camp, filled with a population about twice as great as that of any State in Europe; and if she is going again to pursue a policy of world domination, it will no doubt tax all the statesmanship of the rest of the world to prevent a repetition of the calamities from which we have been suffering. But the only radical cure for this is a change in the international system of the world—a change which French statesmen are doing nothing to promote, and the very possibility of which many of them regard with ill-concealed derision. They may be right; but if they are, it is quite certain that no manipulation of the Rhine frontier is going to make France anything more than a second-rate Power, trembling at the nod of its great neighbours in the East, and depending from day to day on the changes and chances of a shifting diplomacy and uncertain alliances.

A. J. B.

Criticisms of the Draft Treaty were easy to make, and when the violence of the German resistance to its terms became known, many people only found their doubts justified about the nature of this so-called Peace. General Smuts in particular felt clearly that the settlement as it stood was based less on justice than on broken pledges, and that the League Covenant was the only part of it which might redeem the rest. General Smuts could speak with formidable authority. He and General Botha had once been concerned in a settlement which had been a prelude to a real peace. His speech to the

THE FOURTEEN POINTS

British Empire Delegation opened a chorus of criticisms of principle and detail. Balfour from his place by the Prime Minister listened in silence all the morning. He had only spoken once, briefly, at the beginning, when he said that he hoped all would remember that their decisions would be discussed later in the Council of Four. There the French would undoubtedly oppose the removal from the Treaty of some features which the British would regard as indefensible. The Empire Delegations must not bind Mr. Lloyd George too tightly. They must leave him liberty to negotiate.

The morning session closed with a remark by Mr. Lloyd George that the peace of the world might depend upon the result of their discussion.

They resumed it that same evening, the Prime Minister in the Chair as before. Now Balfour took the floor, in the first place replying to General Smuts, and to some specific points made by other critics. He began with a tribute to the impressiveness and importance of General Smuts' indictment. But Balfour thought this had started from too legal an attitude towards the Fourteen Points. The Prime Minister and Balfour himself had been suddenly faced with these on the eve of the Armistice as the proposed basis for peace, and the time had been too short for adequate discussion. They had made some corrections, which had been "supplemented by some perorations," but they had otherwise had no option but to accept the Points. If these were pressed to a legal interpretation, an awkward case might possibly be made out; but it was only necessary to read the Fourteen Points to see that they were incapable of being treated in a strictly legal manner.

Point Nine was an illustration. It laid down that the new Italian frontier should be drawn on a recognisable line of nationality. President Wilson—not at the prompting of Great Britain—had already assented to a line which utterly violated this principle.

Balfour passed on to express his own opinion about the Polish-German frontier. He thought it " impudent " of the Germans to complain of the inclusion of purely German areas in Poland. Their own request for a land connection between East and West Prussia would include some purely Polish territory in Germany.[1] He had no sympathy whatever, he continued, with attacks upon the territorial settlement on Germany's Eastern frontier, which had presented a very difficult problem, on the whole well handled. Mr. Lloyd George favoured a plebiscite in Upper Silesia, and if that suggestion were adopted he thought Germany would then have nothing to complain of.

Passing to the question of the length and extent of the occupation of German territory by Allied troops, he strongly supported the desire of the Dominions to resist the French demands.

Defence of the vagueness of the Reparations Clauses Balfour left to Mr. Lloyd George, merely saying that he did not feel qualified to speak of them.

Reparations were in fact a chapter of the Treaty with which he had not been concerned. But he now delivered himself of some general observations on the economic policy. It was necessary to set industry going again, and he was anxious to get credits for Germany. But he thought it would be wrong for the Committee to fix their minds on the lamentations of the Germans, " when in fact the Germans were responsible for the tragedy of the whole world." Germany

[1] Some notes prepared by Balfour in October 1918, and subsequently printed for the use of the Peace Conference, show that he himself would have been in favour of granting to Germany this land bridge across the " Corridor."

VIEWS ON THE TREATY

was "no unhappy victim of circumstances, she was suffering, and ought to suffer, for her crimes."

Then, turning back to the discussions of the morning, Balfour said that he did not on the whole differ from the views of the British Empire Committee upon the Treaty, but that he was not sure whether some members had not come to the discussion in a temper produced by the pathetic appeals of the Germans, without sufficiently remembering the other side of the case. He recognised that the British representatives had been driven into a peculiar state of mind by the greed displayed by other Allied Powers. It was necessary to get into a more normal condition in order to deal with the problems before them.

These observations are pointers to Balfour's views about the general lines of the Treaty of Versailles—or rather, of the settlement with Germany at which the Treaty aimed. They show him satisfied that, broadly speaking, no injustice was being perpetrated upon the destroyers of the world's peace, and he was therefore concerned chiefly to prevent a reaction which might end in injustice to more innocent sufferers. This preoccupying thought came out clearly a few days later, when Mr. Lloyd George urged the desirability of issuing some declaration to the effect that the Allies would not withhold commercial intercourse and assistance from Germany. Balfour, who very seldom demurred in Committee at any proposal of the Prime Minister, here put in a frigid warning. He was very anxious, he said, in view of the state of Europe, that the Allies should give no pledges to Germany which they were not giving to their own friends. This adamantine attitude in greater matters did not prevent him from taking a lead in courtesy and consideration towards the representatives of Germany in the day of humiliation.

ARTHUR JAMES BALFOUR

1919 A letter written to myself after Balfour's death by Sir Robert Borden, who headed the Canadian Delegation in Paris, says:

> I shall always remember him as a great gentleman. One striking illustration dwells in my memory. At Versailles in May, 1919, when the German plenipotentiaries were about to be admitted in order that the draft Treaty of Peace might be presented to them, it was Balfour from whom emanated the thought and suggestion that we should all rise when they entered the room, and stand till they were seated.

On June 28th the Treaty with Germany was signed at Versailles. The names of the United States Delegates stand first, and then those of the British Empire, beginning with the United Kingdom, where the signature of the British Foreign Secretary stands fourth on the list headed by Mr. Lloyd George and Mr. Bonar Law. Then comes Lord Milner, Secretary for War, and below his name is Arthur James Balfour's. He signed with the gold fountain-pen which the Prime Minister gave him for the occasion, and which he carried in his waistcoat pocket, and used daily for the rest of his life.

On July 1st, 1919, Mr. Lloyd George and President Wilson having already departed from Paris, Balfour took the leadership of the British Delegation in the "Council of Five," on whom devolved the task of bringing order into the increasing chaos of Eastern Europe. Of the original members of the "Council of Four," only M. Clemenceau now remained. Balfour's other colleagues were the American Secretary of State, Mr. Lansing, Signor Tittoni and Baron Makino, the Japanese Delegate.

The Council took over an inheritance of problems some of which were now almost beyond the power of statesmanship to solve satisfactorily. Every small

A DISTASTEFUL POSITION

nationality, except the German Austrians, had some sort of an army in being, and all were remembering how often possession is in fact nine points of the law. There was fighting along nearly every one of the undetermined frontiers, and time and thought which should have been devoted to the permanent settlement had to be spent in futile efforts to exert a dwindling authority over the immediate situation. How distasteful Balfour found the position can be seen from some notes that he made at the time upon the attitude of the " small Allies and the small enemies."

> The former [he wrote] would, one might suppose, obey us through gratitude; the latter through fear. But the gratitude is being rapidly worn away by our persistent efforts to prevent the nations we have saved or created from cutting each other's throats and seizing each other's territory; while the fear cannot easily survive the continual spectacle of our obvious military weakness. Greeks, Roumanians, Poles, Czechs, Jugo-Slavs (I say nothing of the Italians) have all at different times disobeyed our explicit instructions. The Hungarians at the present moment are breaking the Armistice with impunity. The cases are many in which a Division, or a Brigade, or even a Battalion would have made the situation easy which is now difficult, and have effectually smoothed the diplomatic path to peace. But asking the War Department of a Great Power for soldiers is like asking a mendicant for a thousand pounds, and you get much the same reply. The Conference is therefore compelled to talk when action is required. Even the threat of action is denied us; for so notorious is our impotence that we cannot afford to bluff.

This state of affairs put back the Hungarian settlement until long after Balfour had left Paris. He was however much concerned with the final stages of the preparation of the Treaty with Austria, which was signed at St. Germain on September 10th, 1919.

None of the Peace Treaties has met with more adverse

1919 criticism than this, which recognised the existence of a German-Austrian State, and at the same time deprived it of the means and, to a great extent, of the will to live.

Vienna and the few poor Alpine provinces which were all that remained of the Hapsburg Empire could never be complementary to one another, either economically or politically. Between the two million inhabitants of the great cosmopolitan city, once the financial and cultural centre of well-nigh half Europe, and the simple people of the surrounding valleys, there could be little common feeling of patriotism. Hapsburg rule had been succeeded by a Socialist Government in Vienna. Between them and the Catholic population of the country-side there was only one thing in common besides despair at the fate which condemned them now to starve together within a ring fence. That thing was the desire to break through and join themselves to the great mass of the German-speaking race, and thus save their bodies and souls alive.

Later, it became the fashion in England to cry "peccavi" when the Germans of the Reich displayed the wounds inflicted upon their sensitive feelings by the Treaty of Versailles. Yet nothing there can compare for harshness with the clause in the Treaty of St. Germain that condemned Austria to "independence" in 1919.

Since then the desirability of the "Anschluss" with Germany has appeared in different lights even to the Austrians themselves. The end is not yet, but whatever it may be we shall never know what the effect might have been upon Germany herself, and upon Europe, if the German Austrians had been left free by the Peace Treaty at once to merge themselves economically and politically with their brothers in blood and religion in Southern Germany, and if Vienna had thus been able

ECONOMICS

to keep alive a spark which would have brought her [19] unquenchable gaiety and humour to counterbalance the heavy bitterness of Berlin.

Such speculations find no place here, for the Supreme Council of the Allies vetoed any union between Germany and Austria at the end of May, a month before Balfour took Mr. Lloyd George's place at the Conference. British opinion could not have thrown itself into the scales against France on the question of whether the German peoples should be allowed to form a block from the Baltic to the Danube. Moreover the Allied Powers were at one in the desire to give the new-born Czecho-Slovak State every chance of development, and the Czechs saw in the " Anschluss " a danger to their very existence. The fears and feelings of the Czechs provide part of the answer to the question of why the makers of the Austrian Treaty did not do more to secure Austria against a tariff war on the part of her neighbours. Permission for a special customs regime with Czecho-Slovakia and Hungary was indeed given in the Treaty, for a limited period, but there was no effort to enforce any sort of customs union upon the Succession States.

My own Diary of December 1922 records some conversation with Balfour on this and other economic aspects of the Peace Treaties.

> I think [Balfour said] that people talk nonsense when they say economics were neglected in Paris. Things that are evident now were simply not known then—or were mere matters of conjecture. It was agreed then—it is agreed now—that Germany must pay all she could. You *could not* fix the sum in 1919. You have only to look at the difference between the figures that the experts gave. Take our own. Cunliffe put an absurdly high estimate. Keynes, I think, erred the other way. Mind, I'm not saying the results of what was done have not been very bad; but I don't see what we could have done then that was

better. I think all the smaller economic arrangements were fairly good.

Myself. I think you might have seen that Austria must be protected if she was to live. You might have forbidden the new States to kill her with tariffs.

A. J. B. We might have done a little more in that way. But it would have been a very serious infringement of sovereignty. I don't like imposing that sort of thing on Governments.

The results of the lack of safeguards for Austria's economic life must have been quite present in Balfour's mind when he thus defended the Treaty policy, for at the end of 1922 he came fresh from Geneva and from negotiations for a League of Nations loan to the bankrupt country. Indeed this experiment in international finance would have had little chance of support by the League Council but for his bold personal initiative. When the Austrian Treaty was made however the League had not begun to function. It was not thought advisable then to put pressure on the Czecho-Slovaks to help the recovery of Austria. The liberated nationalities of the Dual Monarchy still felt too insecure of their political future to be able to consider their economic interest dispassionately. It was still a question of psychology. As one of the experts in the Political Intelligence Department of the British Foreign Office put it, " Were the Czechs to marry Austria, they would get Germany for mother-in-law."[1]

No help could be looked for from Hungary. Budapest was under the Red Terror of Bela Kun all the time that the Austrian Treaty was in the making, but in any case the Magyars were not interested in the sufferings of

[1] This Minute on the jacket of a Memorandum on the subject of a possible Customs Union bears the initials of Mr. L. B. Namier, author of the chapter in Vol. IV of the *Official History of the Peace Conference*, on " The Downfall of the Hapsburg Monarchy."

SACRIFICES

their former partner in domination. Their one preoccupation, then as later, was to regain their old historic frontiers.

Balfour had pointed out to the Dominions Delegation the practical difficulties of interpreting President Wilson's Fourteen Points as anything more than a guide to general principles which should underlie the Peace settlements. In the case of the German Treaty the " Points" did fulfil at least that function. In the case of the Austrian Treaty no attempt could be made to draw the frontier with any reference to them. President Wilson had early ceased to struggle against Italian claims to the Brenner Pass, which involved robbing Austria of the South Tyrol and of 230,000 Germans, who were German to the core. France and England had been committed to this ever since Mr. Asquith and Sir Edward Grey had found themselves compelled to pay the price demanded by Italy for breaking away from the Triple Alliance, and joining in the War. The strategic frontier of the Alps was only one item in the account, as set forth in the Treaty of London signed in April 1915. The European Allies felt bound to honour it, and President Wilson's acquiescence certainly saved them from some embarrassment. In any case the sacrifice of the Tyroleans was a settled thing before the " Council of Four " handed over the Draft Treaty with Austria to their successors. So also was the inclusion of some three million Germans within the boundaries of Czecho-Slovakia. " Self-determination " of peoples had thus quite gone by the board. In its stead the Treaties with the Succession States all had clauses which put the rights of Minorities of race, religion and language under the protection of the League of Nations. But with Italy there was of course no new Treaty, and Italy was not asked to

1919 undertake any specific obligations in respect of Minorities. The Tyroleans were handed over without any guarantee against suppression of their own culture or language.

In this they were alone among the transferred Minorities of Central and Southern Europe, just as Italy was alone among the States who received such a transfer, in not being asked to accept the international pledges imposed upon the smaller Powers. This exemption greatly increased the indignation with which some of these States—notably Poland and Rumania—regarded the League's right to protect Minorities. The inequality certainly contributed to the imperfect working of the Minority Treaties. Partly for this reason the question was raised later of extending Minority obligations to all Members of the League. But the absence of consent on the part of any great State is the vindication of the politicians in Paris who made no attempt to impose conditions on Italy in 1919. Balfour himself, who was averse to dictating even economic arrangements, would certainly have thought such an attempt to curtail sovereignty as unwise as it would be hopeless.

Moreover the Italy of 1919 made a declaration of her intention of adopting " a broadly liberal policy towards her new subjects of German race, in what concerns their language, culture and economic interests."[1] It was the Fascist Government that began the system of forcible Italianisation of the Tyrolese which sharpened criticism of the neglect to provide them with guarantees for their minority rights.

The Treaty with Austria was signed at St. Germain on September 10th. Balfour admitted himself to be for the moment at the end of his tether. On August 16th

[1] See *The Official History of the Peace Conference*, Vol. V, p. 143.

THE LORD PRESIDENT OF THE COUNCIL

PROBLEMS OUTSTANDING

he had written to Lord Curzon at the Foreign Office :

> Some time ago I told the Prime Minister that I proposed to take six weeks' holiday as soon as the three remaining European Treaties with Austria, Bulgaria and Hungary were ready. It was essential for me to take this holiday partly because I had been in harness continually since 1915, and partly because my doctors insisted on my taking a complete rest this autumn. . . .
>
> The work of the Peace Conference will have reached a definite stage at the end of the month (September). That is the time when I propose to leave Paris. After that date, however, so far as treaty making proper is concerned, we shall have to consider a reply to the Bulgarian observations on our draft Treaty; we shall have to do the same with the Hungarians when they come to Paris. None of these tasks are very formidable in themselves, as 95% of the work of the Treaties has already been completed. If this were all that had to be provided for I don't think that very much difficulty would arise.
>
> It is the other side of the Peace Conference with which I am more concerned. It is evident that the Conference is not going to adjourn, though it may possibly take ten days' recess while the Treaty is going through the French Chamber. The following list of subjects, many of which have nothing to do with treaty making proper, will show you how impossible it is for the Conference to break up altogether at present.
>
> (*a*) Negotiations with the Italians about the Adriatic have just been re-commenced on a far more promising basis than has hitherto been suggested.
>
> (*b*) The whole problem of Turkey, of the administration of Syria and of the evacuation of the Caucasus is untouched, and though it may be possible to postpone the consideration of the main Turkish Treaty for a month or so, events may at any time arise in this theatre which will require prompt consideration and action by the Allies.
>
> (*c*) There is the whole problem of Russia, and our relations with Denikin, Koltchak and the Baltic States. The von der Goltz question is still unsettled.

1919   (*d*) There are innumerable questions arising in regard to the execution of the Treaty with Germany, all of which require the decision of some inter-allied body. For instance, questions about plebiscites, about the occupation of places like Upper Silesia and Danzig, and as to what part each Ally should play. The Agenda is full almost every day with a number of difficult secondary questions of this kind. Another instance is that of the distribution of ex-German ships.

For these reasons I think it is inevitable that the Conference should go on sitting for some time longer.... But if the Conference is going to remain in session, the British Government must clearly be represented by a Minister of authority. We cannot expect Clemenceau, Pichon, Tittoni and Polk to be satisfied with any official, however competent, except possibly for a very few days.

I have now stated the problem. I am afraid I cannot answer it. I write to you because I think the only person who can answer it is the Prime Minister, and I should be greatly obliged if you would discuss it with him and let me know, as soon as you can, the decision at which you have arrived.

Please remember that a holiday I *must* have.

ARTHUR JAMES BALFOUR.

P.S.—Of course what I have said is not intended, by implication or otherwise, to prejudge the question whether I should return to Paris to deal with the intolerable problems of the Turkish Empire.

A few days later Balfour himself settled that question, Mr. Lloyd George had come over to Trouville, and after a talk with him there Balfour wrote again to Lord Curzon that he had told the Prime Minister that his holiday must be complete, and that he could not undertake to resume his work at the Foreign Office in any shape or form. Mr. Lloyd George had accepted this, but had asked him not to resign office at the moment, as he did not wish as yet to deal with the

LORD CURZON SUCCEEDS

Cabinet changes which such a resignation must set in motion.

> This request [Balfour added] I could not well refuse, though the burden of carrying it out will not fall on me. I hope to sign the Austrian Treaty on Wednesday, to leave for London on Thursday, to dine with the American Ambassador to meet Grey on Friday, and to go to Scotland on Saturday night.

This programme he carried out. Passing through London he had a talk with his substitute, soon to become his successor. He repeated his determination not to return either to the Foreign Office, or to Paris.

" He realises," Lord Curzon wrote to Lady Curzon, " that this half and half arrangement is hard on me."[1]

On October 24th the Prime Minister announced in the House of Commons the names of the reconstituted Peace Cabinet. Balfour assumed the office of Lord President of the Council, and Lord Curzon took his place as Foreign Secretary under Mr. Lloyd George.

The " incompatibility of temperament " sometimes held sufficient excuse for dissolving an unhappy marriage more and more dominated the relations of the Prime Minister with the new Foreign Secretary. Lord Curzon discovered that the hardships of his position did not all proceed from the " half and half " arrangement which had undoubtedly been a very trying one, borne by him with dignity and restraint while Balfour and Mr. Lloyd George were in Paris.

In the next two or three years he suffered some personal humiliations which may have increased as it became obvious that affronts could be offered without involving much risk of his resignation. At moments of extreme exasperation Balfour was sometimes the Foreign Secretary's confidant, and even the channel

---

[1] See *Curzon : The Last Phase*, by Harold Nicolson, p. 110.

for his complaints, though Lord Curzon's lifelong knowledge of his friend should have taught him that indignation about personal slights would be apt to suffer dilution on the way, when Balfour was the carrier. In such matters he held that Heaven helps those who help themselves, and that no lesser aid can do much for them. The relations between Mr. Lloyd George and the Marquess Curzon could not be a subject of wholly melancholy reflection to persons endowed with a sense of humour, and familiar with their respective ways of overcoming obstacles. And there was no living man who had more first-hand knowledge of them both than Balfour. He would saunter into Mr. Lloyd George's room at Number Ten, put up his eyeglasses to examine the familiar pictures, and then casually say: "What have you been doing to poor Curzon?" The reply would be listened to with attention, and perhaps met with a faintly sympathetic murmur, but before resuming his study of art preparatory to drifting out of the room, Balfour might say: "Intolerable no doubt, but I fear you have hurt his feelings very much." It is possible to imagine him assuring Lord Curzon when next they met that he had done all he could to present his case.

It did not in fact appear to Balfour that his old friend had been singled out for peculiar misfortune above all his predecessors at the Foreign Office.

> It's the rarest thing [Balfour said one day in 1923] (when we had been talking about the relations between the great Duke of Wellington and Lord Aberdeen), it's the rarest thing when the Prime Minister and the Foreign Minister don't clash. That's what makes me so impatient of all this talk about Lloyd George interfering so much. I don't say Lloyd George didn't often do things he had better not have. But you can't expect the P.M. *not* to interfere with Foreign Office business. It's only when you get a combination of two men who see absolutely eye to eye and work

in perfect harmony that you can avoid it. Lansdowne and myself were one of the rare cases,—but I could give you any number of instances of the other.—The fact is that the Foreign Office cannot be in a water-tight compartment.

It is not, on the other hand, possible to suppose that if Balfour had believed that the relation between Downing Street and the Foreign Office could be restored to what it had been in his own day, he would have spared himself any exertion. Again and again have I heard him declare that close co-operation between a Prime Minister and his Foreign Secretary was essential to a sound foreign policy. I believe that if he were himself criticising the biographer's almost impossible task of appraising the measure of influence which he exercised upon the Paris Conference he might have wished stress to be laid upon this point. And perhaps upon no other. His was a secondary role, played without fumbling or uncertainty. It added little to, and took nothing away from, the confidence his own countrymen already reposed in his judgment and experience. It spread his reputation for these things in the sphere of international politics, and thus laid foundations for diplomatic achievements more remarkable than any for which opportunity had been offered him in Paris.

It was not there, but in Geneva, that the Peace settlement was begun, and Balfour took a leading part.

Chapter XIV

INTERLUDE
1919

Balfour admitted to the Académie des Sciences Morales et Politiques. Letter on the death in action of a friend's son. Balfour's portrait unveiled at Eton. Chancellor of Cambridge University. Rockefeller gift to University Library.

1919

Balfour left Paris at the end of October 1919, tired, but not exhausted. It is interesting to contrast his references to the need for a "holiday" in the letter to Lord Curzon,[1] with the tone in which he had spoken of his future when he resigned the leadership of the Conservative Party in 1911, eight years before. Then, at the age of sixty-three, he seemed to anticipate some decline of energy or health; now, at the age of seventy-one, after four years of unremitting strain, he had no thought, and in truth no desire, for more than the briefest release from harness. Even the friends who knew him best marvelled at the reserves of power he had to draw upon. Lady Wemyss, who visited Paris in the heat of July, when Balfour had just taken Mr. Lloyd George's place in the Council of Five, wrote that "it is a wonderful thing to see A. J. B. at work here, and to realise what the liveliest imagination could not grasp without seeing—the immense burden he carries, and the pressure and strain at which he works—keeping an urbanity which only his special

[1] See above, Chapter XIII.

nature can command." The fact was that Balfour was never too tired to relax, and to this gift the gods had added another, perhaps even greater—he was seldom too tired to change from one form of intellectual exertion to another. At the very climax of the work on the German Treaty, he delivered to the Institut de France an Address which might have been polished in his own book-lined room at Whittingehame, remote from all the controversies of the hour.

The occasion was his admission as an *Associé Étranger* to the Académie des Sciences Morales et Politiques, an illustrious body whose choice of him for membership gave him unfeigned delight, enhanced if possible by the fact that his proposer was the philosopher, Henri Bergson.

Balfour's speech touched on the differences between the French and English character, on the unity of knowledge, the solidarity of spiritual effort. It contrasted the past with the present in which " nothing remains unquestioned : not even the laws of motion," and in which " everything is now permissible, even orthodoxy." The speech, written in English, was delivered in French, in a translation prepared, I think, by M. Bergson himself. The printed report of the proceedings reached Balfour soon after his return home. It was the only relic of his stay in Paris which formed the topic of spontaneous description after his family reassembled at Whittingehame. For a few weeks he revelled in complete idleness. The War had made no gaps in the innermost circle of his family, and marriages had recently enlarged it in a way which increased the happiness of his life during the next ten years. At the end of the War Major Edward Lascelles, the husband of his niece Joan, became his personal private secretary, and, with his wife, was henceforth constantly with

ARTHUR JAMES BALFOUR

1919 Balfour at Carlton Gardens as well as at Whittingehame. I suppose that every family which gathered round its own hearth with no chairs empty, on the first New Year's Eve after Peace was signed, was filled with a thankfulness that was something apart from happiness.

But Balfour's love for young life was not reserved for the circle of his home. It extended to the children of his friends. There were households whose joys and sorrows meant almost as much to him as his own. Among them were those of Lord and Lady Wemyss who had lost two sons, and of Lord and Lady Desborough who had lost two sons. To Lady Desborough, when Billy Grenfell was killed after his brother Julian, Balfour sent a letter which set forth more plainly, more unequivocally than anything else he ever put on paper, his feelings about death.

4, CARLTON GARDENS.
August 5th, 1915.

. . . I do not pretend to offer consolation; in one very real sense there is no consolation to be offered. The blow, the double blow has fallen, and the shock which threatens the very citadel of life can be softened by nothing that I or perhaps any other can do or utter. Who can measure the pain of separation? Who can deny that, normally at least, death *means* separation? And that between the living and the dead there lies an impassable gulf which no longing and no love is able to bridge? For this there is no remedy; we must bear it as we may; but to me it seems that in many cases the sorrow caused by death is due to something more and other than the cause of separation. It is due perhaps to an unacknowledged feeling that the separation is to be unending. Now if this be the settled conviction of the mourner, there is nothing more to be said. But if this is not the case, if the conviction be the other way, if the certainty or even the possibility of a future life be admitted, then we know that there is something wrong if the agonies of bereavement are more than those which should follow on a severance which though complete is temporary.

FLOREAT ETONA

For myself, I entertain no doubt whatever about a future life. I deem it at least as certain as any of the hundred-and-one truths of the frame-work of the world, as I conceive the world. It is no mere theological accretion, which I am prepared to accept in some moods and reject in others. I am as sure that those I love and have lost are living to-day, as I am that yesterday they were fighting heroically in the trenches. The bitterness lies not in the thought that they are really dead, still less in the thought that I have parted with them for ever; for I think neither of these things. The bitterness lies in the thought that *until I also die* I shall never again see them smile or hear their voices. The pain is indeed hard to bear, too hard it sometimes seems for human strength. Yet measured on the true scale of things it is but brief; death cannot long cheat us of love. . . .

The First " Fourth of June " celebrated at Eton after the War was the date fixed for the presentation to the School, by the Old Etonian Association, of the portrait of Balfour by Mr. Fiddes Watt that now hangs in School Hall, and is, I think, the best of all the pictures painted of him in later life.[1] Lord Dartmouth made the presentation, Lord Curzon unveiled the portrait, and Balfour made reply. He spoke of his love for Eton, and went on to say:

> On this day last year I was one of the British Delegates in Paris dealing with the tremendous problems of the Peace. We decided that the day should not pass without celebrating our ancient School, and a goodly number met together. There were soldiers, sailors, diplomats, lawyers, experts in all spheres of administration. Two of us, I remember, were Americans, but Etonians loyal to the back-bone. . . . I am told that similar scenes took place within hearing of the German guns at the front, when this anniversary came round in circumstances of great anxiety and peril. Then Etonians of all military ranks met together

[1] See frontispiece to this volume.

1919 and sent cheerful challenges to their hereditary enemy—I do not refer to the Germans, I refer to the Harrovians—and felt that even in the imminent perils of war they gained strength and cheerfulness and courage from the consciousness of the memory that all held in common, and the inspiration which they brought from their early education within these walls.

The audience listened, as only a youthful audience can listen, and cheered as only a youthful audience can cheer. Balfour's great-nephew, Michael Dugdale, carried him off to tea in his room in Mr. Marten's House, where Lady Desborough joined the family party. Outside the temperature stood at its normal arctic Fourth of June level, but Balfour nevertheless watched the Procession of Boats from Fellows Eyot, with a rug over his knees. The line was only drawn before the fireworks.

A less fleeting renewal of contact with the scenes of his youth took place about this time, when at the end of 1919 he was installed as Chancellor of Cambridge University. He had been Chancellor of Edinburgh University since 1895, and both these were honours which he took very seriously. Ties of family and friendship had kept him in touch with Cambridge University life, and now as Chancellor he succeeded his much loved brother-in-law, Lord Rayleigh, whose death had occurred while he was in Paris.

> I cannot promise [said Balfour in his Inaugural speech], I do not hope to equal, still less to surpass him in what he did for the University. But I will do my best.

He kept his word. In the remaining years of active life he never refused any request from the Cambridge authorities, although this rule sometimes forced him to decline to lend his name, or give his time, to appeals for other objects that he would have liked to support. But, in this as in other matters, he believed in concentration of energy. Few things gave him more unalloyed pleasure than his own part in securing for the new University Library the benefaction of £700,000 made by the Rockefeller Foundation in 1928. The idea of this munificent gift began to take shape at a dinner party in the house of Sir Arthur and Lady Colefax, where Balfour met Mr. Welles Bosworth, the European representative of the Rockefeller Trust, and talked ardently to him of the development of scientific research of which the Library was to be the nucleus.

1920

> It was in your hospitable mansion [he wrote to Lady Colefax], and with your kindly co-operation, that the seed was sown which has so wonderfully blossomed. It isn't easy to amass millions—at least so I am told by those who have done it; but it is far harder to dispense millions so that you do good instead of harm. The Rockefeller Trust is the most wonderful thing ever organised by a wealthy man. He gives over all the world, and he wants nothing in return. He is a poet.

Chapter XV

THE LEAGUE OF NATIONS

The Making of the Covenant. Balfour and Lord Robert Cecil. Balfour's anxiety at American defection. His view of the League's limitations. The First Assembly, 1920. Balfour's public speaking at Geneva. The British Empire votes as one. The Upper Silesian settlement. Balfour's use of League procedure. Balfour's defence of the League.

1920

Readers of the chapter on Treaty-making may have noticed how little mention is made of the one unquestionably constructive achievement of the Paris Conference, the drafting of the Covenant of the League of Nations.

Balfour was not a member of the Committee which, under President Wilson's Chairmanship, defined the sphere of the new effort at international action, and gave it constitutional form. The British Government's representative was Lord Robert Cecil, who, after being Under Secretary for Foreign Affairs, had become Minister of Blockade at the period of the War when inter-Allied co-operation reached its acme of developments in economic matters. No European statesman could rival his knowledge of the administrative machinery which had proved most efficient in these first experiments. More important still, no European statesman was more inspired than he by a passionate hatred of war, or shared so completely the American President's certainty that the way to peace lay through a League of Nations. The faith of these two men was, above every other

THE LEAGUE COVENANT

factor, the driving force that created the League. 1919 Under their impetus and that of General Smuts the Twenty-six Articles of the Covenant were drafted, revised and completed in the space of two and a half months, in time to be incorporated in the Treaty with Germany, for Lord Robert shared President Wilson's resolve that the League should form part of the general settlement. The President's determination on this point had had something to do with the failure of Balfour's attempt to get the Naval and Military clauses of the German Treaty out of the way before the political and financial questions were dealt with. But there is no evidence that Balfour dissented from the general policy of building the Peace Treaties on the League. International organisation on the lines of the Covenant, with the help of the United States, seemed to him to offer the best hope for reconstruction of world peace and prosperity, and it was not his way to be a pessimist about new experiments, nor to handle them timidly. While the League of Nations was in the making, his mind moved along the same lines as Lord Robert Cecil's, much as the mind of an observer deeply interested in the theory and practice of mechanics might move with that of the designer of some new machine. Their respective rôles could not be exchanged, nor the creative power transferred, however great the agreement that might exist about the object in view. Once the new instrument for co-operation was set up, Balfour could show unsurpassed perception of its capabilities. This he demonstrated, from the moment that the organs of the League began to function, at the meetings of the Council and Assembly of 1920, held in London, in Paris, in Brussels, and finally in Geneva.

Between Balfour's own departure from the Peace Conference, and the first of the League Council Meetings

ARTHUR JAMES BALFOUR

1919 he had made the earliest of his speeches on international affairs in the new world order. The date was the first anniversary of the Armistice, the occasion a Meeting at the Queen's Hall organised by the newly formed League of Nations Union. He declared that he was " not prepared to discuss seriously with any man what the future of international relations should be unless he is prepared either to accept the League of Nations in some form, or tell me what substitute he proposes for it." Then he talked of progress.

> I think society may go back as well as forward, I think it requires, and has always required, the constant effort, and the best elements in every society, not merely to improve it, but to maintain it at its level. It is on that condition alone that civilisation, in my judgment, is possible. But the very thought that makes me anxious makes me also hopeful—the very thought that without effort we may slide back assures me that with effort we can press forward.

A note of anxiety comes into the speech at this point. In November 1919, it was already evident that the English-speaking world was not standing solid behind the League, which was so largely the creation of its own ideology. Balfour's next words were addressed as much to Americans as to the enthusiasts in the Queen's Hall.

> If one of the Great Powers begins to make reservations, I confess that I think the future of the League will be dark indeed. . . . The whole sense of equality of effort will be thrown aside, solidarity will be dissolved. Great statesmen will look more and more to the narrower interests which influence public opinion. More and more they will turn their eyes away from the common object for which all must be prepared to make some sacrifice. I therefore venture to say to friends of mine in any country . . . that they ought clearly to understand that unless they are prepared to bear an equal share in an equal task, they are

THE INFANT LEAGUE

threatening with ultimate dissolution the whole of that 1920 new system which all of us most sincerely desire to see work effectively.[1]

The foreboding with which Balfour watched America fading out of the international scene is the measure of the welcome he gave, a year or two later, to President Harding's proposal for a Conference on Naval Disarmament and Far Eastern affairs. But to the end of his life, he held that the defection of the United States from the League of Nations entailed upon European statesmen a duty of perpetual watch lest tasks should be imposed upon the League which it was not capable of performing with its existing membership. Failure must above all things be avoided in the early years, and there were certain questions and certain parts of the world, in which effort by the League to exert authority without a guarantee of American backing would almost inevitably fail. The great political problems of the Pacific stood first upon his danger list. But he was vigilant to prevent as far as possible outstanding fragments of the Peace Treaties from being flung to Geneva for settlement irrespective of whether the League was equipped to deal with them or not.

Thus at the Third Meeting of the League Council (held in Paris in March 1920) telegrams arrived from London, where that relic of the Peace Conference known as the Council of Foreign Ministers and Ambassadors were drafting the attempt at an agreement with Turkey which ended in the abortive Treaty of Sèvres.

Lord Curzon was presiding, and the suggestion that the League might assume responsibility for protection of Turkish minorities, and even of a Mandate over Armenia, seems to have had his endorsement. Balfour repelled both ideas with vigour, basing his arguments

[1] See *The Times*, November 12th, 1919.

ARTHUR JAMES BALFOUR

1920 on the fact that the League had no force at its disposal; that its weapon was public opinion; that Turkey was not amenable to this in the same way as might be expected of the Central European States whose minorities were under League guarantee.[1] In point of fact Balfour was never very happy about the League's responsibility for minorities even in these cases, and he seems to have considered the possibility, although at the eleventh hour, of the Council refusing to accept the responsibilities laid upon it by the Peace Treaties.[2] There is in truth a flaw in the machinery of international action on this point, which could hardly escape his realistic mind, although it does not seem to have occupied him when the Treaties were being drawn up. The League is almost entirely dependent on the good will of the State concerned for carrying out its obligations to minorities. And it is precisely when the good will of a State is lacking that minorities most require protection.

In course of time an acute difference of opinion developed between supporters of the League of Nations who would equip it with physical means of enforcing its authority, and those who believe that to do so would destroy hopes of the reinforcement of its moral powers. Nevertheless in the first three years of the League's life, evolution in the direction of an international force seems to have been contemplated as possible, perhaps even as desirable. The answer sent by the League Council to the Conference of Ambassadors about Armenia may have been drafted by Balfour himself.[3] It contains this sentence:

[1] See *Procès-Verbal* of the Third Council Session, pp. 16, 17.
[2] See *Procès-Verbal* of the Tenth Session of the Council, p. 13.
[3] He had undertaken to prepare a Memorandum at the Third Council Meeting in February 1920. This was probably the basis of the Memorandum agreed to by the Fourth Council Meeting in April. See *Procès-Verbal* of the Fourth Council, p. 27.

GENEVA

> The Council of the League realises its own limitations. 1920
> It realises that it is not a State, that it has as yet no Army,
> and no finances, and that its action upon public opinion
> would be fainter in Asia Minor than in the more civilised
> regions of Europe.

The two words "as yet" would to-day touch a controversy which in itself gives proof of a certain growth in the habit of international thinking on the part of the public. Balfour had a clearer idea of the League's function than most politicians possessed, when he laboured to steer clear of the two dangers which he described thus:

> One that the League may be thought of so little account as to be entirely inefficacious; the other that it may be considered so capable that impossible tasks will be forced upon it to perform.[1]

The League Council had met eleven times, in different capitals of Europe, before November 1920, when the First Assembly was held in Geneva.

Balfour arrived on the 23rd straight from London, astonishing his staff by emerging from his sleeping berth at 7.30 in the morning to breakfast in the buffet at Bellegarde, the French-Swiss frontier station. An hour later they reached Geneva and the British Delegation descended upon the Hotel Beau Rivage, its presence there signalised by huge Union Jacks drooping from all the balconies.

It is difficult to recapture the flavour of intense excitement, curiosity and enthusiasm which pervaded the surroundings of the First Assembly of the League. Thousands of people had poured into Geneva from every quarter of the globe, and turned every one of the

[1] Speech to l'Association Française pour la Société des Nations, Paris. See *The Times* of March 20th, 1920.

big hotels round the Lake into centres of infinitely varied life. The tricolour proclaimed the presence of a large French Delegation in the Hotel Bergues. Its glittering halls were thronged with journalists, and Central Europeans. A more reserved atmosphere hung about the lounge of the Beau Rivage, imported and maintained chiefly by the Messengers from the British Foreign Office, who had accompanied the Delegation. A little automatic gambling machine brightened the hall of this hotel. Fed with centimes it sometimes disgorged more valuable coins. Balfour could never resist it, and finally broke it by pulling the handle too hard, so that all its contents were spilled. After this the Management removed it.

Balfour enjoyed Geneva. He would wander by himself away from the crowded Quaies, up to the University quarter, or to the Gardens where the statues of the Reformers, of Calvin, and John Knox, are set in the wall. There the real Geneva goes its own way, disdainfully unaffected by the international invasion in the lower town. Blessed as he was by the gift of enjoyment of the society of amusing fellow-creatures, he picked and chose among endless invitations. He spoke French well enough for all social purposes.

At Assembly Meetings however where the official languages are French and English, the English-speaking Delegates are somewhat at a disadvantage, as many of their hearers prefer to wait for the French translation. Thus the immense power which the oratory of M. Viviani or of M. Briand used to bestow upon the French Delegation was never given to any Englishman. But there is no audience in the world more sensitive to personal likes and dislikes than a League Assembly, and Balfour became a chief favourite immediately, though perhaps the lively applause which always greeted his appearance at the tribune lacked the deep note of intense feeling in the welcome reserved for Lord Robert Cecil. Yet Balfour was far more versed than his cousin in the arts of speaking which rivet the attention of a continental assembly. When he followed one of the great Frenchmen his style seemed indeed startlingly different. He used practically no gesture; his hands usually grasped the lapels of his coat. His eyes were always on his audience, his voice without much inflection until the peroration—if his closing sentences can be so floridly described. But his utterance was beautifully clear, if sometimes a trifle too hesitating. (A great teacher of operatic singing, Mr. Victor Beigel, once asked me who had trained Balfour's voice production, and would hardly believe that he had never had an elocution lesson in his life.) None of these details were lost on the critical observation of the continental politicians at Geneva. Nor was the unconscious air of immense distinction which invested the tall figure, rather thickened since the years of Balfour's slender youth, the broad shoulders a little rounded, but vigorous, and giving none of the old impression of languor. His hair was by now quite white, and was never cut very short. The foreigners beheld in him the living model of an Elder Statesman in the aristocratic British tradition.

There had been great curiosity, and some suspicion, about the part to be played by the Dominion Delegations at Geneva. Would Australia, Canada, India, New Zealand, and South Africa all take their cue from the Mother Country, and thus constitute a solid block of six votes for the British Empire on every disputed question? Or if not—would the disruption of the said Empire be hastened by the debates in the League Assembly? The chances were discussed at the hour of the *apéritif* from one end of the boulevards to the other, and all the more piquantly because Lord Robert Cecil (who had resigned office at the end of the War) was present at the first League Assembly not as a member of the United Kingdom Delegation, but as a representative of the Union of South Africa, at the invitation of the South African Government. It soon became manifest however that the Dominions were displaying a complete independence of attitude, without any strain upon their mutual relations. Balfour watched the situation with immense satisfaction. When the day did at last arrive on which six British votes were recorded against the overwhelming majority of the Assembly, his amusement knew no bounds. For the subject in hand was the proposal to set up a " Committee of Intellectual Co-operation." Without previous consultation with one another, and with very imperfect understanding of the project they desired to negative, every Delegation from the British Empire proclaimed a terrified " No." They were defeated, for their only supporter was the Delegate from Cuba. The Committee was set up, and Balfour at a later date paid a handsome tribute to its usefulness. At the moment however he welcomed it chiefly as providing a felicitous object-lesson on the kind of proposal that could be reckoned upon to illustrate the solidarity of the British Commonwealth.

The First Assembly revelled in the forms of eloquence in which the Latin races excel. But in the Committee Rooms on the Quai Woodrow Wilson, the League was fed with real problems as well as with flowers of speech. Next year results began to appear. Balfour again headed the United Kingdom Delegation at the Second Assembly in September 1921. Conventions on Social questions such as the Traffic in Women and Children—and on Opium and Dangerous Drugs were now ready for discussion. The international Health work, and especially the campaign against typhus and other such legacies of war and revolution, interested him deeply. But during the Council and Assembly Meetings of 1921 his time was mainly filled by the sequels to the Peace Treaties that began in earnest with the drafting of Mandates, and the fixing of the frontier between Germany and Poland after the plebiscite in Upper Silesia decreed by the Versailles Treaty.

The result of the voting in the disputed area had added to the strain on Franco-British relations, which had undergone much wear and tear in the two years since the French had reluctantly given way to the suggestion of holding a plebiscite in Upper Silesia at all. Even an overwhelming majority of votes for Germany would hardly have reconciled France to handing back to her intact the coal, the iron and the great " industrial triangle" on the Polish border. The plebiscite had given pro-Polish majorities in two out of the five electoral districts in the industrial and mining area, and the position was further complicated by the fact that the German majorities were mainly drawn from the town voters, while the peasantry had voted for union with the new Polish State. Thus, if the plebiscite had been the only guide, it would hardly have given a clear indication for a practicable frontier. But it was not the only guide. The Treaty directed the Supreme Council of the Allies also to take into account the " geographical and economic conditions of the locality."

These interests seemed to point, at any rate in the British view, to returning the " Triangle," with its highly developed network of railways, to Germany which had created it. The French could not agree to the separation of this area from the coal mines where the Polish vote had predominated. Dispassionate consideration of the difficulty was not made easier by a local

1921 insurrection led by Korfanty, a Pole, in the course of which French troops, nominally under the orders of the Allied High Commission, had manifested some active Polish sympathies. Thus when the Supreme Council tried in the summer of 1921 to agree upon a frontier, the effort failed. Mr. Lloyd George had accompanied Lord Curzon to Paris in August for a final attempt to meet the views of M. Briand, then Foreign Minister of France. They had struggled for five days before the Irish question, at that time boiling up for its final crisis, had recalled the Prime Minister to London. On the eve of departure he said to Lord Riddell: " The Silesian question is to be referred to the League of Nations. What do you think of that ? "[1]

Lord Riddell supposed that he was joking, and records how the journalists assembled in Paris greeted the idea with derision. An impartial settlement of a political question already so embroiled, and on which the great Allied Powers had expressed such strong views, seemed much to ask of the League Council, which at this time was composed of representatives of only eight States, namely, Britain, France, Italy and Japan, together with Belgium, Brazil, China and Spain.

But Balfour saw no inherent impossibility in the successful handling by the League of this purely European question. He travelled out to Geneva on August 29th to attend the Council Meeting urgently summoned to consider the case. Mr. Lloyd George's desire to see the industrial districts return to Germany was pretty well known, but the Cabinet issued no instructions fettering Balfour's discretion. Thus left free, he aimed at a settlement on the lines of the plebiscite as far as might be. By agreement with the French representative, M. Leon

[1] See Lord Riddell's *Intimate Diary of the Peace Conference and After*, p. 312.

UPPER SILESIA

Bourgeois, a Committee was appointed of Council Members who had taken no part in the previous discussions. A South American and an Asiatic—they happened to be a Brazilian and a Chinese—were thus for the first time associated with the settlement of a European dispute of major importance.

> The Council [said Balfour] has determined not merely to make an independent examination of the question, but to do so under conditions which will remove any suspicion that it is being dealt with from the view-point of any one country rather than another. The Council will approach the question in that spirit of complete detachment from narrow and individual views which I hope it will always display, and will make a deliberate and determined effort to deal with the problems before it impartially, and in the broadest spirit.

This was undoubtedly done, none the less so because Balfour and M. Bourgeois were in close touch with one another, and with the Committee throughout the six weeks that the recommendations were being drawn up. The interval had a calming effect upon Franco-British relations. Both Governments had agreed to accept the League's frontier line whatever it might be. The decision, when it came, was precisely that which had been ruled out of the Allied discussions, for it divided closely interdependent districts. And even so, dissident minorities were often left on the wrong side of a frontier which had cut in two the living body of Upper Silesian industry, with its network of rail and waterways, mines, factories, workers' dwellings, all as closely woven, and as bound up with private interests as in the " Black Country " of England. Such was the inevitable result of following, in a general way, the indications of the plebiscite. These could only be very roughly taken into account, so mixed was the distribution of the Polish and German-

1921 speaking populations. In fact no frontier could be drawn that was not open to the criticism of disregarding economic interests, without entirely satisfying the wishes of the populations. Had the League Council felt bound to keep strictly to its terms of reference it might indeed have effected a settlement, but only by sacrificing the prosperity of the area. A way out of the dilemma was found. Together with the new boundary line, a detailed scheme was prepared for a transitional regime to last for fifteen years, in order to preserve the economic and social unity of the zone from sudden disruption, and to provide local supervision for the rights of minorities of both races. Such a settlement could not be expected to satisfy either Germany or Poland, although the division left the greater part of the wealth of the district on the Polish side. An effort was made to equalise the minorities of both races, some three hundred thousand Germans becoming Polish subjects, as against a rather smaller number of Polish-speaking people who were left in Germany.

Balfour always defended this method of dealing with the population difficulty, as giving a basis for reciprocity in minority rights. Time on the whole has endorsed his view. Upper Silesia has not reappeared on the danger list of European questions, where it once stood very near the top.

The work of the League Council on this settlement had run concurrently with the Second Assembly through September 1921. When Balfour left Geneva in the middle of October he had founded a reputation for courageous and free use of every opportunity that League procedure offers, especially in skilful resort to public discussion. In his day there was never any question that the power of initiative lay in British hands whenever the British Representatives saw fit to use it.

REBUILDING

As for Balfour himself, a couple of years' experience 1921 of the League and its potentialities infused a brisker tone into his retorts to critics than was traceable before.

> Done more? [he said in a public speech in 1921]. Of course it might have done more. Does anyone know an institution that might not have done more? If so he has the advantage of me. I do not know, for instance, how the Churches would come out.... You cannot shunt the world on to a new track except in favourable circumstances, and the appalling war which has so recently come to an end gave an impulse and impetus without which this experiment would never have been tried....
>
> I feel, as time goes on, not that the war has produced fewer evils than I feared at the time, for the conviction grows on me that the evils are unmeasured. As year succeeds year we shall more and more see how great was the calamity, how inexplicable the crime which brought that war on humanity. There was one bright side to it. The horrors of that war did at least persuade mankind that some great effort must be made to prevent its repetition. Those who with the facile scepticism or easy cynicism of the arm-chair deride the efforts—humble, imperfect, but honest which are being made all the world over to render the repetition of those horrors impossible must be careful that they do not make themselves sharers in the great crime from which we have already so bitterly suffered.

Very far behind the speaker of these words lay the years when the scepticism or cynicism which he had denounced lurked even in the outworks of Balfour's mind. These are not qualities which run in harness with a sense of urgency, and the rebuilding of the defences of world peace seemed to him a very urgent matter indeed. Not because he looked at the post-War world through the eyes of "an old man in a hurry," but rather because he felt convinced that the full extent of the calamity wrought by the War was not yet revealed. He did not outlive that feeling. It spurred him to effort,

313

ARTHUR JAMES BALFOUR

1921 it may have partly inspired that power to perceive and seize opportunities, which was a salient characteristic of his post-War work—at Geneva—in Washington—and in Imperial politics, which, when all is said and done, lay nearest his heart.

Succeeding chapters bring the history of his public service in these matters to its zenith. The motto for them all might be " Work while it is day,"—not the day of a mere human life, but the day whilst those " favourable circumstances " of which he had spoken still made it possible to " shunt the world " out of its accustomed paths.

Fortune had still in store for him some exceptional openings for the kind of work he most wanted to do. The first of them was the Washington Conference of 1921. He came to it with a fervour, and returned from it with a pleasure in its success, greater than any emotion ever inspired in him by the triumphs of his younger days.

" It seems to me," he observed casually about this time, " that nothing ever really happened before 1914."

Chapter XVI

THE WASHINGTON CONFERENCE

Balfour heads the Delegation. The question of the Anglo-Japanese Alliance. The American proposal for Naval Disarmament. Balfour accepts it. The Japanese attitude. The French oppose limitation of submarines. The British case for it. The Four-Power Treaty. Balfour's Speech on termination of the Anglo-Japanese Alliance. The Shantung Question. The Nine-Power Treaty. Balfour returns home. The Garter and the Earldom.

Before Balfour went to Geneva in August 1921, his second journey to America was practically a settled thing. In July the United States Government had issued an invitation to a Conference on Naval Disarmament and problems of the Pacific, to which the British Government had eagerly responded. The fear of a competition in naval strength against the United States had been among the chief anxieties which the withdrawal of America from European affairs had left to the British Empire. The First Lord of the Admiralty, Lord Lee of Fareham, had given the broadest hint to that effect in March, by stating in Parliament that if the United States invited us to come to an agreement on the naval question, he would put aside all other business to help the movement forward. And in June, when the Imperial Conference assembled in London for the first time since the War, the Prime Minister, Mr. Lloyd George, speaking of sea-power as the very basis of the Empire's life, yet added that we would discuss with the

1921

Americans any proposal for limitation of armaments they might wish put forward.

Therefore when the United States Ambassador came to him with the suggestion of calling a Conference of the Powers in Washington on November 11th, Mr. Lloyd George accepted with alacrity. His first intention was to head the British Delegation in person, and his hope of doing so lingered on through the autumn, in spite of the gathering crisis in home politics over the Irish question.

Balfour had been picked out to be the second Delegate, as the front rank Minister already best known and beloved in America. Therefore when the Prime Minister found himself compelled to stay behind, Balfour, as Lord President of the Council, took the leadership of the Empire Delegations. With him the United Kingdom appointed the First Lord of the Admiralty, and the First Sea Lord, Lord Beatty, Lord Cavan, G.O.C. of the Aldershot Command, and Sir Auckland Geddes, British Ambassador at Washington.

The party sailed in the first week of November. Its departure was very different from the embarkation of the Balfour Mission of 1917, revealed to no one and carried out in darkness. Now the whole world watched the ships which brought the European Delegations across the Atlantic to the first Disarmament Conference.

No lengthening of the historical perspective in which the Washington Conference of 1921 is judged should make the contemporary feeling of its importance seem exaggerated. The value of success is often best measured by considering what the results of failure might have been. A breakdown of the first concerted effort to reduce armaments, a deadlock in the first collective attempt to settle the conflicting interests of the Powers in the Far East, would have been a more serious disaster

THE WASHINGTON PROBLEMS

even than later set-backs to progress proved to be. The treaties and agreements made at Washington in 1921 remain an object-lesson in the "new diplomacy," as Balfour defined that much misused phrase—as a departure namely from the "preposterous fallacy that there was a fixed amount of advantage to be got by somebody, and that if one nation got it another nation lost it."[1]

The anxiety of far-seeing people for success at Washington was illustrated in the House of Commons Debate on November 4th. Even Lord Robert Cecil, most courageous of diplomatists, spoke of the possibility of failure as a catastrophe too awful to contemplate, and hoped that the programme would not be too general, too elaborate, or too ambitious.

The programme however was by its very nature bound to raise for the British Empire one question as big, as complicated, and as important in its consequences as any single problem could be. It was clear, when the Delegation left England, that the future of the Anglo-Japanese Alliance must be decided in Washington. Naval disarmament and the problems of the Pacific—the two subjects for discussion—were completely interlocked. In respect of the first, British policy was to await the American proposals with goodwill and an open mind. But in respect of the second, involving the most delicate inter-Imperial issues, it was essential to chart the course well beforehand.

The Government had some pointers given to it in the course of the summer of 1921, when an Imperial Conference met in London. It was still in session when the Washington invitation arrived in July, and enough had already been said to show that the Dominions felt themselves deeply concerned with the policy which

[1] See Speech at the Hotel Cecil in Balfour's honour on his return from Washington, February 17th, 1922.

the Japanese Alliance represented. Their points of view varied considerably, but on the whole the pull of forces worked for putting an end to the Treaty.

This by no means squared with Mr. Lloyd George's inclinations, perhaps even less with Balfour's. There was no living Minister who knew more about the reasons that had made the Anglo-Japanese Treaty the pivot of our Far Eastern policy for twenty years. The Treaty had in fact been largely his own creation, for when it was initiated in 1902 in the last months of Lord Salisbury's Government, Balfour already exercised a powerful influence on foreign policy. To ensure the renewal of the Alliance in 1905 he, as Prime Minister, had taken great risks, and made heavy sacrifices of Party interest.

Although all this lay far in the past[1] in 1921, his own association with the Treaty gave him a strong feeling of personal regret at contemplating its termination. Moreover his belief in its value had not vanished with the changes in the Asiatic situation brought about by the fall of the Russian Empire. His understanding of Japanese psychology, which helped him at Washington to ease the shock of parting by means that rose far above mere tact—showed him also how unfortunate might be the consequences of breaking a particular link with the great Maritime Power of the West which had been a source of pride to the Japanese people.

Another point was the danger of intensifying a cleavage between East and West, between Asia and the rest of the civilised world. Mr. Lloyd George had emphasised that risk in his first speech to the Imperial Conference on June 20th, and his words had clearly impressed the Dominion Premiers, including Mr. Meighen, the Canadian.[2] Nevertheless the difficulties

---

[1] See Vol. I, Chapter XIV.
[2] See *Annual Register*, 1921, p. 62.

THE JAPANESE TREATY

of Canada with regard to the Japanese Treaty were among the serious considerations which Balfour and his colleagues had to weigh. Had a war broken out between the United States and Japan—a possibility which seemed by no means remote in the summer of 1921—Canada would have been in a very difficult position. British Columbia contained some fifteen thousand Japanese settlers living on the coast, or along the waterways and railroads of the sparsely inhabited land. They were feared as well as hated, and defence of the territory, as well as sentiment, would almost certainly prevent Western Canada wishing to remain neutral. The attitude of Quebec and Ontario might remain longer doubtful, but it was hardly possible, nor indeed desirable, that Canada should be divided within herself if such a war broke out. Thus, although by the terms of the Anglo-Japanese Treaty, Great Britain was bound to neutrality if the United States were a party to the conflict, the British Empire might all the more be in danger of losing its unity of action. The Canadian point of view was enough in itself to give the English Cabinet food for thought.

So much for domestic considerations. The wishes of the United States Government were strongly against a continuance of the Alliance as it stood, and it might turn out that the naval agreements themselves would be affected by British insistence on the point. Here the question of the " Freedom of the Seas " entered in, for the American refusal to join the League had left her free to be neutral in a " League war," or a belligerent on her own account.

These were some of the chief arguments for and against the maintenance of a connection which had been satisfactory both to Japan and Great Britain. Before

1921 Balfour left for Washington the Government had decided that the Alliance must be transformed, by merging, if possible, in a more general agreement. No sacrifice was too great at that moment for the object of securing peace in the Pacific. The only difference between Ministers had been as to whether Great Britain should try to hold the balance, and the power of mediation, by maintaining the neutrality between the United States and Japan enjoined by the Treaty, or whether she should enter at once into some constructive plan for settlement of disputes. Balfour came down in favour of that after a thorough study of the question.[1] Nevertheless members of his staff bear witness to his great disinclination to open the subject of the termination of the Alliance with the Japanese in Washington.

There, before any political discussions were even started, the first spectacular success had been achieved by the American proposal of naval disarmament, and its acceptance by Balfour. It included the scrapping of battleships under construction, a ten-year pause in building more and a limitation of capital ships, which worked out at a ratio of 5, 5, 3 for the United States, Great Britain and Japan respectively.

This offer was utterly unexpected in magnitude. Its welcome " in principle " by the head of the British Delegations at the opening of discussion, created an atmosphere for the Conference such as the post-War world had not seen. Balfour used to say that the boldness and generosity of the American proposals subsequently made the negotiations at Washington comparatively easy. He would remark that disarmament is simple enough when people have nothing to be afraid

---

[1] See *The Nineteenth Century and After* for April 1932; an article on " British Policy in the Pacific," by H. Wickham Steed, giving quotations from a Memorandum submitted to Balfour.

of, as must always be the case between ourselves and the United States.

In spite of the truth of this, he perhaps underestimated his own personal share in the initial success. He cabled at once to the Cabinet that the United States proposals should be accepted in principle and without reservation as far as the capital ships were concerned. His own speech at the second meeting of the Conference gives some reasons why this advice required courage from the British point of view.

> Suppose [he said to the Americans] that it was a familiar thought in your minds that there never was at any moment of the year within the limits of your State more than seven weeks food for the population, and that that food had to be replenished by oversea communication. . . . Then you will understand why every citizen of the British Empire, whether he comes from the far Dominions of the Pacific, or the small island in the North Sea, can never forget . . . that without sea communication he, and the Empire to which he belongs, would perish.

The crowded galleries of the hall in the Pan-American Building were watching him with growing enthusiasm as he spoke. Some of his audience had thought, when he first took his place at the big horse-shoe table where the Delegates sat, that he looked older and frailer than on his first visit to Washington, nearly five years before. At the opening session when Mr. Hughes, the American Secretary of State, had made his dramatic proposals, Balfour sat making notes on one of the long envelopes he always used for that purpose. (Sir Maurice Hankey had thoughtfully procured him some American ones of the right size, in time for the meeting.)[1] But Balfour had said nothing at the moment, and there was some feeling that when he did there might be an anti-climax. The

[1] See Lord Riddell's *Diary of the Peace Conference and After*, p. 335.

impression was quite dispelled. At this second meeting his voice was full of warmth.

> Do not suppose [he went on] that I am uttering laments over the weakness of my country. Far from it. We are strong, I hope, in the vigorous life of its constituent parts. We are strong, I hope, in the ardent patriotism that binds us all together.

When he sat down after welcoming the United States' proposal there was round upon round of applause from the Americans and from the British Delegations, filled with pride in their leader.

It could scarcely be hoped that even Anglo-American agreement would do away with every objection on the part of other Powers to reducing their naval strength on the scale proposed. Relinquishment of capital ships caused the least difficulty, largely because of the moderation and power of self-sacrifice shown by the Japanese at Washington.

Balfour had received a private letter from Sir Charles Eliot, the British Ambassador at Tokyo, and a personal friend. Its date—November 10th—two days before the opening of the Conference—made it a particularly valuable picture of feeling in Japan.

> The most remarkable feature about the Delegation [wrote Sir Charles] is that not one of the chief Delegates, who alone have power to decide what the Japanese vote is to be, is a military man. The principal military representative, who no doubt is entirely opposed to disarmament, can only advise his seniors.
>
> . . . . . .
>
> The Navy seems to be sincerely in favour of a reduction of armaments. The Army are as a whole opposed to any reduction. The general public do not agree with this, they feel the burden of taxation, and would like to see troops withdrawn from Siberia, ex-Saghalin, but still they

FRANCE OBJECTS

believe Japan has a mission on the mainland of Asia, and if they were made to feel they were abandoning that mission by any policy of retrenchment, patriotic sentiment would probably get the better of prudence and financial considerations.

Balfour did not reply until December 19th, at a moment when the disarmament discussions seemed to have lost some of the inspiration that had launched them.

" We are at present at logger-heads with the French," he wrote. " It is rash to say how the matter will end." The refusal of France to join in the ten-year naval holiday, or to accept the ratio allotted to her for battle-ships did indeed look like upsetting the whole agreement. That extreme disaster was prevented by a direct appeal from Mr. Hughes to M. Briand, who had been obliged to quit Washington for Paris soon after the Conference opened, leaving naval policy in charge of Admiral le Bon, as intransigeant a character as the French race and the naval profession ever bred. M. Briand, determined that France should not bear the blame for a breakdown of the Conference, promptly cabled that with regard to the tonnage of capital ships he had sent instructions to his Delegation to give way. But he added : " So far as the defensive ships are concerned (light cruisers, torpedo boats and submarines), it would be impossible for the French Government, without putting itself in contra-diction with the vote of the Chambers, to accept reduc-tions corresponding to those which we accept for capital ships under this formal reserve."

This pronouncement, though not altogether a sur-prise, was a blow to the British. Balfour and Lord Lee had by now resolved to make a strong bid for the total abolition of submarines. But if this were not agreed, Balfour informed the Cabinet that he intended to state

1921 that Great Britain could accept no restrictions on light classes of ships, nor upon the arming of the mercantile marine for defence. In that case the naval limitations would be confined in practice to battleships and large cruisers. Therefore much hung on the submarine question.

The British Delegation went into the discussion knowing that the essential condition for victory was lacking, for the United States Government would not go with them as far as total abolition of submarines. Balfour was made aware, before the question was opened at the Conference, that whatever Mr. Hughes' personal feelings might be, the American naval experts were against abolition, and would prevail. American public opinion was awake but divided, for some of the people who most condemned the abuse of submarine warfare, believed that submarines were the best defence of a weak State with a long seaboard. On the other hand the Churches and some other bodies showed signs of coming out for abolition, and the question seemed about to become an issue in domestic politics.

All this created a delicate situation for the British. Balfour's first intention had been to raise the question in open plenary Conference, but on second thoughts he persuaded the Dominion Delegations that it would be wiser to meet defeat in a private Session of the Armaments Committee, and fall back there on an agreement for limitation, coupled with the stipulation of complete freedom for building anti-submarine craft. The next stage would be a Conference session where the British would put their case, admit that they had failed to carry it in full, and state their belief that the world would some day come round to their view. The immediate object must be to get the best compromise they could in respect of submarines. This required the goodwill of the

SUBMARINE QUESTION

United States Government, who would have preferred the question of abolition not to have been raised at all. On that Balfour would not give way. Nothing in the course of the Conference raised a more difficult point of tactics for his decision than this. If the United States Government were against us, how much more all the others represented in Washington, who had behind them only a negligible quantity of national moral indignation on the subject of the submarine sinkings. Unless the case were very skilfully presented it would be easy for would-be wreckers of the Conference—and there were plenty—to persuade the American public that Great Britain had no thought but for her own interests, and was working to deprive weaker States of the humblest weapons of defence. All this was considered, but Balfour and Lord Lee went firmly forward. Their thoughts were fixed ten years ahead, when they hoped abolition might be attainable, if opinion were now given material to work upon.

Lord Lee opened the British case, illustrating from war experience the weakness of the submarine as a weapon of defence, proclaiming the British readiness to scrap what was " the largest and probably the most efficient submarine navy in the world." The offer was a greater contribution to humanity, he thought, than even the limitation of capital ships. The First Lord ended by saying that failure to carry his point did not mean that Great Britain would refuse to consider anything less.

The French and Italians showed no disposition even for compromise. Mr. Hughes read a Report from an American Advisory Committee in favour of retaining submarines, against limiting the size, but advocating the outlawry of unlimited submarine warfare, and the necessity for it being subject to special laws and rules.

1921 Balfour then got up. He made short work of the idea of relying on the honour of submarines to distinguish between merchantmen and warships. Most of his speech was addressed to the French and Italians, who both, he said, seemed to have forgotten some facts.

> The whole war [he reminded them] had turned upon keeping open communications between Europe and the United States, and on supplying Italy with the absolute requisites of national life. . . . You had to develop to the utmost your auxiliary craft which deal with submarines.

Here were the comparative contributions to that object during the world war. France 257 ships. Italy 288 ships. Great Britain 3676 ships. Admiral le Bon had observed that you could not stop the progress of humanity.

> I confess [Balfour said] that as far as the progress of humanity consists in inventing new weapons of war, I would stop it to-morrow if I could. . . . I believe it can be stopped in the matter of submarines, if we all decide to do it. I believe the conscience of mankind would help us.

He confessed however that he had given up hope of support at that Conference. Great Britain would not, as people were apt to think, be the country likely to suffer most by the retention of submarines. No other country had the same means of defence against them.

> This great naval population, this great fishing population, these innumerable craft, these admirable sailors, who showed on every occasion that when their country's allies required it of them, there was no danger or peril of battle they were not prepared to face.[1]

This speech was too plain-spoken to be popular. Balfour's letter-bag was filled with congratulations from many American citizens, but he was criticised for having,

[1] See *Washington Post*, December 24th, 1921.

BRITISH SACRIFICES

as it were, appealed to American feeling over the head of the Government. He had reckoned with this, and did not greatly care. His feelings on the submarine question were strong, and he had taken his precautions against the failure of the British effort interfering with the naval agreements on other classes of armaments.

The submarine debate took place at the very end of December 1921. It dispelled any faint hope that the Washington Conference might be able to close the door upon competition in naval armaments of all classes, as it was about to do for battleships. In respect of these the original American proposals were modified in nothing but detail when the Five Power Treaty on Naval Disarmament appeared in final form at the end of January 1922. For Great Britain it involved the scrapping of ships amounting in all to nearly 600,000 tons, and including the four new *Hoods*, between them totalling 172,000 tons, for which money had been voted and partly spent, although their keels were not yet laid. It was a bold sacrifice for the country accustomed to know herself the greatest naval Power of the world, in that sphere of armaments where the maritime nations had hitherto been most jealous of their power and their freedom.

While the work on the Naval Treaty was still proceeding, Balfour had been immersed in even more exacting discussions in the Committee on Pacific and Far Eastern questions.

The advantages of thinking out a policy beforehand, even though it was not a wholly agreeable one to the British Cabinet, are illustrated by the history of the demise of the Anglo-Japanese Alliance at Washington. American feeling on the subject was found to be as strong as had been expected. Therefore Balfour was relieved by the account sent him by our Ambassador

ARTHUR JAMES BALFOUR

1921 in Tokyo of the effect produced in Japan by the tactful manner in which the first hints of coming events had been presented. This letter was dated November 10th, and has been partly quoted above. Sir Charles Eliot wrote:

> When the proposal to hold a Conference about Far Eastern questions as well as disarmament was first announced last July, the Japanese Government saw at once that they must participate, but the official and popular attitude was hardly disguised hostility. The whole business was regarded as an attempt to arraign Japan before an Anglo-American tribunal. In a month or six weeks there was more confidence, and it was felt that Japan could take her place with the other Powers in a Conference of equals. This developed into the phase which still prevails, namely, a friendly feeling towards America. It is not a very sincere friendship no doubt, but it is thought that America's real interest in the Conference is disarmament, and that to effect something in that matter she will be willing to avoid raising questions about China and Siberia disagreeable to Japan. When the proposal for the Conference was first brought forward, I am afraid the feeling towards Great Britain was one of great bitterness and almost unfriendliness. Things grew better when it was announced that Lloyd George had said we would either maintain the Anglo-Japanese Alliance, or substitute something better for it, but still in spite of our desire to discuss the agenda proposed for the Conference fully and frankly with Japan, I could not induce the Minister for Foreign Affairs to take part in such an exchange of views; they seemed to prefer not to be too intimate with England for fear of offending America. Yet I do not doubt they are most anxious to continue the Anglo-Japanese Alliance. They do not believe that there can be any lasting friendship with the United States, and they fear that if their alliance with us is terminated, they will be isolated. But though they prefer a simple Anglo-Japanese Alliance I think that they will consent to a tri-partite agreement with America.

Balfour found the Japanese Delegation as reluctant to discuss matters with him as the Tokyo Foreign Office had been with the Ambassador, and it took him some time to overcome the feeling. Then he threw himself entirely into the preliminary talks with Prince Tokugawa, head of the Japanese Delegation.

This nobleman had been for twenty years President of the House of Peers, his influence was immense, his international outlook sagacious. With him was Baron Shidehara, one of the most outstanding of Japanese diplomatists, and Admiral Kato, described to Balfour by Sir Charles as " notoriously silent, even in Japanese." His part in the political negotiations was small, but it was he who, after the signature of the new Quadruple Treaty, called upon Balfour by order of his Government, to thank him for his friendship with Japan.

The difficulty of diplomatic achievement is sometimes in inverse proportion to the apparent simplicity of the final document. The Treaty contained only four clauses and merely engaged the parties to respect the integrity of the island possessions of the others in the Pacific, and in the event of dispute to invoke each other's good offices. The fourth Party was France.

> The Treaty [wrote Balfour to Sir Charles Eliot] as I originally conceived it, was of course tri-partite. It was Hughes' idea to bring in the French in order to soothe their somewhat ruffled pride. The difficulty was to let them in without seriously offending the other Powers who were kept out. This exclusion was necessary, as the Japanese had given us to understand that the Treaty would lose much of its sentimental value if it was made the common property of all the Powers, great and small.

An agreement was linked to the Treaty which provided that the strategic islands in the Pacific should not be fortified. This involved long and delicate negotiation. The heart-burning behind it all can be traced between the lines of Balfour's speech to the Conference on

ARTHUR JAMES BALFOUR

1921 December 11th, 1921. He recalled the origins of the old Japanese Alliance, the dangers from Russian aggressiveness, from German ambitions in the Far East, perils now wiped out by history, as the people of the United States could perceive. Americans therefore asked themselves, "Why is this Treaty continued? May it not prove hampering and injurious in case strained relations should become yet more strained?"

> I understand that point of view [Balfour went on]. But there is yet another point of view which I want you to understand. . . . After all, that Treaty, or its predecessors, has been in existence twenty years. It has served a great purpose in two great wars. It has stood the strain of common sacrifices, common anxieties, common efforts, common triumphs.
>
> When two nations have been united in that fiery ordeal, they cannot at the end of it take off their hats one to the other and politely part as two strangers part who travel together for a few hours in a railway train. . . .
>
> So that Great Britain has found herself between the possibilities of two misunderstandings, . . . and we have long come to the conclusion that the only possible way . . . of removing those suspicions and difficulties which are some of the greatest obstacles to that serene peace, which is, after all, the only tolerable condition for civilised peoples, the only possible solution was that we should annul, merge, destroy, as it were, this ancient and outworn and unnecessary agreement, and replace it with something new, something effective, which should embrace all the Powers concerned in the vast area of the Pacific.

The Four Power Treaty did not however touch the root of the danger in the Far East which lay in the disappearance of central government in China, in the disorganisation of Chinese relations with the foreign Powers interested in her trade, and no less in the absence of agreements between those Powers themselves. Unless these two last points could be regularised at Washington,

SHANTUNG

the foundations of the new Treaties would be laid on a quicksand. Above all it was necessary to remove causes of quarrel between China and Japan which had remained open ever since the Treaty of Versailles had assigned to Japan the rights, privileges, and property, formerly held by Germany in the Shantung Peninsula by virtue of the Agreement of 1898, under which the port of Kiao-Chow had been leased by China to Germany.

The surrender of these rights had been claimed by Japan in Paris in virtue of a Treaty with Great Britain and France made early in 1917, when neither the United States nor China had entered the War, and secondly by right of arms, the Germans having been expelled from Shantung by forces mainly Japanese, and containing no Chinese contingent.

China, on the other hand, held that as Shantung was Chinese territory, she could claim direct surrender of all the rights which Germany had obtained in the leased territory. These included, besides the harbour of Kiao-Chow, an important railway, mines, submarine cables, and other property. The promises of Japan that she would give up every privilege in the Shantung Peninsula which involved interference with China's sovereignty did nothing to reassure the Chinese, especially as no pledge was incorporated in the Treaty of Versailles. The Japanese held that their promises, repeated verbally to the Supreme Council in Paris, were implicit in Treaties made between themselves and China in 1915 and 1918, and had nothing to do with the Peace Conference.

The transfer of Shantung had not however been implemented by 1921. The Chinese had twice rejected proposals from Japan to begin negotiations, on the ground that China had not recognised Japanese occupation of Kiao-Chow as valid. As soon as the Washington

ARTHUR JAMES BALFOUR

1921 Conference opened, the Chinese Delegate, Mr. Wellington Koo, presented a Memorandum demanding restoration of Chinese sovereignty, the " open door," and the end of foreign interference with China's national affairs.

Balfour knew all about the beginnings of the Shantung controversy. He had been personally concerned with it during the Peace negotiations and much of his time in Paris had been spent in trying to reconcile the opposing conceptions of national honour. It was in private discussion with him that the Japanese had reached a formula for handing back Shantung in full sovereignty to China, retaining only the economic privileges formerly granted to Germany. On the other side he had listened to the Chinese view that the Treaties of 1915 and 1918, which the Japanese persisted in taking for the basis of future agreement, had been extorted by threats and had inflicted on them a grievous wrong. He did not dissent from that opinion as regard the Treaty of 1915, which followed on the " Twenty-one Demands " which had done much to alienate sympathy from Japan. But as regards the Treaty of 1918, concerned mainly with the provision of Japanese capital for the building of railways in Shantung and Manchuria, Balfour took a different view. In a Despatch to Lord Curzon from Paris, dated May 8th, 1919, he had written:

> They (the Chinese Delegation) could never be got to understand that, whatever might be said of the Treaty of 1915, the Treaty of 1918 between China and Japan was a voluntary transaction between sovereign States, and a transaction which gave important pecuniary benefits to China; nor did they ever adequately realise that by the efforts of Japan and her Allies, China, without the expenditure of a single shilling, or the loss of a single life, had restored to her rights which she could never have recovered for herself.

THE TWO GERALDS

A. J. B. with his brother Gerald in the garden at Fisher's Hill.
1917

A. J. B. with his great-nephew Gerald on the terrace at Whittingehame.
1928

TREATIES WITH CHINA

This opinion was only meant as a historical comment even at the date when it was written, for in the same Despatch Balfour remarked that no agreement seemed possible between Chinese and Japanese with regard to the past. " Nor did this seem necessary. It was only the future which concerned us."

This was still more true at Washington. There for three months, Balfour and the American Secretary of State laboured as principal supervisors of negotiations which, at last, on February 4th, 1922, led to the Sino-Japanese Treaty that restored the Shantung Province once more to China. At the same time Balfour announced that Great Britain was handing back her own lease of Wei-hai-wei.

This agreement was hailed with relief by a weary Conference. The only one of the big settlements still unfinished was the Nine Power Treaty to be signed by the United States, Belgium, the British Empire, China, France, Italy, Japan, Holland and Portugal, for maintaining the territorial integrity and open door for commerce in China. With it went a whole group of smaller Resolutions, "a mighty mass of things apparently trifling, and things of the deepest importance, ranging from discussion of the nationality of a traffic manager of a Manchurian railway to questions touching not merely the immense area of the Pacific, but of the whole civilised world." So Balfour said, in his final speech at the end of twelve weeks hard labour, the results of which he described as "an absolute unmixed benefit to mankind, which carried no seeds of future misfortune." [1] Time has proved this true. If armaments have increased once more, if fear and suspicion once more threaten peace in the Far East, it is not on account of anything

[1] See *The Times* of February 4th, 1922. Speech at the Pilgrims' Dinner in London.

1922 that was done at Washington, but rather because the work of Washington was not consistently carried forward and developed.

The Conference ended on February 6th, 1922.

Balfour was far from being above personal satisfaction in work well done, and his voyage home was almost one of pleasure.

The Prime Minister and the Cabinet were on the platform at Waterloo to greet the return of the Delegation, and outside a crowd waited to cheer them. Balfour drove away with Mr. Lloyd George, and a little later the family collected round him at Carlton Gardens. He had been somewhat surprised by the warmth of his reception in the street, and though pleased, rather glad that it was now, as he thought, all over. He presently went out for a walk with Mrs. Lascelles, and they strolled up Waterloo Place, Balfour scanning the outline of roofs as his habit was, when he perceived people on the tops of some omnibuses standing up and looking towards him. " There must be something interesting," he said. " What can it be ? " " You," answered his niece, whereat he took hasty cover in Hugh Rees' bookshop.

It was on this same day of his return that he heard of King George's intention to bestow on him the Order of the Garter. This was followed in May by an Earldom and Viscountcy, graciously given with Remainder to his only surviving brother, Gerald, and to his heirs male, and to the heirs male of his brother Eustace. The ancient cradle of the Balfour family, Balfour in the County of Fife, was the place chosen for the title of the Earldom. The second title was Traprain, taken from the name of the hill, Traprain Law, which is a landmark in East Lothian, and lies upon the Whittingehame estate.

HONOURS

Some two months elapsed between the bestowal of the Garter and the Peerage. The time was too short for Balfour to accustom himself to the new nomenclature of "Sir Arthur," and it was rumoured in the family that a draft of a letter to the Royal Donor of the honour had been discovered beginning "Mr. Balfour presents his humble duty . . ."

His pleasure in accepting the Garter was enhanced by the fact that it formed a unique combination with the Order of Merit, which had been conferred upon him in the year 1916.

Chapter XVII

LAST WORDS ON IRELAND

The Treaty of 1922. Evolution of Balfour's opinions. Twenty years of " Resolute Government." Balfour's speech of 1911. " Nationality and Home-Rule." Balfour refuses compromise.

1922   Balfour's feelings about the Treaty with the Irish Free State, negotiated during his absence in Washington, seem never to have been fully revealed even to those friends or colleagues who had fought under him in the old Home Rule battles. This is hardly a matter for surprise, however unsatisfactory it may be that a chapter of history so interwoven with Balfour's own life should end, in his lifetime, without one word or sign of approbation or disapproval from him, whose study of Ireland had been so deep, and whose labour for the Union so consistent.

He returned home in the middle of February 1922, to find the Treaty a signed document of which no provision could be altered, and he found moreover that, in spite of the overwhelming vote by which the House of Commons endorsed it on February 16th, the prevailing mood had been, as Mr. Winston Churchill has described it: " most of the majority were miserable, and all the minority were furious."[1]

All Balfour's natural inclinations would prompt him to probe as little as he must into past events presented in an emotional setting of that kind, and he could divest

---

[1] See *The World Crisis : The Aftermath*, p. 320.

THE IRISH SPECTRE

himself of any responsibility for the actual negotiations which had opened in London between British Ministers and the Sinn Fein Delegates almost simultaneously with his own departure for Washington in November 1921. Passions were fading before he applied his mind to their cause, which he did only in 1929, when Mr. Churchill's *Aftermath* was first published. The four preceding volumes of *The World Crisis* he had read with great admiration. ("I am immersed," he once remarked, "in Winston's brilliant Autobiography, disguised as a history of the universe.") When *Aftermath* appeared, Balfour's last illness had begun. The book was read aloud to him, and he listened with painful interest to the chapter entitled "The Irish Spectre." He commented on the magnificent prose, and then said that the substance of it put him in some embarrassment. He had meant to write a chapter on Ireland in his own Memoirs, finishing with an all-round blessing on the Free State, as fitting into the general scheme of the British Empire. But now that he had realised for the first time the full story of the Treaty and the events which led up to and followed it, he felt he must make some comment upon how it had impressed him.

> The Irish [he said] had owed their success to crime. Winston practically admitted it. They had defied British rule,—and British rulers had given in to them. How could such a state of things be said to fit in with the scheme of the Empire?

Balfour could not carry out his intention of writing his final comments upon Ireland, but it is nevertheless possible to trace the evolution of his opinion up to the very eve of the settlement. The Treaty of 1922 was the outcome of a sudden capitulation on the part of the British Government which outraged all his traditions

ARTHUR JAMES BALFOUR

1922 and instincts. But had he been asked what alternative was possible in the winter of 1921, he would probably have countered the question by saying that the measure of freedom then granted to Southern Ireland should have been negotiated earlier and not left to be extorted under pressure at the last. For in Irish policy he had always been an extremist, and his loyalty to the Union was equalled in the old days by his scorn for all the administrative compromises by which the Liberal Party had striven to rid themselves of the Irish question in their series of Home Rule Bills.

When the defeat of Mr. Gladstone in 1886 brought Lord Salisbury into power at the head of a Unionist Government, Balfour believed, as in those days many of the Irish leaders themselves believed, that with the removal of the vicious system of land tenure, the Nationalist agitation would wither away. After four years experience in governing the Irish people he seems still to have held this opinion, for when he was combating Mr. Gladstone's second Home Rule Bill in 1893 he spoke of the agrarian question as " the root and origin of the Irish difficulty and very often mistaken for Irish patriotism."[1]

Ten years of Unionist administration followed the Liberal defeat of 1895—ten years in which Mr. Gerald Balfour's Land Act and Mr. George Wyndham's Land Purchase Act carried forward the constructive Conservative programme of 1886.

When Balfour ceased to be Prime Minister in 1906 his diagnosis of the causes of separatist agitation needed no modification, for in the past decade sedition and terrorism had been dormant in Ireland, and the powers given under his own Crimes Act of 1887 had lain dormant too.

[1] Speech at Limehouse, April 18th, 1893.

RESOLUTE GOVERNMENT

Words spoken in the year 1886 by his kinsman and greatest teacher in the art of politics seemed then fulfilled, or nearly so.

1922

> Parliament should enable the Government of England to govern Ireland. Apply that receipt honestly, consistently, and resolutely for twenty years, and at the end of that time you will find that Ireland will be fit to accept any gifts in the way of local government or repeal of the Coercion laws that you may wish to give her.[1]

So Lord Salisbury had prophesied. But he had tinued thus:

> What she wants is government—government that does not flinch, that does not vary; government that she cannot hope to beat down by agitations at Westminster; government that does not alter in its resolutions or its temperature by the party changes which take place at Westminster.

A dream perhaps, even at the beginning of that fatal connection between the Irish question and English party politics riveted under Mr. Gladstone; a dream to which no practical politician could surrender himself for a moment, when the experience of another quarter of a century had shown successive Liberal Governments in this country roped by the eighty odd votes of the Irish Parliamentary Party to the chariot of the Irish Nationalist leaders. The separatism that had been nurtured in the Victorian Age on grievances drew its strength now from power. And moreover on the Continent of Europe nationalist aspirations were becoming every year a more potent political force as the day of the Serajevo murder came nearer.

On November 6th, 1911, Balfour had made a speech on the Irish question.[2] It happened to be the last he

[1] See *Life of Lord Salisbury*, by Lady Gwendolen Cecil, Vol. III, p. 303.
[2] See *The Times*, November 7th, 1911. Report of a meeting of the Nonconformist Unionist Association in London.

ARTHUR JAMES BALFOUR

ever delivered as Leader of the Unionist Party—his resignation was to be made public forty-eight hours later. But this is not the chief reason for the biographical interest of this speech, though it may account for the frankness with which he revealed the very bones of his thoughts on Ireland, and on the Imperial Constitution into which the Irish fragments must be fitted.

Never, he declared, could that be accomplished by means of the "rotten hybrid system" represented by the Home Rule schemes of which Mr. Asquith's Government had just produced the latest edition. Balfour declared that an Irish Parliament, whether dependent or independent, had been tried in the course of history, and in both forms it had failed. "What folly it all is to go over the same series of failures again, to end with the same conclusions."

He stood therefore for the Union Parliament. He argued, as he had always argued, that owing to the course of Irish history every political idea in Ireland was of English growth, that England had been the giver, not the robber, of any and every political institution that Ireland had ever possessed. Then a new note entered the speech, a note never so clearly heard before. Irish nationalism was still, in his view, basing itself on premises unjustified by historic fact; nevertheless he recognised a reality to which English Home Rulers still remained blind, but which was forcing itself now upon his own vision.

> If this be, as I am sure it is, an attempt of a certain section of the population of Ireland to work on a purely national basis, and to have in their Parliament and their Government a centre round which national feelings are to crystallize, it cannot remain dependent. . . . When Mr. Parnell said, "No man can put a limit to the march of a nation," he spoke words of statesmanlike wisdom. And if

NATIONALITY AND HOME RULE

Ireland is really the nation which that sentence assumed, 1922 then no man could put a limit to its march, and certainly the paper limitations of your Act of Parliament are as powerless to stop the development of the separatist and Nationalist feeling as a child's sand castle is to stop the advance of the sea.

And what of Ulster? Balfour in this speech of the year 1911 was deliberately refraining from speaking of Ulster, or of the evils that would come upon her if the Union were dissolved. He was avowedly taking the broad view of a constitutional statesman.

Once again before the Great War, he expressed his views in an article published in the University magazine of Montreal in the year 1913. This was reproduced at the time as a pamphlet, under the title of "Nationality and Home Rule."[1] In 1920 the Home Rule Act of 1914 was replaced by the Act that set up separate Legislatures for Northern and Southern Ireland, and thus provided at last the real and only solution of the Irish problem. Balfour, in common with all the Unionist leaders in Mr. Lloyd George's Cabinet, accepted a Bill which gave Ulster control of her own destiny. During its stormy passage he put some of his views upon it into a letter to the Prime Minister, dated February 10th, 1920. He argued for a frontier line that should create a homogeneous Ulster. On finance he wrote: "I would pay neither conscience money nor blackmail."

This was the last official paper that Balfour ever wrote on the Irish question. If the bitterly unwilling but loyal acceptance by the North of the 1920 Act had been imitated by the South, the "Irish Spectre" would have been laid. But it continued to haunt the British Government in a more grisly shape than ever before, through

[1] See above, Chapter VII.

1922 murder, and reprisals for murder, until the Government suddenly decided to abandon the attempt to quell resistance by force. In May (1921) the whole power of the State . . . was used to hunt down the murder gang, in June the goal was "a lasting reconciliation with the Irish people."[1]

Mr. Winston Churchill, himself a member of the Cabinet which made this sudden change of policy, explains how no middle way was now left between " war with the utmost violence, and peace with the utmost patience." The Cabinet was divided upon the terms on which the choice should be laid before the Irish. Some Ministers felt that the alternative to repression should be the offer of nothing less than the maximum of Irish demands.

" Let us (so they argued) make it clear that the Irish people are being forced by Sinn Fein to fight . . . not for an Irish Parliament under the Crown, but for a revolutionary Republic."

A debate took place in Cabinet upon this issue. The extremists were in a minority, Balfour among them. One of his colleagues has told me that Balfour thought at this time of reprinting *Nationality and Home Rule*, and refrained reluctantly, because the views expressed in it were not in line with the decision of the Cabinet.

To sum up. Balfour refused to consider any compromise between the maintenance of the Union and complete autonomy for Southern Ireland, " requiring her " (so he had written in *Nationality and Home Rule*) " to manage her own finances, pay her own bills, borrow on her own credit, control her own rebels, settle her own Constitution, remaining, if she so desire it, a self-governing Colony within the limits of the Empire."

With these words a long story draws to its end.

[1] See Churchill, *The Aftermath*, p. 290.

THE FULFILMENT

The beginning was in May 1882, when a young backbencher ran down the corridors of the House of Commons to fling the word "infamy" in Mr. Gladstone's face, on the news that Mr. Parnell was let out of Kilmainham Gaol.[1] Very, very few were left within the walls of Westminster who remembered that scene of forty years back, or the faces of the men who took part in it. There had been Charles Stewart Parnell, with "eyes of red flint," and William Ewart Gladstone, flashing indignation from under his tremendous brow. Still it may have been easier for survivors to recall the looks and tones of those dead leaders than to believe in the identity of their irresponsible young assailant with the venerated figure whom his countrymen were now accustoming themselves to speak of as Lord Balfour. For he had moved with his times so naturally, so harmoniously, so readily, that it needed an effort to remember that he had accumulated his beliefs, and learned to fight for them, on the far-away battlefields of nineteenth-century politics.

And now he leaned upon his spear, sometimes glancing back, but oftener gazing ahead towards the next stage in the development of the constitution of the British Empire, which was to set the coping stone upon his life-long labour for Imperial Union. That stage was nearing the fullness of its time in 1922. Already Balfour could discern how it must be accomplished by seeking the unity of the whole through the complete independence of the parts. The history of his share in framing the Constitutional Declarations of 1926 will be the epilogue to the history of his work for Ireland.

[1] See Vol. I, Chapter III.

Chapter XVIII

THE ELDER STATESMAN

Part I

Discontent of Conservatives with the Coalition in spring of 1922. Balfour supports Mr. Lloyd George. Reasons for Mr. Lloyd George's unpopularity. The " Balfour Note " on War Debts. Balfour and the League of Nations' Guaranteed Loan to Austria. The fall of the Coalition, October 1922.

"It is in old age that power comes. An old man in English politics may exert enormous power without effort, and with no drain at all upon his health and vital force. The work of thirty or forty years of political life in England goes to the building up of political reputation and position. During that long period no power is exercised except by irregular means such as the use of threats of resignation. It is in old age only that power comes that can be used legitimately and peacefully by the once strong man."

1922

This quotation is taken from a letter of Sir Charles Dilke's written in 1885.[1] At the moment of its writing the House of Commons held two men destined to illustrate in their own persons the truth and error in the aphorism. Lord Randolph Churchill, at the age of thirty-eight, was already hacking out a short cut to leadership, with the very weapons indicated. It was indeed a resignation that brought about his downfall. But until that fatal miscalculation had been made, the shrewd judge of

[1] See *Life of Sir Charles Dilke*, Vol. II, p. 153.

COMING CHANGES

parliamentary promise might most probably have pointed to him as the fighter whose ambitions were most likely to be fulfilled. Assuredly the choice would not have fallen on the languid figure lounging beside Lord Randolph on the front bench below the gangway, waiting there as if on the off chance of some intellectual exercise, but seeking nothing so little as power. Yet forty years later, Balfour was wielding an immense influence in the State, precisely in the effortless and almost unconscious manner born of life-long habit.

Nevertheless personal ambitions, with their joys and humiliations, their defeats and their victories, remained as much outside the ambit of his experience in his old age as in his youth. Never in his life had he had to strive for opportunity to prove his capacity, or to advance his career. Perhaps he would never have so striven; but it is a curious fact that this opening page in the average politician's life remained blank to the end in the richly varied book of Balfour's experience.

While the ship that carried him home from the Washington Conference was pursuing a placid course across the Atlantic, the approaching break-up of the Coalition Government was heralding itself by warnings, unmistakable to the Party leaders. When Mr. Bonar Law had returned to London after the recess in February 1922, he found "a complete change of opinion" among the Conservatives with regard to Coalition. He had spoken to the Prime Minister on the subject, telling him that in the present mood of the Conservatives it was impossible that things should go on as they were. Mr. Lloyd George had not expressed dissent.[1]

Lord Riddell noted in his Diary a conversation with the Prime Minister about this time.

---

[1] This is taken from some notes by Balfour of a conversation between himself and Mr. Bonar Law in December 1922.

ARTHUR JAMES BALFOUR

1922   A great deal will depend on Arthur Balfour [remarked Lord Riddell]. If when he returns, he says to the Conservative Party, " Unless you stand together you are going to smash the things you regard as vital. Close your ranks and follow your leaders," that will have a great effect.

It will be interesting to know what line he is going to take [said Mr. Lloyd George]. He may wish to become Prime Minister. If he does, I shall support him. I am in agreement with Birkenhead and Chamberlain. They wanted me to see A. J. B. and secure his support, but I declined. I shall do nothing to influence him. He must do just as he thinks best.[1]

After the first breakdown of Mr. Bonar Law's health in 1921, the Conservative leadership had devolved upon Mr. Austen Chamberlain. There is little doubt that if Balfour had shown the least willingness to resume his old position at the head of the Party, the self-effacing comrade of many years would readily have made way. Then as regards Balfour and Mr. Lloyd George, their complete agreement about the importance of a united front in a world still torn by war, might well have made an exchange of offices practicable between them.

Probably therefore the insurmountable obstacle to Balfour becoming Prime Minister once again was his own view of the part he was prepared to play in his remaining years of political life. If any of the hopes or speculations about his intentions were put to him after his return from America, he would certainly have pointed to his acceptance of a Peerage as proof of his withdrawal from the list of possible leaders. For he felt strongly that Lord Salisbury had been the last Prime Minister who could combine that office with membership of the House of Lords, and he was wont to say that even Lord Salisbury could hardly have

[1] See Lord Riddell's *Diary of the Peace Conference and After*, p. 356.

DISINTEGRATION

maintained to the end the necessary touch with the currents of modern politics, unless he himself, in his peculiarly close relations with his uncle, had been Leader in the House of Commons. As will be seen later on, this consideration weighed decisively with him when his advice was sought in 1923 upon the appointment of Lord Curzon in succession to Mr. Bonar Law.

Balfour could not fail to feel the change of atmosphere that had taken place during the three months of his absence at Washington.

> When I came back [he said] I at once found I was in a different political world from that which I had left. No cause was assigned, no obvious cause existed, but nevertheless the movement towards disintegration had made obvious and serious advances.[1]

Balfour exhibited an aloofness towards the specific discontents of his Conservative friends which some of them found a little exasperating. To many Conservatives the causes for disintegration of the Coalition seemed not only obvious, but so numerous that malcontents could pick and choose among grievances which all in the end were rooted in distrust of Mr. Lloyd George. For some the Irish Treaty, for some suspicions about methods of selection for the Honours List. The failure of the Genoa Conference to do anything for the reconstruction of Europe was also put down to the Prime Minister's mounting account. His desire for an understanding with Russia, the deadlock in Reparations, the rising uneasiness about the results of the Greco-Turkish War, for which his pro-Greek policy was blamed—these were grounds of offence, to which many more trivial were added. Balfour wrote to Lady Frances Balfour, one of Mr. Lloyd George's most passionate critics.

[1] Speech in Edinburgh, November 1st, 1922.

ARTHUR JAMES BALFOUR

4 Carlton Gardens.
26-10-22.

There is no doubt of course that Ll. G. is violently disliked by great bodies of his fellow-countrymen. In the case of the vast multitude this is partly no doubt because they get, at least temporarily, sick of any statesman or Party who has been long in power; but also it is largely due to the scandalous campaign of personal calumny to which he has been subjected. Your story about his taking money for Honours is a good illustration of the lies that have been propagated and apparently believed. *Your* quarrel with him I confess I don't understand in the least. You think he has destroyed the Commons as a debating Assembly. That, believe me, is in the power of no man to do, were he Prime Minister a hundred times over. If the House of Commons has temporarily gone down hill as a theatre of vigorous debate, it is partly no doubt because no questions of principle have divided the historic Parties; but largely also because, so far as I can make out, it is very poor in debating talent. Asquith won't make speeches, Maclean can't, and the Labour people do not appear to have produced any orators of power and authority. It really is nonsense to talk either of Ll. G. or his Secretaries having anything to do with this state of things one way or another.

This letter shows Balfour, as was often the case, less unaware of what people were thinking and saying than some of them imagined. He was more out of sympathy than out of touch with the clamour. There is the authentic ring of indignation in a speech at the City Carlton Club on March 7th, when, speaking of the Prime Minister, he said:

What is the use of abusing him? You will certainly not pull him down from the proper niche he is destined to occupy in the historic gallery. But are you going to do either your Party or your country a service? You say he has made mistakes. I am not going to deny it. We do not produce in this country impeccable angels to lead our counsels, to help in our debates.

PARTY

These are the concluding sentences of an eulogium not easily matched among Balfour's speeches. He was the most impersonal of politicians, in respect of others as much as of himself, never permitting loyalties which, in his eyes, were secondary, to interfere with arrangements that seemed best in the public interest. To hound Mr. Lloyd George out of the political arena seemed to Balfour revolting in the case of one who, as he said, " had impressed the authority of his country on all the nations of the world." But he would not have hesitated to bow the Prime Minister courteously off the stage, if he had thought that his work for the time being was finished. The personal tributes in this speech are therefore not detachable from the main arguments by which he defended the continuance of Coalition Government through the aftermath of war.

> The difficulties [he said] are incomparably more complicated than the problems of war; I am not sure they do not require a . . . statesmanlike insight which cannot get inspiration from party watch-words, important and relevant as they were before this world crisis began, important and relevant as they may become if, and when, the present state of things resumes its normal.

These observations were far from being out of tune with the temper of the people. The approaching fall of the Coalition was not mainly due to a burning desire to return to Party government. Yet many among those who were scheming for the restoration of Party government against Balfour's advice, could hardly share the sentiments or the associations that the very word " Party " called forth in the politicians of Balfour's generation. Belief in the system as practised in England before the War had been of the very essence of his political tradition. To preserve the unity of his Party had seemed to him the primary duty of his years of

1922 leadership, when the rift opened between Tariff Reformers and Free Traders. "I cannot be a second Sir Robert Peel," he had exclaimed when Mr. Lloyd George offered a bargain to secure a united front against the German menace in the year 1911.

This very speech in the spring of 1922 contains great passages upon the political philosophy of Party. "But remember," he concludes, "it is a fair weather system." And in this warning lies also a farewell to the world of his youth.

Every generation must buy its own experience. Having once delivered himself, Balfour said no more throughout a summer full of labour troubles at home, and in Ireland of civil war. In foreign policy a series of Conferences apparently ended in nothing but bickerings with the French, and rebuffs from the Bolsheviks.

In addition there was another legacy of the War which every taxpayer felt to be his own particular affair. The question, namely, of War Debts.

The Government stated its policy on this in August 1922, in a document, famous as "The Balfour Note."

Normally it would have been "The Curzon Note," for although it was primarily a statement of financial policy, it was addressed to the French Ambassador and the representatives of Britain's other debtors in Europe, and was therefore issued from the Foreign Office, of which Lord Curzon was now the head. But he was out of England recovering from illness, and Balfour was in charge of his post. Thus it happened that in much of its phraseology the Note bears the hall-mark of his literary style.

In the sound sense of its initiative against war-debt payments, the Balfour Note has outlived criticism.

THE BALFOUR NOTE

As a political gesture however it failed of its purpose, 1922 being before its time, and in discord with the psychology both of France, obsessed by her hopes of German Reparations, and of the United States, whose people were far as yet from facing the economic consequences of their intention to collect their debts. America could see nothing in the "Balfour Note" except an attempt to evade obligations, coupled with an implied rebuke to herself, a rebuke all the more exasperating for being delivered back-handedly to the address of the French. For the Note was a statement of the British desire to remit all sums due to Great Britain from her Allies, or from Germany in respect of Reparations, and an explanation of why the American refusal to do the same must reluctantly compel us to collect from our European debtors only as much of what they owed as was required to fulfil British obligations to the United States.

> In no circumstances [runs the Note] do we propose to ask more from our debtors than is necessary to pay to our creditors. And, while we do not ask for more, all will admit that we can hardly be content with less. For it should not be forgotten, though it sometimes is, that our liabilities were incurred for others, not for ourselves. The food, the raw material, the munitions required for the immense naval and military efforts of Great Britain, and half the £2,000,000,000 advanced to allies, were provided, not by means of foreign loans, but by internal borrowing and war taxation. Unfortunately a similar policy was beyond the power of other European nations. Appeal was therefore made to the Government of the United States; and under the arrangement then arrived at the United States insisted, in substance if not in form, that, though our allies were to spend the money, it was only on our security that they were prepared to lend it. This co-operative effort was of infinite value to the common cause, but it cannot be said that the rôle assigned in it to this country was one of special privilege or advantage.

ARTHUR JAMES BALFOUR

1922 No passage in the Note is more stamped with Balfour's authorship than the wording of the British view of war debts.

> To generous minds it can never be agreeable, although, for reasons of State, it may perhaps be necessary, to regard the monetary aspect of this great event as a thing apart, to be torn from its historical setting and treated as no more than an ordinary commercial dealing between traders who borrow and capitalists who lend. There are, moreover, reasons of a different order, to which I have already referred, which increase the distaste with which His Majesty's Government adopt so fundamental an alteration in method of dealing with loans to allies. The economic ills from which the world is suffering are due to many causes, moral and material, which are quite outside the scope of this despatch. But among them must certainly be reckoned the weight of international indebtedness, with all its unhappy effects upon credit and exchange, upon national production and international trade. The peoples of all countries long for a speedy return to the normal. But how can the normal be reached while conditions so abnormal are permitted to prevail? And how can these conditions be cured by any remedies that seem at present likely to be applied?

The truth of this is now very generally accepted, but at the time the Balfour Note obtained little intelligent support even from the City of London. America's reaction was shown in her renewed insistence on immediate arrangements for funding the British debt. This was done in December 1922, but Balfour was not a member of Mr. Bonar Law's Cabinet which was responsible for the settlement.

One more piece of international work fell to be done by Balfour before the Coalition Government broke up in October. The stability of the whole Peace settlement in Europe was threatened that autumn by the imminent collapse of the Austrian State's finances. The country could not indeed have supported the burden of existence

THE AUSTRIAN LOAN

for the past three years but for charity and credits which were now both exhausted. Vienna was starving, and the Government almost helpless, for want of funds.

In 1921 the Allies, beginning to take alarm at the prospect of the breakdown of all administration in Austria, had waived for twenty years even the claims to Reparations which had never been exacted. In the spring of 1922 the bankruptcy of the State was so near that several Governments advanced money, Great Britain sending in two million pounds, repayable out of the first loans that Austria might succeed in raising. Other lenders took their security on assets (such as railways) which the Reparations Commission released for the purpose. But all these sums only staved off the crisis, and put fresh burdens on the Budget. The currency slumped, and the Austrian Government appealed to the Allies for a loan guarantee which would reassure the banking houses, who doubted now whether Austria could survive as an entity at all. But the Allies replied that they could severally do no more. The League of Nations, they said, must consider the problem. Its Council would meet at the end of August.

Balfour went out to Geneva, heading the British Delegation for the last time. All his attention was concentrated on Austrian affairs. He studied the documents as he travelled, and asked his principal colleague, Mr. H. A. L. Fisher,[1] to take over most of the work at the forthcoming Assembly of the League, so that he himself could devote all his time to the Council, where Austria's case would be considered.

When Balfour arrived in Geneva the Austrian Chancellor, Monsignor Seipel, was there before him. For the previous fortnight he had been touring the capitals

[1] Then Minister for Education in Mr. Lloyd George's Cabinet. Afterwards Warden of New College, Oxford.

353

of Europe, begging for the very life of his country. Few Churchmen who have filled high secular office have ever kept the esteem and affection of all those who came in contact with them like this dignified old man. Personal sympathy sprang up at once between him and Balfour,[1] who was however already quite prepared to take great risks, financially and politically, for the chance of saving Austria.

For the next five weeks Balfour presided over a Committee of the League Council which evolved a scheme for a guarantee by certain Member States calculated to restore enough confidence in the stability of Austria to enable loans to be raised without further currency inflation until the Budget should be balanced. This was to be done within two years, years of increased taxation and drastically reduced expenditure for the impoverished country. It was a hard programme for Austria to face, and no Government would have had the strength to impose it upon the people, without outside help—which meant outside authority. The League of Nations appointed its own Commissioner, representative of the League, not of any single guarantor. Only so could such infringement of independence have been accepted even temporarily by an Austrian Government, or tolerated by other European States. The idea was not easy to work out in detail on the political side; the financial part of it was even harder. But the will to succeed was there, and the faith in the League's power to do things that had never been done before. The same freedom in experimenting with the new international machine which Balfour had shown during the Upper Silesian settlement enabled him now to take the

[1] I met Monsignor Seipel in Vienna a few years later, and was introduced to him as a relative of Lord Balfour's. He let his coffee cup fall to the floor, in order to hold out both hands. " Your dear uncle saved my country," he exclaimed.

CHANAK

lead for Great Britain in overcoming the difficulties of the Austrian settlement.

> The League of Nations has not failed us [exclaimed the Austrian Chancellor]. The great idea lives,—the idea that a Supreme Court exists, which, when a people is in dire need, will effectually call upon others to help, and perhaps by so doing unostentatiously relieve the world of burdens laid upon it by the sins of the past. Yes, the great idea lives.

That was in 1922.

The speech which Balfour made on October 4th, announcing the success of the Council's labours, was his last at Geneva. No accomplishment in an international gathering such as the League can be put to the sole credit of any one man. But Balfour left a reputation behind him which did not fade. It was the reputation of a man who was sparing in general professions of faith in the League, but who had never shrunk from putting its capacities to every test that his times provided.

When he returned to England at the close of September, Mr. Lloyd George's Government was very near its end. Its fate had really been sealed in August by the popular indignation at the handling of a crisis caused by the rout of the Greeks in Anatolia before the forces of Mustapha Kemal. When the survivors of King Constantine's army had fled from the Asiatic shore, the only foreign troops left on Turkish soil were a handful of British and French, occupying the zone of Constantinople and the Straits, and in grave danger from the advance of the Turkish Nationalist levies. At the most critical moment the French hauled down their flag and withdrew. The British Cabinet was not deterred by news of this desertion from their resolve to resist to the uttermost any threat to the Straits, and any attempt on the part of the Turks to cross to the European side.

ARTHUR JAMES BALFOUR

1922 Telegrams were sent from London to the Allied Powers, to the Balkan States, and to the British Dominions warning them that the freedom of the Straits was in danger, and inviting them to join in defending it by arms.

British policy at this juncture was framed by some half-dozen Ministers. Balfour was one of them. Once again, in the last decade of his life a familiar theme recurs. His first introduction to foreign politics had been at the Congress of Berlin in 1878 when he had watched Lords Salisbury and Beaconsfield achieve that " Peace with Honour " which, for Britain, meant the freedom of the Straits. For the freedom of the Straits, nearly fifty years after, Balfour would still have been prepared to fight. At the moment however a large number of his countrymen were not disposed to take the long view. It is admitted now that the firm stand made by the British Government probably saved Europe from a fresh outbreak of war, for if our troops had retreated out of Anatolia before the Turkish advance, it is unlikely that Mustapha Kemal would have halted on the Asiatic shore. When our troops held their ground, he hesitated before attacking, and his moment passed. But the British Press and public, uninformed, and badly startled, were in no mood to distinguish between courage and mere rashness. The danger to the Allied contingents, which had been precipitated by the unauthorised advance of the Greek army into the interior, was most unfairly put down to Mr. Lloyd George's championship of Greek claims upon the coast. The cup of his unpopularity brimmed over.

In October Mr. Austen Chamberlain summoned the Unionist members of Parliament to the Carlton Club. There had not been such travail within the Party since the revolt against Balfour in 1911. Now Balfour was

LLOYD GEORGE RESIGNS

arguing for a trust in Mr. Chamberlain's leadership which had failed him for his own. He was unheeded. His speech at the Carlton Club did not sway a vote. The decisive voice was that of Mr. Bonar Law, who now came out of his retirement. " I think," he said, " that the time has come to break up the Coalition."

The Meeting rallied to him, and by a majority of nearly two to one, passed a Resolution that the Conservatives, while willing to co-operate with the Liberals, should fight the forthcoming Election as an independent Party. That same day—October 20th, 1922—Mr. Lloyd George tendered the resignation of his Government to the King.

A few days later Balfour spoke at a dinner given to the retiring Unionist Ministers by their supporters who had voted with the minority at the Carlton Club. To them he foretold the return to Coalition which in 1931 began to be called National Government.

> I believe [he said] that again you will come to that system of co-operation, but I believe it will be under circumstances far less favourable than we find at this present moment. We shall come to it in the face of dangers which we shall have to face.[1]

[1] See *Daily Telegraph*, October 24th, 1922.

Chapter XIX

THE ELDER STATESMAN

Part II

Balfour and the House of Lords. Lord Curzon and the Premiership. Unionist defeat of 1923. Balfour visits Palestine. Lord President of the Council once more. Scientific Research.

1922

Balfour took his seat in the House of Lords on May 30th, 1922, introduced by the Earl of Midleton and the Earl of Selborne.

It took him, like most House of Commons men, a little while to get accustomed to his new audience. " It's like talking to a lot of tombstones," he complained to Lord Riddell.[1] Moreover the bad acoustics of the Chamber afflicted him at first, for he was becoming slightly deaf. He rejoiced therefore when ear-phones were fixed at intervals along the backs of the red benches, and eventually he became acclimatised to the House of Lords.

He did not often return to the precincts of the House of Commons after he left it. I do not think he ever entered the Peers' Gallery, and the first time he was seen again in the Inner Lobby was in the year 1927, when he unveiled the statue of Mr. Joseph Chamberlain. That ceremony over, he walked away with me. " It is rather nice," he said, " to be near the old place again." I asked him if he wished he were back in it. " I'm

[1] See Lord Riddell's *Diary of the Peace Conference and After.*

OUT OF OFFICE

quite content where I am," he answered, and pointing over his shoulder to the entrance into the Lower Chamber, he added: " They tell me it's like shooting at sitting pheasants in there nowadays."

After the fall of the Coalition in November 1922, Mr. Bonar Law had formed a Government. Balfour was out of office for more than two years.

The first of them was given up to much needed rest. He went in the spring to Cannes with his niece, Mrs. Edward Lascelles, an expedition which became annual after the War, always in her company. No one knew better than she how to arrange the exact mixture of solitude and frivolity, of long silent motor drives, of gay little dinner parties, and the right amount of lawn-tennis, which made these holidays perfect for him. He came back to London before Easter 1923, much refreshed, and at Whitsuntide went to Sheringham with friends, some of whom had for many years been in the habit of going together to some golfing centre at that season. This year the party consisted of Lord and Lady Wemyss, Lady Desborough, Lord D'Abernon, Mr. Evan Charteris[1] and Mr. and Mrs. Edwin Montagu.

Balfour had hardly arrived at Sheringham when he was laid low by an attack of phlebitis, and was compelled to remain for some weeks in the hotel. He was visited there by a succession of friends and relations, but, as far as most of them knew, he was a complete prisoner in his bedroom throughout the early summer. As a matter of fact however he had gone by motor to London for a day in obedience to an august command. King George desired to consult him about the appointment of a new Prime Minister.

On Saturday, May 19th, 1923, Mr. Bonar Law had received a verdict from his doctors, which caused him to

[1] Lord Wemyss's brother; afterwards Sir Evan Charteris.

ARTHUR JAMES BALFOUR

1923 submit his resignation without delay. The King, who was at Aldershot, received his Prime Minister's letter on May 20th. He was precluded, by the state of Mr. Bonar Law's health, from following the usual practice of the Sovereign in such emergencies, and consulting the outgoing Prime Minister before appointing his successor. The King therefore telegraphed at once to Balfour, a past Prime Minister, and a senior member of his Privy Council, asking him to come up to London the next day.

Only two names were under serious consideration: those of Lord Curzon of Kedleston and Mr. Stanley Baldwin. The one had a long and illustrious career behind him, the other was an untried and an almost unknown personality. But the one was a Peer, the other a Commoner. This, as it turned out, was a fatal handicap to Lord Curzon's claims, especially so in the circumstances of the moment. The Labour Party had not as yet any adequate representation in the House of Lords, and it happened also that the Secretaries of State for Foreign Affairs, the Colonies, and War, as well as the Secretary for Scotland, were Peers. These objections to appointing another Peer as Prime Minister must have been present in the King's mind before he asked for Balfour's opinion, which was given against Lord Curzon, but was no doubt founded on a judgment formed long before the concrete case arose. Balfour believed, and often said, that even in Victorian times, under a more restricted franchise, and before the appearance of a Labour Party, Lord Salisbury could hardly have kept proper touch with the feeling of the country unless Balfour himself had been leading the House of Commons. There is no question therefore which way his advice was given. It seems probable that its effect was simply to reinforce the Sovereign's decision.

A. J. BALFOUR ON THE COURTS AT CANNES
1913

BALFOUR CONSULTED

It has been suggested that Balfour intervened unasked.[1] 1923 The narrative shows that this was not the case. Various accounts have appeared in print about the hurried events of the days between Mr. Bonar Law's resignation on May 20th and Mr. Baldwin's appointment on May 22nd; therefore the exact chronology has a certain interest.

On Sunday, May 20th, the King's Secretary, Lord Stamfordham, telegraphed to Balfour at Sheringham. On Monday, 21st, Balfour came to Carlton Gardens and was visited by Lord Stamfordham in the afternoon. It was on the evening of Monday that Lord Curzon, then in Somerset, received a message from Lord Stamfordham asking him to come to London the next day. The interview between them took place on Tuesday, 22nd, at 2.30 p.m., the King having arrived from Aldershot that day at noon. Lord Curzon then learned that Mr. Baldwin had been summoned to go to the Palace at 3.15. Between the Sunday and the Tuesday voices had been raised in London against Lord Curzon's appointment. Balfour was on the road from Sheringham when, on Monday morning, Mr. Amery and Mr. Bridgeman, then respectively First Lord of the Admiralty and Home Secretary, visited Lord Salisbury, the Lord President of the Council, and expressed their hope that Mr. Baldwin would be Mr. Bonar Law's successor. These views reached the King that same day through more than one channel.

On Tuesday, 22nd, Balfour returned to his peaceful bedroom in the Sheringham hotel. He perhaps never realised the full bitterness with which his old friend was that day seeing " the cup of honourable ambition

---

[1] See *Curzon: The Last Phase*, by Harold Nicolson, p. 355, where it is said: " Balfour had intervened to suggest that Curzon was temperamentally unsuited to guide the destinies of the country in a democratic age."

1924 dashed from his lips."[1] It is probable also that Lord Curzon never knew that Balfour had been asked to play any part in inflicting upon him the greatest disappointment of his life.

Mr. Baldwin's first Government was not long-lived. The year 1923 brought within the range of everybody's vision the economic catastrophe which had overtaken Europe. The lessons of the "Balfour Note" were pointed more sharply in another signed by Lord Curzon from the Foreign Office in August 1923, expounding the burden imposed on this country by the dislocation of her foreign trade, due largely to the French occupation of the Ruhr, and to the fall in the French exchange. The number of unemployed in Great Britain was 1,350,000 at that time, and it seemed an appalling figure. In these circumstances the Prime Minister felt it his duty forthwith to seek a mandate from the country to use tariffs for protection of British industry in the home market. Mr. Baldwin dissolved Parliament in November, but at the General Election the country denied him the mandate. The Unionists, although the strongest Party in Parliament, were in a minority in the new House of Commons, and on January 23rd, 1924, Mr. Ramsay Macdonald, assured of a majority by Liberal support, formed the first Labour Government.

Balfour commented sparingly in words upon the tactics which had produced this abrupt reversal of the Unionist fortunes, contenting himself with throwing up his hands and casting his eyes to the ceiling. His attitude towards politics was rather detached at this time, and he probably never contemplated any return to office. His mind continued to range with its usual freedom and ardour, and my note-books of 1923,

[1] See Lord Ronaldshay's *Life of Lord Curzon*, Vol. III, p. 352.

CONVERSATIONS

1924 and 1925 are full of his talk on all manner of subjects.

One of these conversations is remarkable partly on account of its date—December 1923—when the result of the General Election had made it clear that within a few weeks there was to be a Socialist Administration for the first time in this country.

> I don't myself worry much about this class antagonism we hear so much of [said Balfour]. I think it's getting out of fashion already. It's not the big problem that one predicts for the future. But on the other hand the race problem is getting more difficult everywhere.
>
> *Gerald Balfour.* Not in Great Britain. I don't think we shall ever be much bothered by that.
>
> *A. J. B.* No—perhaps not here. But we can't dissociate ourselves from the Empire. Honestly I don't see what the future of South Africa is to be. And India—though I know absolutely nothing about India. I wish I did.

While this talk was going on some of the party were looking at a handful of cigarette ashes placed in a "Designator" kaleidoscope, which in turning, showed the ashes in a variety of geometrical patterns. Balfour looked down the cylinder and remarked: "I dare say that's how this horrible welter of a world looks to a Higher Intelligence."

Another fragment of conversation is dated April 25th, 1925; its origin was a discussion of the future of the Arab countries, and the possibility of their federation.

> As you know [said Balfour] many people have dreamed dreams since the War ended.

Then, after a pause:

> It's partly the fault of the British nation—and of the Americans; we can't exonerate them from blame either—that this idea of "representative government" has got into the heads of nations who haven't the smallest notion of what its basis must be. It's difficult to explain, and the

1925 Anglo-Saxon races are bad at exposition. Moreover we know it so well ourselves that it does not strike us as necessary to explain it. I doubt if you would find it written in any book on the British Constitution that the whole essence of British Parliamentary government lies in the *intention to make the thing work*. We take that for granted. We have spent hundreds of years in elaborating a system that rests on that alone. It is so deep in us that we have lost sight of it. But it isn't so obvious to others. These peoples—Indians, Egyptians, and so on—study our learning. They read our history, our philosophy, our politics. They learn about our Parliamentary methods of obstruction, but nobody explains to them that when it comes to the point all our Parliamentary parties are determined that the machinery shan't stop. " The King's government must go on," as the Duke of Wellington said. But their idea is that the function of opposition is to stop the machine. Nothing easier of course, but hopeless.

This conversation arose on the morrow of the day he returned to England from a visit to Palestine, where he had gone, at the invitation of the Zionist Organisation, to attend the opening of the Hebrew University on Mount Scopus, outside the walls of Jerusalem.

Balfour started on this his first and only visit to Palestine towards the end of March 1925, accompanied by his old friend, Dr. Weizmann, President of the Zionist Organisation, and Mrs. Weizmann, and by Major and Mrs. Edward Lascelles. They embarked at Naples for Alexandria, where a great concourse of Jews awaited the ship. The voyage had been abnormally rough, and Balfour was so prostrated that there was a doubt whether he was fit to receive the deputation that boarded the vessel.

" But," he objected, to those who wished to spare him " considering that I have come all this way to visit the Jews, it would be a bad beginning not to see them."

PALESTINE

At Alexandria, therefore, he had a foretaste of the welcome that met him in every one of the Jewish settlements which he afterwards visited in Palestine.

The party spent a couple of nights with Lord and Lady Allenby at the Residency in Cairo before going on to Jerusalem. The greater part of the Middle East was in a state of unrest at that time, and the police protection which they had thenceforth to endure must have reminded Balfour of old times in Ireland. But he allowed it to impinge as little as possible upon his enjoyment of Palestine. There was no disorder there, although in protest against Jewish immigration the local Arab leaders had organised a one day strike, when all Arab shops were closed, and Arab newspapers appeared with mourning borders, to signify their feelings towards the author of the "Balfour Declaration."

Among some of the Moslem populace there was a certain confusion of mind about the reasons for this demonstration. One English lady in Jerusalem was told by her Arab cook on the morning of Balfour's arrival, that it would be impossible to buy anything that day, as the King of the Jews had arrived at last. The enthusiasm of the Jewish population on the other hand was almost embarrassing. At Tel Aviv, the new Jewish city on the coast, which already contained some thirty thousand people, the streets were packed with roaring crowds, and illuminated in the evening when Balfour went to the Opera House for a gala performance of the third act of *Samson and Delilah*. At Jerusalem, too, Balfour heard a performance of Handel's *Belshazzar* in Hebrew, the same oratorio of which, as a young man, he had financed the performance at the Albert Hall. With intense curiosity he observed the beginnings of a Palestinian culture drawing its elements from every country, but imitating none. Interest in

ARTHUR JAMES BALFOUR

1925 the new social phenomena of Palestinian Jewry helped him to survive the speechifyings which were an inevitable part of his welcome in every agricultural colony. Fatigue was not mitigated by the fact that these orations were often in Hebrew, which was already being modernised into a living language of daily life. No achievement of the Jewish colonists impressed Balfour more deeply than this, and he dwelt upon it in his own speech to the ten thousand people assembled on the slopes of Mount Scopus on the day the Hebrew University was opened.

From that hill the Roman destroyers of Jerusalem had conducted the siege of the City which ended the epoch of Jewish national life that had begun when the Children of Israel first entered the Promised Land. The very spot where the Jordan had been crossed could be seen from the great natural amphitheatre where Balfour spoke, proclaiming his belief that a new era had opened in the history of the scattered People.

The scene was splendid. Its background was the vast panorama formed by the mountains of Moab, the dark valley of Jordan, and the glittering waters of the Dead Sea. A procession entered the arena on the hillside, headed by Dr. Weizmann and Balfour, who was wearing the scarlet robes of the Chancellor of Cambridge University. Next came Lord Allenby the liberator of Jerusalem, the British High Commissioner Sir Herbert Samuel, the Chief Rabbis of many countries, and representatives of Universities and Governments. When Balfour rose to speak it seemed as if the cheering of the multitude would never cease. He was very much moved. And indeed it has seldom fallen to the lot of any statesman to see within his own lifetime the fruits of a policy so rooted in faith in the qualities of an untried nation as Balfour's Zionism had been. The Hebrew

TOURING

University (barred to no one, whatever his race or religion) seemed about to fulfil all his hopes for a revival and a concentration of Jewish culture. He rejoiced frankly in his own share in the political settlement of Palestine which had made its foundation possible. He knew that when the Jews cheered him there was deep feeling beneath, the feeling of a homeless people, who for the first time in two thousand years were welcoming an honoured guest in their own National Home.

In Jerusalem Balfour and his companions were the guests of Sir Herbert and Lady Samuel at Government House. When touring the country their entertainment was provided by the Zionist Organisation. Great publicity had naturally followed them everywhere and the arrangements of the Palestine Government for Balfour's safety had inevitably made complete freedom an unattainable luxury. Before returning to England he had set his heart on visiting Baalbec in Syria, and on doing so as an ordinary tourist. Passages had been taken on board the *Sphinx*, a Messageries boat due to leave Beyrout for Marseilles, on April 12th. On the 8th, the party took leave of their Palestinian hosts and crossed the frontier into the territory of the French Mandate. They travelled in a special coach attached at Samakh to the Damascus train, accompanied by Mr. George Antonius, who, although he was then in the service of the Palestine Government, came in no official capacity, but at the suggestion of Sir Herbert Samuel, as the best of cicerones for the Syrian sight-seeing to which they were looking forward.

No hint had been given to any of the party before they left Jerusalem that Balfour's arrival in Syria as a tourist could occasion any embarrassment to the French, or be likely to cause any political unrest. So far were

1925 they from suspecting such possibilities that as Major Lascelles bade farewell to the officer of the Palestinian Police Force who accompanied them to the frontier station, he jokingly said that he expected the Government was as tired of protecting them as they were of being protected. Something in the officer's response struck him as odd, and he elicited the information that some hostile demonstration might be expected at Damascus on the part of Arab nationalists. Balfour was already seated in the train, which was almost due to start. He was somewhat annoyed by the rumour which Major Lascelles immediately brought him, but refused to take any notice of it, saying that his intention to pay a private visit to Syria had been known for weeks to the Colonial Office at home, to the Government of Palestine, and to the French military authorities in Syria. As none of them had raised any objections so far as he knew, he was bound to assume that no objections existed. Balfour was not then aware that the Palestine Government had actually consulted the French within the past few days, and had received assurances that his visit to Syria would be welcome.

The Damascus train therefore departed with the party on board. But the pleasure trip ended before it was begun. What happened next may be told in the words of a letter from Mrs. Lascelles to Miss Balfour, written from the Hotel Victoria in Damascus.

> From the moment we crossed the frontier the whole train was full of soldiers, and three (French) officers in our private coach. They bundled us out of the train suddenly at a station before Damascus, and rushed us here in motors; as A. J. B. said, "the Arabs will have to be dangerous indeed before they are worse than that motor drive in crowded streets." The point was to get us here before the train got in. They succeeded. . . . All night the hotel has been surrounded by a regiment of soldiers. . . .

RIOTING

> They let Eddy and me go for a walk with Mr. Antonius this morning, as long as we get back by eleven, as a demonstration is to take place then; though there are still heaps of soldiers I doubt their getting near the hotel. . . . The bazaars are all shut in our dishonour. It is very hot.

1925

This letter was written before midday. At that hour a crowd of some six thousand Arabs was advancing on the hotel. They were excited, but unarmed, and Major Lascelles, watching from a balcony, felt no doubt that they could have been easily handled without the use of fire-arms. But the order was given to shoot, and the French cavalry fired over the heads of the mob, hitting some people behind. Three were killed and more injured by these shots. The rioters retaliated by heaving paving-stones at the heads of the cavalry horses, and for one brief moment there seemed to be a risk that the crowd would get past the soldiers and rush into the hotel. But the danger was soon over. Balfour was both distressed and annoyed and determined, of course, to leave Syria as soon as possible. In the meantime invited guests had succeeded in reaching the hotel and he lunched in the restaurant with Mr. Smart, the British Vice-Consul, Mr. Merton, *The Times* correspondent, and their wives. In the street all had become quiet, and at half-past three General Sarrail, the Military Governor of Syria, paid a call which appeared somewhat long delayed. He showed himself eager for the departure of the party, and at a quarter-past four the luggage was in the motors. Surrounded by a cavalry escort, they left Damascus for Beyrout, where the *Sphinx* was already in harbour. Relays of troops in lorries accompanied them through the peaceful country-side all the seventy miles to Beyrout, causing much delay by continual ceremonial changing of the so-called "guards of honour." For the next three days Balfour remained on

1925 board the *Sphinx* until she was due to sail. Nothing could have been more exasperating to him than this adventure. He had been put in a false position, partly perhaps through misplaced unwillingness to interfere with his arrangements on the part of the Palestine Government, but more through the behaviour of the French. That they expected some hostile demonstration was obvious, but they were evidently unprepared for the size and excitement of the crowd on the following morning, and their nerves seemed considerably shaken by realising that a deplorable incident might turn into something far worse, if the mob succeeded in rushing the hotel.

If the French authorities had indeed not been unwilling to advertise some mild display of Arab feeling, the explanation would have to be sought in the intricacies of Anglo-French relations in the Middle East at that time. By comparison with Syria, Palestine under British administration was already more prosperous economically, largely through the inflow of Jewish energy and capital. Both Mandatory Governments had their own difficulties with nationalist agitation, but French methods of government were highly unpopular, and it might be that some jealousy prevailed, and no unwillingness on the part of the French to draw attention to the solidarity of Arab sentiment on both sides of the frontier. The affair however had no further political consequences, and Balfour soon dismissed it from his mind.

Immediately after his return to England he was once more a Minister of the Crown.

Lord Curzon died on March 20th, 1925, and Mr. Baldwin (who had returned to power after the General Election of October 1924) asked Balfour to fill the vacant post of Lord President of the Council. Balfour

RESEARCH

agreed, only stipulating that he should not take up office until his return from Palestine. Perhaps no other office would now have tempted him, but he had held this one already in Coalition days, and knew its routine duties to be no heavier than he cared to make them. He felt entirely capable of taking his due share of work in the House of Lords, as well as in Cabinet. Moreover the Lord President's office held for him a special attraction, since it carried with it responsibility for two branches of scientific work under Government: the Departments, namely, of Scientific and Industrial Research, and the Medical Research Council.

Already, while a member of the Coalition Government, he had shown how seriously he meant to take his headship of these two bodies. When he came back from America in 1922, the Medical Research Council had just moved its headquarters into the house in Queen Anne's Gate which had once been the Irish Office. Balfour's own old room overlooking St. James's Park was now occupied by Sir Walter Morley Fletcher, Secretary of the Council.[1] To him one morning entered a messenger, slightly excited, slightly dubious.
" A gentleman to see you, Sir."
" Who is it ? What does he want ? "
" He wants to know if he can be of use to you, Sir. But I didn't like to ask him his name, because I *think* it's Lord Balfour."

It was. He had walked down from Carlton Gardens at the earliest possible moment, and crossed the well-known threshold intent upon an answer to his question.

> The Council [wrote Sir Walter Morley Fletcher] had worked previously under some six or seven Ministers, variously eminent, but none, I think, had ever made himself aware of the geographical position of the Office.

[1] The late Sir Walter Morley Fletcher, K.B.E., C.B., F.R.S.

ARTHUR JAMES BALFOUR

1925 ... Need explanation be offered for the affectionate devotion his courtesy and simplicity won from all his subordinates?[1]

The fall of the Coalition Government had not broken Balfour's connection with the Medical Research Council for long. In 1924 he was appointed its Chairman in succession to Lord Irwin. Thus when Balfour joined Mr. Baldwin's Government, he was Chairman of a body constitutionally advisory to himself as Lord President of the Council. He continued to occupy this anomalous dual position until the end of his public career, for, as he informed his medical colleagues, he so much enjoyed his first-hand insight into their work that he would connive at his own presence among them unless objection were raised by others.[2]

He set himself to increase effective contact between the scientists themselves and to put them in touch with the administrative Departments, just as had been done twenty-five years before in the naval and military sphere through the Committee of Imperial Defence. With care and much personal attention he promoted the establishment of its counterpart, the Committee of Civil Research. The two bodies were constituted on the same advisory principle, operating by means of a flexible organisation of *ad hoc* sub-Committees. There was naturally less need for secrecy about much of the work of the Civil Research Committee, and, after a year or two, Balfour was able to review in the House of Lords a long and varied list of activities, ranging from investigation of the life history of the tsetse-fly, to the preservation of foodstuffs on ocean voyages. He expounded with gusto, almost as if he were unveiling the plot of one of his favourite detective stories, how two hundred and fifty thousand pounds' worth of Australian apples had

[1] See *British Medical Journal*, April 5th, 1930. [2] *Ibid.*

RESEARCH

perished in transport in one year from unexplained causes. Research had shown the clue to the mystery:

> These apples [Balfour explained] are alive, are breathing —are breathing exactly like the Noble Lords whom I am addressing. They are breathing in oxygen, they are breathing out carbon dioxide. And these apples were dying of suffocation. It was the old problem of the Black Hole of Calcutta.[1]

It was not with a dilettante's interest that Balfour encouraged work upon such problems. The men of science who devoted their time and energy to his Committees have testified to the encouragement they derived from the novel experience of finding in a layman and a politician, not only the power to give practical help to research, but the imagination to understand its value to the State, combined with the gift of words to illuminate its patient discoveries.

The Imperial Conference of 1926 is remembered for its results upon the constitution of the Empire. Balfour said at the time that he regarded the work of the Research Sub-Committee of the Conference (over which he presided) as only second in importance to that of the Committee on Inter-Imperial Relations. He wrote the vital parts of both Reports with his own hand. In the more famous document the political bonds between the Dominions and the Mother Country were loosened. In the proposals for co-ordinating research he sought to forge new cultural links between all parts of the Empire, through the Departments and individuals performing scientific work in every field. In this (as in the research side of the Empire Marketing Board set up in 1926) Balfour saw eye to eye with much younger politicians in discerning the germ of great developments.

[1] See House of Lords Reports, May 12th, 1927.

Chapter XX

IMPERIAL RELATIONS

The Imperial Conference of 1926. Its problems. Balfour's views of Imperial relations. The drafting of his Report. Effect upon the Dominions. Balfour in 1927. Essay on Francis Bacon. Balfour's views on Nationality.

1926   The record of half a century of public service draws to its close. The fiftieth anniversary of Balfour's maiden speech in the House of Commons fell in August 1926. In October of that year an Imperial Conference was held in London which became a milestone on a road far longer than the span of any life, for its beginnings were made three hundred years back, when parliamentary institutions were first established in a colony of the British Crown.

In 1926 the nations of the British Empire had worked through the immediate problems of their War and pre-War association, and had reached a point of new departure. Before they could lay their new courses a re-statement of their relationships had to be made. The task was delicate, it required courageous guidance. In Balfour the Overseas Dominions found a leader as frank in exposition as the boldest of them could desire. Seven years had passed since the signature of the Dominion and Indian representatives to the Treaty of Versailles had made them independent members of the League of Nations. Since then, in 1922, the Irish Free State had come into being with a position analogous to

EVOLUTION

that of Canada within the Empire. But that position 1926 had not been regularised; it had actually evolved since the Anglo-Irish Agreement was made, as was shown by the appointment of an Irish Minister Plenipotentiary at Washington, and the Canadian signature of the Halibut Treaty with the United States in 1923. Loyal as had been the co-operation of the Overseas Dominions throughout the War, they emerged from it determined never again to be dragged automatically into armed conflict by decisions over which they had no control. The unity of the Empire could no longer be based on either the theory or the practice of a single responsibility for foreign policy. What then was its foundation? Some attempt to answer that question could not be put off, for the Cabinet knew that it would be raised as soon as the Conference met.

Nevertheless there were at least two reasons why an examination of the structure of the Empire might seem to the Mother Country a perilous undertaking at that juncture.

In the first place there was at the moment nothing to counteract the centrifugal forces which must be released by a purely political discussion of inter-Imperial relationships. The opposite pull of economic interests was at its weakest in 1926. Preference Resolutions had been passed at the last Imperial Conference in 1923, but there had not been much vigour in them on the Dominion side, and they had been killed by the vote of the United Kingdom Parliament under the Labour Government of 1924. Nor was there any irresistible will to revive them. The conditions were lacking, as it is easy now to perceive. It required a world slump to generate the amount of external pressure and internal goodwill which made possible even the discussion of trade agreements at the Ottawa Conference of 1932.

ARTHUR JAMES BALFOUR

1926   In 1926 Joseph Chamberlain's dream of the Empire as an economic unit still seemed as far, perhaps farther, from realisation than it had appeared twenty years before. It could certainly offer nothing to modify any tendencies towards political separatism which might manifest themselves. Moreover, for two of the Governments represented at this crucial Conference, the unity of the British Empire had no sentimental or traditional appeal. Nationalist parties founded on hostility to Britain were in power in South Africa, and in the Irish Free State. From Mr. Kevin O'Higgins the United Kingdom Cabinet could not reckon upon much sympathy. General Hertzog was the heir, and possibly the executor, of the old Boer Republican party.

These were some of the considerations which the English Ministers reviewed in their own minds when the Conference opened on October 19th. The Secretary of State for Dominion Affairs and for the Colonies in Mr. Baldwin's Government was Mr. Amery. Initiative for the plan of the Conference was his not only by right of his office, but by right of his long study of Empire affairs. The suggestion for a Committee of Dominion Prime Ministers to discuss the future of inter-Imperial relations came from him. It was essential, in his view, that Balfour should be the Chairman. The Committee was set up on October 25th, 1926. A month later it issued the Report from which dates the opening of a new era in the political development of the second British Empire.

The warnings of history contained in the word "second" give some measure of the importance of what was done. Some hundred and thirty years before, the American colonies had asked questions and advanced claims in respect of their constitutional position which had fallen upon heedless or unsympathetic ears in the

THE REPRESENTATIVE SYSTEM

Mother Country. The consequence had been a war which destroyed for ever the political unity of the English-speaking world. The first British Empire was shattered as it rose. Another grew, from communities distributed through every continent, and infinitely more varied in their character. Soon the inevitable question recurred, the question of parliamentary representation which had lain at the root of the American War of Independence, which could never remain unsolved among men of Anglo-Saxon race, sharing the same political tradition, however far apart their homes might lie.

It was to the United Provinces of Canada that the first grant of responsible government was made in 1840, on the advice of Lord Durham, whose Report opened the stage of constitutional development from which Balfour and his colleagues had now to make a further advance. The line between evolution and revolution is notoriously blurred in English history, and events may seem to fall on one side of it or the other, according to the perspective in which they are viewed. Thus Lord Durham, advocating that the Crown should yield its claim to over-ride the representative body of British Canada, prefaced this great and far-reaching renunciation with the remark that—

> it needs no change in the principles of government, no invention of a new constitutional theory. . . . It needs but to follow out consistently the principles of the British Constitution and introduce into the government of these great Colonies those wise provisions by which alone the working of the representative system can . . . be rendered harmonious and efficient. . . . The Crown must . . . submit to the necessary consequences of representative institutions, and if it has to carry on the government in unison with a representative body, it must consent to carry it

on by means of those in whom that representative body has confidence.

With the acceptance of this principle, the Empire set out along a road where there could be no real halting-place, short of the entire and complete autonomy of the self-governing Dominions. This had long been Balfour's conviction. He had expressed it publicly even before the end of the old order in world affairs. The speech of 1911 already quoted in its connection with Irish Home Rule,[1] contains passages still more prophetic for the future of the British Commonwealth:

> We depend as an Empire upon the co-operation of absolutely independent Parliaments. I am not talking as a lawyer; I am talking as a politician. I believe, from a legal point of view, the British Parliament is supreme over the Parliaments of Canada, of Australasia, or the Cape, or South Africa. But in fact they are independent Parliaments, absolutely independent, and it is our business to recognize that, and to frame the Empire upon the co-operation of absolutely independent Parliaments.

This speech of 1911, little noticed at the time it was made, is the real introduction to the Report of 1926, which embodies the Twentieth Century conception of the relation between Great Britain and the Dominions.

Balfour had been getting ready for this Conference for some fifty years. He had no need to make a preliminary study of its problems. The evolution of the Empire had influenced, perhaps determined, the evolution of his own opinions, which had already outstripped the comprehension of the average Englishman of that day. Balfour's apparently reckless disregard of every constitutional bond but one—the common allegiance to the British Crown—may even have alarmed those Dominions where the feelings of kinship with the

[1] See Chapter XVII.

SEARCH FOR A FORMULA

Mother Country were strongest. New Zealand was as the poles apart from the Irish Free State in tradition, and in political ideals. Now the representatives of the two sat opposite one another at the table in the Lord President's room at the Privy Council Office, and each may have viewed with suspicion and alarm any re-definition of mutual relationships which could be acceptable to the other. At first no step could be taken in this direction which did not arouse the objections of somebody. The search for a formula seemed to be creating its own dangers. But the Chairman confidently allowed it to proceed for many days. Drafts were amended and rejected. Phrases approved in one quarter roused unpleasant associations in another. Thus the word "independence," welcomed by the South Africans, reminded Canada too much of the history of her great neighbour on the American Continent.

A more thorny question was how to word the acknowledgment of free association of the self-governing parts. The phraseology must be proof (some people thought) against any implication of freedom to dissociate. The discussion in Committee made it clear that no such implication was in mind, and Balfour was content to leave it at that.

Anyone who has ever joined in what is fondly called "co-operation" between several persons in drafting a Resolution of the slightest importance, knows the perversity of words when they are expected to obey too many masters. The Committee on inter-Imperial Relations struggled for more than a fortnight with the paragraph which was to be the basis of future relationships between the self-governing Dominions.

At last it was ready:

> Autonomous communities within the British Empire, equal in status, in no way subordinate one to another in

any aspect of their domestic or external affairs, though united by a common allegiance to the Crown, and freely associated as members of the British Commonwealth of Nations.

Every word had been weighed. The intention had been to make the paragraph the opening sentence of the Report. But Balfour perceived that it needed a setting which would bring out its full importance. It must be introduced, it must be expounded, it must be made the central point in the Committee's Report. He carried it away with him from the Privy Council Office to his own room in Carlton Gardens. He started to write, late in the afternoon. After tea a message was sent to Sir Maurice Hankey, Secretary to the Committee, who came and found him tearing sheet after sheet out of the loose-leaf note-book he always used for his original drafts. Presently he was satisfied, and began to read out what he had written. It was the section on " The Status of Great Britain and the Dominions " which stands in the Report word for word as he then wrote it.

" There ! " said Balfour, giving it to Sir Maurice. " Do what you like with it. I am through." He meant, so far as that passage of the Report was concerned. It was written on a Friday, and he went off to the country until Monday, when, by dint of Sir Maurice's infinite capacity for taking pains, all the Dominion representatives had seen and accepted it.

Balfour had laid down another principle as important as the doctrine of equality. A foreigner [he says] might think that the formula of equality of status was " devised rather to make mutual interference impossible than to make co-operation easy." But such a criticism would ignore the history which made the tendency towards equality inevitable and right. Geography forbade the

STATUS AND FUNCTION

federal solution. The only other way was through 1926 autonomy. Co-operation could be attained along that road, by acceptance of the fact that equality of *status* does not imply similarity of *function*. Balfour, in his opening address to the Committee, illustrated this second fundamental point:

> There are always moments in the conduct of fleets, of armies, and of negotiations, when decisions, if they are to be of any use, must be rapid, and when consultations if they involve delay are a danger rather than a strength. If this be so, it must be on one of the seven self-governing communities that the greatest share of responsibility must be thrown"; and so long as the centre of difficulty is Europe, and the present distribution of population in the Empire suffers no overwhelming change, it seems impossible to ask any other portion of the Empire to bear the major responsibilities which devolve upon Great Britain.

Equality of status, diversity of functions. Acceptance of this definition in its turn brought up other questions. The Report goes on to say:

> It is the right of the Government of each Dominion to advise the Crown in all matters relating to its own affairs. Consequently it would not be in accordance with constitutional practice for advice to be tendered to His Majesty by His Majesty's Government in Great Britain in any matter appertaining to the affairs of a Dominion against the views of the Government of that Dominion.

In some responsible quarters this paragraph seemed to carry the logic of freedom dangerously far. Supported though Balfour was by colleagues in close touch with him, it may be that only he could have carried the draft Report through Cabinet. Respect for his experience, and trust in his judgment had reached their peak in 1926, and he was sure of what was required, and of what

1926 could safely be done. It is true that the Covenant of the League of Nations, with its obligations for collective security, now provided new safeguards and created new duties in the event of war, for the seven self-governing parts of the Empire as for every other member State. But the League had never been put to the ultimate test, and Balfour did not seek to justify his policy by his reliance on any written pledge.

> My view most strongly is [he told the House of Lords[1]] that the British Empire is now a more united organism than it has ever been before, . . . held together far more effectually by the broad loyalties, . . . and by devotion to great world ideals of peace and freedom. A common interest in loyalty, in freedom, in ideals—that is the bond of Empire. If that is not enough nothing else is enough. . . .

This quotation is from Balfour's first exposition of the work of the Conference which had just dispersed.[2] It was almost the last speech of the debate in the House of Lords—a fact not quite without significance. Only a comparatively small number of people in the Mother Country grasped at the time the far-reaching nature of the new conceptions of Empire which the Report announced with no flourish of trumpets. In political circles in London the Dominion Prime Ministers and Balfour's other colleagues had talked with enthusiasm of the tact and the consummate skill with which he had led the two Committees on inter-Imperial Relations and Scientific Research, and some friends had realised that a big thing had happened. Lord Esher, for instance, a most sagacious observer, whose memory stretched back to the beginning of Balfour's career, wrote:

[1] See *Parliamentary Report*, December 8th, 1926.
[2] *Ibid.*

A CROWNING ACHIEVEMENT

1926

My dear Arthur,

Of all your great and manifold services, the Report which has your *imprimatur* throughout is one of the greatest. A crowning achievement. You are really very splendid.

> Yours always affecly.,
> Esher.

Upon the whole however Englishmen took the opening of the "New Era" with remarkable placidity. It was not until five years later that the bulk of the nation really awoke to the nature of the surrenders which Balfour had recommended with so much confidence. The time had then come for these to be cast into legal form, and the debates which accompanied the passing of the Statute of Westminster in 1931 showed how little even Parliament had realised all that the doctrine of equality of status carried with it. Balfour was no longer there to expound or defend it. But his policy was already bearing fruit, for in the Dominions the reactions to it had been instantaneous.

Nowhere were they more dramatic than in South Africa. The nation—Dutch and English alike—eagerly awaited the return from the Conference of the Prime Minister, General Hertzog. When he had set out for England the very word "Imperial" avowedly stank in his nostrils. What did he say to it now? His ship berthed at Cape Town on December 13th, 1926. From on board he circulated his first message.

> I can only state that I hope the epoch-making Declaration by the Imperial Conference has brought to a happy close the century old struggle for South African national freedom, and paved the way for a fuller South African spirit.[1]

[1] See *The Times*, December 13th, 1926.

ARTHUR JAMES BALFOUR

1926   Next day he made one of the most remarkable recantations that have ever fallen from the leader of a political party in power:

> He said emphatically that he no longer feared the Empire. He had been a life-long opponent of Imperialism and had feared the Empire. That was because the Empire had been represented as a sort of super-State, but this conception had been scotched at the Imperial Conference. There was no question any longer of domination or superiority over the Dominions.... That made all the difference to his thoughts of the Empire.[1]

And again next day, at one of the huge mass meetings which gathered to hear him up and down the country:

> As a result of the work of the Conference the old Empire no longer existed.... All that remained was a free alliance of England and the six Dominions co-operating as friends.... The Englishmen need not fear that they should say farewell to the Empire, because it was in their interests not to do so. He felt that if the old Empire had been persisted with there would have been a probability of its going to pieces.[2]

The new Empire has yet to be tested. The last piece of work to which Balfour put his hands is still in the looms of current history. So far as the pattern can be traced, it seems as though the purely political difficulties in inter-Imperial relationships have disappeared, at any rate in the Overseas Dominions where the formula could be accepted without the hampering necessity of fitting it into the framework of any more rigid Agreement. It seems as though Balfour's immediate successors in Imperial statesmanship will have to concern themselves less with separatist tendencies inside the British Commonwealth than with the harmonising of economic

---

[1] See *The Times*, December 14th, 1925.
[2] See *The Times*, December 15th, 1925.

FRANCIS BACON

interests, so that these may exert their full pressure in the opposite direction.

A year or so of health and activity remained to Balfour after the close of the Imperial Conference of 1926. His physical vigour was becoming remarkable in a man now nearing eighty. The mere catalogue of the subjects on which he spoke outside the House of Lords in the year 1927 would be enough to show how innumerable were the facets of his interest in life. In an address given in Edinburgh on the work of Lister, Pasteur and Sir James Simpson, he observed that in the past few months he had joined in memorial celebrations of five other great men, Bacon, Newton, Faraday, Beethoven and Richard Bright.[1] On each and all of these he spoke with the ease that came of long familiarity with their work and study of their personalities. In his remarks upon Bacon this was conspicuously evident. Among Balfour's prose writings there is no better example of the power of his critical faculty, the lightness of his touch, the sincerity of his beliefs, the sharpness of his humour and the brilliant polish of his prose, than can be found in his Essay on Francis Bacon.[2] The speech of 1927 faintly reflects its sparkle. It contains no such gem as that which in the Essay concludes a rather disparaging reference to Bacon's political career:

> However low some may rate hereditary honours, everybody will I think admit that it is better to be made a Viscount than to be burned.

But both speech and Essay ring with that veneration for scientific truth which was so potent in Balfour's character. In the Essay he called Bacon a " seer."

[1] Speech at the Lister Centenary Celebration. See *The Scotsman*, July 21st, 1927.
[2] See *Essays Speculative and Political* (Hodder and Stoughton, 1920).

ARTHUR JAMES BALFOUR

1927

He saw, as none had seen before, that ... you must laboriously climb to a knowledge of great principles before you can descend to their practical employment. ... He created, or greatly helped to create, the atmosphere in which scientific discovery flourishes. If you consider how slightly science was in his day esteemed; if you remember the fears of the orthodox, the contempt of the learned, the indifference of the powerful, the ignorance of the many, you will perhaps agree that no greater work could be performed in its interest than that to which Bacon set his hand.

Balfour's literary style was at times so like his conversation that the very tones of his voice seem to sound again in the little fling at the philosopher Hegel with which the Essay on Bacon finishes. It was always possible to get a rise out of Balfour by mentioning Hegel; here he seems determined to get a rise out of himself.

I will not dwell, as I had partly intended, on such tempting subjects as the criticisms passed on Bacon, and, I may add, on Bacon's countrymen, by a great metaphysician of the last century. It may be enough to say that if Hegel thought little of Bacon, Bacon, had he known Hegel, would assuredly have returned the compliment. He would have regarded him as exhibiting the most perfect example of what he most detested in a thinker—the *intellectus sibi permissus*. Assuredly these great men were not made to understand each other; though to us the very magnitude of their differences, by making them incomparable, may allow us (if we can) to admire both.

Balfour's speeches about this time emphasised his own conception of patriotism and national sentiment with an insistence significant of his uneasiness about the racial problems which he considered among the gravest for the modern world. No man was prouder than he of his own racial inheritance, but it was for him only the natural starting-point for wider loyalties.

BALFOUR THE SCOT

> Nationality [he had once said] is valuable so far as it is a centripetal principle, and in so far as it produces closer co-operation between members of the human race. It has another side, and it must not be put on an absurd pedestal.[1]

1927

He put the point in a different way in one of his last public speeches. He was discussing the evolution of the Empire. The passage seemed on the face of it to be in a lighter vein than the rest of what he said, but something in his tone conveyed the impression that a message was being delivered. He was speaking to a great audience in Edinburgh:

> I am a Scotsman addressing Scotsmen, and I feel therefore peculiarly qualified to speak on this subject. I maintain, and I appeal to the history of my country to show that I am right; ... that although different streams have met together to make our kingdom and our Empire, none of them need feel that that difference destroys the unity of the stream which has resulted from their coalescence. I absolutely refuse to allow any man, be he English or be he Scottish, to rob me of my share in Magna Carta and Shakespeare because of Bannockburn and Flodden.[2]

It was not only in speeches on subjects of his own choosing that the vigour of Balfour's mind showed itself in 1927. In January of that year a crisis developed in China, where central government had completely collapsed and the armies of six rival generals were devastating the country, and endangering the lives and property of foreigners in the Treaty Ports. A Cabinet was summoned to consider the situation. Balfour was in Scotland, but came back to London at the urgent desire of the Foreign Secretary, Sir Austen Chamberlain. Before his return, and before the military authorities had

[1] In a discussion of the Problem of Nationality at Oxford, September 28th, 1920.
[2] See *The Scotsman*, January 28th, 1927.

ARTHUR JAMES BALFOUR

1927 delivered their report, Balfour had sent off a Memorandum, which was commented upon by Sir Maurice Hankey:

> I must say I was immensely tickled by the way you had foreseen the military situation without having had a military appreciation. . . . Your Memorandum reads exactly like a commentary on the Report of the Chiefs of Staff Committee . . . but as a matter of fact the two documents were being prepared at a distance of some hundreds of miles at precisely the same moment.

Such evidences of his continuing value in council, and of the special position he had attained among his colleagues, were a source of unaffected pleasure to Balfour in the last year of his full activity. This the year 1927 proved to be. After its close his physical powers began to fail, but the vigour of his mind remained undimmed for long enough to spare him the pang of leaving the Government before Mr. Baldwin's Administration came to its natural end in 1929.

Chapter XXI

THE LAST TWO YEARS
1928-1930

First decline in health. Work on the Autobiography. Reminiscences. Attack of illness at Taplow Court. Recovery. The eightieth birthday. The last autumn at home. Move to Fishers Hill. Resignation of office. Visit to the King at Bognor. India Debate and letter to Mr. Baldwin. Conversations. The approaching end. Visit of Dr. Weizmann. Death, March 19th, 1930.

The Christmas holidays of 1927 were the last of the family gatherings at Whittingehame free from shadows of anxiety about the Head of the House. When he was laid up with an attack of what we called laryngitis in the first week of the New Year we believed it to be merely a passing trouble. In point of fact it was a first symptom of the illness from which, more than two years later, he died.

Lord Dawson of Penn, who was in touch with his case to the end, has kindly contributed a brief account of it.

> Rather more than two years before Lord Balfour's death the circulatory system began to fail. This was due not to disease, but to wear. In the vigour of life the circulation is maintained not only by the heart but by the vessels, which are elastic, and can dilate or contract according to the varying needs of the body. With the passing of the years the vessels are liable gradually to lose these qualities, and in the vessels thus affected the stream of blood is apt to become thin, and from time to time so dwindled that the parts of the body which it should supply fail to function aright. The vessels of the brain are par-

1928 ticularly liable to suffer from this process. Thus it was that in January 1928 there was an intermittent difficulty in swallowing, and the voice was uncertain from weakness in the movements of the tongue and palate. This trouble passed, and his general health remained excellent.

The progress of the weakness here described was very slow at first, and indeed the year 1928—Balfour's eighty-first—was by no means one of steady decline in strength. This was the period when he wrote the greater part of the fragment of Autobiography from which I have liberally quoted in the first volume of this book. But gradually composition became a strain on his physical strength, and soon we had to try to persuade him to give it up; for his standard of perfection in word and phrase remained as high as in the prime of his years, when no pressure of work had ever deterred him from polishing and re-polishing every sentence intended for the printer.

The Autobiography, although unhappily the story is broken off on the threshold of his political life, was the means of reviving much that would otherwise have been lost. In the first place it involved delving into the vast confusion of his papers—work which he entrusted to me—and even the first survey of the accumulations of fifty years revealed unexpected treasures. Realising very soon that we were working against time, I counted every day's excavation lost unless it produced some document or letter which might rouse his curiosity or recollection. The bundles tied with faded tape, or with elastic bands that crumbled at a touch, came at random out of big tin boxes stored in an empty room at Whittingehame. Some of these boxes bore the initials "V.R." and the Crown, printed in white upon their lids, and it was indeed by the lettering of three reigns that it was easiest to guess what the contents might be.

AUTOBIOGRAPHY

Balfour's way of dealing with papers had always been of the simplest: " Where the tree falls there let it lie," whether on the counterpane of his bed, or the floor of his sitting-room. Secretaries, or his servant, would gather them up, State papers, private letters, invitations to dinner and all. Most of them somehow or other got preserved, and some of them roughly classified[1].

There was a day, quite at the beginning of my explorations, when the string round a big bundle of Irish Police Reports broke and disclosed in the middle of them, a letter in Lord Salisbury's handwriting, proffering advice on the administration of the new Crimes Act of 1887.[2] I flew with it to Balfour, whose only observation, after reading it several times, was, " Dear me ! I wonder if I did what he suggested ! " It seemed to me that the serious awakening of his interest in his own memories began with the discovery of that letter. Nevertheless, although the interest grew as the boxes gave up their secrets, Balfour never showed an old man's absorption in the past. Indeed it sometimes appeared that his thoughts now reached more than ever towards the solution of the great problems of the future, and that he had to make a fresh effort every time to bring them back to the years whose difficulties and achievements were over and done. Some sign of ignorance on my part was often the best stimulus. " You've still got a lot of history to learn," he would say with his radiant quizzical smile, and then perhaps would proceed to supply the deficiency. One day I tried a successful experiment in provocation.

" Did you make anything that lasted in your first twenty-five years of Parliament," I asked him, " except your reputation ? "

[1] This thanks to the efforts of Mr. W. M. Short, Balfour's personal Secretary for many years.
[2] For this letter see Vol. I, p. 150.

1928 "An Education Bill," he answered lazily, "and you seem to forget Ireland."

"But what is Ireland now?" I said. "And what remains of your Irish policy?"

He sat up, thoroughly roused.

"Everything. Everything!" he said. "Look at the position of Ulster now. That remained to us. And what was the Ireland which the Free State Government took over? The Ireland that *we* made. Why—even the Land Purchase Act which the Liberals stopped (that was a wicked thing they did)—even that had gone far enough to save the country. The Irish Government could have done nothing with Ireland but for our work. Fetch me that book on the mantelpiece—that book about the Congested Districts Board. Take that away and read it. Give it to me a minute."

He turned the pages for a quarter of an hour, reading attentively some pages of the story of planned relief for Irish poverty, a story thirty years old, yet so remarkably modern. Finally he looked at the frontispiece of the book, a photograph of himself in the 'eighties, with neat little dark mutton chop whiskers. "Look at that," he said. "Do you think it's like me still?"

It struck me, as he said this, that I had never heard him make an unprompted remark about his personal appearance before, or indeed express any opinion in the family controversies about likeness, which arose each time his portrait was painted. It was, in this as in other ways, impossible to plumb the depths of his un-self-consciousness. He continued to examine the photograph which had started so unwonted a train of thought, with dawning amusement in his eyes. I wondered what was coming.

"Do you know," he said, "that all through my first Parliament the communications that came to me from the Whips were addressed to ' Captain Balfour ' ? I was in the Lothian and Berwickshire Yeomanry, as you know."

We burst out laughing. " You *must* put that in your Memoirs," I said.

" Why ? You think a touch of pure farce would be an improvement ? "

" There used to be a legend," I said, " that you spoke at a Yeomanry Dinner, and were so shy that you had to sit down."

" I don't remember ever speaking, or trying to speak, at a Yeomanry Dinner. But I was thinking last night that I ought to say something about how I neglected the Cambridge Union. I think it was the only part of Cambridge life I didn't make the most of. I never went to the Debates, and I never spoke. Result —that when I stood for Hertford I had only twice been on my legs in public."

" And those times ? " I asked.

" Once at a tenants' dinner in the Marble Hall at Hatfield when I was about sixteen, and my grandfather made me get up—and the other time at home when I came of age."

This was the kind of talk that became more frequent in the two years of his old age which I am attempting to describe. It gradually became tacitly understood between us, as his strength waned, that many of the things he said about the past were meant to be recorded. The time came when I knew that he would not dislike the idea of notes being taken of his conversation, and that he sometimes even desired it.

Balfour did not relinquish active life with the relief at the laying down of a burden, which eases the transition for some old people. In the first year of his illness he was keenly anxious to recover strength, and exulted in

1928 each period of temporary improvement. But when the relapses came his cheerful equanimity never failed. In sickness as in health the strong sweet reasonableness of his nature carried him through without any apparent effort. The interest which he took in his symptoms had never any touch of the morbid preoccupation of an invalid. Medical science had always been a favourite subject, and no doctor was ill-advised enough to try to conceal from him the real state of affairs at any stage of his last illness. "Knowledge always helped him," writes Lord Dawson, when relating that Balfour discussed the medical problems of his case "with acumen and detachment."

The first note of real alarm sounded on Sunday, March 17th, 1928, a few days after the conversation recorded above. Balfour was convalescent after the illness of the early spring, and went for the week-end to Taplow Court, to stay with Lord and Lady Desborough.

Lady Desborough has recalled the events:

> He was much better, and in very good spirits. A girl—Anthea Skinning—came to play the piano in the evening. He was delighted with her, and went on and on asking for more, and went to bed late. The next day, Sunday, was very lovely and hot. He sat out for a short time before luncheon, watching the tennis on the red court. After luncheon we sat on at "coffee" in the library, until four o'clock, and he and Winston and Mr. Fisher[1] had an enthralling conversation—starting with Napoleon. Mr. Fisher has often reminded me of how brilliant Arthur was that day. Then I went out for a walk with Winston, and A. J. B. started to walk round to the tennis court with Venetia Montagu.[2] It was then that he had the sudden difficulty in finding the right words, and used the wrong ones. He was much troubled, and went up to his room to rest. I

[1] The Rt. Hon. H. A. L. Fisher, Warden of New College.
[2] The Hon. Mrs. Edwin Montagu.

went up there on returning, a little after five. His speech was then all right, but he was very agitated, and looked ill. We got our doctor, Gilbert Moore, at once. All adverse symptoms had then vanished, and temperature and pulse were normal; but A. J. B. was insistent on going back to his own house at once, and he motored up before dinner.

Nothing of this kind recurred in that year, and Balfour was soon able to leave London again and spend the late spring staying with Lord and Lady Wemyss at Stanway and in Lord and Lady Astor's house at Sandwich. Intimate friends came down to see him, and these weeks under the roofs of people whom he loved were full of enjoyment.

Balfour wrote the greater part of the Cambridge chapter of his Autobiography at this time. One of the scenes that remain in memory is of him lying on a couch in the garden at Stanway—matchless in its beauty on a May morning—a heap of books of all sorts by his side, and among them some proofs of Mr. L. B. Namier's *Structure of Politics*, which interested him profoundly. He was talking to Lady Wemyss and Lady Desborough with a gaiety beyond the reach of illness or old age to touch.

"I've been thinking," he said, as conversation turned on his own book, "that one of the most unusual features in my life has been its continuity. I have never been forced to break the thread of any of my interests. That was one advantage of being without academic distinctions, for while I was at Cambridge I read books that interested me, as I went on doing when I left."

After some five weeks of complete rest Balfour came back to London in June 1928, eager to resume his normal way of life. He attended Cabinets, dined out, even returned to his habit of walking home from dinner parties, all through that summer.

1928   July 25th was his eightieth birthday. On the 24th he went to the large public luncheon given in his honour by the British Academy. The Prince of Wales proposed his health in a speech which delighted him by its allusion to "the half-century in which he had maintained his golf handicap at a lower level than mine is ever likely to attain." Balfour's reply was a tribute to youth and to learning, subjects on which it was always easy for him to speak with conviction. But the effort, and the heat of the room, tired him. The next day opened with a spate of messages from all over the world. King George telegraphed:

> It is a great pleasure for the Queen and me to send our heartiest greetings on his eightieth birthday to an old friend like yourself, and one who has been a faithful and valued adviser to three successive Sovereigns. We trust you may continue to be blessed with those powers of mind and body which have long been the delight and admiration of your many friends.   GEORGE R.I.

The birthday was the date fixed for the presentation of a Rolls-Royce motor car given by friends of all political parties in both Houses of Parliament. The ceremony took place in the Speaker's Courtyard at Westminster, at the end of Question time. Balfour walked from Carlton Gardens across the Horse Guards Parade with Mrs. Edward Lascelles, arriving hot, and a trifle agitated lest he should be, as he was, a little late. The speeches accompanying the gift struck more than one chord of feeling which affected him deeply. The Prime Minister, Mr. Baldwin, spoke of the labour of love it had been to collect the offerings of more than 160 members of the House of Lords, and more than 150 of the House of Commons. Mr. Lloyd George talked of old fights across the floor, and of their war

LOYALTY

service together; Mr. Clynes[1] ended by assuring him that if he had political enemies he had not a single personal foe.

1928

Balfour had, as usual, prepared nothing of his own speech—the last, as it turned out, that he ever made. Considerably moved, he failed to marshal all the reminiscences of parliamentary life that he afterwards wished he had given to an audience which included recruits as well as veterans of the political battlefield. He said not one word of the great figures already legendary to almost all the men who stood round listening curiously to the benign-looking statesman who had measured his youthful strength against Gladstone and Parnell. Yet psychologists might have noticed that nearly the whole of the first part of his speech was addressed almost personally to Mr. Lloyd George, who may well have been the only Commoner present to remember the giants, and was certainly the only living man to be called their equal in debate.

The speech failed to satisfy him. He criticised himself as he drove out of Palace Yard seated in the new car. I do not think he ever entered those gates again. Nevertheless his closing words had been a fitting leave-taking. Recalling that since the year 1874 he had never (with the exception of three weeks after the defeat of 1906), ceased to be a member of one or other of the historic Chambers, he said:

> I feel that of my eighty years of life by far the largest part of my time, energies, hopes, strivings, and, as far as they exist, of my ambitions, have been spent within these walls. I have never for a moment failed in my loyalty to Parliament, however that Parliament was constituted. . . .
> I am eighty. I cannot take much more part in public affairs, but I rejoice to think I see growing up younger

[1] The Rt. Hon. J. R. Clynes.

1928 generations, one by one, who instinctively follow the great example of their forefathers, and are predestined with undiminished lustre to carry to future ages the glories of the British Empire.

It was Lord Randolph Churchill's son who, at the end, called for " Three cheers for A. J. B."

The new car became a feature in daily life at Whittingehame during the last autumn that Balfour spent there. Exhibiting it to the family provided an excuse for afternoon drives with no particular objective, and these became a daily habit. We soon perceived that it was best to avoid the roads leading to old haunts of golfing days. We explored instead every by-road in the Lammermoors, often coming down into Berwickshire, and returning home along the Great North Road by Cockburnspath and Dunbar. Balfour always sat in front beside Frederick Mills, who had driven him for more than twenty-five years. Every now and then he would stop the car at some point where the wide curve of Belhaven Sands and the Tyninghame Woods lay spread below, and would glance back at us smiling. But he disliked talking in a motor car, as much as he disliked being forced to ask the way. There was a day when both these mishaps befell, which took its place among the jokes of which the family never tired. Miss Balfour had undertaken to guide the expedition by map. In the heart of the hills we reached a village which upset her calculations. "Ask the name of this place," she said to Mills. After consultation with a man standing on his own doorstep, Mills reported the place to be " Cranshaws."

"Impossible!" Miss Balfour exclaimed. "If this is Cranshaws I don't know where we are. Ask him if he is sure he is not mistaken."

Balfour turned round in his seat, and said with some

vigour: "No, my dear. No! To ask a man once whether he knows where he lives is permissible. But it cannot be done twice. We must go on."

Sometimes on these drives Balfour would get out and walk a little, but pain in his leg made even that amount of exercise increasingly difficult, and this was the chief trial to his spirits during an autumn which was otherwise by no means unhappy.

When Cabinet meetings began again after the summer holidays Balfour was naturally anxious to attend them. But the doctors forbade London life. Lord Dawson had paid a week-end visit to Whittingehame and entirely agreed with the verdict of Balfour's own medical attendant there, Dr. Wedderburn of North Berwick. Upon this Balfour offered his resignation, but the Prime Minister would not listen to the suggestion. Whether able to attend Cabinets or not, Mr. Baldwin wanted Balfour to receive the Papers, and be available for consultation.

Under these circumstances Balfour decided to come for a time to Fishers Hill, the home of his brother Gerald, in Surrey, where he would be accessible to his colleagues. In January 1929, he made the move, which turned out to be the last of his life. The fifteen months that still remained were spent under his brother's roof. Only once or twice in the course of the spring he was able to come up to London. The pain in his leg and the paroxysms of coughing were both becoming more troublesome, and his movements were more and more confined to the daily drive.

Early in May Mr. Baldwin's Government resigned, and with this Balfour's official life came to its natural close. King George was then at Bognor, recovering from his own serious illness. Balfour was summoned thither, and drove over from Fishers Hill to deliver up

1929 in person the seals of his office. He had luncheon with the King and passed some part of the afternoon sitting in the garden with him. Emotion was not far below the surface when the time came for leave-taking. Strong links had been forged in more than forty years of service to the Crown. "It was a moving thing," he said that evening to Major Edward Lascelles, "to do what one knows to be one's last public action, after fifty years of public life."

He came back to Fishers Hill however as cheerful as usual, and spent the evening downstairs, listening to the adventures of his great-niece, Frances Dugdale,[1] just returned from a visit to New Zealand. Next morning however he woke up with the pain in his leg greatly aggravated. A fresh attack of phlebitis had developed, and from that day onwards he never left his own rooms.

His sitting-room immediately became a centre for family and friends. The tale of his visitors that summer and autumn was large and various. Sir Maurice Hankey, Sir Austen Chamberlain, Mr. Baldwin, Mr. Lloyd George, Lord Midleton, and other ex-colleagues would come down of an afternoon and talk of current politics. He was intensely interested by what Mr. Winston Churchill told him of his forthcoming book on Marlborough. Another day Mr. Philip Snowden[2] amused him vastly with Yorkshire stories. Lord and Lady Salisbury, Lady Wemyss, Lady Desborough, were often there. Dame Edith Lyttelton, widow of his beloved friend Alfred, was living very near by.

Much as he enjoyed such company, he lost none of his appreciation for solitude, even when the power of reading diminished with an increasing difficulty in

---

[1] Afterwards Mrs. James Fergusson.
[2] Then Chancellor of the Exchequer in the Labour Government, afterwards Lord Snowden.

KING GEORGE V AND LORD BALFOUR AT BOGNOR,
MAY 11TH, 1929
(Photograph taken by H.R.H. Princess Victoria)

CO-OPERATION WITHOUT JEALOUSY

focusing print. He was content to lie on his sofa 1929 absorbed in thought, often continued in words when one of us came into the room. With his amazing power of adapting himself to conditions he began to tolerate reading aloud, a thing he had never done in all his adult life. It was not difficult to devise interests and amusements for an invalid who carried inside himself such well-springs of contentment.

I noted many fragments of his talk during the autumn of 1929. Conversations were not so sustained as of old, on account of his throat, and sometimes they broke off still tantalisingly undeveloped. He started one day talking about Russia. The date was September 1929.

> I'm not much alarmed by Russia [he said]. I admit nobody knows much about it, and the most ignorant seem to be the Russians themselves. But I'm not afraid from the military point of view—they've never succeeded yet in waging a big war. I suppose you *could* draw a world picture in which they, in collaboration with the yellow races, might form some kind of economic tyranny. But that doesn't seem to be plausible.
>
> The Kaiser conjured up a Yellow nightmare. It's quite easy to conjure up a black one. But where do you get the centre for a movement? I mean a centre with a solid economic position as well as aggressive capacity.—But everything turns upon genius. Suppose a man arose with power of blood—with biological continuity, who had the power of inflaming vast populations. What would the English speaking world put against that? I am nothing if not an apostle of the English-speaking world,—but it does not mean England only. I don't know that the Americans are faithful to the ideal.—
>
> The whole thing depends on there not being jealousy but co-operation. We must work together or not work at all.

Some interruption must have occurred, for the notes break off. The theme of "co-operation without jealousy" recurs however.

ARTHUR JAMES BALFOUR

1929 "I should like to make that the motto of the British Empire," he said on one occasion.

The future of India was becoming a burning political question in the autumn of 1929, and it was often evident from Balfour's talk that his thoughts had been running on it, but he never could now be drawn into expressing opinions about details of policy on any current subject. He knew, as only those who have lived long behind the scenes can know, the difference between inside and outside knowledge. But he followed the debates on Indian affairs with unusual concentration, especially that of November 7th following the pronouncement regarding Dominion status.

The sanctioning of this phrase in the Viceroy's speech had crystallised the uneasiness of a section of the Conservative Party about Indian constitutional reform. It was known, moreover, that the Prime Minister, Mr. Ramsay Macdonald, had written to Mr. Baldwin, now leader of the Conservative Opposition, before the Viceroy's statement was made, and that Mr. Baldwin had replied from Aix that he personally was prepared to concur in the use of the phrase, provided the Government of India and the Simon Commission did the same. As regards the Commission this condition was not fulfilled, and Mr. Baldwin had no easy task in the conduct of a Debate, which was a severe test of parliamentary judgment as well as of larger statesmanship. Mr. Baldwin did not, on this question, command the full confidence even of all his own colleagues on the Front Opposition Bench.

Many a time Balfour had asserted his own authority as leader under conditions of similar difficulty. It seemed to me as he lay on his couch in the sunny room at Fishers Hill listening to the reading of Mr. Baldwin's speech, that the atmosphere of the House of Commons enveloped him, and that all the trained instincts, all the technical knowledge of the great Parliamentarian were alert once more. He listened with an absorbed, a critical attention. The speech presently passed from the thorny ground of the Viceroy's statement to a survey of the past history of the Indian and English peoples, and the ideal of their future relations. Balfour's face glowed with pleasure, for here were the very thoughts which had been filling his own mind. I do not know whether he had ever listened to a speech of Mr. Baldwin's, for although he had served under him in two Governments they had never been together in the House of Commons after Mr. Baldwin became a prominent figure there. This, far more than the difference in age, was a bar to the knowledge that Balfour was always eager to increase, about a personality which both charmed and mystified him. Seldom perhaps he had worked with any man whose processes of arrival upon their common ground were more widely divergent from his own. In this Indian speech however he found the very message that he had no longer the power to give.

I had no sooner finished reading than he exclaimed that he must write to Mr. Baldwin.

FISHERS HILL.
Nov. 8th, 1929.

MY DEAR BALDWIN,

I am very unnecessarily troubling you with a letter intended to express the feelings which I cannot keep to myself of intense admiration for your great utterances in the House of Commons yesterday. You treated the greatest of political themes in a way, and with an inspiration, which will for all time give you an unchallenged position among the orators of the English-speaking race. No more can be given even to those who are greedy of posthumous fame. It is a delight to me to think that on a subject which has so greatly occupied the thoughts of my declining years, it

ARTHUR JAMES BALFOUR

1929

has fallen to you, as leader of the Party, to give utterance in fitting language to great thoughts of the greatest of all subjects.

Yours ever,
BALFOUR.

This letter was dictated to me. It was one of the last, if not the very last he ever wrote in connection with public affairs.

A few weeks before that time my diary records some talk which I repeat, although with hesitation. In earlier years such flourishing of the conversational rapier was like a game, and only after it became a rarity did I ever try to fix on paper the irreproducible flash of his weapon. To those who remember his talk when he was determined not to be serious, this sketch will seem drawn with a heavy hand. Yet to some who never encountered him, or saw the playful mockery of his smile when in this mood, some notion may possibly be conveyed of the agility and ease with which he could evade pursuit.

The talk arose from an article in *The Times* Literary Supplement of September 26th, 1929, on "Toryism." He listened to the reading of it with some impatience, saying several times that it was "pretentious stuff," but "it rather amuses me all the same. Go on."

At the end I asked him what *he* thought the principles of Toryism were.

A. J. B. "Do you think that a profitable speculation?"
Myself. "I don't care. I want to hear what you have to say about it."
A. J. B. "I suppose the principles of common sense, to do what seems to be the right thing in a given case."
Myself. "But can't you find any sort of general principle to guide judgment as to what is the right thing?"

THE AUTHOR OF *PHILOSOPHIC DOUBT*

A. J. B. " Aren't you making judgment needlessly complicated by that question ? "

Myself. " I won't have you dodge my point. Do you think there is no common denominator in the outlook on politics of all the different groups that have been called Tory through the centuries ? "

A. J. B. " Can you find one ? "

Myself. " Start again. You were born in a definitely Conservative milieu. Is your Conservatism simply the result of the influences that surrounded you, or is it the result of independent thinking ? "

A. J. B. " The result would have been the same."

Myself. " Suppose that instead of being born Uncle Robert's nephew you had been Gladstone's son."

A. J. B. " Then Gladstone would have cut his throat at an early stage."

Myself. " Oh dear ! Oh dear ! Try to imagine this. An intelligent young man comes and says to you : ' I have read English history, but I know nothing whatever about the present position of English political parties. I want to go into politics. Which Party would you advise me to join ? ' What would you say ? "

A. J. B. " Of course I should say, choose the party that appeals to you most. And of course he would answer that they all appeal to him to some extent. Then I should have to throw him back on his history which you tell me he has read, and tell him to judge for himself on that. But if you ask me to give him principles to guide himself, I will answer that men have been asking for those ever since history began. They have been asking for clear simple rules,—but the more effort has been made to produce those abstract rules,—the greater has been the confusion and the controversy. So I should decline."

Myself. " Poor young man ! But serve him right for coming to you."

A. J. B. " Ah ! Not for nothing was I the author of *Philosophic Doubt !* "

Another day about this time we began talking of art, and Balfour described how his interest in the work of Burne-Jones and William Morris had been started through the influence of his brother, Eustace, who was their ardent admirer.

> That circle [he said] opened certain doors to me. Morris's poetry, B.-J.'s painting. They are the same thing in different mediums. I could read William Morris—and did with great pleasure. I expect I could still. I loved B.-J.'s use of colour. That romantic movement meant a good deal to me.
>
> *Myself.* "I knew Burne-Jones meant a good deal to you, but when you put it like that you startle me. I have never thought of you as a romantic. I always think of you as a lover of the eighteenth century in literature and thought."
> *A. J. B.* "But don't forget I have always loved Scott."
> *Myself.* "Quite true. But one thing at least you are *not.* You are not an Elizabethan. Shakespeare is never at your elbow."
> *A. J. B.* "Quite true.—I dislike a number of poets. Donne for example, and Crabbe."
> *Myself.* "And Browning?"
> *A. J. B.* "I've read *The Ring and the Book,* which I fancy is more than you have."

Then presently he went on:

> "I am ashamed now of my enthusiasm over Ruskin at one time."
> *Myself.* "I remember though how you prevented me from reading Ruskin when I was quite young. You said he mixed up ethics and æsthetics in a confusing way."
> *A. J. B.* "I rather agree with that verdict still. His philosophy was certainly not mine."

This talk presently took a more serious turn, and I asked him how he wished his philosophical work to be dealt with when his Life came to be written. It was clear by this time that the Autobiography would remain the mere fragment that it is, and I had been waiting for an opportunity to put this question. Consultation

THE SUNSET

between Balfour and his brother Gerald led eventually 1929
to a request to Balfour's old friend, Professor Pringle-Pattison, to write the appreciation which is printed at the end of this volume. The name of M. Bergson was also mentioned when the brothers first talked the matter over. "There are no two men I had rather be understood by," Balfour explained eagerly, and more than once recurred with evident pleasure to the idea of asking one of them to write something. Yet, left to himself, I doubt whether it would have struck him that his philosophical work required any special reference in his Biography. When the subject was first mooted he said to me:

> I don't very much care whether there is an appreciation of my philosophy. Do not worry your head with expecting permanence for philosophic thought. Not even relative permanence. All that any man's thought is, is a contribution greater or less to the stream of thought of his own time, which flows on and turns into the thought of the next generation. There is a fashion in thought—as impermanent as a fashion in dress. Something remains—goes into the stream; but it is no use to spend time in measuring the value of the fashion itself. So do not worry your head about what need be said about my philosophy.

Indeed the idea of "worry" was now more than ever out of place in Balfour's company. The tranquillity of spirit which had always seemed an active rather than a passive quality in him, appeared in the last months of his life to well more copiously from its hidden springs. As the end came nearer, the discomfort in his throat practically ceased, and with the certainty that he would be spared any increase of physical pain the last clouds vanished which might have obscured for us the splendour of the sunset.

The paraphernalia and atmosphere of a sick-room never intruded themselves, thanks very largely to the

1930 tact and understanding of Dr. Thorn of Woking, and of Sister Margery Gowans, who was with him after July 1929. His other attendant was James Coleman, who had been his personal servant for over thirty years, accompanying him everywhere, treating him always with the air of indulgence shown by a fond guardian for a helpless child, and possessed of a sixth sense for his every physical need.

The winter of 1929-1930 went calmly by. As the months passed, more of Balfour's waking hours were spent in listening to music, fewer in talk. A large gramophone stood in the passage outside his rooms, and through the open door he listened to the classical music he liked best, returning oftenest to Beethoven, and his beloved Handel.

Although his ready, unaffected interest for the things of the moment did not wane, it often seemed at this time that his thoughts, when he was alone, or listening to music, were elsewhere. Assuredly they were not fixed upon the past. The expression of indescribable eagerness which sometimes illuminated his face was not a glow of reminiscence. Had it been so he would have been changed indeed; whereas to the end he was always the same, except in as far as the decline of mere bodily strength brought its inevitable changes. To those who could read the familiar signs there seemed no possible doubt that he was often absorbed in the thought that he was on the brink of knowledge of the ultimate mystery of life. He would not now have drawn back one step, even had that step been in his power to take.

Readers of his own books, or of the letter to Lady Desborough written after the death of her sons,[1] know that Balfour was convinced of the existence of a personal God—" a God " (as he wrote in his Gifford Lectures)

[1] See above, Chapter XIV.

A FAREWELL

"who answers prayer." Nothing was more interwoven with the texture of his being than this belief, but it was no surprise to us that he desired no external aid for its realisation as the end of his earthly life drew near.

From his young manhood onwards he had followed with the very closest attention and knowledge the scientific investigations, with which some of those nearest to him were connected, into the evidences of survival of personality after death. The very nature of those investigations precluded discussion of their results with those who were not engaged upon them. Therefore my own first-hand knowledge of his beliefs on that subject is far from complete. Nevertheless, since first-hand knowledge is the only right way of approaching so intimate a question, I will here record my conviction that he utterly rejected the idea of death as an end of personality or of service, and that he did not think of its partings as eternal. I believe too that as his own death approached he dwelt more and more upon the prospect of recognising, and being recognised by, those whom he had loved.

Early in March 1930, his strength began to ebb faster. He slept many hours of the twenty-four, the same sound natural sleep which had never deserted him at any time of stress. When awake he spoke very little, but never failed to greet us with a smile. A few days before the end he received for a few moments a visitor from outside the circle of his family. This was Dr. Chaim Weizmann, the Zionist leader.

No one but myself saw the brief and silent farewell between these two, so diverse from one another, whose mutual sympathy had been so powerful an instrument in the history of a nation. The privacy of their last meeting would not be broken here except for one reason. A few days later, millions of poor Jews in the ghettoes

ARTHUR JAMES BALFOUR

1930 of Eastern Europe and the slums of New York were bewailing with deep personal grief the loss of a British statesman whose face they had never seen. All over the world the ceremonial candles were lit in the synagogues, and the Prayer of Remembrance, the A'skara, was chanted. Never in living memory had this been done for any Gentile. For the sake of the people who repaid his understanding of them with the greatest tribute in their power to bestow, it is right to record the visit of Chaim Weizmann to Balfour's death-bed. It was not the love or sorrow of an individual alone which was expressed by the tears of one Jew that day. No words passed between them, or could pass, for Balfour was very weak, and Dr. Weizmann much overcome.

But I, who saw the look with which Balfour moved his hand and touched the bowed head of the other, have no doubt at all that he realised the nature of the emotion which for the first, and only, time showed itself in his sick-room.

> When great men die,
> A mighty name, and a bitter cry
> Rise up from a nation calling.

There were no other visits of farewell. He always disliked good-byes. The end came rather suddenly early in the morning of March 19th. He had slept almost continuously for the two days before, but there was no reason to suppose that this state might not have gone on for some time, and no special summons had been sent to those of the family who were absent at the moment. He died holding the hands of the two of his own generation who were dearest to him, his brother Gerald,[1] and his eldest sister, Mrs. Sidgwick. Gerald Balfour's wife, Lady Betty, their son Ral with his wife,[2] and

[1] Afterwards second Earl of Balfour.
[2] Afterwards Lord and Lady Traprain.

myself, were also in the room. We thought that he recognised us almost till the very last moment. When that moment came we hardly knew.

The offer of burial in Westminster Abbey was made by the Dean and Chapter within a few hours of Balfour's death. It was gratefully declined, for his own wish was to be buried at Whittingehame in the family burial ground, where were the graves of his mother, and of his brothers Frank and Eustace.

The spot is of extraordinary beauty. The stems of tall beeches rise round it like the columns of a cathedral, but no walls shut out the view of the woods of Whittingehame and the hills beyond. The bones of many generations of dead lie under the short grass, for the place is consecrated soil, although the church and churchyard are half a mile away, and the old burial ground is now entirely hidden from any public road or pathway.

A little fresh snow lay on the Lammermoors on the morning of Balfour's burial, the sky was the pale blue of an East Coast spring, the bank of the glen below the House was still white with masses of snowdrops. His body had been taken straight from the railway train to the church, which was filled by the people of Whittingehame and by friends from farther parts of the county. Outside waited a larger throng. After the service, conducted by the Minister of the parish, the Rev. Dr. Marshall Lang, the coffin was carried on one of the estate carts, drawn by big Clydesdale horses, along a short stretch of public road, the family and friends following on foot. Two more of the farm carts were piled with flowers. It is the fashion nowadays to discourage the sending of wreaths. We could hardly have done so even if we had wished it, for they came from all parts of the Empire and the world, and they

ARTHUR JAMES BALFOUR

1930 added immeasurably to the beauty of the scene. There was a point where the procession turned at right angles off the public road into the policies of Whittingehame, and the crowds of strangers were debarred from following farther. As the carts rounded the corner carrying their coloured loads I thought I had never seen anything more lovely. And later in the day, when the burial ground was once more in solitude, the brightness of the flowers seemed more astonishing still. They had been spread all over the grass under the beeches, and could be seen from far off, blazing like a summer garden surrounded by the soft austere colouring of the leafless trees.

Appendix I

NOTES ON LORD BALFOUR'S PHILOSOPHY

By the late Professor Pringle-Pattison

"As for philosophy," said Lord Balfour in sketching out the early chapters of an Autobiography, only fragments of which he lived to complete; " of course I shan't describe it in a book like this. But if the thing is to be a portrait of me at all, it will have to go in. It has been continuously in my mind—I've worked at it off and on—well! since I was at Eton. No! really *before* Eton I believe I began muddling about with those ideas. You know, when I look back at myself, I'm appalled by how little I've changed in eighty years."[1] Certainly in any portrait of the man a serious attempt must be made to portray in the proper perspective the philosophy to which he so persistently returned. It was, I think, nearer his heart than anything else.

It is not necessary for the purpose to go further back than 1866, in the autumn of which year he went up to Cambridge and began his undergraduate career as a Fellow-Commoner of Trinity College. The reference to " Eton " and " before Eton " just quoted must be taken quite simply—it is so treated by Balfour himself in the context of these autobiographical chapters —as referring to the first awakening of the boy's mind to reflective thought, to the first consciousness of the existence of an important problem, rather than to any conscious endeavour to solve it. Balfour was a little over eighteen when he entered Cambridge, and he could not have reached that age without noting the sharp divisions of contemporary thought in regard to the theology of the churches and the very foundations of a

[1] *Chapters of Autobiography*, Foreword, xii.

ARTHUR JAMES BALFOUR

religious view of the world. " In the sixties of the last century," as he reminds us, " the so-called 'conflict between religion and science' was in a very acute stage. . . . On the side of Biblical criticism the writings (for example) of David Strauss and Renan had begun to ferment in the minds of many educated people. On the scientific side such works as Lyell's *Geology*, and Darwin's *Origin of Species* had raised cosmological issues which profoundly stirred the religious world. The times (from the point of view of religious speculation) were stormy, and every dabbler in theology or science was profoundly conscious of the fact. Among these dabblers was I."[1]

In Balfour's case his appreciation of the situation was intensified by the atmosphere of the home in which he had been reared. " My mother," he tells us, " was a woman of profound religious convictions, and it was in an atmosphere saturated with these convictions that our home life was spent." He was not, therefore, prepared to acquiesce in the current negations without an independent investigation of the evidence upon which they were based. But so far as his time at Eton was concerned, the result of any reflections he had on the subject had been little more, he intimates, than " to direct my wandering curiosity to philosophy and, in particular, to the philosophy of beliefs."

It was at Cambridge, under the arrangements of the then newly instituted Moral Sciences Tripos, that he found the opportunity, while reading for his degree, of following his bent in this direction. At Cambridge, too, he made the acquaintance of his future brother-in-law, Henry Sidgwick, already a Fellow of Trinity, who was appointed Lecturer in Moral Science in 1867. Sidgwick, who was ten years Balfour's senior, had himself about this very time, after a somewhat prolonged intellectual struggle, renounced his earlier allegiance to Mill. " Take notice," he wrote to a friend in December 1866, " that I have finally parted from Mill and Comte, not without tears and wailings and cutting of the hair."[2] Balfour has acknowledged in the warmest terms how much he owed in these formative years to the stimulus and encouragement of the older man, both in his informally conducted lectures and in innumerable private conversations.[3] In his Gifford Lectures of 1914, in what he calls

[1] *Chapters of Autobiography*, p. 17.
[2] *Henry Sidgwick: A Memoir*, by A. S. and E. M. S., p. 158.
[3] See *Memoir*, pp. 309–311, also *Chapters of Autobiography*, pp. 50–60.

ARTHUR JAMES BALFOUR

"an autobiographical parenthesis," he has put on record the impression left on his mind by the philosophical situation as he gradually explored it in these undergraduate years.

I went to Cambridge in the middle sixties [he says] with a very small equipment of either philosophy or science, but a very keen desire to discover *what* I ought to think of the world and *why*. For the history of speculation I cared not a jot. Dead systems seemed to me of no more interest than abandoned fashions. My business was with the groundwork of living beliefs; in particular with the groundwork of that scientific knowledge whose recent developments had so profoundly moved mankind. And surely there was nothing perverse in asking modern philosophers to provide us with a theory of modern science!

I was referred to Mill; and the shock of disillusionment remains with me to the present hour. Mill possessed at that time an authority in the English Universities, comparable to that yielded forty years earlier by Hegel in Germany and in the Middle Ages by Aristotle. Precisely the kind of questions which I wished to put, his logic was deemed qualified to answer. He was supposed to have done for scientific inference what Bacon tried to do, and failed. He had provided science with a philosophy.

I could have forgiven the claims then made for him by his admirers; I could have forgiven, though young and intolerant, what seemed to me the futility of his philosophic system, if he had ever displayed any serious misgiving as to the scope and validity of his empirical methods. If he had admitted, for example, that when all had been done that could be done to systematise our ordinary modes of experimental inference, the underlying problem of knowledge still remained unsolved. But he seemed to hold, in common with the whole empirical school of which, in English-speaking countries, he was the head, that the fundamental difficulties of knowledge do not begin till the frontier is crossed which divides physics from metaphysics, the natural from the supernatural, the world of "phenomena" from the world of "noumena," "positive" experiences from religious dreams. . . . For my own part, I feel now, as I felt in the early days of which I am speaking, that the problem of knowledge cannot properly be sundered in this fashion. Its difficulties begin with the convictions of common sense, not with remote, or subtle, or otherworldly speculations; and if we could solve the problem in respect of the beliefs which, roughly speaking, everybody shares, we might see our way more clearly in respect of the beliefs on which many people are profoundly divided.

That Mill's reasoning should have satisfied himself and his immediate disciples is strange. But that the wider public of thinking men, whom he so powerfully influenced, should, on the strength of this flimsy philosophy, adopt an attitude of dogmatic assurance both as to what can be known and what cannot, is surely stranger still. Thus, at least, I thought nearly half a century ago, and thus I think still.[1]

Though long, I have quoted this passage practically in full, because it reproduces so vividly the temper and attitude of Balfour's first book, and summarises at the same time so clearly the main drift of its argument and the nature of the conclusions to which it seemed to its author to lead. Clearness on these points is the more desirable, seeing that the title of the volume and the method of argument followed were, to a certain extent, open to misconception—especially by those who did not take the trouble to read it. Balfour himself described it in the Preface as "a piece of destructive criticism formed by a series of arguments of a highly abstract character." The first point to note is that with science as such, with science proceeding on its own suppositions, Balfour has no quarrel either in this book or in any of those that followed it. Every scientific argument presupposes, for example, the law of Universal Causation or the regularity of nature; and the truth or accuracy of its conclusions depends entirely on this assumption. Balfour nowhere questions the propriety of this assumption as a necessary part of scientific method, or the necessity, for the same purpose, of that other assumption of an independently existing external world in whose processes the operation of the law may be traced. It is indeed absurd to suspect any lurking antipathy to science in one whose scientific interests were so conspicuous from first

[1] *Theism and Humanism*, pp. 137–40.

ARTHUR JAMES BALFOUR

to last. As Sir J. J. Thomson wrote, in his obituary tribute in *Nature* : " No statesman ever did so much to promote the development of science or kept in closer touch with its progress," and this is more than borne out by Lord Rayleigh's more detailed and intimate account in his *Lord Balfour in relation to Science*. It is not science, therefore, but the inadequate philosophy of science put forward by Mill and the English empirical school, that is the subject of Balfour's sustained attack ; and the method adopted to expose the inadequacy is, fundamentally, to thrust them back inexorably upon the Humian scepticism which is their common point of origin.

> Nothing in the history of speculation is more astonishing, [he says, in the chapter of *The Foundations of Belief* which resumes for a wider audience the more technical arguments of the earlier book] nothing—if I am to speak my whole mind—is more absurd than the way in which Hume's philosophic progeny—a most distinguished race—have, in spite of all their differences, yet been able to agree, *both* that experience is essentially as Hume described it, *and* that from such an experience can be rationally extracted anything even in the remotest degree resembling the existing system of the natural sciences. . . . Having reduced our belief in the fundamental principles of scientific interpretation to expectations born of habit ; having reduced the world which is to be interpreted to an unreated series of impressions and ideas ; having by this double process made experience impossible and turned science into foolishness, [Hume] quietly informs us, as the issue of the whole matter, that outside experience and science knowledge is impossible, and that all except " mathematical demonstration " and " experimental reasoning " on " matters of fact " is sophistry and illusion ![1]

Balfour's own conclusion, on the contrary (as he states it in the same chapter of *Foundations*) is that

> a purely empirical theory of things, a philosophy which depends for its premises in the last resort upon the particulars revealed to us in perceptive experience alone, is one that cannot rationally be accepted.[2]

[1] *Foundations*, pp. 96–7 ; 8th edition, 102–3.
[2] *Ibid.*, p. 133, 8th ed. 141.

ARTHUR JAMES BALFOUR

And so much any competent philosophical tribunal would adjudge that he had successfully established. He himself adds:

> A full and systematic attempt, first to enumerate, and then to justify, the presuppositions on which all science finally rests, has, it seems to me, still to be made, and must form no insignificant or secondary portion of the task which philosophy has yet to perform.[1]

It will be observed that he does not claim to have performed, or even positively to have attempted, that task in the *Defence of Philosophic Doubt*. That volume consisted almost entirely, as he himself pointed out, of destructive criticism of attempts made by others—in particular a radically destructive criticism of the currently accepted accounts of the foundations of scientific knowledge, as given by English philosophers of the empirical persuasion. With the collapse of these supposed foundations, the procedure of the same philosophers in arrogating to " positive science " the name of knowledge, and setting it up as the " norm of certainty by which all other departments of belief are to be judged," is necessarily invalidated. Science, in point of fact, so far as empirical philosophy can show, is no better equipped with a rational foundation than are other beliefs which we as firmly hold. With this conclusion, the writer appears for the present to consider his work accomplished. He is content to add at the close certain " practical results "—changes in mental attitude—which legitimately follow from his demonstration of the rationally foundationless character of modern science and all its doctrines. And when we turn to these " Results " what we find offered us is the somewhat unsatisfactory consolation that " religion is, at any rate, no worse off than science in the matter of proof,"[2] seeing that the system of science at any rate has been shown to be, " as a whole, incapable of any rational defence."[3] We have as much right, therefore, to believe the one as the other. " In the absence," he says, " of reason to the contrary, I am content to regard the two great creeds by which we attempt to regulate our lives as resting in the main upon separate bases."[4] Both science and theology

---
[1] *Foundations*, p. 98, 8th ed. 104.
[2] *Defence*, p. 319.   [3] *Ibid.*, p. 315.   [4] *Ibid.*, p. 322.

ARTHUR JAMES BALFOUR

have "claims on our belief" but these claims are not to be considered as reasons.

> Whatever they may be, they are not rational grounds for conviction, raised by their very nature above the reach of criticism. It would be more proper to describe them as a kind of inward inclination or impulse, falling far short of —I should perhaps rather say, altogether differing in kind from—philosophic certitude, leaving the reason therefore unsatisfied, but amounting nevertheless to a practical cause of belief, from the effects of which we do not even desire to be released.[1]

Or again, the position may be stated thus:

> I and an indefinite number of persons, if we contemplate Religion and Science as unproved systems of belief standing side by side, feel a practical need for both; and if this need is, in the case of those few and fragmentary scientific truths by which we regulate our animal actions, of an especially imperious and indestructible character—on the other hand, the need for religious truth, rooted as it is in the loftiest region of our moral nature, is one from which we would not, if we could, be freed. But as no legitimate argument can be founded on the mere existence of this need or impulse, so no legitimate argument can be founded on any differences which psychological analysis may detect between different cases of its manifestation. We are in this matter unfortunately altogether outside the sphere of Reason.[2]

The phraseology throughout these passages deserves the closest attention. To find a parallel to it, we have to go back to Hume, the Hume of the "Treatise," who seeks to resolve reason itself into a psychical force.

> After the most accurate and exact of my reasonings, I can give no reason why I should assent to it, and feel nothing but a *strong propensity* to consider objects strongly in that light in which they appear to me. . . . I may, nay, I must yield to the current of nature in submitting to my senses and understanding, and in this *blind submission* I show most perfectly my sceptical disposition and principles. . . . If

[1] *Defence*, p. 317.   [2] *Ibid.*, p. 320.

ARTHUR JAMES BALFOUR

we believe that fire warms or water refreshes, it is only because it costs us too much pains to think otherwise.[1]

In a precisely similar strain, Balfour is careful to warn us that "an ultimate impulse to believe a creed is in no sense to be regarded as a reason for believing it, nor can we argue that this ultimate impulse is a better reason, the more people there are who feel its influence."[2] It is not, therefore, altogether surprising that his position should have been taken by the majority of his readers, or at least, by the majority of his critics, at its face value as undiluted scepticism, and the "practical results" which he sought to deduce from it, as only a new version of the many specious but dangerous attempts made in the past to found religious faith upon universal doubt. He was charged, as he complained on a later occasion, with "recommending mankind to believe what they wish, since all beliefs alike are destitute of proof."[3] It was in vain that he protested that this was not what he had ever wanted to say, for he acknowledges himself, in the same context, that, "taken by itself" the tendency of the augmentation in the *Defence of Philosophic Doubt* may easily appear to be sceptical. The truth is, that he was not yet in possession—not yet at any rate in conscious possession of a really constructive principle, such as is central in the *Foundations of Belief* and in all his subsequent writings.

The *Defence of Philosophic Doubt* represents, therefore, only a temporary halting-place in the author's thought. In it he is content, as we have seen, to contemplate religion and science as unproved systems of belief, standing side by side, and "resting in the main upon separate bases." But neither philosophy nor religion can permanently acquiesce in such a solution. Philosophy demands a unity, a system of some kind, in what it recognises as knowledge, and religion claims for its foundational certainties a paramountcy in experience as a whole, which forbids it to accept a merely departmental rôle. The all-important advance made in the *Foundations of Belief* is precisely the recognition of this fact. Balfour there explicitly discards what he now calls the "patchwork scheme" of "simply setting up, side by side with the creed of natural science," another and supplementary set of beliefs which may minister to needs or aspirations which

[1] *Treatise of Human Nature*, Part IV, section 7.
[2] *Defence*, p. 319.   [3] *Theism and Humanism*, p. 137.

science cannot meet,—a scheme in which " the two regions of knowledge lie side by side, contiguous but not connected, like empires of different race and language, which own no common jurisdiction nor hold any intercourse with each other, except along a disputed and wavering frontier where no superior power exists to settle their quarrels or determine their respective limits."[1] As opposed to this unconsidered division of the 'Whole' of Knowledge into two or more unconnected fragments,"[2] he accepts the philosophical demand for " the unification of all belief into an ordered whole, compacted into one coherent structure under the stress of reason " as " an ideal which we can never abandon," even though it is " one, which, in the present condition of our knowledge, perhaps even of our faculties, we seem incapable of attaining."[3] He proceeds accordingly, in the last of the four parts into which the book is divided, to put forward his own " suggestions towards a provisional philosophy." These do not claim, he everywhere admits, to be a " system," after the fashion of the great masters of metaphysical thought; yet the arguments and the conclusions are philosophical in nature. He carries with him the negative results of his previous volume. He had shown there that the current empirical philosophy was unable to supply a foundation for the necessary assumptions of scientific theory. The whole fabric of the sciences depends upon the principle of universal causation, but it is impossible to extract from particular experiences anything more than the habit of expecting

> among sequences familiar to us in the petty round of daily life, the accustomed recurrence of something resembling a former consequent, following on the heels of something resembling a former antecedent. . . . When we come to the more complex phenomena with which we have to deal, the plain lesson taught by personal observation is not the regularity, but the irregularity, of Nature. . . . This apparent irregularity of Nature, obvious enough when we turn our attention to it, escapes our habitual notice, of course, because we invariably attribute the want of observed uniformity to the errors of the observer. And without doubt we do well. But what does this imply? It implies

[1] *Foundations*, pp. 186–7, 8th ed. 198–9.
[2] *Ibid.*, p. 187, 8th ed. 199.   [3] *Ibid.*, p. 233, 8th ed. 249.

that we bring to the interpretation of our sense-perception the principle of causation ready made. It implies that we do not believe the world to be governed by immutable law, because our experiences appear to be regular; but that we believe that our experiences, in spite of their apparent irregularity, follow some (perhaps) unknown rule because we first believe the world to be governed by immutable law. *But this is as much as to say that the principle is not proved by experience, but that experience is understood in the light of the principle.*[1] " The uniformity of nature," in short, " cannot be proved by experience, for it is what makes proof from experience possible."[2]

The man of science approaches the facts which he investigates with the " presupposition " that they constitute a rational or intelligible system. But, if that is so, the relations of Science to a doctrine like Theism appear at once in a totally different light from that in which they are represented by Naturalism. Instead of being an unnecessary hypothesis, Theism now appears as the fundamental postulate on which all scientific procedure rests.

In the *Foundations of Belief* Balfour starts from the distinction, of which he had already made effective use in the *Defence of Philosophic Doubt* between the *causes* of a belief and the *reasons* which may be brought forward to justify it. Otherwise expressed, the distinction is between the origin of our beliefs and their validity. Naturalism is concisely defined by him in one place[3] as " this theory of the non-rational origin of reason "; and throughout the volume the author is engaged in pressing home the " incoherence " of the theory, " the ineffaceable incongruity, between the origin of our beliefs, in so far as these can be revealed to us by science, and the beliefs themselves."[4] Here again, for the proper understanding of the argument, it is important to remember that Balfour does not profess to challenge the biological theory of human evolution, as formulated by the scientific expert. He is prepared, as a layman must be, to accept that account, on the testimony of the expert, as provisionally true, taken as science or as history. It is the attitude of

---

[1] *Foundations*, pp. 129–32, 8th ed. 137–40.
[2] *Ibid.*, p. 295, 8th ed. 282.
[3] *Ibid.*, p. 67, 8th ed. p. 72.   [4] *Ibid.*, p. 321, 8th ed. p. 310.

naturalistic philosophy which he condemns for accepting this bit of natural history as a complete metaphysic of the process, and "*refusing to allow us to penetrate beyond the phenomenal causes by which, in the order of Nature, our beliefs are produced.*"[1]

Reason, it must be remembered, is, for biological science and for a naturalistic philosophy, only a faculty developed in a certain species by " the blind operation of material causes "[2] —to serve, to some extent at least, as an aid in the struggle for existence. But when once we have realised that reason, from a scientific point of view, is itself a natural product, and that the whole material on which it works is due to causes physical, physiological and social, which it neither creates nor controls, we are, Balfour argues,

> driven in mere self-defence to hold that, behind these non-rational forces, and above them, guiding them by slow degrees, and, as it were, with difficulty, to a rational issue, stands that Supreme Reason in whom we must thus believe, if we are to believe in anything.[3]

The first of the four parts into which the book is divided, entitled " Consequences of Belief," is an exposure in all its nakedness of the naturalistic theory of the origin of all our beliefs and sentiments. On the basis of his analysis, Balfour proceeds to argue, that, however sincerely individual naturalists may profess their homage to ethical ideals, the sentiments and the creed are in their case antagonistic, and that " the more clearly the creed is grasped, the more thoroughly the intellect is saturated with its essential teaching, the more certain are the sentiments thus unnaturally associated with it to languish or to die." In a passage of rare beauty and eloquence,[4] he urges that, even if we suppose the perfection and happiness of humanity to be the all-inclusive object of human endeavour, the ideal fails to satisfy our ethical imagination. The fortunes of the human race, so far as science can tell us, are too transitory and unimportant an accident in the general scheme of things to satisfy aspirations and emotions nourished upon beliefs in the Everlasting and the Divine !

I know not, [he says, in concluding this section of the book] how it may strike the reader : but I at least am left

[1] *Foundations*, p. 322, 8th ed. p. 311. [2] *Ibid.*, p. 296, 8th ed. p. 283.
[3] *Ibid.*, p. 322, 8th ed. p. 311. [4] *Ibid.*, pp. 29–32.

sensibly poorer by this deposition of Reason from its ancient position as the Ground of all existence, to that of an expedient among other expedients for the maintenance of organic life; an expedient, moreover, which is temporary in its character and insignificant in its effects. An irrational Universe which accidentally turns out a few reasoning animals at one corner of it, as a rich man may experiment at one end of his park with some curious " sport " accidentally produced among his flocks and herds, is a Universe which we might well despise, if we did not ourselves share its degradation.[1]

The rationality of the Universe is thus reached not as the conclusion of any " inferences " of the ordinary pattern,[2] as when we infer from a cathedral the existence of an architect, or from any special work of design the existence of a designer. It is itself the condition of the possibility of any inference whatsoever. " Something," he says, " may be inferred from the mere fact that we know—a fact which, like every other, has to be accounted for."[3] There is no escape from the incoherences of the materialistic theory—" the impossible task of extracting reason from unreason "—" unless we are prepared to bring to the study of the world the presupposition that it was the work of a rational Being, who made *it* intelligible, and at the same time made *us*, in however feeble a fashion, able to understand it."[4] " Some such presupposition," he repeats, " is not only tolerated, but is actually required by science."[5] And in concluding his Gifford Lectures twenty years later, he returns once more to emphasise, almost in the same terms, the nature of his conclusion. " It is the criticism of our common knowledge," he urges, " which brings us ultimately to Theism."[6] " God," he says, in his concluding page, " must not be treated as an entity which we may add to, or subtract from, the sum of things scientifically known, as the canons of induction may suggest. He is Himself the condition of scientific knowledge."[7] And he instructively compares his own procedure with that of Descartes, who, after his attempted start with the independent certainty of

---

[1] *Foundations*, p. 75, 8th ed. p. 80.   [2] *Ibid.*, p. 186, 8th ed. p. 197.
[3] *Ibid.*, p. 296, 8th ed. p. 283.   [4] *Ibid.*, p. 301, 8th ed. p. 288.
[5] *Ibid.*, p. 321, 8th ed. p. 310.
[6] *Theism and Humanism*, p. 252.   [7] *Ibid.*, p. 274.

he *Cogito, ergo sum*, found himself driven to seek the ultimate guarantee of all our beliefs in the truthfulness of God.[1]

The *Foundations of Belief* was a conspicuous literary success. Edition after edition was called for, and the newspapers and reviews overflowed with articles discussing its arguments and conclusions. But most of the critics seem to have brought to their task eyes which could see in it only what they were prepared to find. Anyone looking back may well deem it incredible that, on its first appearance, the impassioned vindication of Reason and theistic faith, which I have just sketched, and which is the very heart of the whole argument, was, by the majority of the reviewers, ignored, if not misrepresented. They concentrated their criticism instead upon certain passages in which they professed to find only the reputed scepticism of the author of *Philosophic Doubt*, or upon particular chapters in which they discovered such a muster of the forces of reaction as they supposed might be expected from the leader of the Tory Party in the House of Commons. It must be acknowledged however that Balfour himself, by the phraseology he used and the licence he allowed himself in certain sections of the book was, to some extent at least, responsible for the misconceptions of his critics. As we have just seen, the main thesis of the volume *was* precisely the *irrationality* of Naturalism, as a final account of our

[1] I cannot forbear citing at this point a more recent parallel to Balfour's position in the " theistic faith " of my own father in philosophy, Professor Campbell Fraser. This faith is presented by Fraser also, " not as a principle by which we eke out the defects of knowledge, but as the fundamental presupposition of all knowledge and reasonable action." The whole procedure of science, as well as the activities of ordinary life, depend, he constantly urges, on the supposition that we are living in " a cosmos," not " a chaos." Our reliance on the laws of nature implies an ultimate trust in " the reasonableness of interpretability of nature," and is, therefore, unconscious faith in God omnipotent in nature. And so, he tells us in his *Biographia Philosophica*: " I gradually came to think of this theistic faith, not as an infinite conclusion empirically found in finite facts, but as the necessary presupposition of all human conclusions about anything." I refer to this parallel the more readily, because Fraser was, I think, the first (outside the circle of Balfour's personal friends) to do justice to the dialectical subtlety of the *Defence of Philosophic Doubt* and the sweep of its argument. He invited Balfour, a year after its publication, to address the Philosophical Society of the University of Edinburgh, and, eleven years later, he was foremost among those who promoted his election to the Chancellorship of the University.

cognitive and ethical experiences. Yet we find a long and prominent chapter of the book expressly devoted, and devoted with manifest gusto, to the glorification of Authority, as contrasted with Reason. The beneficent and all-pervading influence of the former is contrasted with " the comparative pettiness of the rôle played by reasoning in human affairs."[1]

> To Reason [he concludes] we are in some measure beholden, though not perhaps so much as we suppose, for hourly aid in managing so much of the trifling portion of our personal affairs entrusted to our care by Nature as we do not happen to have already surrendered to the control of habit. By Reason also is directed, or misdirected, the public policy of communities within the narrow limits of deviation permitted by accepted custom and tradition. . . . Yet, if we are to judge with equity between these rival claimants, we must not forget that it is Authority rather than Reason to which, in the main, we owe, not religion only, but ethics and politics; that it is Authority which supplies us with essential elements in the premises of science; that it is Authority rather than Reason which lays deep the foundations of social life : that it is Authority rather than Reason which cements its superstructure.[2]

It is obvious that, in this passage and in others like it, Reason is used as strictly equivalent to " reasoning " or conscious logical rationalisation. The two terms, reason and reasoning, sometimes cross and re-cross one another several times on the same page without any distinction between them.

This usage is no doubt common in our older English thinkers, but it is equally true that, in recent philosophical writing, Reason, if it does not always explicitly convey a larger meaning, at all events constantly tends to assume that sense. When Balfour himself speaks, as we have just seen him doing, of " Reason " as " the Ground of all existence," as " the roof and crown " of things, of the universe as " the creation of reason," and of all things as working together " towards a reasonable end," it is clear that he has something more in mind than the " intellect " or the " discursive reason " which is only " permitted to have

---

[1] *Foundations*, p. 228, 8th ed. p. 242.
[2] *Ibid.*, pp. 227–229, 8th ed. pp. 240–43.

ARTHUR JAMES BALFOUR

a hand in the simplest jobs."[1] It is the limited range of the latter which he intends to contrast with the omnipresent action of "Authority." But, by insisting, as he does repeatedly, on the "non-rational" character of the causes which he groups under that name, he conveys to an unwary reader the impression that they have no relation to Reason in the larger sense. If however the meaning of the term Authority is extended, as he proposes, so as to include "custom, education, public opinion," "the contagious convictions of countrymen, family, party or church," as well as "habit" in the management of our personal affairs, that at once disposes of any absolute opposition between the two groups of causes. An action is first performed consciously, with minute supervision of every step or detail. But, according to the beneficent provision of nature, the action goes more smoothly the oftener it is repeated, and the active supervision of consciousness is no longer required. The action has become habitual, and the higher energies of the living creature are set free for the performance of new tasks, for the acquirement of new dexterities. This applies to the humblest bodily exercises: but Aristotle's definition of virtue as a habit is enough to remind us that it holds equally in the highest reaches of the ethical life. Habit, being thus in its origin the creature of reason, cannot be opposed to it as an alien force. And the same is true of custom, tradition, public opinion, the spirit of the age, etc. They are non-rational causes of belief certainly, in the sense that their determining influence over the individual does not depend upon a conscious process of reasoning on his part—a progress from premises to a conclusion. But customs and institutions are themselves originally products of the conscious activities of thinking beings, and are intended to be the embodiment of a rational purpose. Doubtless, no customs or institutions are an adequate or final embodiment of reason, and hence they are subject to progressive modification, in which the old becomes opposed to the new, and may even come to be regarded as a mere obstruction in the path of rational reform. But they have their birth from reason originally, and remain throughout accessible to its transforming influence. Lord Balfour's own view of human history, in a theistic setting, as "an instrument for carrying out a Divine purpose,"[2] transcends in fact the opposition

[1] *Foundations*, p. 72, 8th ed. p. 77.   [2] *Ibid.*, p. 324, 8th ed. p. 313.

between Reason and Authority which, for a temporary purpose, he chooses to emphasise.

Taking Authority in the sense he did, it was easy for him to prove its vastly preponderating influence in determining the ordinary beliefs of the mass of mankind, and to make sport of the idea of a community setting out to put in practice Descartes' ideal of founding the conduct of life on a logically concatenated system of truths. One might almost be tempted to say that in this chapter he is disputing without an antagonist. But that would be to forget the historical perspective in which the bearing of passages like those quoted above can best be understood. Balfour's contribution to what we may call the philosophy of religion was, as we have seen, in the first instance, a demonstration of the insufficiency of Mill's empirical philosophy as a foundation of our scientific beliefs, and a consequent repudiation of the agnostic attitude assumed by members of that school towards the main articles of religious belief. But his revolt was no less, intellectually and temperamentally, a revolt against the social philosophy of the philosophical Radicals, of whom Mill was the last representative. "The speculative outlook of the philosophical Radicals," he tells us, in his recent chapter of autobiography, "filled me with contempt." And small wonder, seeing that, for Bentham and his followers, the past represented only the incorporated spirit of evil, the fountain of unnumbered abuses, which it was their function, as the champions of reason and utility, to make an end of. It is against this narrow and individualistic rationalism and its reading of history that this section of the *Foundations of Belief* is directed: and Balfour employs all his powers of epigram and irony to expose the ineptitude of the language habitually indulged in by those devotees of pure reason. By his glorification of Authority, as the principle of cohesion and continuity in human society, he proposes actually to invert their habitual reading of the antithesis between Authority and Reason as that between the powers of darkness and of light respectively. The section in question is brilliantly written and full of the wisdom of life, and no lover of good literature would wish it away. Just for that reason however one can understand how its phrases may have lingered in the memory and tended to acquire undue prominence in the mind of the ordinary reader. But, in the case of critics more

ARTHUR JAMES BALFOUR

fully equipped, one must suspect either their perspicacity or their candour, if, by quotation from an argument whose application is so strictly limited, they sought to create the impression that the fundamental inspiration of the volume was a desire to flout Reason in all its manifestations, or, in the language of one of the critics referred to, to " smite Reason to the ground."

Up to this point we have studied Lord Balfour's philosophy, chiefly, if not exclusively, in its relation to the Naturalism of which he is the avowed and relentless critic. But any account of his thought would be incomplete which did not touch also upon his attitude to the Idealism, based on Kant and Hegel, which was, for the better part of half a century, the chief constructive movement in contemporary British philosophy. The effective study of Kant and his idealistic successors had little more than begun in this country when Balfour went up to Cambridge in 1866. Hutchison Stirling's pioneer work, *The Secret of Hegel*, was published in 1865, and T. H. Green's first piece of philosophical writing appeared in the *North British Review* in 1866. His *Introduction to Hume* was not published till 1874. Wallace's *Logic of Hegel* (1874), Bradley's *Ethical Studies* (1876), and Edward Caird's *Philosophy of Kant* (1877), belong to the post-graduate years in which Balfour's chief occupation was the working-out of his *Defence of Philosophic Doubt*. A long chapter on " Transcendentalism " in that volume is evidence that, after parting company with Mill and the empirical school, he had turned, with curiosity and a certain amount of sympathy, to investigate this new way of ideas. There is a corresponding chapter, on " Idealism; after some recent English writings," in the *Foundations of Belief*, based to a considerable extent on an article on Green's " Metaphysics of Knowledge," contributed to *Mind* in the interval between the two volumes. The article was written in 1883, after the premature death of that philosopher, and in it Balfour takes Green as the most prominent representative of what he calls there the " Neo-Kantian " school, and as the first to give (in the posthumously published *Prolegomena to Ethics*) a systematic statement of the metaphysical doctrines of the school, disengaged from the exposition and criticism of preceding thinkers. He acknowledges his own sympathy with the conclusions which Green seeks to establish, and also his sense of their common starting-point from the bankruptcy of Sensationalism in Hume and his English successors. He goes so far as to say, " I do not refuse to accept in their most general sense, and with some qualifications, the conclusions on which Green insists." But he adds, " we are specially bound to examine with anxious and impartial care any system with whose conclusions we are in general sympathy." Hence his " technical discussion of the technical arguments by which they are sustained " ; in spite of the general sympathy he must " demur to their being regarded as portions of a reasoned philosophic system."[1]

In the article referred to, he had indeed touched with the keen lance of his criticism some of the more serious ambiguities in Green's otherwise attractive theory of the " spiritual principle " from whose active combining agency Nature, as a system of thought-relations, results. All objects, Green constantly argues, are constituted by relations, and the realisation of these relations is due to the relating activity of a single self-conscious intelligence. The transcendental Ego, which Kant proclaimed as the necessary implicate of all experience, is identified by Green with the one eternal divine Subject to which the universe is relative. Its constant presence to the relations which constitute the contents of the universe communicates to these relations their permanence and objectivity. It is their " medium and sustainer " ; the objectivity of the universe just means its existence for such a consciousness. It is " the eternally complete consciousness," of which all other self-conscious intelligences are partial " modes " or " manifestations." In this fashion, it makes the animal organism of man a vehicle for the reproduction of itself; and Green habitually attributes to this eternal Self a constitutive activity which is tantamount to creation. It is said to " make nature " ; or nature is said to result from the activity of the spiritual principle. Yet, if we consider the method by which the existence of this Self was reached, such predicates appear more than questionable. Green himself, in discussing the applicability of the term " cause " to describe the relation between God and the world, warns us that there is no separate particularity between the agent, on the one side, and the determined world as a whole, on the other, such as characterises any

[1] *Mind* (January 1884), p. 92.

agent or patient, any cause or effect, within the phenomenal world.
That the unifying principle should distinguish itself from the manifold which it unifies is indeed a condition of the unification, but it must not be supposed that the manifold has a nature of its own apart from the unifying principle, or the principle another nature of its own apart from what it does in relation to the manifold world.

Hence "the concrete whole," he tells us, "may be described indifferently as an eternal intelligence realised in the related facts of the world, or as a system of related facts rendered possible by such an intelligence." What the unifying principle does in relation to the manifold world is, in short, simply to unify it: Green says himself in one place that we know the spiritual principle only as a principle of unity in relation. It is in fact the case that the transcendental analysis of knowledge, taken by itself, can tell us no more about it. So far as the argument goes, if we consider the unity apart from the manifold which it unifies, it is, Balfour argues, no more than "the bare geometrical point through which must pass all the threads which make up the web of possible experience"; or if we take it in the concrete, as qualified by the multiplicity whose unity it is, then "in its all-inclusive universality it holds in suspension, without preference and without repulsion, every element alike of the knowable world."[1] In neither case, Balfour argues, can such a principle of unity be regarded as a fitting object of love, reverence or devotion. We cannot but feel, therefore, that in many of the expressions he uses, Green tends to read much more into his conclusion than the premises will warrant. The actual result reached does not satisfy in any real sense the requirements of Theism. A God thus morally indifferent can never be the God of religion. God, even in Matthew Arnold's diluted phrase, remains a Power that makes for righteousness. However difficult it may be to understand, religion seems everywhere to imply what Balfour calls, in the concluding sections of *Foundations*, "the preferential exercise of Divine power."[2]

In any case Balfour leaves us in no doubt as to the implications of the Theism on behalf of which he argues. His dissatisfaction

---

[1] *Foundations*, pp. 145–6, 8th ed. 154–5.
[2] *Ibid.*, p. 316, 8th ed. p. 304.

with Green's argument and its conclusion may be said to extend, more or less, to the typical metaphysical arguments for theism in general; the conclusions reached are, even if true, too meagre for his purpose.

> The highest conceptions of God [he says, in the Introduction to his Gifford Lectures of 1914] seem to approximate to one of two types, which, without prejudice, and merely for convenience, I may respectively call the religious and the metaphysical. The metaphysical conception emphasizes His all-inclusive unity. The religious type emphasizes His ethical personality. The metaphysical type tends to regard Him as the logical glue which holds multiplicity together and makes it intelligible. The religious type willingly turns away from such speculations about the Absolute, to love and worship a Spirit among spirits. Which of these types is contemplated in the argument that follows?
>
> To this question I would reply by another. Are the two conceptions incompatible? Must we abandon the second if we accept the first? If so, it is of the second I propose to speak. It is the God according to religion, and not the God according to metaphysics, whose being I wish to prove. . . . For myself, I must admit that I have never succeeded to my own satisfaction in fusing the two conceptions. Yet I do not profess to be content with their separation. The attribution of personality to God, though much truer, I think, than the denial of it, is manifestly inadequate to the full reality we are struggling to express. Some of the greatest religious teachers, Christian and non-Christian, that the world has seen have more or less explicitly held both, or at least have leaned towards neither exclusively. . . . This may well represent the highest wisdom. But, the argument of these lectures has a narrower scope; and when, in the course of them, I speak of God, I mean something other than an Identity wherein all differences vanish, or a Unity which includes but does not transcend the differences which it somehow holds in solution. I mean a God whom men can love, a God to whom men can pray, who takes sides, who has purposes and preferences, whose attributes, howsoever conceived, leave

ARTHUR JAMES BALFOUR

unimpaired the possibility of a personal relation between Himself and those whom he has created.[1]

He would not, I think, claim that his own argument, any more than that of an idealist like Green, is sufficient philosophically to establish conclusions so far-reaching; nor does it seem probable that results quite so definite are likely to be reached by any philosophic method. He repeatedly, and indeed almost punctiliously, tells us that he does not pretend to offer his readers a complete philosophy. The constructive ideas outlined in Part IV of the *Foundations of Belief* are expressly put forward as " Suggestions towards a Provisional Philosophy." In his prefatory remarks to the volume, he says that his purpose in the book has been " to recommend a particular way of looking at the world problems which, whether we like it or not, we are compelled to face . . . to delineate and if possible to recommend a certain attitude of mind."[2] And, similarly, at the end of his Gifford Lectures in 1914, he describes the outcome of the lectures as " a point of view " rather than " a philosophical system."[3] A philosophical system " rationalised throughout," assuming nothing which requires proof, and admitting no inexplicable residues, he holds it is impossible for us, at our present stage of development, to achieve.

> The philosopher conceives that within the unchanging limits of his system an appropriate niche can be found for every new discovery as it arises. My view is that the contents of a system are always reacting on its fundamental principles, so that no philosophy can flatter itself that it will not be altered out of all recognition as knowledge grows. . . . We must not conceive the development of knowledge as a process of adding new truths to old truths, in the course of which old truths are supplemented but are not changed. It rather resembles the increase of some plastic body which, wherever it takes place, involves a readjustment of every part. Add brick to brick, and you may finish your house, yet never alter its foundation. Add belief to belief, and you will set up strains

---

[1] *Theism and Humanism*, pp. 19–21. [2] *Foundations*, pp. 3–4.
[3] *Theism and Humanism*, p. 261.

and stresses within your system of knowledge which will compel it to move towards some new position of equilibrium.

Accordingly, "we must recognise that our beliefs must be provisional because, till we approach complete knowledge, all beliefs are provisional. We cannot claim that they are good, 'so far as they go'; but only that they are good as we are at present able to make them. And we must recognise that the two statements are profoundly different."[1]

Need we wonder, then, that in spite of any sympathy he might feel for the avowed aims of the neo-Hegelian idealists Balfour felt himself worlds removed from the unabashed claims put forward by Hegel himself that his system represented the very insight of the Absolute Being into his own existence and history. The consistent temper of Balfour's own philosophy is finely exhibited, by contrast, in a characteristic passage with which this chapter may fitly close:

> I like to think of the human race, from whatever stock its members may have sprung, in whatever age they may be born, whatever creed they may profess, together in the presence of the One Reality, engaged, not wholly in vain, in spelling out some fragments of its message. All share its being; to none are its oracles wholly dumb. And if both in the natural world and in the spiritual the advancement we have made on our forefathers be so great that our interpretation seems indefinitely removed from that which primitive man could alone comprehend, and wherewith he had to be content, it may be, indeed I think it is, the case that our approximate guesses are still closer to his than they are to their common Object, and that far as we seem to have travelled, yet, measured on the celestial scale, our intellectual progress is scarcely to be discerned, so minute in the parallax of Infinite Truth.[2]"

[1] *Theism and Humanism*, pp. 263-6.
[2] *Foundations*, p. 276, 8th ed. 375.

Appendix II

THE PEACE SETTLEMENT IN EUROPE

MEMORANDUM BY THE RIGHT HON. A. J. BALFOUR.
NOVEMBER 1916

The Prime Minister asked the Members of the War Committee to express their views on the peace settlement; and the present paper is an attempt—a very tentative and halting attempt—to comply with this request.

Even the most tentative suggestions must however proceed upon some hypothesis with regard to the military position of the combatants at the end of the War. What this will be no human being can foresee with any assurance. But inasmuch as it is convenient to proceed upon a hypothesis which is clear and determinate, I shall assume in what follows, though merely for the sake of argument, that the Central Powers, either through defeat or exhaustion, have to accept the terms imposed upon them by the Allies.

Let me add this further preliminary observation. The number of questions which will have to be discussed at any Peace Conference is obviously very large. In what follows I desire to do no more than to offer some stray reflections upon the most important group of these questions—that which is concerned with the redistribution of population in the European area. By this limitation will be excluded not merely such subjects as the restriction of armaments, the freedom of the seas and the revision of international law, but also Heligoland, the Kiel Canal, strategic modifications of frontiers,[1] and the

The Balfour Memorandum

Allied victory assumed.

---

[1] Of course, such strategic modifications might involve transfers of populations, which could not properly be described as negligible. But their object would not be to acquire territory, but to increase security by making frontiers more defensible.

ARTHUR JAMES BALFOUR

extra-European problems connected with Asia Minor and Germany's Colonial Empire.

On some of these subjects I may perhaps trouble the Committee at a later date.

<small>Strip Central Powers of non-German territory.</small>
The principal object of the War is the attainment of a durable peace, and I submit that the best way of securing this is by the double method of diminishing the area from which the Central Powers can draw the men and money required for a policy of aggression, while at the same time rendering a policy of aggression less attractive by rearranging the map of Europe in closer agreement with what we rather vaguely call " the principle of nationality."

The second of these methods, if successfully applied, would secure many objects which are universally desired by the Allies. It would give Belgium her independence, restore Alsace and Lorraine to France, provide some kind of home rule for Poland, extend the frontiers of Italy, and establish a Greater Serbia and a Greater Roumania in South-East Europe; I should greatly like to see it applied in Bohemia also. To Bohemia, Germanic civilisation is profoundly distasteful. The Czechs have been waging war against it for some generations, and waging it under grave difficulties with much success. Whether an independent Bohemia would be strong enough to hold her own, from a military as well as from a commercial point of view, against Teutonic domination—surrounded as she is at present entirely by German influences—I do not know; but I am sure the question deserves very careful consideration. If the change is possible it should be made.[1]

<small>A new map of Europe.</small>
Now, a map of Europe so modified would not only carry out the second of the two methods of preserving peace which I have described above, but would also help to carry out the first. The resources of men and money on which the Central Powers could draw for purposes of aggressive warfare would be greatly diminished. Alsace-Lorraine, Austrian Poland, with possibly, parts of German Poland, Transylvania, Italian Austria, Bosnia and Herzegovina would cease to be recruiting grounds for supplying German or Austrian Armies; and the men of military age

---

[1] I presume that arrangements will be made by which the frontier of Bohemia would, to some small extent at least, become coterminous with the New Poland.

ARTHUR JAMES BALFOUR

thus withdrawn from the Central Armies would be added to the nations with which the Central Powers are now at war; thus, as it were, counting two on a division.

The populations thus transferred would, I suppose, be more than twenty millions. I take no account in this argument of the non-Italian population which Italy will no doubt obtain if the Allies are successful; nor do I discuss the uncontested zone coveted by Bulgaria. If the principle of nationality be rigidly applied, I suppose that, without doubt, Bulgaria ought to have it. Whether she deserves it, and whether, in view of Serbian sentiment we can give it to her, is quite another question.

I conceive that this general scheme is, broadly speaking, what public opinion in this country would desire to see carried out. The point on which there might be most difference of opinion would perhaps be the fate of Poland—since the fate of Constantinople and the Banat is already settled so far as the Allies can settle it. Almost the only thing on which Russia and Germany seem to be agreed is that the status of Poland should be altered by the War, and that, while receiving some measure of autonomy, it should remain dependent upon one of its two great neighbours. But as to what the limits of the new Poland should be, and on which of its two great neighbours it is said to be dependent, there is, it need hardly be said, a fundamental divergence of opinion between Petrograd and Berlin. *Problem of Poland.*

Looking at the Polish question from a purely British point of view, I should like to see the new State include not merely Russian Poland, but as much of Austrian and German Poland as possible. This, of course, is in strict accord with the two principles laid down earlier in the paper. But I should *not* like to see the old Kingdom of Poland restored. I should fear that the new Poland would suffer from the diseases through which the old Poland perished; that it would be a theatre of perpetual intrigues between Germany and Russia; and that its existence, so far from promoting the cause of European peace, would be a perpetual occasion of European strife.

Moreover, even if such a Poland were capable of playing the part of an efficient buffer State (which I doubt), I am not sure that a buffer State between Germany and Russia would be any advantage to Western Europe. If Germany were relieved of all fear of pressure from Russia, and were at liberty to turn her whole strength towards developing her western ambitions, France and Britain might be the sufferers; and I am not by any means confident that cutting off Russia from her western neighbours might not divert her interests towards the Far East to an extent which British statesmen could not view without some misgivings. The more Russia is made a European rather than an Asiatic Power, the better for everybody.

I therefore conclude that the solution of the Polish question which would best suit our interests would be the constitution of a Poland endowed with a large measure of autonomy, while remaining an integral part of the Russian Empire—the new State or province to include not only all Russian Poland, but also Austria's and (part at least of) Prussia's share in the plunder of the ancient kingdom.

Schleswig-Holstein. Personally I should like to see the Danish portions of Schleswig-Holstein, filched by Prussia and Austria from Denmark in 1863, again restored to their former owner. But Denmark would hardly accept the gift unless it was accompanied by some form of territorial guarantee which she would think effective; and even then the memory of Belgium might act as a deterrent. But the question should be seriously considered. I ought, parenthetically, to add that unfortunately the region through which the Kiel Canal passes is German both in language and sentiment.

So far I have indicated the kind of changes which I should like to see attempted when peace comes to be discussed. But there are some projects advocated by those who believe in the complete victory of the Allies which I regard with great suspicion. Among these perhaps the most important are the projects for breaking up or reconstituting the German Empire. If I had *No internal interference with Germany or Austria.* my way, I should rule out any attempt to touch the internal affairs either of Germany or of Austria. It may be that, under the stress of defeat, ancient jealousies—forgotten in the hour of victory—will revive. South may be divided from North, Roman Catholic from Protestant, Wurttemberg, Bavaria and Saxony from Prussia, or from each other. A revolution may upset the Hohenzollerns, and a new Germany may arise on the ruins of militarism.

Any or all of these things are possible, but I would certainly deprecate any attempt on the part of the victorious enemy to bring them about. One of the few recorded attempts to crush

ARTHUR JAMES BALFOUR

militarism in a defeated State was Napoleon's attempt to destroy the Prussian Army after Jena. No attempt was ever less successful. As everybody knows, Napoleon's policy compelled Prussia to contrive the military system which has created modern Germany. It may be—I hope it will be—in the power of the Allies to strip Germany of much of her non-German territory; but, whatever be the limits of the new Germany, I hope no attempt will be made to control or modify her internal policy. The motto of the Allies should be " Germany for the Germans—but only Germany." *[sidenote: Napoleon's failure to crush Prussia.]*

This formula however, even if it be accepted, does not solve the problem of Central Europe. It says nothing, for example, of the future relations between Germany and Austria. I should myself desire to see the Dual Monarchy maintained, shorn indeed of a large portion of its Slav, Italian, and Roumanian territories, but still essentially consisting of Austria and Hungary. If this were to occur, we should have in the future, as we have had in the past, a German Empire and an Austrian Empire side by side and probably kept in close alliance—political if not also economic—for the purposes of mutual protection. Other possibilities however have to be considered. The result of the War may be the complete break-up of the Dual Monarchy; and if the Dual Monarchy breaks up, it is reasonable to suppose that the German portion of it would coalesce with the German Empire, leaving Hungary either isolated or dependent. Apparently such a change would create a great German-speaking State more formidable than Germany before the War; and this may be, in fact, what would happen. On the other hand, it must be remembered that such a change would profoundly modify the position of Prussia. The Roman Catholics and South German elements would become overwhelmingly strong; and if the driving force behind the German aggression be due, as most observers think, to Prussian organisation and Prussian traditions, the change might in its ultimate effect be a defeat for German militarism. *[sidenote: Possibility of German-Austrian Unity.]*

But I do not disguise from myself either that the dangers of such a Teutonic reorganisation are considerable, or that the likelihood of its occurring may be increased if the result of the War is to convince the German-speaking peoples that their only hope of national greatness lies in their consenting to forget

439

all causes of difference and welding themselves into a single powerful State. Those who think the future must necessarily resemble the past may perhaps be disposed to remind us that for the five centuries preceding the Bismarckian era the political tendencies prevailing in Germany have been, on the whole, centrifugal and separatist.

They will argue that this inveterate tradition, interrupted though it has been for forty-five years by a united and triumphant Germany, nevertheless represents the real tendencies of the race; and that to this tradition it will revert after a war for which Prussian policy and a Prussian dynasty have been responsible.

Personally, I am inclined to doubt this conclusion, plausible as it seems; nor do I believe that anything which we and our Allies can accomplish will prevent the Germanic Powers, either united by alliance or fused into a single State, from remaining wealthy, populous, and potentially formidable.

For this reason I do not share the fears of those who think that the triumph of the Slav countries is likely to menace German predominance in Central Europe. When we remember that the Slav populations are divided by language, religion and government; that they fought each other four years ago; that they are fighting each other at this very moment; that the only one among them which can count as a Great Power is Russia; and that Russia, according to most observers, is likely to be torn by revolutionary struggles as soon as the pressure of war is removed; when (I say) we remember these things, we shall probably be disposed to think that the Germanic States will be very well able to take care of themselves, whatever be the terms of peace to which they may have to submit.

Slav races too divided to threaten Europe.

This is a fact (if it indeed be a fact) which is sometimes ignored. Many of those who speculate about the future of Europe seem to fear that Germany will be so weakened by the War that the balance of Power will be utterly upset, and Britain will be left face to face with some other dominance. I doubt this. In any case it seems to me quite clear that, measured by population, Germany—and still more, Germany in alliance with Austria— will be more than a match for France alone, however much we give to France alone, however much we take from the Central States. If, therefore Europe after the War is to be an armed camp, the peace of the world will depend, as heretofore, on

ARTHUR JAMES BALFOUR

defensive alliances formed by those who desire to retain their possessions against those who desire to increase them. In that event the Entente is likely to be maintained. Germany may suffer a spiritual conversion; Russia may break up; France and Britain may be rendered powerless by labour troubles; universal bankruptcy may destroy universal armaments; international courts may secure international peace; the horrors of 1914, 1915, 1916, and 1917 may render the very thought of war disgusting to all mankind. On these subjects it is vain to speculate. All I would for the moment insist on is that the greatest territorial losses which the Allies can or ought to inflict on the Central Powers will leave them powerful both for defence and offence. Whatever trouble Russia may give us in Mesopotamia, Persia, and Afghanistan, I do not think she will attempt the domination of Europe, still less succeed in securing it.

There are two subsidiary points on which I may say a word before concluding—rights of way and indemnities. If the shores of the Adriatic are in Italian hands, if Salonika is in Greek hands, how are we going to provide the Central Powers with commercial access to the Mediterranean and the South? That they should not be denied such access seems to be fairly clear. It is one thing to cut off Germany from her megalomaniacal designs upon Asia Minor, Mesopotamia, Persia, and India; it is quite another to put the commerce of Austria-Hungary with the Eastern Mediterranean and the Suez Canal at the mercy of the States which lie between it and the sea. There could, it seems to me, be no more powerful incentive to new wars. Some method of guaranteeing to States which have no convenient seaboard the free flow of commerce through selected channels is therefore urgently required. I have had no time to give to the subject, but I have sometimes idly wondered whether the treaties which apply to navigable rivers flowing through different States might not with the necessary modifications be applied also to ports and railways. *Need to secure access to sea for Central Powers.*

My last topic is war indemnities. I have, for the sake of argument, assumed that the success of the Allies is going to be complete. On this assumption—ought indemnities to be demanded? *Problem of Indemnities.*

Germany has never made any secret of her intention of beggaring her enemies and reducing them, if she got the power to complete commerical subservience. My own inclination would be strongly against imitating Germany's behaviour in 1871 and imposing a commercial treaty on my opponents for my own advantage. Such treaties are needlessly humiliating, even when they are not onerous. When they are, they are sure, sooner or later, to be broken.

But there are two things I should like to do and which in the interests of international morality I think ought to be done. I think the Central Powers should be made to pay for the damage they have done in Belgium, Northern France, and Serbia; and I think they ought to surrender shipping equivalent in amount to that which they have sent to the bottom in the course of their submarine warfare. These are charges which it should be within their power to meet; and if within their power to meet, then certainly within our right to demand. Whether more can or ought to be exacted is a point on which I feel incompetent to give an opinion; but it may be worth remembering that to take territories from the German or Austrian Empires free of debt, is in effect to increase the burdens on the States from which they are taken, and to relieve the burden on the States to which they are added.

A. J. B.

Oct. 4, 1916.

INDEX

Acland-Hood, Sir A., 30, 44
Admiralty in the War, 144 *et seq.*, 171
Air Board, 158
Akers-Douglas, Rt. Hon. A.
  See Chilston, Lord
Alexander, Professor, 224
Allenby, Lord, 365–6
  enters Jerusalem, 234
Alliance v. *Entente*, Balfour on, 105
Amery, L. S., 361, 376
Anglo-French staff conversations, 105–7
Anglo-Japanese Alliance, 317 *et seq.*
Anti-Zionists, 214, 227, 233
Anschluss, 284–5
Antonius, Mr. G., 367
Arabs in Palestine, 218 *et seq.*, 220, 368
Arabs join the Allies, 219
Armenia, 255, 303–5
Armistice, 262
Army, the, 79
  and Ireland, 101
Ashbourne, Lord, 68
Asquith, Rt. Hon. H. H., 50–4, 64, 115, 138 *et seq.*, 164, 171 *et seq.*
  Prime Minister, 40
  and the Navy, 52–4
  and King George, 61
  and Home Rule, 94, 97, 102, 120, 340
  falls from power, 138, 156, 167 *et seq.*
  and Second Coalition, 178 *et seq.*
Astor, Lord and Lady, 395
Australian apples, 373–4
Austria, 247–8, 266, 284 *et seq.*, 439
Austrian loan, 352–5
Autobiography, 390, 395, 406

Baker, Mr. R. S., 201, 264, 270
Balcarres, Lord, 68, 83, 86–8
Baldwin, Mr. S., 360 *et seq.*, 370, 388, 396, 399, 400, 402–3
" B. M. G.," 86
Balfour, Miss Alice, 16, 30, 83, 121, 205, 368, 398
Balfour, Countess of, 30, 410
Balfour Declaration, 213, 215 *et seq.*, 227, 233–4, 365
Balfour, Rt. Hon. A. J.,
  in Opposition, 13 *et seq.*, 20 *et seq.*, 41
  elected for the City, 14, 26 *et seq.*
  secret of charm, 17, 203
  and Chamberlain, 21 *et seq.*
  speech at Manchester, Jan. 1905, 23
  on Sir Robert Peel, 25, 74–7, 350
  on House of Lords Reform, 34–5
  on Campbell-Bannerman, 40
  on Licensing Bill, 40
  as Party leader, 41–7
  speech at Birmingham, 48
  on naval policy, 52 *et seq.*, 149 320
  on Land Valuation, 56
  and the Finance Bill, 57 *et seq.*
  on Home Rule, 62, 96 *et seq.*, 340
  on Royal prerogative, 64
  resigns leadership, 71, 83–93, 294, 340
  rejects coalition with Liberals, 72
  on conscription, 80
  at Bad Gastein, 82
  speech at Haddington, 98
  on Anglo-German relations, 107
  on Imperial Defence Committee, 104, 125, 131

INDEX

religious attitude, 109, 408, 423, 432
at outbreak of war, 113 *et seq.*
on expeditionary force, 117
on Kitchener, 119–20, 157
First Lord of the Admiralty, 125, 134, 139 *et seq.*
and War Council, 125 *et seq.*, 168
on western front, 130
supports Jellicoe, 149
on Gallipoli, 153
on Asquith, 156–7, 166, 170
on Air Board, 158–9
Jutland statement, 160–2
on Mr. Lloyd George, 170 241, 348–9
resigns Admiralty, 172 *et seq.*
and Second Coalition Government, 178 *et seq.*
Foreign Secretary, 181, 186 *et seq.*, 236 *et seq.*
on Peace Settlement, 186, 189, 435
goes to America, 194 *et seq.*, 220, 226, 231, 314 *et seq.*
at Mount Vernon, 203
in Canada, 207
and Zionism, 213 *et seq.*
on the Arabs, 220–2
opens Hebrew University, 235, 364
on unified command, 237 *et seq.*
rebuke to General Staff, 245–6
in Paris, 250, 270
and Lansdowne Letter, 249 *et seq.*
on Russian collapse, 25
at Peace Conference, 263 *et seq.*
and British Empire Delegation, 276
on Peace Treaties, 279 *et seq.*, 285, 289
with Lloyd George at Trouville, 290
Lord President of the Council, 291, 370 *et seq.*
at Geneva, 293, 305
at Institut de France, 295
power of sympathy, 296
Fiddes Watt portrait, 297
Chancellor of Cambridge, 298
at Queen's Hall, 302
on Japanese Alliance, 329–30
receives Garter and Earldom, 334
at City Carlton Club, 348, 356
in House of Lords, 358, 371, 382
at Cannes and Sheringham, 359–61
on representative government, 363–4
in Palestine and Syria, 364
and Imperial Conference, 378
interest in science and medicine, 385
on nationality and patriotism, 387
last illness and death, 389, 399, 410
on his Irish policy, 392
Rolls-Royce presentation, 396
goes to Fishers Hill, 399 *et seq.*
resignation at Bognor, 399
burial at Whittingehame, 411
Balfour, second Earl of, 15, 17, 27, 334, 338, 363, 399, 410
Balfour, Lt.-Col. E. W. S., and Lady Ruth, 15, 123
Balfour, Eustace, 15, 334, 406
Balfour, Lady Frances, 30, 90, 347
Balfour Note, 350–3, 362
Balfour, O. H. C., 122, 126
Balkan States, 128 187–8, 356
Battle cruisers at Rosyth, 126
Beatty, Earl, 126, 148–51, 164–5, 316
Beaverbrook, Lord, 167–8, 177, 181–2
Beigel, Victor, 307
Belfast Lough incident, 96, 102
Belgium, 116, 186
Bergson, Henri, 295, 407
Berlin Congress, 356
Bernstorff, Count, 190
Bikanir, Maharajah of, 275
Birkenhead, Earl of, 36, 68, 87, 346
Birrell, A., 97
Blockade, 135

INDEX

Board of Invention and Research, 152
Bonar Law, Mr., 68, 94–6, 100–1, 114, 120, 137 *et seq.*, 166, 167, 275, 282, 345–7, 352, 359
   and Second Coalition, 179 *et seq.*
"Book of Bosh", 19
Borden, Sr R., 275, 282
Bosworth, Mr. Welles, 299
Botha, General, 274–5, 278
Bourgeois, M., 311
Bowles, Mr. Gibson, 29
Brandeis, Mr. Justice, 230–1
Breckenridge Long, Mr., 200
Brest-Litovsk, 247
Briand, M., 306, 310, 323
Bridgeman, W. C., 361
Bridges, General, 198, 205
British Empire Delegation, 274, 281, 287, 316
British fleet in the Channel, 113
British Peace Delegation, 267
Buckingham Palace conference, 177–83
Budget of 1909, 41, 50, 55 *et seq.*
Burnham, Lord, 251

Cabinet secretariat, 240
Callaghan, Sir G., 148
Cambridge, 298–9
Campbell-Bannerman, Sir H., 30, 31, 52
   death, 40
Canada, 207, 307, 377–9
   Japanese in, 319
   See Dominions
Carnock, Lord, 115
Carson, Sir E., 68, 104, 120, 141, 145, 167–8, 209
Cavan, Earl of, 316
Cawdor, Earl of, 57
Cecil of Chelwood, Lord, 36, 169, 171, 184–8, 193, 236–9, 242–4, 252, 300–1
   Minister of Blockade, 187, 300
   and Zionism, 232
   at Geneva, 307
   and disarmament, 317
Cecil, Lord Hugh, 36

Chamberlain, Rt. Hon. Sir A., 22, 27, 47, 68, 82, 87, 115, 141, 243, 346, 356, 387, 400
Chamberlain, Rt. Hon. J., 21 *et seq.*, 184
   illness, 48
   statue, 358
Chamberlain, Mrs. J., 22
Chaplin, Lord, 68–9
Charteris, Hon. Sir E., 359
Chilston, Lord, 68, 74, 88
China, 331–3, 387
Choate, Mr. J., 206–7
Churchill, Lord R., 344
Churchill, Rt. Hon. W., 50, 103–4, 113, 124, 127, 138–9, 142–4, 152, 185, 264, 336–7, 342, 394, 398, 400
   and Fisher, 127, 138, 145 *et seq.*
   and Dardanelles, 128
Clemenceau, M., 269–71, 282, 290
Clynes, Rt. Hon. R. J., 397
Coalition Government, first, 125, 132, 137, 156, 166
   second, 176, 236, 345, 352
Cole, Lady Eleanor, 15
Cole, Hon. Galbraith, 15
Colefax, Sir A. and Lady, 299
Coleman, J., 408
Committee of Intellectual Co-operation, 308
Convoys, 151
Cook, Sir J., 275
Cooper, Mr., 205
Council of Five, 282, 294
Council of Four, 271–2, 287
Crewe, Lord, 63, 131, 177
Cromer, first Earl, on Zionism, 228
Cunliffe, Lord, 205
Cunliffe, Sir F., 124
Curling, 16
Curragh incident, 101
Curzon of Kedleston, Lord, 57, 68–9, 87, 158, 236, 297, 303, 310, 347, 360–1, 370
   and Kitchener, 146
   Foreign Secretary, 241, 262, 289–92, 350
   in Paris, 310

INDEX

Czecho-Slovakia, 285–7
Czecho-Slovaks in Russia, 260–1

D'Abernon, Lord, 359
Daily Telegraph, 250
Dangerous Drugs Convention, 308
Danzig, 290
Dardanelles, 127, 131, 137, 141, 202, 356
Dartmouth, Lord, 297
Dawson, Mr. G., 251
Dawson of Penn, Lord, 389, 394, 399
de Chair, Admiral, 205
Derby, Earl of, 68
Desborough, Lord and Lady, 296, 298, 359, 394–5, 400, 408
"Die-Hard" revolt, 66–8, 82, 86, 356
Dilke, Sir C., 344
Disarmament, naval, 303, 315 *et seq.*
Dominion Delegations, 269, 273, 307
Dominion status, 378 *et seq.*, 402
Dominion trade, 373 *et seq.*
Dreadnoughts, 50, 53
Drummond, Sir E., 194–5, 244
Dugdale, Frances, 400
Dugdale, Michael, 298
Durham, Lord, 377

Education Bill, 1906, 32, 35
Edward VII, King, 57, 59, 63
  death, 60
Edward VIII, King, 396
Eliot, Sir C., 322, 328–9
Empire Marketing Board, 373
Entente Cordiale, 104, 106
Esher, Lord, 248, 382–3
Eton, 297–8, 413
Expeditionary force, 116 *et seq.*

Feisal, Emir, 219
Fiddes Watt portrait, 297
Finlay, Sir R., 68
First Sea Lord, 127, 143–7, 164–5
Fiscal policy, 23, 41 *et seq.*, 85
Fisher, H. A. L., 353, 394
Fisher, Lord, 113, 127–9, 133, 138, 143–6, 152, 185

Fletcher, Sir W. M., 371
Flood, Mr., 204
Four Power Treaty, 330
Fourteen Points, 279, 287
France, 104 *et seq.*, 115, 244, 260, 329
  and Polish-German frontier, 309
  and disarmament, 323, 325
  and reparations, 351
Freedom of the Seas, 249, 319
French fear of Germany, 277
  on the Ruhr, 362
French, Lord, 130
Frontiers, new, 278–80, 309

Gallipoli, 141, 152 *et seq.*, 184
  See Dardanelles
Garvin, J. L., 77
Geddes, Sir A., 316
Geddes, Sir E., 170
General Election, 1905, 13, 20
  1910, 50, 53, 58, 63–7
  1918, 263
  1924, 362, 370
Geneva, 105, 305 *et seq.*
George V, King, 60, 63, 66, 82, 89–90, 99, 175, 178–9, 334, 359–61, 396
  at Bognor, 399
German Navy, 51
  Jutland statement, 162
  Peace offer, 188, 246–7
  colonies, 264, 439
Germans in North Sea, 148
Germany, 107, 116
  Allied occupation, 280
Gibbs, Alban, Mr., 14
Gibson, Mr. H., 205
Gifford Lectures, 15, 108–11, 135, 408
Gladstone, Viscountess, 30
Gladstone, W. E., 45, 338–9, 343, 405
Golf, 14
Goodwin, Mr., 204
Gowans, Nurse, 408
Gramophone, 13
Great War, 80
  outbreak, 112

446

INDEX

Greek defeat, 355
Grey of Falloden, Lord, 51, 54, 104, 107, 115, 118–19, 183
  Note on submarines, 163
  and Zionism, 225

Haldane, Lord, 116–18
Halsbury, Lord, 67, 82
Halsbury Club, 88
Hankey, Col. Sir Maurice, 126, 128, 131, 140, 144, 242, 271–2, 321, 380, 388, 400
Harding, President, 303
Hardinge, Lord, 243–4, 250–1, 267
Headlam-Morley, Sir J., 240
Henderson, Rt. Hon. A., 178
Hertzog, General, 376, 383
Hibbert Journal, 83
Home Rule, 61–2, 73, 77–8, 94 *et seq.*, 120, 337–8
House, Colonel, 188, 194, 200–1, 211, 263, 270–3
House of Lords Reform, 33, 58 *et seq.*, 82
  veto, 58 *et seq.*
Hughes, C. E., 321–5
Hughes, Mr. W. M., 275
Hungary, 268, 283, 286
Hussein, Emir of Mecca, 219, 225

Imperial Conference, 273, 318, 374 *et seq.*
Imperial Defence, 51, 104, 125, 145, 372
Imperial Preference, 23–4, 47–9, 375
India, 275, 307, 402
Ireland, 95, 203, 336 *et seq.*, 391–2. *See* Home Rule
Irish Americans, 204
Irish Free State, 336, 374, 376
Irish Party and Lords' veto, 58
Irish Treaty, 336–47
Irwin, Lord, 372, 402
Islington, Lord, 216
Italian claims, 202, 270–2, 279, 287–9
Italy and disarmament, 325

Jackson, Admiral Sir H., 144–6, 148, 164
Japan, 209–10, 255, 258–9, 315 *et seq.*, 322, 327 *et seq.*
Jellicoe, Lord, 144 *et seq.*, 151, 160–1, 164–5
Jewish National Home, 213, 217, 219
Jutland, 141, 148, 159 *et seq.*

Kato, Admiral, 329
Kerr, Philip, 77, 272
Keyes, Sir R., 152
Kiao-Chow, 331
Kitchener, Lord, 119, 131, 134, 141, 157, 184
  and Curzon, 146
  death, 166
Kitchener's Army, 121
Knollys, Lord, 20, 90
Koo, Mr. Wellington, 332
Korfanty, 310
Kühlmann, 246, 249

Labour Party, rise of, 21, 38, 47, 360, 362
Labour problems in the War, 135
Land Valuation Bill, 55–6
Lang, Rev. Dr. M., 411
Lansdowne, Lord, 27, 34, 39, 58, 60, 63, 67–8, 81, 88, 100, 114–16, 171, 293
Lansdowne Letter, 249 *et seq.*
Lansing, Mr., 206, 270, 282
Lascelles, Hon. Edward, 15, 295, 364, 368, 400
Lascelles, Hon. Mrs. Edward, 15, 295, 334, 359, 364, 368
Lawford, V. A., D.S.O., 205
Lawn tennis, 14
League Council, 301 *et seq.*, 310
League of Nations idea, 190, 196, 287, 300 *et seq.*
  Covenant, 270, 278, 300, 382
  and Austria, 352–5
League of Nations Union, 302
le Bon, Admiral, 326
Lee of Fareham, Lord, 315, 323–5
Leeper, R. and A., 240

447

INDEX

Lenin, 233, 257–60
Levin, Dr. Schmarya, 223
Liberals and Lords Reform, 38–40
Licensing Bill, 40
Lichnowsky, Count, 119
Linthicum, Mr., 204–5
Lloyd, Lord, 115
Lloyd George, Rt. Hon. D., 40, 50, 55 *et seq.*, 67, 116, 281, 290, 355–7, 396
   proposes coalition, 72 *et seq.*
   and national defence, 78–9
   and munitions, 133, 170
   and Balfour's appointment, 139, 182–3
   on submarine campaign, 150
   at War Office, 166
   Unionist distrust of, 168
   Prime Minister, 184
   and Italy, 202
   and Zionism, 215, 226
   and unified command, 238
   relations with Balfour, 241, 266
   in Paris, 247, 266, 275, 310
   and Empire Delegation, 275
   and Curzon, 291–2, 310
   and naval disarmament, 315–16
   and Genoa Conference, 347
Lockhart, Bruce, 257–60
Lodge, Senator, 21
Long, Rt. Hon. W., 67–9, 87, 141
Lothian, Lord. *See* Kerr
Louis of Battenberg, Prince, 144
Lyttelton, Rt. Hon. A., 68, 77
Lyttelton, Dame E., 400

Macdonald, Ramsay, 362, 402
McKenna, Rt. Hon. R., 50
MacMahon, Sir H., 219, 225
Makino, Baron, 282
Malcolm, Sir I., 196–7, 205–7
Mandates, 274, 303, 309. *See* Palestine.
Marconi, Signor, 144
Marne battles, 244
Masterton Smith, Sir J., 144, 171
Maxe, Leo, 85
Medical Research Council, 371–2
Meighen, Mr., 318

Mensdorff, Count, 248
Mercer, Mrs., 16
Merton, Mr., 369
Mesopotamia, 242
Mexico, 191, 244
Midleton, Earl of, 358, 400
Mills, F., 398
Milne, Mrs. Arthur, 15
Milner, Lord, 57, 77, 215, 270, 282
Minorities, 287–8, 303–4
Montagu, Mr. E., 214, 216, 233, 275
Montagu, Hon. Mrs. E., 359, 394
Mount Vernon, 203
Munitions, 132–4, 170
Murmansk expedition, 261–2
Mustapha Kemal, 355

Namier, L. B., 240, 286, 395
Nationalism, 98
Nationality and Home Rule, 96–7, 341
National Review, 85–6
Naval policy, 50
   disarmament, 323 *et seq.*
Newton, Lord, 32
New Zealand, 379
Nicolson, Sir A. *See* Lord Carnock
Nine Power Treaty, 333
Nord and Sud, 107
Northcote, Lord, 21

O'Higgins, K., 376
Old Age Pensions, 47
Oliver, F. S., 77
Oliver, Sir H., 148
Orlando, Signor, 271
Ottawa Conference, 375
Oxford and Asquith, Lord. *See* Asquith

Page, Mr., 188, 192–4, 211
Palestine, 213 *et seq.*, 364
   Mandate, 213, 217, 225, 231
   development of, 218–19
Parliament Bill, 59, 66, 81 *et seq.*
Parnell, C. S., 204, 340, 343
Peace Conference, 201, 263 *et seq.*
Peace offers, Germany, 188, 246–7
   Bulgaria, Turkey, Austria, 246

INDEX

Peace Settlement, 186, 435 *et seq.*
Peers, creation of, 65, 70
Percy, Lord Eustace, 231
Phillips, Mr., 205
Philosophy, 83, 108, 385–6, 406, 413 *et seq.*
Pichon, M., 290
Poland, 280, 309, 437
Politicians and the War, 167
Porter, Mr., 204
Prince of Wales's Fund, 124
Pringle-Pattison, Professor, 407, 413

Rayleigh, Evelyn, Lady, 30
Rayleigh, John, Lord, 136, 298
Reading, Lord, 257
Redmond, Mr., 58–9
Reparations, 267, 280, 351–3, 442
Rhine frontier, 278
Riddell, Lord, 167, 310, 345, 358
Roberts, Lord, 79
Robertson, Sir W., 239
Rockefeller Trust, 299
Rogers, Mr., 204
Rothschild, Lord, death, 135
Rothschild, second Lord, 213, 232
Roumania, 187–8
Runciman, Rt. Hon. W., 157
Russia, 115, 130, 154, 187, 202, 247, 253 *et seq.*, 289, 347, 401, 438
  Jews in, 214, 227
  murders of Imperial family, 262
Russian Revolution, 233, 254 *et seq.*

St. Germain, Treaty of, 283 *et seq.*
Salisbury, Marchioness of, 20, 400
Salisbury, third Marquess of, 68, 184, 187, 236, 338–9, 346, 356, 360, 391
Salisbury, fourth Marquess of, 361, 400
Samuel, Sir H., 214, 223, 366–7
Sandars, J. S., 43, 83, 89
Sarrail, General, 369
Scientific and Industrial Research, 371, 382
Scott, C. P., 223
Secret Treaties, 201–2, 220

Seipel, Monsignor, 353–5
Selborne, Earl of, 68, 358
Sèvres, Treaty of, 303
"Shadow Cabinet," 42, 66, 68, 82, 85
Shantung, 331–2
Shidehara, Baron, 329
Siberia, 255, 260
Sidgwick, Mrs., 410
Simon Commission, 402
Sinha, Sir S. P., 275
Smart, Mr., 369
Smith, F. E. *See* Birkenhead
Smith, W. H., 87
Smuts, General, 215, 248–9, 274–5, 278–9
Snowden, Lord, 400
Sokolow, Mr., 223, 228, 230
South Africa, 308, 376, 379, 383
Spain, 246
Spender-Clay, Major, 205
Spring Rice, Sir C., 189–90, 192, 211, 231
Stamfordham, Lord, 361
Statute of Westminster, 383
Steel-Maitland, Sir A., 68, 83, 86
Strutt, Admiral Hon. A. C., 122
Submarine campaign, 149–52, 187, 190, 208
Submarines, abolition of, 324–6
Supreme War Council, 238–9
Sykes, Sir Mark, 215, 228
Sykes-Picot Agreement, 202, 220, 225, 230
Syria, French in, 219, 289, 367–8

Taff Vale judgment, 38
Talbot, Lord Edmund, 180
Tariff Reform, 22, 44
Tchlenow, Mr., 223
Temple, Mr., 204
Theism and Humanism, 15, 108
Theism and Thought, 108
Thorn, Dr., 408
Times, The, 81, 251, 369, 404
Tittoni, Signor, 282, 290
Tokugawa, Prince, 329
Trades Disputes Bill, 38
Traffic in Women and Children, 308

449

INDEX

Traprain, Lord and Lady, 410
Treaty of Mutual Assistance, 210
Trotsky, Leon, 233–4, 257–60
Tsetse fly, 372
Turkey, 153, 202, 289, 303, 355
Two-Power standard, 52
Tyrol, South, 287–8

Ulster, 95 et seq., 121, 341
   frontier question, 103
Ulster Covenant, 1912, 95
Unemployed, 362
Unified command, 236 et seq.
Unionist Free Traders, 48–9
United States, 135, 261, 301, 375, 378
   enter the War, 151, 188 et seq., 193 et seq., 244
   and League of Nations, 190, 300 et seq.
   Missions to, 194 et seq., 226, 314 et seq.
   naval arrangements, 208–11
   and Japan, 210
   and Zionism, 226, 230–2
   and naval disarmament, 315 et seq.
   and Japanese Alliance, 319, 327 et seq.
   and China, 333
   and War debts, 351
   See Wilson
Upper Silesia, 280, 290, 309–12, 354
" Us Four," 15–16

" Valentine Letters," 28
Versailles Treaty, 265 et seq., 270, 281
   criticisms of draft, 278

Victory Loan, 192
Viviani, M., 203, 306

Wagner, Frau Kosima, 224
War aims, 252
War Cabinet, 241
War Council, 125, 128, 131–3, 168, 171, 180, 238
   members, 131
War debts, 350
Washington Conference, 314
Wedderburn, Dr., 399
Weizmann, Dr. C., 216, 222–34, 364–6, 409–10
Wemyss, Countess of, 82, 118, 135, 263, 294, 296, 359, 395, 400
Wemyss, Sir W., 152–5
Whittingehame, home life at, 13 295, 389, 398
Wilson, Admiral Sir A., 144
Wilson, Sir H., 115, 239, 260, 275
Wilson, President, 188, 191 et seq., 200 et seq., 220, 232, 244, 256, 261, 264, 269, 287, 300
   at Peace Conference, 201
   at Geneva, 308
Wiseman, Sir W., 209
Wolfe-Murray, General, 131
Women's Suffrage, 90
World Crisis, The, 337
Wright, Sir Almroth, 113
Wyndham, Rt. Hon. G., 51, 68, 338

Zimmermann telegram, 191, 244
Zionism, 213 et seq., 364 et seq.